Purple Solutions

Purple Solutions

A Bipartisan Roadmap to Better Healthcare in America

Coauthored and edited by
Daniel Sem

 Remedium eXchange

Remedium eXchange
A Healthcare Economics Think Tank

The Remedium eXchange is a think tank, abbreviated as the Rx Think Tank, with a vision to increase Quality, Access, and Affordability of healthcare for all, in a patient-centered and consumer-driven healthcare delivery model.

rxthinktank.org

For Lucas, Camille and Isaac

Be yourselves, because you are all inspiring to me.

*Be strong, find happiness in small things,
spread love, and work hard.*

*Don't be fence-sitters, but also don't be afraid to listen
and compromise when it makes sense.*

*It is in your hands to make the world a little better,
and find peace on that journey.*

You're already off to a good start!

Contents

Acknowledgments

I would like to thank all of the contributors who have written excellent and thought-provoking chapters for this book. I would also like to thank my wife Teresa for supporting and tolerating my countless hours of typing into the wee hours of the morning on my laptop, and my assistant Janet Mushall at Concordia University who helped run the school of business during my brief periods of "writing hibernation." And I am indebted to the army of editors who helped with formatting, citations, and more, including especially Amy Reid at ProofREID, along with Savanna Elsbury, Erin McCraw, Rachel Lutz, and Bailey Smith. I owe special thanks to the many speakers and members of the *Rx Think Tank* who provided the inspiration, information, and support that led to this project, along with Robert Graboyes, Elise Amez-Droze, and Leck Shannon at the Mercatus Center at George Mason University. Finally, I am grateful to my siblings Tom Sem, Terry Chelstowski, Kathy Lange, and Marianne Reimer, for their support and those November meetups in Florida where we relax, solve world problems, and remember Dad.

Disclaimer

The various authors and coauthors of this book have diverse and sometimes opposing views of healthcare policy. The submission and inclusion of a chapter in this book in no way indicates that one author condones or approves of what another author has written. Indeed, this diversity of perspectives is why the book is entitled *Purple Solutions*. It brings together a robust exchange of ideas, views, and logically supported and researched* arguments of thought leaders, scholars, and practitioners on both sides of the political aisle, or increasingly within different subdivisions on one side of the aisle.

---

* You will find an extensive list of citations for each chapter at the end of the book.

Introduction

I should tell you that I began writing this book while I was teaching in Shanghai, China, in mid-December of 2019, just as (unbeknownst to me) the coronavirus pandemic initiated. China, an autocratic society, dealt effectively with the epidemic; but as a society, the country has little freedom, suffers from human rights violations and, while capitalistic, is ironically also socialist. As I write this, the jury is still out as to whether the United States, a country that rightfully values freedom, liberty, and human dignity, will deal as efficiently with the pandemic. What we do know is that another Asian country, Singapore—whose healthcare system delivers quality care at 2.5% GDP versus the United States' 18%—set a shining example of success in controlling Covid-19 and is discussed in this book as an example of how creatively implemented market forces can be channeled toward positive ends. So is the better solution to effective healthcare socialism or market forces? What, if anything, can be learned from other countries, and what should be uniquely American? Well, if you are curious, please read on.

This book is about finding bipartisan, or *Purple* (i.e., red and blue) solutions to healthcare problems in the United States. It begins with the premise that the best healthcare reform—and likely the only viable healthcare reform, from a political perspective—will require Democrats and Republicans to roll up their sleeves and compromise to find the best path. Hard to imagine, I know. Our country seems irreparably polarized, as are most of us—even within our respective families.

I come from a family of five, and we all shared a father who was a staunch Republican—albeit not a fan of some of our current political theatrics. Ever since my father passed away in November of 2016, the five of us have gathered every November in Florida for family-bonding time and to remember Dad. This last November, after sharing my plans for this book, I discovered that we are as divided as any American family. About half of us generally vote on the Red side, and the other half on the Blue side. As the fifth child of a (loving) father with strong and sometimes polarizing political views, my role in life has evolved into being the peacemaker and the person looking for reasonable and compromise solutions. Such was the nature of our family discussion in Florida last November. I mostly listened as my siblings debated in sometimes heated ways the benefits of essentially single-payer healthcare versus free markets. Where do I stand? I try to stand for reasonable compromise, for Purple solutions. While I confess I have somewhat libertarian leanings at times, in practice I end up voting pragmatically, almost as often for Democrats as Republicans. So, I suppose, I stand in the middle. In our polarized political world, that probably means I may be in the minority. Please hear me out.

I am certain that you—the reader—are equally familiar with this heated political debate about healthcare in America, and perhaps you have strong opinions. In writing this book, when I speak in the *first person* to "you" (*second person*), I am speaking directly to *you* as a healthcare consumer. I suspect that you may believe that our healthcare delivery system is broken, and that the cost is too high for what you get in terms of medical outcomes. You probably feel the increasing pain of paying more and more out of pocket for your healthcare, through high deductibles and co-pays, and you likely feel powerless to do anything about it. As a country, we spend $3 trillion per year for healthcare, and per person we spend around $10,000 per year (see chapter 1), with the total cost such that 20 cents of every dollar we earn in the economy is going to healthcare. This is more than any other developed country.

So, what is the solution? Those on the Red side of the political aisle may say "repeal and replace" the Affordable Care Act (also known as Obamacare) and let market forces sort things out, because only a free market can address all the moving pieces of the healthcare market and set prices to reasonable and accurate values. Advocates for a free market solution would silence skeptics by saying *the current system we have does not function like a free market yet and should be given a chance to truly compete.* Those on the Blue side of the aisle may say that the market is cold and heartless and does not apply to something like healthcare. So, they say, we need a simpler single-payer system paid for by the government, like Canada has. On one end of that spectrum is "Medicare for All," fully government sponsored, which would expand what some view as an already-successful Medicare program. The more moderate camp on the Blue side may suggest we keep private insurance companies and private provider options while also expanding a form of Medicare. So, which side of the political aisle has the correct solution to America's healthcare dilemma? Or is it possible the best solution(s) would be a compromise between both proposals, which I will call Purple solutions.

While our politicians are more polarized than ever before, I would like to believe that the average American citizen is more reasonable and open-minded. Is that true? I'm not sure. We did elect our leaders, so perhaps we are also just as polarized? I hope not. Only *we*—as citizens, consumers, everyday folk—can drive the kind of change and compromise that is needed to create a healthcare system that actually works and reflects what is good about America. That is the purpose of this book. It is a call to action. Maybe even, in the words of John Torinus, a call for a grassroots healthcare revolution. It is a roadmap to assist American consumers as they search for and discuss intelligent and informed solutions to healthcare that are not all Red or all Blue but are more likely to be Purple solutions.

This brings me to the central thesis of this book. I truly do believe that each side of the political aisle brings some value to the healthcare reform debate. In fact, we need both sides to balance the other and offer solutions to the blind spots that each may have.

I believe we need some sort of competitive market to foster innovation and produce realistic pricing and value in what everyone agrees is an incredibly complex system of services. This is the topic of section 2 of this book, which is on the Red side of the discussion. I also believe we need some sort of safety net to protect the poor as well as all of us against catastrophic events, like an expensive cancer treatment, infusion therapy, or even costly end-of-life care. With regard to the latter, a majority of those in nursing homes end up on Medicaid, which can only happen when you reach poverty level (i.e., all your assets have been depleted by our healthcare system). That is not a good way to end one's life with dignity. This safety net discussion is the topic of section 4 of this book, which is on the Blue side of the debate. Section 1 of the book provides an introduction to the current state of healthcare in America, and section 3 provides on overview of high drug prices.

So where do we point an accusing finger for the creation of our dysfunctional healthcare system in America? It is likely true that for the most part those in government and those in the medical provider world sincerely want to help patients and provide quality, accessible healthcare. They likely have good intentions. But there are dysfunctional incentives in our system, and there are also those who are gaming the system for financial gain. Is it big government or big corporations at fault? Perhaps both. Too much concentrated power and decision-making in government or large corporations is equally bad. We need power and decision-making in the hands of patients and the providers (e.g., physicians, nurses) who directly help them and are on the frontlines of healthcare delivery. This book presents a case for Purple solutions that aim to empower the consumers of healthcare (the patients) and the providers (physicians, nurses, and the like), rather than big government or big corporations, with the clear goal of providing more accessible, higher-quality, and more affordable healthcare. Unfortunately, there is no powerful lobby group for this goal.

Finally, what was the inspiration for this book and the source of information for it? It is a product of the *Rx Think Tank* (RxThinkTank.org). In full disclosure, a fraction of the profits from this book will go to support the activities of the Rx Think Tank, whose mission is "to increase Quality, Access, and Affordability of healthcare for all, in a patient-centered and consumer-driven healthcare delivery model." The Rx Think Tank at Concordia University has held *Healthcare Economics Summits* for four years, hosting discussions with the brightest minds in healthcare policy, from physicians to hospital CEOs to healthcare delivery entrepreneurs to those in the pharmaceutical supply chain, to state and federal politicians. The content of this book is informed by those speakers, as well as discussions with the hundreds of Rx Think Tank members, attendees, and panelists who have participated in these summits over the years, along with research into the healthcare policy literature. While this book is largely my writing, based on research and insights from these many scholars and practitioners, there are also many guest-expert-authored chapters. For these chapters, I typically provide a preface that provides context, and there is a brief biography of each author at the end of the book. Many of these guest authors are of differing political views and might be opposed to what other authors have submitted and written; but the goal of this book is to provide a diversity of perspectives. I attempt to provide a common thread and coherence between, before, and after chapters. And at the end of each section, a roadmap for compromise— *Purple solutions*—is also presented, so that we can have better-informed, intelligent, and respectful conversations about healthcare in America.

You may wonder if I am qualified to write and edit a book on this topic? Probably no more than a lot of other people. I do have a PhD, MBA, and a JD degree, so you would think I might know a thing or two about law, regulations, pharmaceutical science, business, and healthcare. I even started several biotech companies, and now I serve as a dean and professor of business, with a passion for healthcare policy. But I am finding there is far more that I do not know than what I do. I learned this lesson especially when I decided to take on this project, asking, "What is wrong with healthcare in America, and how do we fix it?"

Healthcare administrators often say "healthcare is complicated," then they go on to use complicated terminology only they understand, like ICD-10 codes, CPT codes, reimbursements, chargemasters, risk pools, capitation, value-based care, stop loss insurance, population health, EHRs, RVUs, and of course they reference the giant tome we call the Affordable Care Act, which few people have ever read. These administrators get paid big salaries to use these terms and to master their small siloed piece of this large healthcare system. No degrees helped me understand this healthcare system. I just talked to a lot of smart people working in the field, outside the field, and even some looking to disrupt and change the field. I have to confess that last group was the most fun. This book is an attempt to summarize the gems of those conversations as well as some relevant healthcare policy and medical-business literature.

When we are told that "healthcare is complicated," we often throw up our hands and say, "I'm just glad someone else smart is handling this." Please don't do that. Healthcare is not so complicated that we can't discuss how it all works at a high level and identify the problems. The last time somebody told me something was complicated, and they talked fast with a lot of confusing words and asked me to trust them, I found out they were embezzling money. Sometimes I wonder if healthcare is like that. This book is an attempt to explain healthcare in America, and I am certain it is not so complicated that you can't understand it. Read this book cover to cover, or just use it as a reference and move between chapters depending on what interests you. I have tremendous respect for the intellect of Americans, even if our politicians do not speak to us as if we are intelligent. Let's rise above their low expectations and characterization of us and push them to find effective bipartisan solutions to America's broken healthcare system.

I am looking forward to my family discussions this next November, and then for all of us to vote our consciences for what we think makes the most sense for healthcare reform. I hope we elect politicians who can rise above the current political theatrics and dysfunction, with the courage to reach across the aisle to find ways to fix healthcare in America, using truly bipartisan Purple solutions that work.

Purple Solutions

SECTION 1

Where Are We Now?
The Good and the Bad

CHAPTER 1

Why Healthcare in America Is More Expensive Than It Needs to Be

DANIEL SEM

This chapter provides an introduction and a broad overview of the history of healthcare and insurance in America and how and why it is so expensive compared to other countries. The chapter is really a foundation for the rest of the book, which includes a wide range of guest authors who are experts and leaders in their fields and who go deeper into different aspects of the issues that I present in this chapter. Guest authors in subsequent chapters sometimes take differing views on the problems and solutions to healthcare cost and access problems, but that is the goal of this book—to explore a range of bipartisan, Purple solutions.

Who Pays for Healthcare in America?

Before addressing the cost of healthcare, we should consider first how we pay for healthcare in America because that affects the cost. Although *price* is probably the more accurate term because price is what you or some surrogate acting on your behalf pays, irrespective of what it actually costs. You might say that your employer, your insurance company, or the government pays for your healthcare, and then you contribute something in the form of a co-pay and deductible. You, of course, also pay insurance premiums. Well, actually, you are paying for all of it, either directly or indirectly. Right now, $18 of every $100 you earn at your job goes to healthcare, while in many other countries that have better health outcomes the amount is much less (typically half) per person. So, the real problem with healthcare in America is not who pays for it (you, your company, the government, or your insurance) but the actual cost. Ultimately, though, you are paying no matter what. If the cost keeps increasing without justification, you pay. As a result of inflated prices, which may or may not be the result of increased real costs, others who are part of what has been referred to as the Medical-Industrial Complex benefit (see chapters 4 and 5) (Relman, 1980). How did we get to this state of affairs, and why is it this way? To address this question, let us briefly review the history of healthcare delivery and insurance in America

3

over the last 100 years. After that, we will return to this topic of cost (and the price you must pay), which is the real and more significant problem.

The History and Role of Healthcare Insurance

The way we deliver and pay for healthcare in the United States has changed a lot over time. So has the cost. Going back only as far as 1960, we spent a modest 5% of gross domestic product (GDP), or $146 per person on healthcare, versus 18% of GDP and $10,739 per person now (Amadeo, 2020). How was this paid then and now? There was a time at the beginning of the twentieth century when people paid cash for healthcare and did not rely on insurance. So it all started with us paying for healthcare directly, and healthcare was not that expensive (less than 5% of GDP). I am not suggesting we should return to those days, but it is interesting to note and remind ourselves that *healthcare and access to healthcare is not the same as insurance*. News flash: You actually can get (typically lower cost) healthcare without using insurance! This is called *self-pay* or *direct pay* healthcare, and it is a growing trend among consumers who cannot afford high co-pays and deductibles, even with Affordable Care Act (ACA) plans (Parnell, 2014). As healthcare consumers, we typically assume that the only way to get healthcare is with insurance and that access to good healthcare is synonymous with access to good insurance. That, after all, is what the ACA is all about. It is about making sure that everyone has insurance, not necessarily about making sure everyone has access to good healthcare. But these are different concepts, even if you do not see that yet. Please bear with me on this, as a central thesis of this chapter is that how we *do* insurance, by letting surrogates act on our behalf, is at the root of why healthcare is so expensive in America.

What Is Insurance?

It seems simple enough—the insurance company, our surrogate—reimburses us for medical expenses. This is for everything from routine checkups to emergency room (ER) visits, to open-heart surgery to infusion therapy for cancer. But how does most insurance, outside of healthcare, work? Think of your car or home insurance. If you totaled your car or your home was destroyed in a fire, insurance pays to help you recover from these rare but catastrophic and financially devastating events. For more routine problems, like a dead battery or alternator in your car, or a broken water heater in your home, you pay for those directly with cash or credit. Healthcare insurance is not like that. It is not like insurance at all. We expect healthcare insurance to pay for everything, even routine doctor visits that would cost less than $100 if we paid cash but will be billed at much higher prices if we use insurance. But then why do we care as long as it is reimbursed, right? That is a problem that I will get to later, but for now suffice to say that the prices charged to insurance companies are highly inflated and do not likely reflect actual costs, so you do not ever want to pay those prices. And yet you typically probably do pay those inflated prices as you work toward hitting your deductible if you use insurance. On the positive side, though, you think that everything is largely free for you after that deductible. Many of us go on a healthcare spending spree at the end of the year after we have hit our deductibles—and why not? Of course, now that we have increasingly large deductibles and co-pays, we are actually starting to care and would like to avoid these large price tags for doctor and especially ER visits altogether. Interestingly and surprisingly, the co-pays or deductibles that we pay are typically larger than if we used a self-pay approach, but we do not do that because we believe that it is not possible to not use insurance and instead pay directly since we wrongly believe that all healthcare *must* be "purchased" using insurance. The point is, healthcare insurance is not insurance in the way we typically think of insurance, and we have become so accustomed to this idea that we as healthcare consumers are paralyzed in the absence of insurance, even when the most logical thing to do is to not use it. Unfortunately, the healthcare system is not currently set up to let us easily purchase without insurance, often forcing us to pay the inflated prices that providers charge insurance companies and not telling us, up front, what things would cost if we did want to pay cash. That is changing now. This phenomenon, and the potential solution of paying directly and only using insurance for expensive needs, is the central thesis of a 2013 book by David Goldhill entitled *Catastrophic Care*. Goldhill argues that we would be better off treating healthcare insurance like other forms of insurance and paying for routine healthcare needs using cash, perhaps from health savings accounts (HSAs) paid for by employers and others. This leverages market forces to control cost and makes the patient the real customer rather than some disinterested surrogate (government or insurance company). Goldhill is probably in large part correct, but I am getting ahead of myself. Back to the history of healthcare delivery and insurance in America.

The History of Healthcare Insurance
During World War II, President Franklin Delano Roosevelt (FDR) passed the Stabilization Act (1942) as part of his wartime effort to control inflation by freezing wages, salaries, and prices. To deal with a labor shortage, companies needed to find creative ways to attract employees, and since they could not offer increased wages or salaries, they offered benefits in the form

of healthcare insurance. That is how healthcare insurance became linked to employment, and it has been that way since. So the fact that we get our insurance from our employers is a "wartime accident" (Mihm, 2017). In this regard, the United States is somewhat unique in the world, since most other countries, with the exception of Japan (Ellis et al., 2014), do not couple healthcare insurance with employment. To address frustrations with this system, some have proposed national healthcare.

There was no national healthcare in the United States until the introduction of Medicare and Medicaid on July 30, 1965, when President Lyndon B. Johnson signed into law the bill that created it. It started as Medicare Part A (hospital insurance) and Part B (medical insurance) and was expanded further in 1972; Medicare Part D, created under the Medicare Prescription Drug Improvement and Modernization Act of 2003, added prescription drug benefits (Centers for Medicare and Medicaid [CMS], 2020). Today, Medicare and Medicaid are managed under the Department of Health and Human Services within the CMS, currently under the leadership of Alex Azar II and Seema Verma, respectively (U.S. Department of Health and Human Services [HHS], 2019a). Medicare is available to anyone age 65 or older, and Medicaid is available only to low-income families under the age of 65, with income at or below 133% of the federal poverty level (CMS, n.d.). The only other public and federally funded national healthcare insurance in the United States is TRICARE, for current and former members of the military (TRICARE, n.d.). Medicare, Medicaid, and TRICARE are kinds of national public insurance.

Private insurance, typically paid for by employers since World War II, has evolved significantly over the years. One interesting period of development was in the 1970s and 1980s, when HMOs became popular. HMOs began in 1970 as a response to concerns over increasing costs and because of growing public demand for national healthcare. President Richard Nixon's administration responded with the HMO Act of 1973, which led to the growth of HMOs in the 1980s with around 30 million participants in 1987 (Gruber et al., 1988). But consumer frustration over limited choices for providers and services began to kick in around 1987 (Gruber et al., 1988). Around that time, HMOs began to decline in popularity. The decline and dissatisfaction peaked in the 1990s. The generally accepted reason for the decline of HMOs was summarized in a *CommonWealth Magazine* article:

> Patients complained about services denied and referrals refused, but the disgruntlement actually started among physicians. Most doctors working under HMOs . . . preferred the traditional practice model (choice of

provider, choice of treatment, fee-for-service payment), but that model had become too costly for many employer groups. Feeling coerced by market forces, doctors complained to their patients. (Enthoven, 2005)

On a more positive note, the National Bureau of Economic Research (2020) reported how medical spending decreased during the time when HMOs were popular. After HMOs went out of vogue, healthcare costs resumed their relentless increases, much higher than inflation. Two clear lessons from our exploration into HMOs emerged: (a) Some logical constraints on healthcare spending actually help to control costs, and (b) Americans do not like constraints on their healthcare choices (Enthoven, 2005).

The failure of the HMO system, which was intended to provide more efficient and effective healthcare, led some to conclude that we needed more portable health insurance that was separate from employer-based insurance, like the statewide nonemployer-based plan proposed by Republican Curt Gielow and Democrat Jon Richards in Wisconsin (Enthoven, 2005). That plan, called the Wisconsin Health Plan (presented by Curt Gielow in chapter 20), would have provided a choice of health plans and would have supported and created integrated-delivery HMOs without as many restrictions as the HMO system that was once prevalent. But it never became a reality and was controversial because it was, at the state level, universal care that was to be financed by a payroll tax. It was a failed attempt at a Purple solution for a safety net.

After HMOs, healthcare costs resumed their continued rise, and the industry continued its trend toward increasing levels of consolidation, facilitated by a number of factors that included federal regulatory constraints and incentives that favored large consolidated providers (see more on this in chapters 4 and 5). This situation led to the growth of what some have cynically called the Medical-Industrial Complex (MIC). This term is a reference to President Dwight Eisenhower's 1961 warning about the "military-industrial complex," which he feared would have excessive economic and political power. Dr. Arnold Relman wrote an article raising concerns about how the increasingly consolidated healthcare industry is focused too much on profit maximization and is putting physicians under pressure to themselves be financially motivated to provide excessive services and procedures, even if not in the best interests of the patient (Relman, 1980).

Most recently we had the passage of the Patient Protection and Affordable Care Act of 2010 (ACA), which permits people to buy private insurance on private exchanges. It was an attempt at universal healthcare but using publicly financed private insurance purchased on exchanges. These insurance plans, as well as the most prevalent employer-sponsored insurance plans, are evolving increasingly into high-deductible plans (Cohen & Zammitti, 2018). These deductibles are so painfully high for the average American family that it is almost like not having insurance or having what is called *catastrophic care* insurance. The average deductible for a family in 2019 was $3,700 for employer-sponsored plans, with 14% of deductibles being more than $6,000 (Masterson, 2019). Within the ACA exchanges, the high-deductible plans, called the bronze plans, require you to pay 40% of your healthcare costs, with an annual out-of-pocket maximum of $7,900 in 2019 (HealthPocket, 2020). How many families can afford $7,900 or even $3,700 in a given year, in addition to their monthly insurance premiums, whether through the ACA or their employer? This is not sustainable. We are at a tipping point.

These high-deductible plans are almost like catastrophic care plans that provide coverage only for very expensive procedures. Perhaps that is how we should view them, rather than paying the inflated prices coming from hospital chargemaster (aka proprietary) price lists for more routine doctor visits. That is to say, now might be the time, finally, for consumers to rethink how we do insurance, because the insurance we now have is essentially forcing us to overpay for care that can be purchased at much more favorable rates if we just purchased them without insurance. Indeed, many are opting to not use insurance and instead pay cash for services to save money (Rosato, 2018). While you can ask your current provider what they would charge you if you paid cash, there are also resources to help consumers shop for direct primary care (direct pay) options on their own, such as:

- MDsave: https://www.mdsave.com
- PricePain: http://www.pricepain.com
- SimpleCare (from American Association of Patients and Providers): https://simplecare.com/providers.asp
- Association of American Physicians and Surgeons (AAPS): https://aapsonline.org

And soon you will be able to get reasonably priced primary care at retail drugstores like CVS, Walgreens, and Walmart (see chapter 10).

With the now high level of consumer spending on healthcare through high-deductible plans, we seem to be at a tipping point, or perhaps more accurately a breaking point, in healthcare in the United States. This is why healthcare is the top concern for 36% of voters in the upcoming elections (Cannon, 2019), and it is why we need politicians to begin reaching across the aisle to find solutions—Purple solutions.

How Other Countries Do Insurance

The evolution of healthcare insurance in the United States was clearly convoluted and has led us to the very nonoptimal place that we are in now. As mentioned earlier, Japan and the United States are unique in the world in that they predominantly finance healthcare insurance through employers, although in Japan it is mandatory (Ellis et al., 2014). How do other countries handle healthcare insurance? Contrary to popular belief, countries with universal healthcare that is paid for by the government vary significantly in how they implement it and the extent to which they involve private-sector insurance companies and competition. Some countries (e.g., the Netherlands and Switzerland) require purchasing of private insurance offered by competing private insurance providers, without offering public options, similar to the ACA (Tikkanen, 2019). Pure public (i.e., government run and funded, paid for by taxes) single-payer national plans are less common, but are offered by countries that include the United Kingdom, Canada, Norway, and Sweden (Tikkanen, 2019). Yet even in these countries with single-payer public plans, most (with the notable exception of Canada) have secondary private insurance options to cover noncovered services and for faster access to care—or in some cases for prescription drugs that are not covered on the public plan (Tikkanen, 2019). Canada is unique in that it has publicly funded universal healthcare and does not allow supplementary private insurance and does not even allow consumers to get healthcare services (e.g., MRI scans) outside of the public plan. This is much more restrictive than most countries in the European Union, for example, which typically allow consumers to either purchase additional private insurance or purchase healthcare services directly with cash to avoid the waits or suboptimal care of publicly funded plans. This has led to problems for Canadian healthcare consumers who often go to the United States for care to obtain treatments that are not covered under their restrictive universal public plan or in situations where waits are too long. In one conversation with a Canadian physician, I was informed that he saw a significant number of patients who were not willing to wait for procedures such as hip or knee surgeries, which typically had a wait time of 6 to 12 months in Canada in his experience. He saw, directly or through his colleagues, roughly four patients a week going to the United States for these procedures. And in a study by the Frasier Institute, 63,459 Canadians chose to receive healthcare outside of Canada, which was thought to be due to the long wait times Canadians had for procedures—10.6 weeks after seeing a specialist, for medically necessary procedures. In one example, otolaryngologists saw 2.1% of their patients going abroad for procedures (Ren & Labrie, 2017). This would not happen if Canada allowed supplemental private insurance options or direct pay options in addition to its universal public plan, as is the case in many other countries.

Contrasting with the universal care provided by public single-payer plans like Canada's, Germany has a more flexible universal multipayer system that is also paid for by the government, and there are on the order of 200 plans available (Ellis et al., 2014). Singapore has even more flexibility, with both public and private insurance providers, and with the services from public-sector providers focused on inpatient, outpatient, and emergency care while the private sector is focused more on primary and preventative care. As mentioned earlier, Singapore has one of the lowest-cost healthcare systems. It relies on a model where Singaporeans must buy insurance through government-sponsored HSAs, with the insurance being subsidized by the government (Ellis et al., 2014). While government-sponsored, it does make the patient the consumer and introduces some market forces in that way. Overall, there are very few peer countries to the United States (again, excepting Canada) that have implemented a single-payer system without private or direct pay options also being made available to supplement and fill coverage gaps or other deficiencies in the public universal healthcare options. And while a handful of countries (e.g., the United Kingdom and Canada) have only public single-payer plans, most with universal care actually have private or a mixture of public and private insurance options to choose from, even if they are mandated and paid for by the government. Given the American culture that values freedom, individuality, autonomy, and choice, if you favor government-sponsored universal care, as most Democrats do, then the more appropriate option seems to be a hybrid version, like those offered in Germany, Switzerland, and Singapore, rather than those that offer only one public single-payer plan, like the United Kingdom and Canada. Very few developed countries have restricted healthcare consumers so as to completely limit them to public options by not even permitting private insurance options to supplement what the public option does not offer. While America does not need to do what other countries do, we would be foolish to avoid the lessons learned in those countries, and we should think about what fits best with our unique culture and values as Americans.

Back to Considering Who Pays for Healthcare and Who the Real Customer Is

This chapter began by asking the question "Who pays for healthcare in America?" In America, the current political debate seems to be about insurance, which is either employer-financed insurance (the status quo) or government-sponsored insurance, including the exchanges offered in connection with the

ACA. But the insurance companies or the government are our surrogates, making healthcare decisions and making payment decisions for us and then asking for our money to do this. We ignore cost or price and maintain the illusion, with insurance or the government, that someone else is paying for our healthcare. But, in fact, as healthcare costs rise, insurance premiums just increase, which we pay because our employers pay them. Some have argued that wage stagnation in America is the result of this because what employers would have paid us in raises has gone to pay for increased benefits, in the form of healthcare insurance (MarketWatch, 2018). All along, the insurance companies make more money because as costs and prices rise they simply charge us higher premiums. Insurance companies do what they can to reject claims, which is a problem unto itself, with around 200 million claims rejected each year (Mayer, 2009). But as insurance company expenses rise, they simply charge higher premiums, which is why premium rates paid by employers have increased significantly faster than inflation (National Conference of State Legislatures, 2018). There really is no market force to keep prices low, as there would have been if we were paying directly and were personally responsive to prices. This is again explained most eloquently in Goldhill's book. According to his logic, it would be better for the government or our employer to provide us with money (in a health savings account) and then for us to spend that money on our healthcare directly, as is done in Singapore, rather than insert a surrogate to make purchasing decisions on our behalf (e.g., those in the insurance company who decide if claims should be reimbursed or rejected) (Goldhill, 2013).

The Incentives Are Wrong in Our Current System

Free market advocates would say that accurate prices paid by actual end-user consumers provide correct incentives and ultimately lead to better products and services at lower cost. Our current healthcare system does not have the actual end-user consumer (patients) making decisions and paying actual market prices. Even our doctors are not aware of and are not sensitive to prices. So there is no free and competitive market; only a reimbursement-driven system that rewards for more medical procedures. One might argue whether there should be a free market for healthcare. My point is simply that since the introduction of insurance in the 1950s, there never was. We, as healthcare consumers, do not even know how much healthcare costs and neither do our doctors. And even if we did, we would still make our decisions based only on whether the healthcare is reimbursed by insurance (or Medicare/Medicaid), which has pre-negotiated contracts with our providers. We would rather get the in-house $2,000 MRI scan than go outside for an equally high-quality $700 MRI if the former is reimbursed and the latter is not. Those are accurate representative numbers (see specific examples to follow) that illustrate the dysfunctional nature of the incentives in our current system that is driven by reimbursements (insurance or Medicare/Medicaid). Compounding this problem, physicians in large provider groups typically get penalized if they refer out for procedures, which—in the language of the providers—is referred to as "leakage." Physicians are not to be blamed for their complicity, since they typically do not know how much procedures cost or how they impact their patients financially. They are experts in medical diagnoses and treatments, not in finance. So they tell us to get the MRI in-house because they are told by their administrators to refer internally. It is much easier, and all of the information is in-house in the electronic medical record (EMR), so the care you get is said to be much more coordinated. Sounds good. Makes sense. One could also view this as a powerful anticompetitive tool used by larger hospitals and providers to hinder competition, allowing them to charge more for procedures. And we consumers do not care because as long as insurance companies reimburse via pre-negotiated contracts and prices with large providers, what does it matter? Hospitals are in constant battles with insurance companies, fighting to get services reimbursed, while insurance companies push back to turn down reimbursements and reject claims. This administrative war, manned by large teams of billing and medical coding experts (whose salaries we pay), ultimately puts others (our surrogates) in charge of deciding what care we will get that is covered. If you doubt it is a war, ask any physician who has had to lobby on their patient's behalf for reimbursement of a procedure that their "peer" in the insurance company has denied, or ask any patient who has had their claim coverage denied as one of the 200 million annually rejected claims mentioned earlier.

Adding to the misguided incentives in our healthcare system, physicians in large provider networks are often compensated, even with Medicare, based on the quantity of services they provide in what are called *relative value units* (RVUs), as discussed in chapters 3 and 4 (Centers for Medicare and Medicaid Services, Medicare Learning Network, 2017). Physicians in large provider groups are perversely incentivized in this fee-for-service model (versus a salary model) to have patients get more healthcare services, and especially more expensive procedures, in what is sometimes referred to as, using the wonderfully cynical phrase describing how they get compensated, "eat what you kill" (Ali, 2019). I truly believe that physicians go into medicine predominantly for noble reasons, to help patients. But putting them under the pressure of this dysfunctional incentive is a problem. All of these well-intentioned government-created dysfunctional incentives, discussed further in chapter 3, conspire to have you as a patient get more unnecessary care from the hospital (which makes more money), where the incentive is to have more procedures done and billed and reimbursed, but never with an eye to overall cost. As long as it is reimbursed, you or the hospital do not care. And when the hospital loses its battle with the insurance company or Medicare and it is not reimbursed, then you are stuck needing to pay an inflated price that comes from the hospital's chargemaster list of prices. In a nutshell, the incentives in our system were designed with good intentions (see chapter 3), but they are wrong, and you the patient do not have much say in the process of determining what healthcare you will or will not get, and how much you will have to pay in the end. And in the midst of all of this dysfunction, the cost of healthcare in the United States continues to rise. So should we be focusing our political debate only on deciding who pays—insurance or government or you (well, it is always you)—or determining why the cost is so high? Perhaps we should be discussing cost also.

The Real Problem Is Cost, and the Absence of Price Transparency and Markets

The United States spent $3.5 trillion on healthcare in 2017, more than any other developed country in the world (Amadeo, 2020). That is roughly $10,000 per person and typically includes contributions from our employers and from us directly in the form of deductibles and co-pays. Those deductibles and co-pays have increased significantly in recent years because of the increasing prevalence of high-deductible plans. This spending is starting to put unbearable strains on the average American family. For all of this spending, does the United States have the best healthcare in the world? No. We may lead the way in medical innovation, new drugs, and new surgical procedures, but in terms of health outcomes not so much. We rank poorly in the world relative to peer countries (Woolf & Aron, 2013), although some have argued that these rankings are misleading because they ignore other factors, like lifestyle and social determinants of health, that are uniquely poor in the United States and have nothing to do with our healthcare system directly (Price & Norbeck, 2018).

The Major Contributors to the Cost of Healthcare

The largest overall contributors to healthcare spending are physician and clinical services (20%) and hospital care (33%) (Centers for Medicare and Medicaid Services, Medicare Learning Network, n.d.). Increasing hospital costs are thought to be caused by some of the factors described in the previous section, as well as from the trend toward consolidations (Gee &

Gurwitz, 2018). These problems and trends are discussed in chapters 3 through 5. Some have argued that this trend toward overconsolidation is leading to anticompetitive behavior and pricing abuses (Gee, 2019). To address these problems, in part, the Donald Trump administration and HHS proposed a new CMS rule on price transparency and competition on November 15, 2019. Hospitals would have to make public all charges, including payer-specific negotiated charges and the amount the hospital would accept in a cash payment from a patient. Hospitals would also be required to provide a "display of shoppable services in a consumer-friendly manner" that must be "easily accessible. Without barriers and . . . searchable. Item descriptions must be in 'plain language'" (HHS, 2019b). Not surprisingly, hospitals, which include the American Hospital Association, are suing the Trump administration to keep this information secret (Abelson, 2019). The response by Caitlin Oakley, speaking for the Department of Health and Human Services, was that "hospitals should be ashamed that they aren't willing to provide American patients the cost of a service before they purchase it" (Abelson, 2019). This regulatory step is a small positive one toward price transparency, to better inform and empower patient-consumers.

Cost Relative to Other Countries

Overall cost of healthcare continues to rise in the United States, now at 18% of GDP. That equates to $10,222 per person, with the next highest-spending country being Switzerland ($8,009), followed by Germany ($5,728) and six other wealthy European countries, Canada, Australia, and Japan, all in the $4,200 to $5,500 range (Sawyer & Cox, 2018). On the whole, we spend about twice what our peer countries spend and seven times what Singapore spends, per person. Singapore is a uniquely positive success story, since Singaporeans spend only 2.5% of GDP on healthcare (Ministry of Finance Singapore, 2019), and yet they have a healthcare system and outcomes that compare very favorably with ours in the United States (Carroll, 2019). Singapore also out-performed the United State in their initial response to the 2020 coronavirus pandemic. There are aspects of the healthcare system in Singapore that have been highlighted by other authors (Goldhill, 2013) as providing useful lessons for us as we rethink our healthcare system in the United States. These will be discussed in more detail later in the chapter.

Putting U.S. Spending in Perspective, Internally

If we spend 18% of GDP on healthcare, that means for every $100 of your paycheck $18 of it goes to healthcare. That $18 goes to cover not just your insurance premiums and co-pays, but also tax dollars to cover Medicare and Medicaid. Medicare and Medicaid themselves already consume $1 trillion per year (HHS, n.d.). It is also worth noting that Medicare and Medicaid should probably be considered as *costing* even more than this, since the level at which they reimburse hospitals is so low that hospitals need to charge more for non-Medicare and non-Medicaid services to make up the loss in what is called *cost-shifting* (Roy & The Apothecary, 2019). In any case, $1 trillion, 40% of which is Medicare, is a significant fraction of the total United States federal budget of $4.7 trillion (Amadeo, 2019). Try to imagine the impact of expanding Medicare across the whole population, such as in the Medicare for All proposal of Senator Bernie Sanders. Right now, we spend $0.4 trillion on Medicare to treat everyone age 65 and over, which represents 52 million people in 2018 (Mather et al., 2019) or only 16% of the population. Scaling for the whole population of 327 million, in a crude calculation, that would be $2.5 trillion if everyone was on Medicare and at the same spending level. Like I said, this is a crude calculation, since it ignores the fact that Medicare is a lower estimate of actual cost, and the competing factor that more healthcare spending occurs as we get older—30% of Medicare spending itself happens as end-of-life care (Davis et al., 2016). Previously reported estimates of the cost of Medicare for All per year (over 10 years) have ranged from $2.5 trillion to $3.6 trillion (Committee for a Responsible Federal Budget, 2019). The bottom line is that our healthcare is too expensive, and it is far more expensive than in other countries. How we pay (ACA, Medicare for All, private insurance) is important. But expanding Medicare, or proposing other public options, does not get at the real problem, which is cost, and the fact that there is not enough money to pay for a dramatically increased version of what we already have. As Democratic presidential candidate Pete Buttigieg commented in a political debate in response to a discussion about the justification for the large spending in Medicare for All: "We've got to move past the Washington mentality that suggests that the bigness of plans only consists of how many trillions of dollars they put through the treasury" (Hellmann, 2020). Medicare for All, if expanded, would certainly cost a significant amount of money, and many would argue it is not financially sustainable and would not necessarily provide better healthcare. Those who favor universal healthcare need to devise plans that are at least fiscally feasible. The debate continues. But the debate, which is mostly about how to pay for the healthcare, needs to also include more discussion of why it is so costly and how to decrease the cost, because we only have around $15 trillion to spend for everything—from defense to education to healthcare. Purple solutions that discuss government-sponsored universal healthcare also need to consider a role for the private sector and real functional competing markets for insurance, as well as for buying healthcare without insurance.

A Government-Regulated, Reimbursement-Driven Market

The current political debate avoids the root problem of cost and is focused only on insurance and, more generally, reimbursement strategies. That is, it is focused on whether we should use private insurance or public insurance, and in the extreme case Medicare for All. The ACA itself is mostly about insurance, although it proposes to use private insurance, subsidized by the government. Insurance is important, but the underlying and bigger problem in the United States is the high cost of healthcare, whether we pay for it directly or through employer-sponsored insurance or through the government from the taxes we pay. Whoever is getting rich off of America's inflated healthcare costs must be very happy that Democrats and Republicans are only talking about how to pay them (i.e., public or private insurance) and very little about how and why people are charged so much. The high charges are not necessarily from malicious intent, but rather from a lack of market forces, price transparency, and ground-level decision-making by the patient-consumer and the physician or other frontline provider. Increasingly, decision-making in healthcare is through bureaucracies: (a) government regulatory agencies demanding compliance (see chapter 3) and (b) a highly consolidated, sometimes anticompetitive Medical-Industrial Complex with great economic and political power demanding compliance with its internal policies (see chapters 3 and 5). Arguments can be made that we would have better healthcare and lower cost if control and decision-making were at the level of the consumer, at the patient-provider interface, and if the consumer could know prices (including co-pays and deductibles) up front. This price information, combined with medical-quality information interpreted with the help of a nonbiased (i.e., not financially conflicted) physician or a healthcare navigator—a new kind of healthcare service provider, explained later in this chapter—could be used to guide our healthcare decision-making (see chapter 9). This would lead to a world where we as consumers are in charge (see chapters 8 and 10), and because of market forces it would lower healthcare costs and also cut administrative waste. It would be a healthcare market that is better and more responsive to our needs than our purely reimbursement-driven healthcare market.

Transparent Market-Driven versus Opaque Reimbursement-Driven Markets

The former puts patient-consumers in control, and the latter puts government or insurance companies in control. While the current healthcare system in the United States includes some competitive markets for private healthcare insurance (e.g., in the ACA exchanges), there is no competitive market for the actual healthcare services, where consumers can see realistic and accurate prices and what they get for those prices—although, with the pending CMS rule that demands that hospitals provide price transparency, this may be changing. For example, ProHealth Care in Wisconsin is doing rather innovative work to develop new easy-to-navigate, consumer-facing tools for price shopping that are exactly what the market needs and seem to be what the CMS rule on price transparency is asking for (see figure 1.1).

Market-driven trends that empower consumers—to *consumerize* healthcare—are now beginning to go beyond simply offering healthcare services in traditional settings, like hospitals, to include remote medicine via telemedicine and, as covered in chapter 10, clinics in drugstores across the country in places like CVS, Walgreens, and Walmart (Paavola, 2019). We will get our care wherever we are: at home, at work, or while traveling. Delivery of healthcare remotely via telemedicine is increasing dramatically due to the 2020 coronavirus pandemic. One hope is that after the pandemic, which has forced us to adopt a new paradigm in healthcare delivery, we will become more open to creative and perhaps better ways to obtain healthcare. We are also being asked to get diagnostic tests (in this case for Covid-19) via drive-up services at drugstores, another positive paradigm shift in healthcare delivery (i.e. in retail settings; see chapter 10) that we might otherwise have been slow to adopt, had it not been for this unfortunate crisis.

Transparent Pricing and Competition to Consumerize Healthcare—for Individuals and the Companies That Buy It for Their Employees

This trend toward consumerizing healthcare is occurring both at the level of individual patient-consumers and at companies that are buying the healthcare for their employees and are tired of paying too much for insurance policies. In his two books *The Grassroots Healthcare Revolution* and *The Company that Solved Healthcare*, John Torinus discusses how he, as CEO of Wisconsin-based Serigraph, took on the high cost of healthcare at his company (Torinus, n.d.b). His motivation came from the fact that healthcare premiums for his employees were becoming his most significant expense, and it kept rising to the point where his company would have

FIGURE 1.1 Consumer-facing price transparency tool being developed at ProHealth Care.

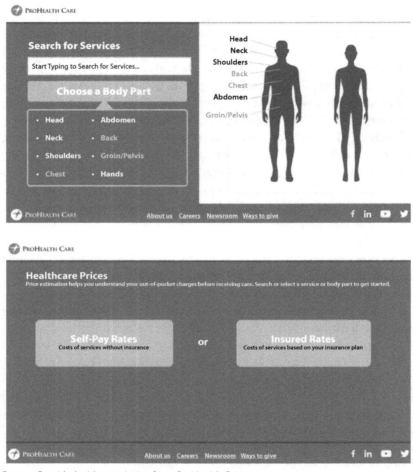

Source: Provided with permission from ProHealth Care.

trouble competing and would also be constrained in how much it could pay employees. So Torinus began looking at the cost of actual services, and he himself began shopping to find the best value for his employees. Just as one example, the price of hip surgeries varied from $26,000 to $46,500, and there was no correlation with quality that he could see—it was arbitrary because prices were not transparent and no market forces were in place (Torinus, n.d.a). For most healthcare consumers and payers, like employers who self-insure, it is almost impossible to get a straight answer on the price for a procedure, whether knee replacement surgery, bypass surgery, or whatever, because there are so many fees that even the hospital that is doing the procedure and that will later charge you cannot tell you the fee up front. But after it is done, you see the bill—often a surprise bill—for the surgeon, the anesthesiologist, the nurses, the hospital bed, various supplies, and on and on. Nobody knows exactly what anything costs, and even if they did the costs are typically inflated prices from the chargemaster list that they created to get maximal reimbursement from the insurance company. Torinus began demanding up-front pricing, called *bundled pricing*, so he would know his options for common procedures. This saved his company significant money and was the topic of one of his books, *The Company That Solved Healthcare* (Torinus, 2010). It is simple: Define and negotiate the price up front. If you think about it, how crazy is it that in healthcare we select services but we have no idea what they will cost us, and we play no role in the process of differentiating what services to get, but then months later we get convoluted and complicated bills that shock us with the actual prices that increasingly have us paying full and inflated costs because of our high-deductible plans. That would be like shopping in a grocery store that had food items with no prices listed and us having only a vague sense that some things may or may not be free, and some things we would have to pay for, but we would have no idea about the actual cost because it is not told to us. Torinus now shops for the best value for his employees up front or enlists the help of an agent who works on his behalf, like Eric Haberichter at Access HealthNet (Access HealthNet, n.d.), to negotiate bundled prices for a fixed and transparent fee (chapters 8 and 9). Haberichter is acting like a healthcare navigator for a company, just like could be done for individual healthcare consumers. A healthcare navigator is a person who acts as an independent agent to help individuals or companies navigate and choose the best healthcare services in a medically and financially sound, holistic, and nonbiased way, whether they go in network or out, with insurance or without. It is a new position in healthcare that is emerging and is discussed in chapter 9. Thus, the vision of consumerization of healthcare is to allow both individuals and the companies that often pay for their healthcare to shop for the best value in transparent and competitive markets with real and accurate prices that can be obtained for exactly what they want: a full procedure—with an easy-to-understand bundled price.

Why Do We Need Transparent Markets and Competition?

When consumers can make informed purchasing decisions based on actual accurate prices that they have to pay, in what are called free markets, this has always led to lower cost and higher quality and the development of new innovative products, and it is the main reason for the prosperity of countries that have allowed capitalism to flourish. This ironically includes socialist China, which only recently (in the late 1990s) allowed somewhat free markets and capitalism to take hold, and this began to increase the prosperity of the country as measured by GDP per person. China is unique in the world in the way it embraces both socialism and capitalism, which typically are mutually exclusive contradictions. I do not mean to suggest anything other than that the increasing prosperity in China was a clear result of the introduction of capitalism and markets. There are obviously other problems from the perspective of a country, like the United States, that values liberty. This role of markets and capitalism in decreasing cost and increasing prosperity was noted by Steve Forbes, who commented that free markets have reduced poverty worldwide, lifting one billion people out of poverty in the last 20 years, and these free markets can turn scarcity into abundance. For example, they are responsible for turning the cell phones of the 1980s (the size of a shoebox, costing $3,995), into something nearly every consumer owns (Forbes, 2019). This same logic is why, unlike for the rest of healthcare, the prices for the top 10 cosmetic surgeries, which are typically paid out of pocket (no insurance, free and competitive markets), have decreased since 1998, based on inflation-adjusted numbers from the American Society for Aesthetic Plastic Surgery (n.d.; Perry, 2017), whereas other medical procedures have increased in cost.

For Markets to Work, Real Prices Are Needed

In healthcare, prices are not transparent and consumers cannot shop, so there is no constraint on price and no market force. Prices are also somewhat arbitrary and often reflect the waste within a given hospital or the extent to which hospitals cost-shift to cover expenses elsewhere, like for under-reimbursed Medicare or Medicaid expenses, or emergency room overuse by the uninsured. Whatever the cause, prices are arbitrary. In one study that looked at 10,155 knee replacement surgeries and 5,013 hip replacement surgeries from 61 hospitals in 2008, a large price variation was found both for the knee replacement surgeries ($1,797 to $12,093) and the total hip replacement surgeries ($2,392 to $12,651). The variability was due predominantly to hospital characteristics (61%) or, within hospital factors (36%), with very little of the variation having to do with the patient characteristics, diagnoses, and comorbidities (Robinson et al., 2012). Similar variability was found for hospital MRIs in California, which varied in price from $255 to $6,221, also in a seemingly arbitrary way. One patient-consumer noted that they were told their MRI would be $1,850 and they had a deductible of $7,500 (so they would pay the full $1,850), but then they discovered they could pay up front at $580 if they agreed to not tell the insurance company (Aliferis, 2014). This seemingly random variation in prices charged for MRIs has been reported in other places, such as Philadelphia ($264 to $3,271), New York City ($416 to $4,527), and Washington, D.C./ Richmond, Virginia ($193 to $2,009) (Proval, 2014). Price seems to have no meaning and varies in an uncontrollable way because it is dictated only by reimbursement levels or other factors unique to a hospital, and they are opaque to the patient-consumer. This might not have mattered to the patient-consumer in past years when insurance covered everything, but now for the first time patients have to pay these arbitrary and inflated prices because of large co-pays and deductibles. As noted by Jennifer Schneider, MD, "There's no way today for someone to know what things will cost if they simply follow the rules and go in-network . . . . It's like letting someone shop on your credit card without any sort of limit" (Proval, 2014). And yet physicians, who don't typically know prices, are told not to refer out of network, in what is termed by the industry as leakage. This term, leakage, should be troubling to you as a consumer and to your doctor, because it suggests an anticompetitive practice that is not in your best interest.

The healthcare industry tries to avoid leakage because it leads to revenue loss for the provider, which has even led to the creation of software to identify which physicians are referring out and why. The stated goal is to rectify the situation because "the patients whom you are referring out may not return back which means you are losing your valuable patient." One software solution vendor recommends "using data analytics . . . that will help prevent leakage" so that they can then "educate in-network providers to minimize the referral leakage" (HealthViewX, 2020). It is argued on one "anti-leakage" software vendor's website that:

> Referrals impact adversely in the revenue cycle of providers, and they most often fail to realize the importance of losing a patient and revenue while directing patients to a specialist outside of their network which could be prevented by building clinically integrated networks that will help to analyze problems within the network and [which] prevents referral leakage. (HealthViewX, 2020)

This mindset is a bit frightening. The benefit that is stated is the value of the "clinically integrated networks." The prospect of providing this seemingly noble benefit is likely why physicians succumb to this practice, believing it is in the best interest of the patient. A more cynical person might view it as "drinking the Kool-Aid." It is a way to keep revenue in the large provider and eliminate smaller providers—like small physician groups—that many would argue provide a better patient experience. But these smaller physician groups are being squeezed out of business (see chapters 4 and 5). This is a rather candid statement of what is done in the industry and could be viewed as an anticompetitive system that leads to more revenue because now providers can bill insurance companies more, with inflated prices from their chargemaster price list.

What Is a Chargemaster?

Chargemasters came into use in the 1950s and provide a listing of all the services that patients use in a hospital setting, along with their prices, which are based on negotiated rates with insurers. The purpose of the chargemaster is twofold: "compliance with public reporting and establishing baseline rates in negotiations with insurers" (Association of American Medical Colleges [AAMC], n.d.). The chargemasters (which are not readily viewable by the public) are an example of the opaque and distorted world of prices billed to insurance companies, in contrast to the real world of prices if patients were to pay directly. The chargemaster prices are inflated prices negotiated with insurers to increase reimbursement for the hospital (see chapter 8). But if a patient either wants to pay directly because they have no insurance or goes out of network accidentally, then these fantasy-world prices become their nightmare—in the form of surprise bills! As noted in an article by Richman and colleagues (2017), "Many healthcare providers seek to collect exorbitant chargemaster rates from uninsured and insured out-of-network patients. These efforts impose significant burdens on financially vulnerable patients and hinder efforts to create affordable narrow-network insurance plans." The authors suggest that the hospitals are actually breaching contracts with their patients, and this could be a mechanism to provide relief from these exorbitant surprise bills, because they argue that "contract law does not support the collection of chargemaster rates, which have little relation to either actual costs or market prices. Instead, proper contract law supports imputing market-negotiated rates" (Richman et al., 2017). Even if these prices were posted online for consumers, they would be of little help since they are artificially inflated prices. Rather, patients need to know what they would actually pay with their insurance based on co-pays and deductibles, and they would also have to put together all of the various costs that go into a procedure in a bundled price—like "the particular blood tests, the particular medicines dispensed, the facility fee and the physician's charge, and more" (Appleby & Ostrov, 2019; Pear, 2019). Compiling all of the separate prices that go into a procedure, say, a hip surgery, is called *price bundling*. The only way that providing transparent prices is useful to consumers is if providers give them bundled prices, then tell them what they would pay without insurance (or out of network) and, if they have insurance, what they would pay in terms of co-pays and deductibles. That information is never easily obtained, unless you use direct pay physicians. Yet this exact kind of price transparency is being required under the pending CMS price transparency rule that would "require hospitals to provide patients with clear, accessible information about their 'standard charges' for the items and services they provide" (HHS, 2019b). It would require the item and service to be in "plain language" and should also include what the hospital is willing to accept if patients pay directly in cash or use insurance. It would, for the first time ever, allow patients to shop for services using accurate prices. And, if prices are displayed openly by all hospitals, it is likely that the arbitrary variation or overly inflated prices would go away because of consumer pressure (i.e., market forces). This assumes there is no implicit price collusion, a concern raised by Robert Graboyes in chapter 14.

If Consumers Know Prices, Will They Shop?

Why would patients ever shop for healthcare services? That is not how things were ever done in America (well, it might have been that way 100 years ago). And it seems like healthcare is different and shopping should not apply and you should not be thinking about money when it comes to healthcare. Well, maybe you would not shop for something urgent, like a bypass surgery, and perhaps you would tend to go with whatever your physician recommends in most cases. That is fine, but if a 10-minute perusal using an online tool that you discuss with your non-financially conflicted physician can save you thousands of dollars, or even $1,000 on an MRI, I think patient-consumers might begin to do it. Especially patient-consumers who have been burned by previous $2,000 surprise bills. People increasingly have high-deductible plans, where they pay full price for services up to their deductible. This is relatively new, and it is financially debilitating for most families. If you have a $2,000 deductible and your doctor says you need an MRI, do you want to gamble and helplessly wait and see if you need to pay the $1,900 for the MRI that is in their chargemaster and is inflated because it was the negotiated price the hospital has with the insurer (and probably also reflects cost-shifting), or would you like to sit down with your doctor and explore an easy-to-navigate web interface or software app, like *Healthcare Bluebook*, that identifies other places that charge as low as $200 and also do quality MRIs? That is the new world we will live in. At the moment, patient-consumers do not know they can shop. They think that they must helplessly wait for and live in fear of the surprise bill they cannot afford. That will all change if the new CMS rule goes into effect and hospitals begin to post their prices up front, and if patients begin to realize they are empowered to shop on their own with the help of a healthcare navigator and software tools and maybe also with the help of their physician.

Rescue From Chargemaster Prices (Surprise Bills), Co-Pays, and/or Large Deductibles

There is no way to avoid them, right? You are trapped in a world with large deductibles and surprise bills, right? That is what most people think, but that is not the reality. Besides someday being able to shop with tools like *Healthcare Bluebook* (figure 1.2), which will hopefully drive down prices, patients can entirely avoid the world of chargemasters, where prices are inflated because of insurance reimbursement battles. There are providers, often smaller providers, that bypass insurance altogether, and they have better rates. Did you know that you can pay directly, with cash or credit card, a direct pay physician with whom you can get 24/7 access for an entire year at $50 to $150 per month (Hunt, 2019)? Compare this to a single ER visit, which in 2007 cost on average $1,389 (Alltucker, 2019). Paying out of pocket for the direct pay physician often costs less than using insurance, which also runs the risk of surprise bills or large deductibles.

A story shared with me recently by a family friend illustrates well an all-too-common scenario, highlighting problems with the lack of price transparency and patient empowerment in our healthcare system. Her small company does not offer insurance, so she purchased insurance that had premiums of around $500 to $600 per month, less than that offered through the ACA exchange, with better benefits and a deductible of $5,000. One day she hurt her toe and dislodged the nail, which she tended to at home but then decided to go to urgent care. At urgent care, a nurse bandaged her toe and suggested it might be fine, but to be safe, suggested she should go to the ER in case of infection. At the ER, a nurse looked at the toe, rebandaged it, and then called a doctor in. The doctor, who did not look at the toe, stepped in briefly and said it should be fine and released her. In the end, the ER visit did nothing that urgent care did not do and was truly unnecessary. But it was recommended, so she did it. Then she got a $2,000 surprise bill that she is now paying off. This unnecessary mistake, which cost $2,000, could have been handled by a $100/month concierge direct pay doctor paid for without insurance.

FIGURE 1.2 Interface for the Healthcare Bluebook software application. A tool to enable price comparisons for healthcare services.

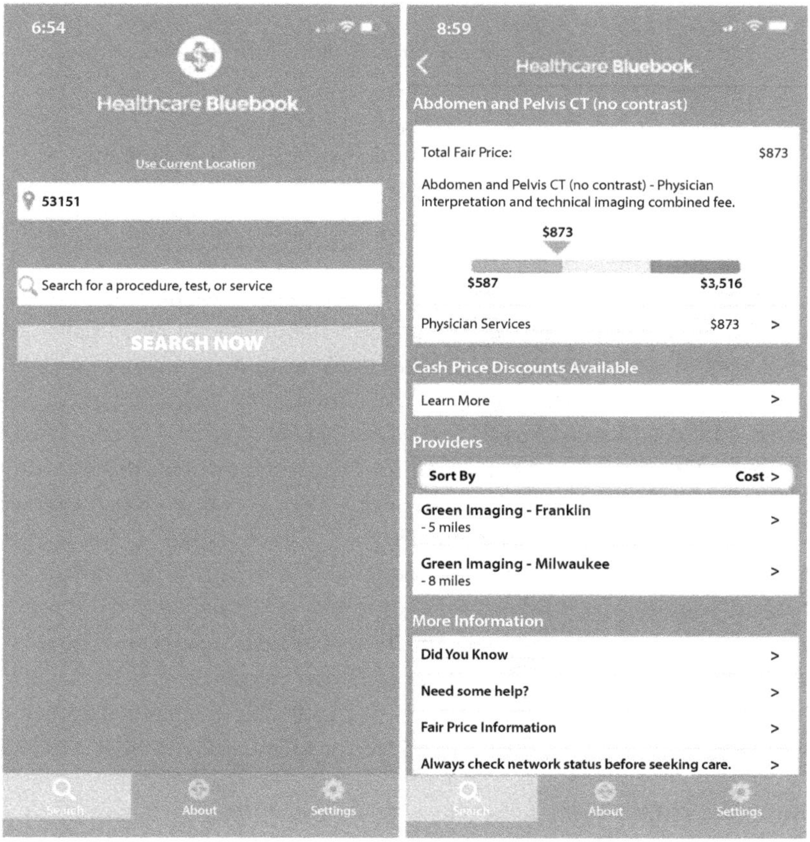

Source: Provided from the Healthcare Blue Book: https://www.healthcarebluebook.com/

The concept of concierge doctors is described more in later chapters, but briefly they are physicians who are not part of large provider networks and offer excellent 24/7 direct pay services at very reasonable prices. Direct pay concierge medicine is a grassroots revolution, attempting to return medical practice and the patient-physician relationship to what it used to be in the good old days, and providing better healthcare at much lower cost.

As price transparency and competition become a reality, and consumers have increasingly high-deductible plans, we will move to a world where healthcare becomes more consumerized and where it is making more use of low-cost and high-quality direct pay options, including healthcare services

obtained at a local CVS, Walgreens, or Walmart clinic, or through a growing number of direct pay physicians. For patient-consumers wondering how
to find this network of direct pay resources, there are some useful websites
for concierge doctors that charge around $100/month for 24/7 services:

- Concierge Choice Physicians: https://www.choice.md
- American College of Private Physicians: https://www.acpp.md
- MDVIP: https://www.mdvip.com
- Premier Private Physicians: http://premiermd.com

In conclusion, our healthcare system that lacks price transparency and
competition and relies only on an opaque reimbursement model has led to
ridiculously inflated prices for all aspects of healthcare. Changes are now
underway that could help to create a more transparent and competitive free
market of consumerized healthcare, where patients and their providers are
empowered to make decisions for themselves, rather than being powerless and
at the mercy of their surrogates. This seems like a good trend, but are markets the entire solution? What about the poor or unemployed (as due recently
to Covid-19) who cannot afford even basic care, or middle-class workers who
struggle to afford basic healthcare, or those who are intimidated by or unable
to navigate this consumerized and complicated world of healthcare? Should we
not have some baseline level of healthcare? Even economist Friedrich Hayek,
the staunchest of free market advocates, saw a need for a safety net for something like healthcare. And if a safety net were justified, what would it look like?

Universal Healthcare, Medicare for All, and the Safety Net Concept

The previous discussion makes a case for the importance of price transparency, free markets, and competition as being the best way to set prices in
healthcare and to control costs. But if it lets some people fall between the
cracks or does not ensure basic care for everyone, is that something we as
a society can tolerate? Whether you think healthcare is a right or not, do
we not as a society have an obligation to provide some baseline of care for
everyone? We provide public and private options for education, so should
we not do that for healthcare as well? At some level, we already do this by
providing ER access to everyone, which is the most expensive way to provide healthcare (see chapter 18). Access to emergency rooms, irrespective
of ability to pay, is required by law as a result of the Emergency Medical
Treatment and Labor Act of 1986 (EMTALA), passed under the Ronald
Reagan administration (CMS, 2012). It is a form of universal healthcare that

is already "offered," and it is a tremendous financial burden on hospitals. It is a very expensive safety net and needs to be replaced with something more sustainable.

What would a die-hard free market economist say about a healthcare safety net? The most respected free market economist from the Austrian school of thought is Friedrich Hayek. While Hayek probably would not be a fan of universal healthcare provided only by the government, he might actually be open to some sort of safety net as a Purple solution based on this comment from his famous text *The Road to Serfdom* (Caldwell, 2007, pp. 120–121):

> Where, as in the case of sickness and accident, neither the desire to avoid such calamities nor the efforts to overcome their consequences are as a rule weakened by the provision of assistance, where, in short, we deal with genuinely insurable risks, the case for the state helping to organize a comprehensive system of social insurance is very strong . . . there is no incompatibility in principle between the state providing greater security in this way and the preservation of individual freedom.

This has been interpreted to mean Hayek might support some form of universal healthcare as a safety net (Yglesias, 2010). Is it possible that universal healthcare as a publicly funded safety net can be created, operating in parallel and along with a free market?

Medicare for All and Its Variants

Is Medicare for All without any private option or competition the right kind of safety net? To be clear, Medicare for All was not being proposed in the 2020 election as a safety net, but rather as America's only source of primary healthcare, unlike almost any other developed country except Canada. But perhaps variations of Medicare for All could be used as a safety net as part of a Purple solution. Let us explore various publicly funded and managed universal healthcare options, like Medicare and its proposed variants, as potential safety nets.

Perhaps you would say that Medicare is perfect and does not limit care, and therefore Medicare for All would be the same. Well, Medicare does not pay enough to cover all of the expenses of healthcare right now. As discussed earlier, hospitals make up this deficit by charging others more, which is called cost-shifting. That is, they make up the money they lose because of low Medicare (and Medicaid) reimbursement levels by charging more elsewhere. If we expand Medicare so there are no other sources of revenue for hospitals, then they will have to charge actual costs. If we did Medicare for All, we would also have to adjust Medicare so it was in line with what other countries do, which typically put more (hopefully reasonable) restrictions on coverage in place and also reimburse at levels that cover costs. Some proposals for modified versions of Medicare for All are presented in section 4 of this book. Examples are the "Medicare for All Who Want It" proposal (Pete Buttigieg for America, n.d.) and the YoungMedicare proposal of David Riemer (see chapter 21). If some variant of expanded Medicare is someday adopted, should voters and legislators ever go that route, it will be important to realize that in the past Americans were not happy with constraints and limits put on healthcare services covered. As discussed earlier, in the 1980s we had HMOs that limited spending, often in somewhat reasonable ways. That worked at some level, since that was the one brief period in recent U.S. history where cost of healthcare slowed its unrestricted growth. But American consumers did not like those constraints, just like they will not like the added constraints in an overly restrictive Medicare for All system that will be fiscally feasible. If the United States someday adopts a public universal healthcare solution, it is doubtful Americans will tolerate a solution as restrictive as Canada's, which limits patients to only use the universal public plan and does not even allow supplemental private insurance or direct pay options for healthcare. An American universal healthcare system would need to be more flexible than Canada's, like those offered in the Netherlands, Germany, Switzerland, or even Singapore.

Some Sort of Safety Net Is Needed

Some who are proposing Medicare for All are advocating that it is all that is needed and there should be no private insurance anymore. Senator Elizabeth Warren is in this camp. Other 2020 presidential candidates, including former vice president Joe Biden and former South Bend, Indiana, mayor Pete Buttigieg, are proposing hybrid and flexible solutions. Buttigieg's Medicare for All Who Want It proposal allows consumers to opt out and use private insurance instead or to supplement a public option with private insurance (Pete Buttigieg for America, n.d.). Biden's proposal is to add a public option to the existing ACA. The YoungMedicare proposal of David Riemer and the associated Wisconsin Plan of Curt Gielow, presented in chapters 21 and 20 respectively, are models that resemble what Biden is proposing, requiring everyone to participate but allowing flexibility through selection from several tiers of private plans. Thus, there is a range of universal healthcare proposals that are promoting some type of Medicare or public option expansion to everyone, regardless of age. Some proposals are rigid like Canada's, and some are more flexible. If the plan provides some baseline quality healthcare and allows supplementary insurance and direct pay to be obtained on top of the baseline of care, then these universal options can be viewed as safety nets. Some people might say we should require everyone to use only a single universal public plan (Medicare for All) so that everyone has exactly the same healthcare. That is to say, complete government control of an essential resource for society (the definition of socialism). Others argue that the lessons from HMOs and the Canadian system suggest that approach is too rigid and not a good fit for the American culture, which prioritizes individuality, choice, and freedom.

Since cost keeps increasing, if we had a safety net/universal system like Medicaid for All (or a private analog), there would likely be limits on what is covered that we would not like. That is why most countries that have a publicly funded universal healthcare system also have supplemental private insurance options, so that people can still buy access to the excluded services or medicines (not on the formulary) either using supplementary insurance or by paying directly out of pocket. Even the United Kingdom allows this to some extent, and in countries like Germany and Switzerland private insurance instead of public insurance is an option. A case could be made, distinct from what the most die-hard Medicare for All advocates are asking for, that there should be some very basic level of coverage for everyone, especially the poor, and that this coverage could be supplemented with additional private insurance, whether in the open market or the ACA exchanges. To be clear, that is not what Senators Warren or Sanders are proposing. But some variation of the universal healthcare plans that Biden and Buttigieg, or Gielow and Riemer, are proposing could be used to serve that function, as a safety net, given their more flexible structures.

Lower Cost Using a Supplemental Direct Pay Option, in or Outside of the Country

As mentioned earlier, it is typically less expensive to purchase healthcare using direct pay options in the United States because those prices reflect actual costs and are responsive to market forces. Such direct pay options should always be made available to supplement any government-sponsored universal healthcare plans, which will inevitably have some limits and constraints, such as the excluded services or long waits that have been seen in some cases in Canada. In the extreme, China, Mexico, and India have government-sponsored care, but based on my discussions with students and faculty using their healthcare, it is of such poor quality or requiring long waits that they prefer to pay out of pocket for care in direct pay, competitive, and free markets. In one study, it was noted that out-of-pocket direct pay care represents a significant fraction of total healthcare spending in China (35%), Mexico (47%), and India (62%), even though all three have free universal healthcare provided by the government (Peltzer et al., 2014). Interestingly, those direct pay markets have now evolved to the point where healthcare is sometimes so good and so low cost that a field of medical tourism has developed where Americans fly to clinics in Mexico and India for major surgeries (Kelley, 2013). Savings can be significant, with some examples from the World Health Organization (WHO) shown in table 1.1.

A handful of insurance companies have even supported medical tourism programs, including Anthem Blue Cross and Blue Shield (WellPoint) in Wisconsin, with Apollo Hospitals in India (Kelley, 2013).

It is interesting that Canada, which has a very restrictive public universal healthcare system, also has a very active medical tourism industry, with 63,000 Canadians going out of the country for healthcare in 2016, most commonly for surgeries (9,454 people) (Ren & Labrie, 2017). The lesson is simply this: If the United States ever adopts a national universal healthcare system, it should *also* allow consumers to purchase services on a supplementary direct pay (out-of-pocket) market as well, so that consumers can have the option, ideally without needing to resort to medical tourism, to get medical care that they cannot find in the necessarily more limited public option. Other countries allow this, except for Canada, which is why those 63,000 Canadians went abroad for healthcare (Ren & Labrie, 2017).

Both/And: Free Markets and Publicly Funded Universal Healthcare

There are probably many reasons why healthcare is less expensive in these other countries, including fewer regulations and, especially, the fact that they have very active direct pay markets—free markets. It would be better and more convenient to let those direct pay markets, which ultimately will

TABLE 1.1 Medical Tourism Prices (in US$)

	Countries			
Procedure	US	India	Singapore	Mexico
Heart bypass	$113,000	$10,000	$20,000	$3,250
Angioplasty	$47,000	$11,000	$13,000	$15,000
Knee replacement	$48,000	$8,500	$13,000	$14,650

Source: Kelley (2013).

provide better care at lower cost, evolve within the United States also, in parallel with any publicly funded national universal healthcare plan that is created. As noted earlier in this chapter, there is a strong case to be made that unless there is transparent and accurate pricing coupled with incentivized, informed, and empowered consumers making buying decisions, prices will inflate out of control. This is the logic for having a hybrid system, which supplements any publicly funded national universal coverage or safety net (e.g. the Biden proposal) with a direct pay market with transparent pricing (e.g. the Trump and CMS proposal) that encourages providers to control cost and to listen to you, the consumer, directly rather than only to insurance companies and the government. This will normalize and control prices so that if there is a public system such as Medicare for All or a modified ACA (with a public option) paying for healthcare, at least the prices being paid via reimbursements can be benchmarked against realistic market prices that will be constantly driven lower (because that is what free markets do).

The Future: Technology, Personalized Medicine, and Empowering the Patient

Any discussion about healthcare delivery, whether it be via free markets (Republicans) or universal public healthcare plans (Democrats), should consider not just the way healthcare is practiced today, but how it will or might be practiced 5, 10, or 20 years from now. Those changes will be dramatic positive changes that have nothing to do with government or insurance and everything to do with the exciting disruptive innovations going on in science, medicine, information technology, and the biotechnology industries. Already consumers can see the advent of telemedicine, which allows easy access, 24/7, to physicians from our homes (Morris, 2019). Remote monitoring and wearable technologies will increasingly allow us to personally track our health and communicate with our healthcare providers (or navigators) or even get real-time medical information using artificial intelligence. The need to visit doctors in hospitals and to do tests in clinics may decrease in dramatic ways that we can hardly imagine now (Ericsson, n.d.; Solomon, 2017). Even some acute care could be done at home rather than in the hospital using this technology (Klein, n.d.). The 2020 coronavirus pandemic has been forcing us to move in some of these directions but after the pandemic is gone, I hope we will have learned to lean in to this better and more efficient way of delivering healthcare for certain situations.

Couple these telemedicine and "hospital at home" technologies with trends in personalized medicine, which leverage genomic advances and internet of things (IOT) technology to report biological data in real time, and the practice of medicine could be very different from what we currently know (Roth, 2018). Of course, the ultimate in mobile and consumer-facing personalized medicine can only be realized if we can own and carry with us in some secure and useful way our genomic data and our medical record data, the latter of which is currently trapped in proprietary electronic medical records, like Epic or Cerner, and further protected by government regulations like the Health Insurance Portability and Accountability Act (HIPAA) (Biernat, 2019). But a consumer revolution driven by our desire to own and control our health, empowered by seeing and using our own health information more easily, will likely overcome any regulatory and corporate anticompetitive barriers that are now in the way. Not surprisingly, companies like Epic have opposed this trend under the protective cover and justification of HIPAA, but consumers can and should drive this change toward their own empowerment. It will happen just like it did in the transportation industry, when Uber put information and control in the hands of millions of empowered consumers, bringing about industry change that politicians or corporate giants never imagined or wanted. We need an analogous grassroots healthcare revolution.

These exciting advances in medicine and technology, and how they may change the face of healthcare delivery, are the topic of chapter 2 by Robert Graboyes, senior research fellow at the Mercatus Center at George Mason University.

CHAPTER 2

Technological Innovation and the Supply Side of Healthcare

ROBERT GRABOYES

Chapter 1 provided an overview of healthcare delivery in America and the various problems that lead to increased cost. This chapter looks at innovations in healthcare that could change how we deliver care in the future and reshape the entire healthcare delivery world by providing "supply-side solutions." Possible innovations include technology such as telehealth and medical diagnostics, but also healthcare licensure (chapter 7), various regulatory (chapter 3) reforms, and specifically, Food and Drug Administration (FDA) regulations (chapters 15 and 16).

For decades, America's healthcare debate has been rancorous and mired in partisanship. What would it take to get some amicable, bipartisan cooperation on healthcare in Congress or in state legislatures? This chapter explores some possible avenues that can lead to substantive improvements in the quality (and quantity) of care and fiscal impact of providing that care.

The structure of this chapter is as follows:

- First comes a discussion of the difference between demand-side and supply-side approaches to healthcare reform. In essence, this is the distinction between how we pay for healthcare and how we produce healthcare.
- Second is a brief mention of conventional wisdom—tropes— concerning American healthcare. Readers are asked to set those tropes aside for the duration of this chapter and reconsider them later.
- Third is a thought experiment—the Calendar Test—that summarizes the idea of supply-side innovation.
- The fourth section offers 10 areas for supply-side innovations and public policies that can unleash such innovations.

Dr. Robert Graboyes is a Senior Research Fellow and Health Care Scholar at the Mercatus Center at George Mason University.

Demand- Versus Supply-Side Reforms

Since World War II, if not before, the national debate has focused primarily on the demand side of healthcare—especially federal insurance law and how we pay for services. The central goal has been "coverage"—getting insurance cards into the hands of more people. By its very nature, such a debate sets into motion a zero-sum game of winners and losers because policy prescriptions tend to alter patterns of demand without significantly augmenting the supply of resources available for care or the formulas for using those resources.

Payment models are important. However, without large increases in resources (e.g., number and types of providers, hospital beds, medical devices, or new drugs) or newer, more efficient ways of combining those resources to provide care, a new insurance card does little to improve aggregate access to care. One can apply this complaint to the Democratic-sponsored Affordable Care Act of 2010 (ACA) or to the various Republican repeal-and-replace proposals that have been floated and sunk in the intervening years. One can also apply this complaint to proposals for a single-payer (Medicare for All) system, a public option, or the expansion of Medicaid.

With relatively static supply conditions, expanding the quantity or quality of care for one group in society effectively requires us to diminish the care that some other group receives, directly or indirectly. With total expenditures relatively invariant to healthcare reforms, reducing the costs paid by one group necessitates a similar increase in the costs paid by some other group. (Expenditures have risen steadily over decades, but whether healthcare reforms like the ACA have perturbed that path is within the margin of debate.)

Supply-Side Focus

The debate will churn on, but in this chapter, we will take a vacation from the maddening squabble over demand and consider the opportunities inherent in *supply-side* conditions. We will focus on the production of care rather than on the purchase of that care. This includes both the resources that go into the production of care and the formulas for combining those resources into care. For a restaurant analogy, we'll focus on the ingredients and recipes rather than on whether to pay by cash or credit card. We are more concerned with how we make the pie bigger, tastier, and more economical rather than on how to divvy up a fixed pie at a fixed price.

There are several good arguments for taking this approach. First, by breaking out of the zero-sum mold, we introduce the possibility of bipartisanship and calm discourse that seems perpetually absent from discussions of comprehensive insurance reform. Second, there is a good argument to be made over the medium to long term that supply-side issues are more important.

The best analogy lies in the information technology industry. Moore's law describes the remarkable decline in the cost of computing power over the past 50 years. Cheap computing has transformed the world economy and, over the past quarter-century, has transformed human relations and helped fuel the greatest rise out of poverty that the world has ever seen.

The remarkable rise of information technology was fundamentally a supply-side, not demand-side, process. New technologies, new products, new manufacturing processes, new applications, all developed in ferociously competitive, highly decentralized markets, fueling the change. Imagine the difference had we spent the past 50 years arguing over how to finance room-sized mainframe computers and how much computing time should be allotted to each American.

The question that this chapter seeks to answer is not, "How can we expand insurance coverage?" Rather, it is: "How can we make healthcare as innovative in the next 30 years as information technology was in the past 30 years?" The answer lies in changing the technology of healthcare. And "technology" can mean either the physical resources used to produce care or the recipes for combining those resources into care.

Getting Past the Tropes

Before moving on, it is important to cast a bit of doubt on the usual stories—the tropes—that surround American healthcare. Certain facts are well known. America spends more than any other country on healthcare in the aggregate, per person, and as a percentage of gross domestic product (GDP). National health expenditures were $3.6 trillion in 2018, or $11,172 per person, and accounted for 17.7% of GDP (Centers for Medicare and Medicaid Services, 2018). Statistics indicate that America falls short of many other developed nations in certain health metrics, such as average lifespan (Organization for Economic Cooperation and Development [OECD], n.d.a) and infant mortality (OECD, n.d.b). The Institute of Medicine (2012) estimates that American healthcare wastes $750 billion per year—30% of total healthcare spending.

Many take these facts as proof that America's healthcare system is in crisis, that spending levels are unsustainable, that American healthcare is unusually loaded with waste, that Americans receive inferior care, and that massive cost reductions are available simply by reconfiguring our health insurance system. There is also a deep-rooted assumption—incorrect—that the health status of individuals is primarily attributable to healthcare. According to Choi & Sonin (2017), our deficits in lifespan and infant mortality depend more on the genetic makeup of America's population, individual behavior, social circumstances, and environment.

In fact, American healthcare has plenty of problems, but the tropes do not hold up under scrutiny. There is no room in this chapter to demonstrate these points. My suggestion is that readers put these concerns aside for the moment, suspend disbelief, and then reconsider those tropes at another time. A place to start is Graboyes (2018).

The Calendar Test

To explain the difference between demand- and supply-side reforms, I have devised what I call a Calendar Test. It involves picturing a physician's daily calendar and asking whether a particular reform clears time off the doctor's calendar—without reducing the quantity or quality of care provided. If it does not, the reform is mostly on the demand side (and redistributive) and fails the Calendar Test. If it does clear time, it is a supply-side reform.

Here is how it goes. Imagine a primary care physician who works 10 hours each day. For five hours, she sees 20 patients for 15 minutes apiece. For the other five hours, she does other tasks, including administration, travel, training, reading, meetings, editing electronic health records, and so forth.

One day, someone with the authority to do so hands out four gift coupons, each good for one visit with this doctor today. There are three responses that fail the Calendar Test and one that passes. First, the doctor can see 24 patients, shortening each visit to 12.5 minutes, thereby diminishing the care that each patient receives. Second, the doctor can cancel four of the previously existing appointments, thereby eliminating care for those four altogether. Third, the doctor can work an extra hour, which does not compromise the level of care but does increase the aggregate cost of care.

All three of these solutions fail the Calendar Test and all three resemble the familiar reforms that dominate the national healthcare debate. The ACA promised care to 20 million or 30 million new insurance enrollees (and dozens of free services for all Americans) but did little to increase the supply of resources used in their care or the methods of combining those resources into care. Given that, the increased care that one person received was likely matched by decreased care to some other individual in society. (One problem in discussing such reforms is that it is much easier to identify and observe the winners than it is the losers.) The Republicans' repeal-and-replace proposals would essentially have done the same thing.

So would other proposals (e.g., Medicare for All, a public option, Medicaid expansion).

The fourth option is to alter the supply conditions in healthcare markets, thereby clearing time on the doctor's calendar. There are three basic ways to do this: Shift some of the physician's workload onto nonphysician providers such as nurse practitioners, physician assistants, and pharmacists. Shift some of the doctor's workload onto intelligent machines. Or shift some of the doctor's work onto the patients themselves—aided by nonphysicians and intelligent machines. These solutions pass the Calendar Test. They allow the physicians, aided by these additional resources, to provide more for more people.

We can also imagine organizational changes in the physician's practice that allow her to devote more hours to patient encounters and fewer hours to nonpatient tasks. This could include more efficient business models that reduce administrative tasks and reduction of red tape.

Professor John Cochrane of the Hoover Institution at Stanford University once wrote (Cochrane, 2014), "What's the biggest thing we could do to 'bend the cost curve,' as well as finally tackle the ridiculous inefficiency and consequent low quality of health-care delivery? Look for every limit on supply of health care services, especially entry by new companies, and get rid of it."

In the next sections, we take a quick tour of such innovations.

Supply-Side Innovations and Public Policies

[1] Get Out of the Way of Telemedicine. Telemedicine is an umbrella term for the provision of medical care at a distance using electronic communications (Office of the National Coordinator for Health Information Technology, 2017). Categories include videoconferencing, remote monitoring, online prescriptions, asynchronous consultations, emails, or telephone conversations. Telemedicine allows patients to receive medical care anywhere and at any hour, thereby reducing costs and improving access—especially in rural and underserved areas and during emergencies.

Telemedicine can pass the Calendar Test by enhancing demand-smoothing across localities. Suppose that on a particular day, demand for physician appointments are high in Atlanta and low in Dallas. In such a situation, Atlanta patients can contact Dallas physicians via telemedicine, thereby relieving the pressure on Atlanta doctors.

Telemedicine may be less expensive for both doctor and patient than an in-office visit, and the ability to contact a doctor from one's own office or residence or vacation spot can lead to the early detection of serious problems. Yet some states throw up barriers against the adoption of telemedicine.

Ian Tong of Doctor on Demand (Graboyes, 2016b), a nationwide tele-medicine company, spoke (at my invitation) to a national gathering of legislators—many or most of them physicians, and many skeptical about telemedicine. He described how he had saved the life of a young woman who had contacted him on her tablet—by observing the appearance of her eyes and fingernails. Very likely, she would have died had she waited for a conventional office visit to her doctor. (A few years later, my 92-year-old mother's life was similarly saved by a FaceTime video conversation with her grandson—an emergency room doctor.)

In various parts of the world, including sub-Saharan Africa, telemedi-cine has brought prompt, lifesaving capabilities to the remotest villages (Wamala & Augustin, 2013).

Telemedicine offers expectant and new mothers in rural areas consider-able benefits by creating the opportunity to reach subspecialists such as pro-viders in maternal fetal medicine (Bryan, 2019). In-person visits to maternal fetal medicine specialists were reduced by 50% in rural Arkansas thanks to greater telemedicine use (Magann, 2012). The University of Arkansas's telemedicine program helped reduce the incidence of very-low-birth-weight infants, thereby reducing infant mortality (Kim, 2013).

Telemedicine is also especially valuable to non-English-speakers and those who move frequently. Consider the plight of a Spanish-speaking migrant family whose child becomes ill in the middle of the night on a remote ranch. Formerly, the options would be to travel to a distant medical facility or delay care. With telemedicine, the same family can contact a physician immediately—and perhaps a Spanish-speaking one at that. Others who can similarly benefit include those with mobility problems, those poorly served by public transportation, and those busy with childrearing or work.

Other applications include online prescription providers, telepsychia-trists, telepsychologists, and even teledentists.

Despite the promise of these technologies, federal and state regula-tory barriers considerably limit the availability of telemedicine. Some states require an assistant ("telepresenter") to be physically with the patient when a telemedicine encounter occurs, thereby undermining the spontaneity and convenience the technology makes possible (Bryan et al., 2018).

Perhaps the largest obstacle to telemedicine is the frequent requirement that doctors doing teleconsultations must be licensed in the states where their patients are located (Office of the National Coordinator for Health Infor-mation Technology, 2019). Licensure reform is discussed at length in chapter 7 of this book. This licensure constraint considerably limits telemedicine, since 84.5% of physicians are licensed in a single state (Robeznieks, 2019). Some question the constitutionality of legal obstacles to telemedicine, as they may run afoul of the Interstate Commerce Clause (Gupta & Sao, 2012). This barrier to care can be reduced by establishing licensing reciprocity agreements among the states or by redefining the location of a telemedicine encounter to be where the doctor is, rather than where the patient is.

[2] Encourage innovation in diagnostic devices that are less physician-intensive. Another way to pass the Calendar Test is to reduce the time that physicians are engaged in conducting diagnostics.

I personally experienced an episode of atrial fibrillation (afib) in 2016. Immediately thereafter, I purchased an AliveCor Kardia for $99 (Graboyes, 2016a). This device, linked to my cellphone, allows me to perform a clinical-quality electrocardiogram in 30 seconds and to receive an instant evaluation of whether I appear to be experiencing afib. On at least two occasions, the device showed that I had no need to visit an emergency room. This relieved the emergency room physicians, nurses, and other personnel of the need to watch over me for several hours—and the need for my insurer to pay perhaps $10,000 for needless services. Recent Apple Watch models have similar apps built in.

Another device, Cellscope, lets parents determine whether their child has an ear infection and, if they like, send the results to a physician (Cellscope, n.d.).

Intelligent machines offer considerable opportunity to relieve pressure on the physician's calendar. We get a glimpse of that in a fairly recent story from Japan. There, a woman failed for months to respond positively to leukemia treatments. IBM's Watson computer was called to analyze her case (Graboyes, 2017a). Her data were fed into Watson, which then read 20 million medical journal articles on leukemia, concluding that the physicians had misdiagnosed the specific type of leukemia. After changing treatments, the patient went home. Watson's entire reading and analysis took 10 minutes.

However, the availability of some diagnostic devices is limited by a long, slow, uncertain approval process at the U.S. FDA (see more on effects of FDA regulations in chapters 15 and 16). Others hover on the edge of legality. An example of the latter is NightScout, a device developed by a group of computer programmers for use by parents of diabetic children (NightScout, n.d.). NightScout connects to a child's insulin pump and transmits the data to the parents' cell phone, smartwatch, or other device. This continuous remote monitoring gives the child greater freedom of movement and the parents greater peace of mind because they are able to immediately get their child's glucose reading on a smartwatch, for example. NightScout is an example of what my colleague Adam Thierer refers to as permissionless innovation (Thierer, 2016) and technological civil disobedience (Graboyes & Rogers, 2018)—a willingness to conduct innovation, even if regulatory authorities balk at approval.

The approval process could be improved by introducing competition for approval—a process that already exists in the European Union. Private evaluation organizations, which already evaluate products and make approval recommendations, and the FDA can compete to inform patients and doctors about the safety and effectiveness of medical devices (Williams et al., 2015).

[3] Adopt regulations that allow medical drones. In Rwanda, Tanzania, and Vanuatu, unmanned aerial systems are transporting blood products, drugs, and other medical goods at low cost—an especially important innovation in vast rural areas. The United States is only beginning to use this technology for medical purposes (Graboyes & Bryan, 2019). Drones can save lives in situations where time is critical.

Integrating medical drones into America's busy airspace will require significant regulatory and legal actions by federal, state, and local authorities. American airspace architecture was developed more than half a century ago; shoehorning a new class of vehicles into that architecture poses many challenges (Ganjoo, 2019). Ground-to-drone communications must be fast, reliable, and data intensive, so the Federal Communications Commission (FCC) will need to be involved in broadband allocation and satellite access (Poss, 2019). Technology companies and the FCC are currently grappling with the regulatory framework necessary to implement fifth-generation (5G) wireless standards, which will allow faster, more powerful, more reliable wireless communication (Ullah, 2019).

[4] Permit innovative business models such as direct primary care (DPC). Direct care changes the relationship between doctor and patient (see chapter 6). Rather than paying for specific services or specific visits, patients pay monthly fees (often in the range of $60 to $70) and then receive primary care with no additional charges. In addition to in-person visits, patients can often contact doctors by telephone, video link, or email. DPC practices often use nonphysicians (nurses, therapists, aides) to guide patients on health and care (Graboyes, 2016c) and have built dozens of clinics in the Northeast United States. Iora Health, a leading DPC firm, has established around four dozen clinics in 10 states.

Some states have discouraged DPC by threatening to treat such practices as insurers, opening them to prohibitive costs. DPC can offer special benefits in rural and underserved areas (Saslow, 2019). These clinics are typically open for long hours that are more convenient for those who have trouble reaching a doctor's office during working hours. Their telehealth capabilities also help patients and relieve pressure on traditional practices.

[5] Allow nonphysician providers to practice up to the limits of their training without physician supervision. Some states allow nurse practitioners, physician assistants, pharmacists, and others to perform tasks that, in other states, require higher-cost physician labor (Timmons, 2016). Lots of medical services demand the presence of a physician. Many tasks traditionally performed by doctors can be safely, effectively performed by nonphysician professionals. Doing so passes the Calendar Test. Chapter 7 discusses ways to expand scope of practice and licensure for a range of healthcare providers.

In roughly 28 states, nurse practitioners (NPs) must collaborate with or report directly to a physician, significantly limiting the ability of NPs to care for patients. There are also unintended consequences. In Wyoming, a physician assistant was left unable to care for patients after his supervising physician died suddenly (American Academy of Physician Assistants, 2017).

Easing restrictions on nonphysician practitioners who are able to perform tasks currently performed by doctors can free up doctors' time, thereby lowering costs and expanding access. Of course, nonphysician providers should not engage in care beyond the extent of their training.

[6] Eliminate certificate of need (CON) requirements. In roughly 35 states, healthcare providers who wish to offer certain new services must first apply for a certificate of need (American Academy of Physician Assistants, 2017). This can discourage new and innovative hospitals and other providers from competing. A CON application is only approved if the proposed service is deemed to meet a "need" in the population that would benefit from it. CON laws especially restrict access to care in rural communities, reduce quality of care, and increase costs (Mitchell, 2017).

States with CON laws have fewer community hospitals per capita and fewer ambulatory surgical centers per capita, with the greatest impact in rural areas (Bryan, 2019). CON laws are even associated with higher mortality rates from heart failure, pneumonia, and heart attacks (Stratmann et al., 2017).

[7] Welcome international medical graduates. The United States faces critical shortages of healthcare providers in future years. Even now, a surprising number of counties across the nation do not have a single physician within their boundaries. One way of easing these gaps in coverage is to welcome more international medical graduates and lower the barriers they face in obtaining licenses to practice in the United States.

[8] Accommodate trailing military spouses. Military families frequently move across state lines. Then spouses of service personnel can find themselves unable to work until they go through the time and expense of obtaining licenses in their new states because occupational licenses do not generally transfer across state lines. No doubt, a significant number of these spouses work in the healthcare professions. Making their licenses transferrable could help alleviate personnel shortages.

[9] Remove obstacles to charity care. In Mississippi, Carroll Landrum, a semiretired physician, closed his brick-and-mortar office and began providing free or nearly free care to residents of remote and underserved areas from his car—house calls, in other words. Apparently, for making house calls without having a brick-and-mortar clinic, Landrum was threatened with the loss of his medical license (Graboyes, 2017b). While I have no way of verifying an anecdote a Mississippi doctor shared with me, it echoes stories I have heard from other doctors I have taught over the years: A patient, this doctor said, had come in from a distant rural county with a painful, grotesque, potentially life-threatening hernia that had apparently festered for years. The doctor asked what finally made him seek help. The patient said it was the first time he had ever been able to find a ride to the hospital. This is the sort of patient for whom Dr. Landrum (or telehealth) is meant.

To the greatest extent possible, laws and regulations ought to encourage, not discourage, Good Samaritans among providers.

[10] Solve the Narayana riddles: Here is an open-ended recommendation— a process, not an action. It takes the form of a story and two riddles about the story.

One of the most innovative healthcare providers on earth is India's Narayana Health System. Narayana's 20 or so hospitals (plus one in the Cayman Islands [Graboyes, 2017c]) perform a broad variety of healthcare services. Heart bypass surgery at these hospitals costs between $1,000 and $2,000, compared with roughly $100,000 in the United States. Narayana's success rates and quality of care equal or surpass those of almost any other hospital in the world. Note, too, that Narayana is a for-profit enterprise. The essence of this health system's success is that in many ways, Narayana hospitals operate like a Toyota factory, which are textbook examples of quality and continuous improvement.

Inspired by a request by Mother Teresa, the company's visionary CEO, Dr. Devi Shetty, wanted to harness its success to serve an American clientele. His company formed a partnership with Ascension—the largest Catholic hospital system in the United States. But, the companies determined, such a hospital could not succeed in the United States, so they built their new hospital in the Cayman Islands—a 90-minute flight south of Miami. Shetty famously said, "The best location to build a hospital on the planet today is a ship that is parked in the U.S. waters just outside its territory. . . . The site at the Cayman Islands is the closest approximation that fits the bill."

Would-be healthcare reformers in the United States could do well to study Narayana and to ponder two riddles related to its success: How does this innovative enterprise achieve such massive economies? And why can't equivalent success be achieved within the territorial limits of the United States (Das, 2014)?

A reformer who did nothing but ponder those two questions could achieve quite a bit.

SECTION 2

Empowering Patients, Providers, and Payers

Consumerization, Transparency, and Competition in Healthcare

CHAPTER 3

Created (Un)equal
Legislating Quality in Healthcare

GREG WATCHMAKER, MD

This chapter presents the perspective of a physician-provider on the value and the dangers of regulating quality measurements in healthcare from afar. It explores the unintended consequences of this well-intended regulatory exercise—done remotely by legislators in the federal government. Consequences include the creation of a healthcare system that is not always in the best interest of patients but treats diverse and unique individuals with one-size-fits-all restrictive criteria. It also encourages consolidation in the industry, which is the topic of chapters 4 and 5.

The second paragraph of the Declaration of Independence articulates our forefathers' conviction that "... all men are created equal. ..." An important principle when writing laws to govern a nation, but a flawed premise when extended to the realm of healthcare. We are all (aside from identical twins) born differently, with a propensity for high blood pressure or not. Diabetes, mental health, and cancer risk are all different and compounded by personal lifestyle choices we make throughout our lives. Our current system of healthcare, where the patient does not behave like an accountable and educated consumer and where federal policies attempt to legislate quality and medical processes across a heterogeneous population, has increased inefficiency and cost without meaningful improvement in quality. This chapter reviews these past efforts in order to learn from their shortcomings and focus on present and actionable new directions that might provide hope for a better healthcare future.

Good Intent

Little known except to healthcare historians is that the first federal healthcare initiative was enacted shortly after the founding of our country. In 1798, President John Adams enacted *An Act for the Relief of Sick and Disabled*

Greg Watchmaker, MD, is a graduate of Washington University School of Medicine and a practicing hand surgeon at the Milwaukee Hand Center.

Seamen, which taxed seamen 20 cents a month and established the construction of Marine hospitals (Library of Congress, n.d.). Congress reorganized the hospital system several times but it remained underfunded and poor in quality compared with local community hospitals as time went by. Legislators eventually tripled the tax rate and expanded the hospitals' role beyond seamen to include control of infectious diseases and processing of immigrants, but they ultimately cut funding and dissolved the hospital system.

One hundred and fifty years later the federal government entered the arena of healthcare but in a much broader way, serving not just seamen and immigrants but all persons age 65 and older as well as the poor. The Social Security Amendments of 1965 established Medicare and Medicaid as entitlements and stand today, though they have been amended over time to modify who is covered and what benefits are granted.

As a payer of healthcare, policymakers and administrations found themselves intertwined with an increasingly complex and expensive entitlement. In medical school, I first heard the adage, "Medical care used to be ineffective and inexpensive . . . now it is effective but expensive." The Bureau of Health Insurance, the precursor of the current Centers for Medicare and Medicaid Services (CMS), moved to tame spending growth.

Medicare established "Conditions of Participation" rules, Professional Standards Review Organizations (PSROs), and Quality Improvement Organizations (QIOs). Through local and national coverage determinations, the programs attempted to modify utilization of specific tests or procedures. A study found that in only one out of eight procedures for which coverage determination policies were put in place was there a statistical change in utilization by beneficiaries (Foote et al., 2008). The study concluded that "coverage policies have the potential but do not consistently impact utilization as policy makers intend and expect them to do."

These ineffectual efforts were replaced with a series of programs including the Surgical Care Improvement Program (SCIP), the Physician Quality Reporting System (PQRS), the Quality Reporting and Hospital Value-Based Purchasing (VBP) program, and the Medicare Access and CHIP Reauthorization Act (MACRA), among others. No doubt, each new program, with its associated new regulations, was born of good intentions: Provide high-quality care at a lower cost. Legislating health and value in healthcare delivery, however, was too often based on unvalidated assumptions that "sounded good" and may even have been "proven good" in small trials or test projects, yet they were not beneficial and sometimes were harmful when enacted broadly using payment incentives and penalties.

Unintended Consequences of the CMS Regulations of the Last 10 Years

Over the past decade, CMS has taken a more aggressive approach to effect change that has included public reporting and more significant financial rewards and penalties for Medicare-participating facilities and providers. An example of this approach includes the Hospital Readmissions Reduction Program (HRRP) that was established under the Affordable Care Act (ACA) and required CMS, beginning in 2012, to impose financial penalties on hospitals with higher-than-expected 30-day readmission rates for patients with heart failure, acute myocardial infarction, and pneumonia (Wadhera et al., 2018). Chronic obstructive pulmonary disease (COPD) was added in 2014.

Good intent: A patient who is medically well treated and stable on discharge from the hospital will not require readmission soon thereafter. In reality, though, it turned out to be a poor policy that penalized hospitals for readmitting patients because of disease progression, poor compliance, or a new illness. Responsive to the potential 3% payment penalty, hospitals put in place programs to reduce readmissions. They opened observation units adjacent to their emergency departments in which to hold patients who returned within 30 days in hopes of preventing readmission. Hospitals created information exchanges so that they could be notified of potential readmissions across large geographic areas. Third-party vendors offered real-time text services that alerted physicians on the frontlines of a 30-day readmission patient (CRISP Health Services, n.d.).

With the creation of the HRRP, hospital administrators, physicians, nurses, social workers, and third parties became focused on a well-intentioned policy that had little basis in preceding science and associated medical best practice. The policy therefore would best be viewed through the lens of a scientific experiment. At a defined point in time, a new policy was enacted that incentivized a change in healthcare behavior. The results of this experiment, unfortunately disappointed its creators. Other studies found that, "although the 30-day all-cause readmission rates declined, *the mortality rates* increased. Hospitals with lower readmission rates had *higher* mortality rates" (Samarghandi & Qayyum, 2019). The increase in 30-day post-discharge mortality was driven mainly by patients who were not "officially readmitted" to the hospital, suggesting that HRRP might have led to patients being managed in emergency departments or observation units instead of inpatient units. Studies found an increase in post-hospital discharge mortality for COPD (Samarghandi & Qayyum, 2019) and for pneumonia and congestive heart failure (Wadhera et al., 2018).

Simply stated, hospitals avoided penalties by reacting to a federal program and more Medicare recipients died outside of hospitals in their communities or in observation units. This fact was corroborated by evaluation of the full Medicare database, which showed a 1.3% absolute increase in 30-day mortality in patients with heart failure after the implementation of the HRRP compared with a declining mortality rate in the decade that preceded (Fonarow, 2018).

Although data suggested that readmission was not a good surrogate for quality of care, hospitals continued to focus energy and expense on post-discharge care in hopes of reducing their readmission statistics (and penalty). Finkelstein et al. (2020) published a prospective, randomized study that sought to reduce utilization by "super-users" of healthcare at coalition hospitals. To reduce cost and readmissions of high-utilizers—5% of the population accounts for over 50% of healthcare dollars spent each year—this coalition created an intensive hospital/provider-led post-discharge program. This included a team of nurses, social workers, and community health workers who coordinated post-discharge care and included an average of 7.6 home visits after discharge. Among the 800 patients randomly assigned to the control versus the intervention group, there was no statistical difference in readmissions in the six months following discharge. The average cost of the program per enrolled patient was $5,000 (Modern Healthcare, 2020).

Government Efforts to Micromanage Quality Increase Cost and Harm Patients

The disappointing outcomes from the readmission program are not isolated but instead are commonplace for government-led efforts to improve quality. Similar scenarios of good intent, inadequate underlying science, placement of incentives, great taxpayer cost, and disappointing results are occurring at an increasing rate as regulations increase. The Surgical Care Improvement Program (SCIP) was a joint effort between CMS and the Centers for Disease Control (CDC) launched in 2006 based on agreed "core measures" that intended to ensure ". . . quality healthcare for all Americans through accountability and public disclosure" (Weston et al., 2012). This program established over a dozen very specific guidelines on how to practice medicine. Several of these guidelines stipulated when perioperative antibiotics should be administered and discontinued, how medications called beta-blockers should be dosed before surgery, and how blood sugars should be controlled after surgery.

SCIP measures put on full display a governmental belief that micromanagement of the practice of medicine will improve outcomes. Unfortunately, each of us has enough variability in our underlying health and responses to treatment that such broad policies are difficult to craft in a way that are safe and also improve outcomes. Westen et al. (2012) evaluated the success of these measures at the height of the program and found that SCIP successfully incentivized compliance to its reported measures, but they found little evidence that it provided any substantial benefit to patients.

Dr. Karen Sibert, in her article "The Dark Side of Quality," explains the backstory of several of the SCIP measures, including their flawed scientific bases, economic underpinnings, and poor results (Sibert, n.d.). The article lauds one measure (central venous line process) and its positive impact on reducing the rate of infections in critical care patients but also exposes the discredited science that led to the SCIP beta-blocker recommendation. This perioperative medication guideline, which was enacted both in America through SCIP and also in Europe, led to initiation of a course of beta-blocker administration before surgery that unfortunately was found to increase postoperative mortality by 27% (Bouri et al., 2014). I sympathize for the authors of the SCIP guideline; they intended well but are now faced with scientific evidence that the guidelines promoted a change in care that may have led to a significant number of deaths.

Hold the Insulin

The downstream implications of Medicare quality initiatives are that hospitals often apply guidelines broadly to all admitted patients. This touched home in the early morning hours of October 11, 2014. That morning, I found myself sitting in a Cleveland Clinic intensive care unit beside my 20-something, previously healthy daughter who had just undergone urgent and unexpected open-heart surgery. The environment was familiar to me, having cared for many post-cardiac patients when I was a surgical resident: the IV drips, medications, and alarms little changed from the time of my own training. The nurse came to hang a bag of fluid with insulin in it and mentioned to me that my daughter's blood sugar was a little high. I mentioned that my daughter was not diabetic and that a mildly elevated blood sugar is a normal physiologic response following surgery. She responded confidently that keeping my daughter's blood sugar below 200 mg/dl the morning and two after surgery would improve her healing. The nurse looked puzzled when I replied that my 20-something daughter does not have Medicare. Lost on her was the fact that scientific studies, already superseded with newer data, had led to Medicare's SCIP guideline INF-4. This one-size-fits-all federal guideline on glucose control led hospitals to hire quality reporting staff who crafted and implemented hospital protocols to match this glucose guideline to improve the hospital's SCIP reporting. Lost on this unsuspecting nurse was that she had just recited almost verbatim the Medicare SCIP compliance measure guideline back to me. This is an example of the mindless following of federal regulatory guidelines, only for the sake of regulatory compliance, without considering the unique needs of a patient.

Hospitals across the country routinely find it too complex to apply internal processes that are different for Medicare and non-Medicare patients and therefore apply these processes to all hospitalized patients. Unknown to my daughter's nurse was the publication in the *Journal of Thoracic and Cardiovascular Surgery* earlier that very year calling for an end to this SCIP measure based on new scientific evidence. The article was plainly titled, "Surgical Care Improvement Project Measure for Postoperative Glucose Control Should Not Be Used as a Measure of Quality after Cardiac Surgery" (Lapar et al., 2014). This study of 1,700 cardiac surgery patients showed that SCIP-directed glucose control after surgery was not associated with improved risk-adjusted mortality, morbidity, or hospital resource usage.

Fewer Regulations, More Local Physician Empowerment

SCIP- Surgical Care Improvement Program

The nurse consulted with my daughter's surgeon and held giving the insulin. Eventually the SCIP measure itself was rescinded by CMS. The history of SCIP and similar programs demonstrates that it is a generally failed premise that federal administrators, even when supported by bright minds with good intent, can steer medical decision-making in a positive way that withstands the scrutiny of later scientific analysis. Moreover, public policies often take years to implement and remain in force years thereafter. Quality programs constructed along such a time line are unresponsive to newer research and discovery of limitations in older studies.

Pay to Play—Federal Pressure Resulting in Higher Cost and Consolidations

Motivated by incentives, penalties, and promises of public disclosures of quality, hospitals and physicians embraced quality initiatives en masse, but at great expense. The initiatives motivated changes in healthcare across America but also required detailed reporting back to the federal government to assess compliance. Each year, the guidelines were modified to either add new quality measures or modify/drop old ones. The complexity of reporting was beyond the current administrative staffing levels of hospitals and additionally beyond the capabilities and sophistication of many small hospitals. The federal programs therefore birthed an industry of quality reporting consultants, reporting intermediaries, and the rapid addition of hospital and physician practice employees dedicated to program compliance and data submission. This led to increased costs, and pressure on small providers and hospitals to merge or be acquired, as discussed in the next two chapters.

What hospitals and professional providers learned was that reporting is a rapidly changing and expensive endeavor to participate in. An average-size hospital dedicates 59 employees to regulatory compliance of which one-quarter are doctors or nurses (American Hospital Association [AHA], 2017). Health systems must comply with 629 discrete regulatory requirements across nine domains. According to the AHA, community hospitals spend over $7 million annually on administrative activities to support compliance. Smaller hospitals that do not have the financial resources or the technical know-how have difficulty surviving in this expensive new landscape and have consolidated with larger systems at an increasing rate.

This was not an unintended consequence. In 2010, the White House's top healthcare advisers wrote an open letter in the *Annals of Internal Medicine* stating that the ACA "reforms will unleash forces that favor integration across the continuum of care" (Kocher et al., 2010). Kocher and fellow White House advisers laid out an ambitious once-in-a-generation opportunity to change how healthcare is delivered in America and "remove many barriers to delivering high-quality care, such as unnecessary administrative complexity. . . ." In hindsight, the ACA instead greatly expanded administrative complexity. It also resulted in higher cost by loss of competition. By 2016, the letter's lead author, Bob Kocher, wrote a retraction in the *Wall Street Journal* titled, "How I was wrong about Obamacare," where he detailed his misgivings regarding the direction the legislation took and the consolidation it promoted (Kocher, 2016).

Consolidation was also a by-product of "pay for performance" programs, the first of which was the Medicare Physician Group Practice (PGP) project, the precursor to the broader accountable care organizations (ACOs). The intent was to establish quality of care standards with both upside and downside financial risk for the providers who participated (Centers for Medicare and Medicaid Services, 2011). Significant electronic and administrative infrastructure is necessary to participate in an ACO. Small groups were not positioned to participate. The average ACO in the year 2017 consisted of 618 providers with some ACOs having over 4,000 providers. Mixed results regarding quality and cost savings led CMS to build on its initial ACO experience and establish the Next Generation Accountable Care Organization (NGACO) model (Hanson, 2020). In January 2020, CMS released a progress report on the NGACO model and found no improvement in quality and an increase in spending by $93 million. Not only was there an increase in total cost to the payer (Medicare), providers who participated also needed an administrative infrastructure for reporting that, in the absence of this program, may have been directed to direct patient care activities instead. The total financial loss, therefore, was much greater.

More Regulations Mean Less Time Spent With Patients

The high cost of a complex system is paid not only in real dollars but also in lost patient-physician interaction time. Like hospitals, physician practices large and small must comply with federal reporting or accept fines or reduced reimbursement. Casalino et al. (2016) found that U.S. physician practices spent 15.1 hours per physician per week complying with external quality measures, including data collection, tracking, entry into the electronic medical record, and data submission. This translated into an annual $40,069 per physician per year totaling $15.4 billion for all providers in the U.S. (Casalino et al., 2016). Shrank et al. (2019) reviewed the data from 54 peer-reviewed articles on waste in healthcare across all settings of care and found that "administrative waste" was the single largest share at $266 billion.

As a mid-career physician, I have gained the perspective of practicing both before and after implementation of many of the federal quality policies in healthcare. I have watched the evolution of well-intentioned but poorly thought out reporting tools and quality guidelines. As a private practicing physician who puts patients before paperwork and reporting, the downside is that my practice is fined several percent each year for each Medicare patient I treat because of my decision to be a nonreporting provider. On a positive note, my full attention is on patient care. Truth be told, I am surprised that many physicians choose to participate in quality programs at all since studies have shown the high administrative costs associated with them and the lost patient care time.

[handwritten margin note: Tech. MD puts Pt before paperwork]

Back to the Patient . . . or Computer

Fortunately, as data has accumulated over the past several years bringing to light the increased cost and low benefit of the federal quality healthcare policies, not only did the former legislative architects openly question the paradigm but so has the current administration. Better, less complicated, and less expensive care took on new meaning with Executive Order 13771, "Reducing Regulation and Controlling Regulatory Costs" (Federal Register, 2017). In response, Seema Verma, the current director of CMS, launched the

Patients Over Paperwork initiative. Its intent is to reduce burdensome regulations (Centers for Medicare and Medicaid Services, 2018).

Regulations Creating the Wrong Financial Incentives

Beyond making changes in quality reporting programs, CMS leadership chose to take on the deeper underpinnings of administrative burden across multiple levels of the healthcare industry. An example of this is a project moving forward in conjunction with the American Medical Association where CMS is working to simplify the fundamental way physicians document and get paid for patient care. For over 20 years, reimbursement for care has been based on documentation in the medical record. In 1995, CMS published a guideline for physician evaluation and management (E/M) billing that considered the depth of history taking, breadth of examination, and complexity of decision-making. The guideline was a complex grid with requirements that, for example, "at least 2 bullets from each of 6 areas OR at least 12 bullets in 2 or more areas" be documented in the physical exam. Also, the more questions a physician asks and responses they enter into the medical record (whether or not related to the patient's current medical condition), the greater the reimbursement. Documentation of complex but active diagnoses tangential to the current issue is financially rewarded. This policy is why the patient who goes to the emergency room for stitches on a fingertip is first asked about any recent feelings of conflict at home or in the workplace, loss of appetite or weight, changes in bowel habits, or difficulty walking up stairs. Ask 10 or more questions from separate "body systems" of a patient and reimbursement increases even more. Electronic health record (EHR) software has flourished in this environment making it easy to copy and paste a patient's previous medical information into the current encounter resulting in eight-page medical accounts for minor conditions. This leads to more reimbursements for the hospital, more unnecessary care for patients, and increases the overall cost of healthcare. It is a perverse incentive, created by well-intentioned regulations.

The Role of EHR Software Requirements

Though EHR software is well suited to recant previous health information for E/M billing purposes, physicians struggled with its inefficiencies and poor clinic design. Physicians distracted by quality reporting were now additionally diverted to the demands of electronic record documentation. I fault my own profession for allowing the introduction of inefficient, poorly designed EHR software to become entrenched in our hospitals and clinics. There was, however, no stopping this trend. Most clinicians probably did not realize that the digital train left the station in 2004 with President George W. Bush's Executive Order 13335—Incentives for the Use of Health Information Technology and Establishing the Position of the National Health Information Technology Coordinator (Bush, 2004). Health information technology (HIT) became a government priority. On February 17, 2009, the American Reinvestment and Recovery Act (ARRA) was enacted. It included over $20 billion for the development and promotion of electronic health records of which over $17 billion was in the form of provider financial incentives. The caveat was that the federal government would define what "meaningful use" of HIT would look like in order to qualify for incentives (U.S. Department of Health and Human Services, 2017). Providers needed to adopt "meaningful use" on a tight time line since implementation incentives diminished each year.

I strongly agree with the premise that the digitalization of medicine has many potential benefits. As a physician who started my education as a computer science major and continues to develop software (including for federal quality reporting), I see tremendous untapped opportunities in this realm. The tragedy was that a large sum of taxpayer money was spent quickly on software that was not mature in design. Vendors modified their systems to meet the changing definition of meaningful use rather than the clinical needs of the hospitals, providers, and patients using them. Innovation could only occur if it stayed within the bounds of the federal definition of electronic use.

The EHR meaningful use train came to my local hospital over a decade ago. A few years after implementation, during a meeting with the hospital's CEO, I asked what he thought of the digital migration. He responded that the vision of lower cost with fewer support staff and greater provider productivity had not materialized. He explained that low-wage file room clerks were now replaced with high-wage IT support staff that were hard to retain. The cost of computer servers, software licenses, and network infrastructure exceeded the cost of paper copiers and medical record storage. The productivity of physicians declined and remained less even years after EHR implementation because of the amount of time the physicians spent interacting with the software. This last point has been cited as the most frequent reason physicians feel "burnout," and there is a direct correlation between poor EHR usability and burnout (Melnick et al., 2019). A recent time-analysis study of physician-patient interactions using a modern EHR demonstrated that over 50% of a physician's clinic time is spent interacting with the EHR rather than the patient (Young et al., 2018). In addition, family physicians spend an average of 86 minutes of "EHR pajama time" once home in the evening (Arndt et al., 2017).

Our local hospital's experience is emblematic of an unfortunate disconnect that still exists between federal policymakers and healthcare providers. The financial impact is magnified in larger healthcare systems where implementation of EHR platforms consumes dollars that could have been used for patient care. Vanderbilt University and MD Anderson reported high implementation costs, ongoing increased labor cost, and lower operating income related to their new EHR (LaPointe, 2018). Despite direct evidence to the contrary, the official website of the Office of the National Coordinator for Health Information Technology (ONC) still claims on its website today that "electronic health records (EHRs) help improve medical practice management by increasing practice efficiencies and cost savings" (ONC, 2018).

By defining in great administrative detail how providers should use technology, the federal government has committed the same error that has stymied clinical quality improvement efforts for decades. Technology and medical knowledge move at a fast pace. No one person or governmental committee at any point in time understands all there is to know in medicine and technology, nor can an individual in either industry determine the best path forward for the entire industry. Administrations that feel to the contrary ignore their predecessor's shortcomings and risk spending ongoing large sums of taxpayer money with uncertain benefit.

Proponents of the rapid transition to electronic medicine proffer that although the cost (especially initially) is high, the improvement in care outweighs the downside of its cost. Early small studies questioned the validity of this assertion. Large studies, including one conducted at Stanford University, evaluated 255,000 patient encounters and failed to document quality of care benefits from EHRs (Romano & Stafford, 2011). Others studied the impact of EHR implementation on the treatment of heart failure, which is the most common admitting diagnosis in Medicare-aged individuals (Selvaraj et al., 2018). Their study of over 21,000 patients showed no benefit in quality, readmission, or mortality rates.

Let's Talk—A Positive Role for Government, Creating Standards for Communication

Communication is as powerful a tool in healthcare as it is in other industries, and in this realm there is reason to believe the government plays a positive role. Talking the same language creates efficiencies, removes ambiguities, and lowers cost. In the medical field, our predecessors of all nationalities agreed on Latin to name anatomical structures. In the 1800s and early 1900s, efforts to categorize and communicate disease states led to the International Classification of Disease (ICD) now on its 10th revision (History of the Development of ICD, n.d.; Centers for Disease Control and Prevention, 2011). In 1966, the American Medical Association (AMA) published the first edition of the Current Procedural Terminology (CPT) manual to categorize surgical procedures and medical encounters.

The federal government at several critical points has played an important, positive role in standardizing the way physicians, insurers, researchers, and the government itself communicate healthcare information by embracing these "languages." This has included the mandated use of the ICD and CPT code sets. In 1996, the Health Insurance Portability and Accountability Act (HIPAA) extended this into the digital realm by mandating that "any provider who accepts payment from any health plan or other insurance company must comply with HIPAA if they conduct the adopted transactions electronically." In 2009, the Department of Health and Human Services updated electronic standards to version ASC X12 Version 5010 (Federal Register, 2009). These mandates aligned our industry to talk the same. No hospital, insurer, or medical organization has sufficient standing to mandate such sweeping compliance with standards. It is in this role that the federal government shines.

Currently, there remain additional standards that require adoption in the realm of clinical data communication and laws that can be written to promote compliance. Such standards could facilitate growth and innovation in the areas of telemedicine and telehealth, as discussed in chapters 1 and 2. The current administration should be supported in its efforts to promote interoperability and communication standards and admonished when it attempts to define the inner workings and outward function of medical applications. Application programming interfaces (APIs) are widely used by software developers and providers of healthcare to meet the needs of their patients, unencumbered by prescriptive federal definitions such as "meaningful use," and have the ability to be more innovative and economical.

Future Directions—With Empowered Patients

The current administration sounded a familiar healthcare tone with Executive Order 13813. Signed in October 2017, this order seeks "the development and operation of a healthcare system that provides high-quality care at affordable prices for the American people . . . and improve access to and the quality of information that Americans need to make informed healthcare decisions" (Federal Register, 2017). These words, with minor reordering and modification, articulate the thoughts of every administration for the past 50 years. In section I subsection c(2), however, there is a significant break with the past as the order seeks to "re-inject competition into healthcare markets by lowering barriers to entry, limiting excessive consolidation, and preventing abuses of market power." The order also addresses the need for price transparency. In response, the Department of Health and Human Services, the Department of Labor, and the Department of the Treasury jointly authored their analysis of current programs and a blueprint forward. The report included a self-reflective statement: "Unfortunately, government bureaucracies are often slow to change and adapt to healthcare innovations and new payment models. Given the government's large role in the health-care sector, this likely contributes to lower productivity in the sector. . . . Simply put, government has played a large role in limiting the value Americans obtain for their healthcare spending" (U.S. Department of Human and Health Services, U.S. Department of the Treasury, & U.S. Department of Labor, n.d.). This sobering statement is not a partisan rebuke of the previous administration but instead a more overarching statement of how bureau-cracies are not well positioned at any point in time to lead innovation and cost-saving in this arena. I agree with this assessment, and there is now ample scientific data to support the assertion.

Promoting competition among providers by reducing financial incen-tives to consolidate and demanding price transparency so that patients have an opportunity to be educated shoppers is a tectonic shift in paradigm from a single-payer, government-funded policy. No matter the direction our country takes between these two ideologies, at the end of the day, some-one receives and someone pays for healthcare. Whether it is the taxpayer or the employer or the individual, knowing what services cost and what benefit they deliver matters. I applaud all efforts that illuminate and educate patients and make them accountable for their own health. The idea that the government or even a physician group can be "accountable" for an individ-ual's health and health decision-making ignores large variations in health that occur from lifestyle choices such as obesity, smoking, drug usage, and chronic disease. It is not surprising that the return to medical paternalism with ACOs has met with disappointing quality and financial results.

Placing the patient at the center of healthcare reform legislation and ask-ing patients to be active, responsible advocates for their own health will require education and engagement from all stakeholders. Taking "ownership" of one's health is innate for some but will require significant messaging for others. The government can play a large role in establishing a healthcare data "bill of rights" whereby providers in all settings are required to electronically transmit patient clinical data such as lab results, office visit notes, and hospitalization reports to a patient controlled, patient-centered repository. As a provider, I would welcome a proposal that required providers to transmit such data to a secure, HIPAA-compliant repository of the patient's choosing within 48 hours of the encounter. This repository, with patient permission, could then be shared with future providers. Such a paradigm is what is referred to in computer jargon as a many-to-one-to-many relationship, which in this instance has the patient positioned in the center as the "one" and past and future healthcare providers on either side as the "many." It is far less complex and more achievable than the many-to-many relationship current evolving between EHR vendors who maintain healthcare data in protected, proprietary silos.

It is clear that CMS already understands the importance of this shift in the way data flows and is stored in healthcare. The administration should be supported in its newly developed MyHealthEData and Blue Button 2.0 initiatives (Blue Button, n.d.). The MyHealthEData initiative is a fine demonstration project with the government itself serving as the central data repository for Medicare beneficiaries. Hopefully, once standards are developed and providers and patients begin to embrace this many-one-many healthcare data paradigm with the patient in the middle, the administration will empower secure, independent, cloud-based data repositories to assume this important role through bipartisan legislation.

No matter the future landscape of payers, the government should be applauded when it serves the important role of protecting patient rights. The Emergency Medical Treatment and Labor Act (EMTALA) is an excellent example whereby federal law requires anyone coming to an emergency department to be stabilized and treated, regardless of their insurance status or ability to pay. Federal laws establish the rights of patients to have access to their medical record and the right to maintain its privacy from others. Similarly, the administration should be applauded when the patient is placed at the center of healthcare advocacy as it relates to the secure flow of information between providers no matter the setting.

Understanding past failures of government quality efforts, regulations, and paternalism while embracing efforts on transparency and clinical information sharing are bipartisan ideas that are present and actionable. Though we are created biologically unequal from one another, we all benefit from a healthcare system that is patient-driven and delivers better value.

CHAPTER 4

Do We Want a *Medical-Industrial Complex* or a *Healthcare Delivery System* That Empowers Patients?

KATIE NEMITZ AND DANIEL SEM

In chapter 3, Dr. Greg Watchmaker discussed some of the unintended consequences of well-intentioned government regulations in healthcare. These consequences include a trend toward more consolidation of hospital providers into what some have called the Medical-Industrial Complex. This chapter provides a deeper dive into this consolidation trend, along with a brief history of the healthcare industry and an assessment of the effect of consolidation on patient care. It serves as a foundation for chapter 5, which provides a perspective from a physician, the former president of the American Medical Association, who has personally experienced this anticompetitive force on her practice in New Mexico, which is fighting to survive and serve patient needs against this increasingly powerful Medical-Industrial Complex.

Background

Our current national healthcare system or "medical industry" has evolved significantly over the last 100 years. It is unclear, however, if the transformation has been in the best interest of patients and providers or whether the system has evolved to benefit associated industries. One thing is clear: As a nation, healthcare consumers are not happy with the prices they pay for health-related services. Healthcare consumers are also not happy with waiting extended periods of time to see providers, and they feel they should be able to receive healthcare when needed without worrying that they will have to forgo paying a different monthly bill to receive that care. To that end, most would agree that no one should go bankrupt because of a medical tragedy. Yet, healthcare seems to have evolved to a point today where the financial strain placed on individuals is no longer sustainable.

As healthcare consumers, it is important to be informed regarding the history of healthcare in America, what drives the healthcare system, who

---

Katie Nemitz is a doctoral student at Concordia University Wisconsin.

drives the healthcare system, and where we are headed if changes do not occur. Without this information, we will not be able to suggest, construct, and implement an effective healthcare delivery system that will meet everyone's needs and not put undue financial burdens on the average American.

Current U.S. Healthcare System Performance Global Rankings

The United States spends more money per person on healthcare than any other country in the world and yet, when evaluated, our patient outcomes are not better than that of other industrialized nations. In 2017, the United States spent over $3.5 trillion on healthcare (Amadeo, 2019). This equates to more than $10,000 per person. "Healthcare accounts for almost 18% of the GDP [gross domestic product] in the United States and averages between 9.6 and 12.4% in other developed countries" (Ducharme, 2018). While the cost of healthcare in America is the highest in the world, we lag other nations in performance related to important health indicators. This begs the question: What are we getting for our money?

If we were running a business that cost more to run than any other business of its kind in other countries, as business owners we would certainly study other business models, create a business plan that would help to guide operations, and plan for improvement and sustainment of that business. We would also survey customers to ensure what we develop would meet their needs as well. Unfortunately, while that scenario should happen with healthcare, it probably will not. In this chapter we evaluate how our healthcare system evolved over the last 100 years and what drives and supports our current healthcare delivery system. We also identify areas of opportunity and discuss the business implications of the current system on both the healthcare delivery system itself and the healthcare consumer.

The History of Healthcare in America

Healthcare leaders have been debating the best way to design or improve a healthcare system for the last hundred years and have periodically explored different proposals for national healthcare. The history of the U.S. healthcare system is interesting. Under Theodore Roosevelt, the country really started to evaluate what it needed out of our healthcare system. Roosevelt believed that no country could be strong if its citizens were weak or sick, and so he wanted to ensure citizens could get care when needed (Palmer, 2020). In 1915 the American Association of Labor Legislation (AALL) drafted a bill that would provide insurance coverage to the working class and those earning less than $1,200 per year. Coverage was to include physician and nursing services, hospital care, sick pay, maternity benefits, and death benefits. Costs were to be shared between workers, employers, and the state (Palmer, 2020).

The American Medical Association (AMA) worked early on with the AALL committee to introduce a health insurance plan, but the American Federation of Labor was against it (Palmer, 2020). The commercial insurance industry also opposed the AALL bill. By the 1930s we still did not have a universal solution, but the focus did shift to expanding access to medical care. More and more people were starting to use healthcare services as the country started to recognize the importance of expert care and infection prevention.

In 1935 the Social Security Act was signed into law by President Franklin D. Roosevelt. While it might seem natural that the Great Depression would spur the country into passing health insurance coverage for everyone, that was not the case (Palmer, 2020). Roosevelt was reportedly worried that including healthcare in his Social Security bill would ensure that the bill would not pass since the AMA was against universal coverage and carried so much clout (Palmer, 2020).

Harry Truman became president in 1945 and once again healthcare was a topic for discussion and resolution. While Truman supported national health insurance, the opposition convinced the masses that it would prove communist influence if the United States was to pass socialized medicine (Palmer, 2020). Throughout the rest of the 1940s the AMA and its supporters continued to be successful at convincing the public that national healthcare was a link to socialism and, as a result, Truman's plan died in congressional committee (Palmer, 2020).

The United States is somewhat unique in the world for coupling health insurance with employment, and yet this was not part of any strategic design but rather a leftover artifact of World War II that is now central to the American view of healthcare insurance. After WWII employers started to offer coverage and private insurance expanded. Companies offered health insurance as a way to attract workers, since there were wage freezes at the time (Carroll, 2017). This trend also gave citizens a feeling of stability regarding the state of their insurance and medical care during a challenging time. At the same time, the unions were able to negotiate healthcare benefits when contract negotiations occurred (Palmer, 2020). Interestingly, in 1942 employee health premiums were made tax-deductible to employers but not individuals, which discouraged individuals from getting their own coverage from that point forward (Hollaran, 1999).

The 1950s are marked by the presidency of Dwight D. Eisenhower, whose administration opposed socialized medicine but at the same time grew concerned that not all citizens were covered by an insurance plan (Institute of Medicine, 1993). While there was much debate about the best solution, the result of years of talk resulted in Medicare and Medicaid being developed (Institute of Medicine, 1993) in the 1960s. Medicare and Medicaid are still in operation today and service a large portion of the population.

The retired were hit hardest by the cost of healthcare, so Medicare was put into place to ensure our elderly and others not able to work were able to get some form of healthcare. Medicare was created in 1965 by Lyndon Johnson as part of the Social Security Act Amendments, ultimately resulting in what is today know as CMS, the Centers for Medicare and Medicaid Services (n.d.).

By the mid-1970s the Employee Retirement Income Security Act (ERISA) was passed (Institute of Medicine, 1993). ERISA was meant to regulate private employer pension plans. Since that time, court rulings have interpreted the bill in ways that affect a significant number of state regulations on employment-based health plans (Institute of Medicine, 1993). This uncertainty has left employers feeling as if they need to continue offering plans to their employees. Groups of insured employers have grown, as employers see the advantage of self-insuring because of evolving interpretations of ERISA.

Next, health maintenance organizations (HMOs) were introduced more broadly and were designed to eliminate individual health insurance. HMOs became popular in the 1980s (Hollaran, 1999). As a freshman senator, Ted Kennedy proposed that the government should pay for everyone's healthcare and promoted the idea of the HMO. A network of doctors and hospitals who have agreed to accept payments at a certain level for their services is one definition of an HMO, and this structure was created to allow members of the HMO to keep costs lower (Hollaran, 1999). The result of the passing of the HMO Act, however, has sometimes left patients feeling forced into receiving covered care at specific locations, with specific providers, and only when approved by their specific plan (Hollaran, 1999). This situation, ultimately, led to the declining use of HMOs.

Fast-forward to today in a post-HMO world with rising healthcare costs, and we find the 2018 CMS budget at $1.1 trillion, with 52% going to Medicare and 36% going to Medicaid (Health and Human Services Office of the Secretary & Office of Budget, 2017). The amount of money allocated to healthcare is astonishing, especially since these figures do not include private insurance companies. No one can say for sure if Medicare provides enough coverage or the right types of care. What we can say for sure is that, because of relatively low Medicare reimbursement levels (when compared to what private insurance pays out), healthcare organizations are unable to sustain themselves as a business when Medicare patients use most of the healthcare services being delivered. In 2017, private health insurance plans reimbursed at more than twice what Medicare would have paid for those same services (Luthra, 2019).

Medicare is limited to those age 65 and older. The closest thing that we now have to a universal and national healthcare offering is what was created by the Affordable Care Act (ACA), which was enacted in March 2010. Under the ACA, the healthcare delivery system in general would make insurance available and affordable to more people through the exchanges each state put in place. The ACA would effectively expand Medicaid to cover all adults with income below 138% of the federal poverty level and would support innovative medical care delivery methods designed to lower healthcare costs (Affordable Care Act, n.d.). The actual outcome of the passing of this legislation, however, has been increased premiums for those using the plan as well as for the health payers covering those insured, which was obviously not the desired effect (HealthPayerIntelligence, 2016).

America never did get the universal healthcare or "healthcare safety net" that so many wanted for the last 100 years. The bright spot in all of this is that more and more people have had assistance with their medical bills and insurance coverage over the years. Even if the overall cost to purchase and deliver healthcare has continued to rise, we continue to see people advocate for coverage that is cost efficient and available to everyone. It will be important to continue learning from past mistakes and incorporating input from various clinical and business leaders when creating and proposing a new healthcare solution and improvements to what we currently have in place.

Our Current Healthcare Delivery System

At this point in time, America's healthcare system is heavily regulated by the government and paid for by insurance companies (which are themselves typically paid by our employers). In addition to private insurance, there is government-funded insurance in the form of Medicare and Medicaid, managed by CMS. CMS is "managed by the government and is required by law to implement quality payment incentive programs to reward providers that submit bills for service to them" (Quality Payment Program, n.d.). Medicare is one of the largest insurance providers in our nation, with 17.9% of the population enrolled at this time (U.S. Census Bureau, 2019). This system was designed to require physicians to treat patients according to best practice guidelines for a plethora of diseases and procedures. If a healthcare organization wants to find any significant measure of financial success, it must comply with these CMS regulations because of the number of people using government-funded healthcare solutions.

The CMS-mandated patient quality outcomes that must be measured under our current healthcare delivery system are evaluated and ranked according to several metrics. Some are process measures (e.g., screening for colonoscopy, screening for mammogram, or vaccinations), and some people would say these are the easiest results to monitor and measure because a patient either has or has not completed the measure within the specified time frame. Outcome measures are harder to achieve success with because the patient must be more involved in the care plan to obtain the desired result. An example of an outcome measure would be the measurement of a hemoglobin A1c test for diabetes. If the A1c result is < 8%, the patient's diabetes can be considered well controlled by most standards. For the diabetic patient to achieve a test result in this recommended range, they need to make lifestyle changes (e.g., exercise; diet), and that is where the physician/patient relationship starts to become very important. Fostering an effective relationship requires more than a rushed 10-minute visit with your doctor.

An important new trend in healthcare delivery is the focus on population health in America, which has organizations placing even more emphasis on patient outcomes in order to ensure their insurance reimbursements are maximized. Since Medicare began reimbursing providers based on quality outcomes and adjusting payments when goals were not met, providers have had to shift their focus to keeping people healthy in the long term rather than treating them just when they are sick (Livingston, 2017). That is the whole premise of population health—disease prevention through education and connection with appropriate community resources when patients need them. It is about healthcare rather than "sick-care."

Consider that under the population health subset of the healthcare delivery system, just because an organization provides healthcare education does not mean a patient has to or will listen. But getting patients to listen and make lifestyle changes are the only ways for providers to assist with improving their patients' overall health outlook. Looking through the population health lens, organizations believe they can prove that they deliver superior care by having a greater percentage of their patient population show signs that their diabetes is well controlled. What if the measure looked at "the percent of patients attributed to your organization that have the diagnosis of diabetes"? Wouldn't that show a better relationship between the provider and its patient? Maybe that should be the focus that the healthcare industry should take; preventing disease is much better for the patient than curing one. For example, Type II diabetes is largely preventable and if people are getting the counseling they need, it could in theory mean that the disease could be avoided altogether. But a key question is whether there are proper incentives in our healthcare system for this approach to disease management and prevention versus a focus on treatment sick patients. Are the incentives for healthcare or for sick-care?

How Healthcare Organizations Get Paid

It costs healthcare organizations a very large amount of money to meet current government regulations, which were designed in theory to ensure patients are getting the best care. For organizations accepting Medicare payments, healthcare reimbursement is a zero-sum game. There is one pot of money and organizations are competing for their share of the reimbursement dollars. Healthcare organizations that comply with the most regulations while proving they achieve the best patient outcomes receive the largest reimbursements, and those in compliance with the fewest number of measures and regulations receive the least. These are federally imposed incentives. The healthcare organizations at the low end of the performance spectrum even risk penalties or negative payment adjustments, while high-performing organizations will receive upward payment adjustments (money taken from lower-performing organizations). It is important for healthcare executives to ensure they are making the organizational changes that show how effective their care is in terms of outcomes, so they get more in federal reimbursements. It is also important to maximize the care and services being provided, as well as staff time so that the largest gains can be achieved.

One way for organizations to deliver efficient care is for them to become experts at delivering a certain type of service or procedure. If an organization can "package" all the elements that usually allow patients to have the best outcomes, then optimize workflows, education, and patient follow-up, most of the time it leads to good patient outcomes. Because the outcomes are predictable and the program is built to support best practices, organizations realize greater rewards because they have standardized care. The packaging of services and the billing for these packaged services is what the healthcare industry calls *bundled payments*. Bundled payments have allowed healthcare organizations to incorporate best practice standards into their plans of care for similar procedures and diagnoses to specialize in those areas. This has been a wise move for organizations and is evidenced by the fact that for Medicare alone, there is between a 2% to 4% savings in the cost of care (Calandra, 2018). Bundled payments work well for hip and knee surgeries because the patient education, procedures, and recovery are predictable. Evidence of this is shown in figure 4.1; standardizing the implants used for

FIGURE 4.1 Bundled payments save money: savings for joint replacement at the Baptist Health System in Texas. MJRLE is major joint replacement of the lower extremity.

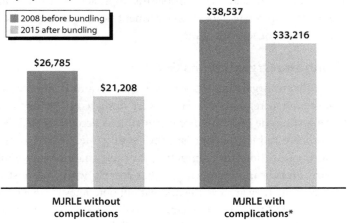

Note: * means not a statistically significant difference. Calandra (2018).

hip and knee replacement surgeries offers even greater savings for organizations. Bundled payments are good from another perspective, in that they provide easier-to-understand billing for the payers as well.

Government regulations and solutions for healthcare, however, are not always the best for each specific patient's case since "one size fits all" solutions are sometimes too rigid. Yes, best practice means that something is considered an acceptable practice standard. However, people are different and healthcare providers should be able to treat each patient uniquely to receive the outcome that best suits them and respects their individuality. For chronic conditions such as diabetes, patients need more specialized care and treatment at times to gain their buy-in before committing to difficult lifestyle changes. Some patients require lengthy educational sessions and emotional support while other patients learn of their diagnosis and make lifestyle changes immediately. No one can easily predict what level of support each patient will need, which is why clinicians are not in favor of "one size fits all" solutions.

Cookie-Cutter (Industrialized) Solutions Versus Personalized (Concierge) Care

Chronic disease processes like diabetes that have a behavioral component are not always managed with the patients' best interest in mind in our current large-scale healthcare system. Evidence suggests that physician practices that are smaller (e.g., concierge medicine), where patients receive more one-on-one attention, have lower hospital admission rates and better out-comes when dealing with chronic conditions than for physicians that prac-tice in larger group practices having more than 19 practitioners (Casalino et al., 2014). "In small practices owned by physicians, admission rates average between 4.3 and 5.1%, but practices owned by hospitals average admission rages of 6.4%" (Casalino et al., 2014). To the extent that this is true, the current trend toward consolidation (see appendix A) into larger and larger healthcare provider practices is troubling, especially for treating chronic disease.

When clinicians are providing care for certain conditions where the best practice is the widely accepted standard, there is no concern or need from providers to spend additional time with patients. For instance, when a patient has a stroke, the standard of care on discharge from the hospi-tal includes prescribing patients a daily aspirin and cholesterol medication. There are rarely times when this is not appropriate for a specific patient. With that in mind, there are alerts in the electronic health record (EHR) that remind clinicians to ensure those medications are ordered on discharge (so organizations can meet government and other health insurance com-pany regulatory metrics). These reminders are called "best practice alerts" (BPAs). When health systems use those alerts, it can be referred to as "cookie-cutter medicine." There is nothing wrong with using technology to make a job easier, but when the cost to purchase and implement these common-sense solutions would cripple a small practice, providers are left feeling pressured to join larger organizations. In other words, the cost of regulatory compliance is making it hard for small physician practices to survive and is forcing "cookie-cutter medicine," which is not effective at treating chronic disease.

Small provider practices do not have the time or resources to ensure they are following regulations and might not have the ability to negotiate the best contracts with external vendors and health plans (Beaton, 2017). This will force consolidations, and pressure small practices to consider being acquired by larger groups, sometimes against their will (see chapter 5). When providers feel their best option to deliver great care is to merge with larger practices or healthcare organizations and give up autonomy, you know they are feeling stress about their business and their ability to provide excellent patient care in a financially sustainable manner. Physician leaders report the most common reason to merge with an organization is to help with capital investments, especially in computers and supporting infra-structure, to succeed with alternative payment models (APMs) and to nego-tiate contracts with health plans (Friedberg et al., 2015). Joining a larger network also provides security when it is unknown what new government regulations will come later, demanding often costly compliance. The threat of remaining solvent as a business and the need for negotiating contracts with health plans can be important reasons to merge (Beaton, 2017). These are some of the many factors that are encouraging this trend toward consolidation of medical providers.

Unfortunately, the assumption that government regulations create proper incentives that operate better than market forces may not be accurate (see chapter 3). Ironically, these well-intentioned regulations are leading to more mergers and acquisitions, which lead to a less competitive marketplace overall and might also be leading to lower-quality and higher-cost care, in some instances. The stresses of working within a large consolidated healthcare provider group, versus a smaller practice, have even been suggested to be a cause of increasing levels of physician stress and burnout (Finnegan, 2018). Learning more about healthcare practice consolidation, the advantages and the dangers (for both patients and providers), will help to identify areas of opportunity when planning a new healthcare delivery system or how to improve our current system. Whether good or bad, there is undeniably a current trend toward consolidation in the industry, via both vertical and horizontal integrations (see appendix A).

Horizontal and Vertical Integration in the Healthcare Industry

Throughout this chapter we have discussed the current healthcare landscape and how we got to where we are, including the recent trend toward consolidations driven by increasingly onerous government regulations. What has not been discussed yet are the business practices that have resulted in physicians changing their practice structure. In order to understand the current healthcare delivery system and repayment structure more fully, it will be helpful to understand horizontal and vertical integration, which both lead to small private physician practices merging with or being acquired by larger practices and healthcare organizations, for the purpose of strengthening their business. This is a significant trend, with healthcare mergers reportedly up 14% in 2018 (LaPointe, 2019) (see appendix A).

In horizontal integration, a company grows by combining with other companies that provide the same service. An example of this in healthcare would be a physician practice with 10 providers offering to buy a practice with two providers. They would all continue to provide the same services they had been in the past but performing them together would both strengthen their market position and improve patient access. An example of horizontal integration on a much larger scale is the recent merger of Aurora (the largest healthcare system in Wisconsin) with Advocate (the largest healthcare system in Illinois) to create Advocate-Aurora, the 10th largest health system in the nation (Milwaukee Journal Sentinel, 2018). Such mergers are touted as being beneficial in that they provide more integrated care and efficiencies of scale. Conversely, these horizontal mergers can at times be viewed as anticompetitive and in those cases would occasionally be blocked by the Federal Trade Commission (FTC), as occurred when Advocate previously attempted a merger with NorthShore—a different Illinois provider network (Schenker, 2018).

Vertical integration is the combination of complementary services normally offered by more than one entity. In healthcare, vertical integration is occurring every day when hospitals hire private practice providers to work for them and often later acquire them. An example would be a hospital that is tasked with providing inpatient services when patients are very ill. When the hospital hires specialty care providers, for instance, the hospital now has a place to refer patients on discharge for follow-up care. This is a strategic move that decreases overall costs of care and keeps more revenue inside the organization. So, if a hospital needs a patient to see a cardiothoracic surgeon, for instance, as part of discharge follow-up and the hospital hired a cardiothoracic surgeon to work for it, the hospital will receive the cardiothoracic surgeon's services cheaper. Referring outside, even if better for the patient, is called "leakage" and results in less revenue for the hospital. Here again, there can at times be concerns that such integrations hinder competition and violate antitrust laws, which are regulated by the FTC. In this regard, antitrust concerns have frequently been raised due to the large number of mergers and acquisitions involving healthcare providers (see appendix B), and these have sometimes led to lawsuits and FTC actions (see appendix C). The recent merger of CVS (a large pharmacy) and Aetna (an insurer), discussed in chapter 5, is another recent case of vertical integration that has raised antitrust concerns (National Law Review, 2018).

The more healthcare systems diversify via vertical integrations, the further their reach and the more they can affect the market. Some industry experts argue this kind of vertical integration provides better coordination of care delivery and lowers cost. Others would argue that the healthcare organizations that are vertically integrated are anticompetitive and sometimes create a monopoly in their market area, especially if they own the pharmacy, the hospital, the specialty care providers, the skilled nursing facility, and other associated businesses.

Healthcare organizations are taking this another step further and are looking into ways to further stabilize their healthcare operations in this difficult landscape by even running their own insurance companies and creating their own clinically integrated networks, analogous to what was being pursued in the CVS-Aetna merger. Does this kind of vertical integration ensure the best interests of the patients are met, or does it just maximize revenue for the large healthcare provider? One study out of Rice University suggests that vertical integration has led to a significant decrease in the quality of the patient experience (Short & Ho, 2019).

One important and cautionary factor to consider is that a vertically integrated organization does everything internally, even if it might be financially or clinically better for the patient to not use all the services within the vertically integrated organization itself. These larger vertically (or horizontally) integrated healthcare organizations stand to make more money if physicians refer work internally, and the organizations put many incentives and checks in place to decrease referrals out of their system in what is known as "leakage." This practice is typically more expensive for the patient, however, since internal referrals can be used as an entry-point funnel for more expensive specialty procedures (Matthews & Evans, 2018). One example would be an MRI that would be billed at more than $2,000 if done internally but can be obtained at an outside clinic or specialty business for less than $700 (Aliferis, 2014).

This area of pricing for services is where the healthcare landscape can start to get confusing. As integrated healthcare organizations grew, when it was time to renegotiate contracts with insurance companies, they were able to receive better contracts because they had more negotiating power because of their size (Beaton, 2017). But what are the actual negotiated prices? Typically, this is not transparent to patients and is part of what the Trump administration is trying to change. One of the reasons we are unable to get a standard "price list" for hospital services is that every hospital charges a different price for a given service, depending on the contracts the hospital negotiated with the insurance companies. Organizations protect this information as a kind of trade secret. Indeed, these internal price lists, called "chargemasters," are not publicly discoverable and are typically inflated prices that are used to maximize an organization's reimbursement levels from insurance companies (Nation, 2016). Of course, at times patients end up having to pay these inflated prices, such as when they end up accidentally using out-of-network services or when they have not yet met their insurance plan's deductible. For this reason, it is often far less expensive to pay for services out of pocket using direct pay options versus having to pay these inflated prices through an insurance plan.

Some Implications of Government Regulations in the Healthcare Industry

Once physicians realized that new legislation relied heavily on quality outcomes and would require extensive and expensive EHR information transfers, they had to decide how they were going to achieve compliance. Physicians choosing not to align with regulations risk losing patients or paying fines to CMS or other insurance companies to participate in reimbursement plans. In some practices, physicians found themselves experiencing inconsistency between financial and nonfinancial incentives. Physician resources allocated to providing each patient service are ranked on a common scale and the output of that scale is a relative value unit (RVU) (National Health Policy Forum, 2015). Typically, organizations give clinicians a productivity goal measured in RVUs.

RVU-based financial incentives for physicians and providers center around patient volumes at the same time as pay-for-quality outcome programs focus on outcomes (Friedberg et al., 2015). The dilemma for providers, then, is should they work to meet their RVU goals or should they concentrate their efforts on quality outcomes? It is very difficult to focus both on volume and quality outcomes since many patient outcomes are linked to time spent between the provider and the patient (Floyd, 2014). Many physicians have reported they would rather have their payments linked to outcomes so they can spend the time necessary with each patient as the pay-for-performance model suggests versus work in an RVU-based model. In the current structure, the incentives are for hospitals to perform as many procedures, measured in RVUs, as possible. Physician pay is linked to volume in terms of RVUs, which is a potentially perverse incentive since it encourages overtreating patients with expensive procedures, for financial gain (Kate R, 2016). The RVU system could also disincentivize providers from seeing patients for certain types of office visits and reward them to set up their appointment templates to favor appointment spots with visit types carrying higher RVUs.

Another twist in the current healthcare reimbursement game is that patients may be incentivized by Medicare or other insurance companies to go to the provider that has the best patient outcomes (according to publicly reported healthcare data). Some insurance companies force patients to switch to higher-performing providers by refusing to pay (or limiting reimbursement) for claims presented by lower-performing providers and health systems. This is evidenced by the Medicare Stars program, which allows patients a way to evaluate providers on quality and performance (eHealth

Medicare, n.d.). Plans that perform better will cost patients less than those that underperform, according to plan requirements.

How Organizations Meet Regulations and Stay Solvent

Because the new regulations set forth in the ACA were so complicated, healthcare organizations needed to hire more employees to assist with navigating the complex reimbursement programs and metrics. These program managers help the physicians learn about their options for successfully implementing such programs as the Merit-Based Incentive Payment System (MIPS) (the program that determines Medicare payment adjustments) and the Meaningful Use program (a government program aimed at financially encouraging practices to electronically share health information), among others. Program managers help organizations decide which metrics they perform the best on and help to ensure proper reporting and regulatory compliance takes place. Program managers also help practice leaders determine how the organization's version of an EHR will meet interoperability requirements in the Meaningful Use program. All these additional staff and infrastructures are a practice necessity but are not directly adding value for the patient, some would argue. Think of the additional cost all these salaries add and they do not increase access to healthcare or directly support clinical outcomes. It makes it more difficult for smaller (and possibly more efficient) physician practices to survive, since they do not have this big regulatory infrastructure in place to administer compliance.

At the same time that small private physician groups were going through the stress of dealing with legislation and regulations, healthcare organizations were also trying to plan for how to remain solvent as a business, considering how regulations (such as those in the ACA) would impact them. Many health systems chose to purchase the practices of private physicians in their market areas to remain solvent. They understood that if they could get more people practicing under their umbrella, they would be able to share costs associated with meeting regulations while also receiving financially lucrative specialty care and surgical services at a lower price since they would have ownership of the physician practices that supported their organization (mentioned earlier in the section on healthcare integration).

What Americans Need and Want From Their Healthcare Delivery System

As a country we have still not decided if healthcare is a "right" or "privilege." We also confuse having insurance with having healthcare, as if it is not possible to obtain healthcare without health insurance (see chapter 1).

Additionally, we have not differentiated care that is "wanted" from care that is a "necessity," and determined if "wanted" care should be covered by insurance. Should plastic surgeries be covered? What about a cancer treatment that costs $100,000 but likely extends a life by only months? Does the risk of a surgical procedure outweigh the benefit to the patient?

Why does all this matter? It matters because whatever the American public decides we need and want out of our healthcare delivery system should be exactly what we design our system to provide for us. Let me say that again, whatever the PUBLIC decides we need and want out of our healthcare delivery system should be the system we end up with—but only if we can afford to pay for it.

The public needs to begin thinking and acting as if we oversee our healthcare delivery system, because we are supposed to be in charge here. No one should rely on a surrogate (e.g., insurance companies or government) to make decisions that affect ourselves and our families. The system we end up with should also be self-sustaining and include checks and balances to ensure it is not abused. Whatever system is designed must be fully funded as well and have a mechanism to control costs (e.g., price transparency in some sort of competitive market, where consumers are empowered and incentivized to make smart decisions). Ensuring healthcare delivery system sustainability for the way we choose to use the healthcare delivery system in this country will be the only way to solve the issues we are facing today. Just as the post office had to evolve to meet consumer demands under consumer-driven market forces created by disruptive innovators like Amazon, so too must our healthcare delivery system evolve to satisfy consumer demands with a competitive market that complements government programs.

What Is Next for the Healthcare Delivery System in America

What does all this mean for the healthcare consumer? The significant trend toward vertical and horizontal integration is leading to a decline in smaller physician practices and the growth of what some have referred to as the Medical-Industrial Complex (Relman, 1980). It is not clear that healthcare is better in terms of quality of care or cost in this new and larger system, however. It means that unless healthcare is dramatically reformed in America, we will not be able to achieve optimum population health at the best price. And as a country we will not be able to ensure that all citizens have access to affordable and accessible healthcare. We need to design a healthcare delivery system that will ensure that no one must go bankrupt in order to receive medical care, and we need whatever system is designed to be collaborative in nature. Effective partnerships between healthcare providers and patients are the best way to ensure improved health outcomes. This requires us to preserve the small physician practices that have defined the healthcare delivery system in the United States for over 100 years and to empower decision-making at the level of patients and their providers. Access to both healthcare and non-healthcare-related resources (i.e., food banks, subsidized housing, gyms, and education) are also mandatory pieces of ensuring excellent population health. Finally, considering and addressing both mental and physical health needs is an important ingredient in achieving optimum overall health.

Conclusion

Patients should be at the center of America's healthcare delivery solution, and they should be empowered in every healthcare service interaction. Patients also need to understand and own their conditions and treatment plans in a responsible manner. Patients need to become knowledgeable in and help to manage more of their care, from both a clinical and financial perspective. For those who may not be capable of this, perhaps we need healthcare navigators to act as their agents to help them navigate our disconnected healthcare system, which is full of dysfunctional incentives that either do not fully consider or in some cases work against the interests of patient-consumers. This will help our nation to become healthier overall, since many chronic conditions today have a component to the treatment plan that must be owned by the patient (e.g., diet and exercise). If patients are unwilling or unable to partner with their healthcare providers, we will continue to have outcomes that are less than optimum. More resources need to be created and then allocated to help people deal with the stresses of life and their medical diagnoses, but these cannot just be provided by the government—we also need the private sector and proper market forces, driven by the patient-consumer, not their disinterested surrogates. Rewards and incentives should also be built into the system so that when patients achieve great improvements, they receive motivation to continue their difficult but rewarding journey to better health.

Does the American healthcare consumer want a "medical industrial complex" with little option for personalized care and highly specialized but siloed practitioners? Or would the public prefer to have a practitioner partnering with them to customize care and treatments based on each person's unique situation and needs, where they as a team are informed and empowered without the hindrance of a large bureaucracy (whether corporate- or government-based)? As a nation, we cannot choose to receive custom care and continue to vote for politicians that want government-run solutions that will have no competition or that encourage the continued consolidation of healthcare systems into a Medical-Industrial Complex that also lacks competition. Those two choices are very different. Perhaps if politicians had to use the same healthcare system they are voting into place, the solutions would look much different than they do currently.

In closing, there are Purple solutions and they are not out of reach. People from both sides of the political aisle want what is best for their family members and for society. They want to make sure loved ones do not go bankrupt because of a medical condition, and they want to make sure no one goes without needed medical care because of insurance or financial challenges. If we can all agree to start there, we can get to a solution that benefits the people that it should benefit. Business aside, this is not the correct industry to try and make big profits on—and that goes for supposed "nonprofit" hospitals as well, which simply fold in large profits. Arguably, if there were truly transparency and competition, these large profits—and administrative waste—would shrink. Healthcare is a service industry that needs to remain pure of heart and intent as well as free from politics and overregulation as much as possible, so that every solution is designed with the patient at heart. In the words of George W. Merck, former president and chairman of Merck: "We try to remember that medicine is for the patient. We try never to forget that medicine is for the people. It is not for the profits. The profits will follow, and if we have remembered that, they have never failed to appear" (Merck, 1950).

Looking Forward

Our current healthcare system is a very complex, fragmented, and expensive structure with many improper incentives, and it needs an overhaul immediately. It is neither what Democrats nor what Republicans want—it is the worst of both worlds. This overhaul should be designed by healthcare providers, nurses, and industry experts from other areas such as law and business to guide clinicians. The need is for a self-sustaining healthcare system that places patients and patient outcomes at the center while empowering and informing the patient as a consumer, and with clinicians using best practice research findings to guide care in a flexible manner that is not dictated from on high by a rigid system that focuses on maximizing RVUs (i.e., care and procedures that generate revenue). We need a system that does not let surrogates in government, the pharmaceutical industry, or insurance companies make decisions that should be made by providers talking directly to patients as the real customers. Additionally, attention should be paid to the provider and nurse experience because without them, there is no healthcare delivery system. Healthcare worker safety, quality of life, and ability to positively contribute to the work they perform are necessary components that are largely missing from the system we have today.

We can see some of the adverse effects of the large consolidated healthcare system that is in operation today if we look at patient outcomes in organizations that are vertically integrated or horizontally integrated. One study noted that 91% of metropolitan areas had such a high level of consolidation that it warranted concern and indicated a need for better enforcement of antitrust laws and elimination of anticompetitive behavior (Fulton, 2017). We need a system that preserves small provider groups that are more flexible and responsive to patient needs, that harkens back to the days of the fictional character Marcus Welby, MD. The television show by the same name was set in a time when doctors and nurses were able to get to know and spend time with their patients, and during a time when healthcare was less expensive and more accessible than it is now.

Although, right now, consumers can get 24/7 access to a physician using direct pay concierge medicine (direct primary care) for an entire year, for less than the cost of one visit to the emergency room using their current insurance, in most instances (Roberts-Grey, 2019). Consumers have been conditioned to believe they cannot do anything without insurance and without approval of their doctor. That leads to letting ourselves remain captive to a medical industry that simply does not work for how we should choose to use the healthcare system, if we were empowered. Perhaps we as consumers need to change our mindset as well.

Providers have many stories to tell about how their patients are not getting the recommended care because of limitations within the current healthcare system, such as the need for prior authorization, the difficulty in transferring our medical records, or because the service or time a patient requires is not available from a doctor when the patient needs it. Chapter 5 highlights examples from these scenarios and will serve as further proof that our healthcare delivery system, with growing levels of consolidation, is not designed with the patient and with frontline providers of care in mind.

APPENDIX A

Upcoming Mergers and Acquisitions Data for 2020— The Trend Continues

Proposed or Completed Mergers	Outcome of Discussions	Costs Associated/ Dollars at Stake	Other Details
2020—Michigan's Beaumont Health and Summit Health set to merge 1st quarter of the year (McGrail, 2020).	Hospital leaders want to expand market share, improve care quality and overall population health. Goal is to expand into northeast Ohio and further in Michigan down the road.	Beaumont is Michigan's largest healthcare system with $4.7 billion in total annual patient revenue. Summa is one of the largest integrated health-care delivery systems in Ohio with annual revenue of $1.4 billion.	Once merger is complete, the system will employ 45,000 staff and over 6,000 physicians."Summa's health insurance option will continue to be a vital part of Summa and it will retain board oversight" (McGrail, 2020).
2020—Louisiana's Lafayette General Health and Jennings American Legion Hospital to merge starting October 1 (LaPointe, 2020). Lafayette General Health also expected to merge with Ochsner Health System— deal to close in beginning of 2020.	Executives cited "strengthening partnerships, what the provider networks already do together, and to protect organizations in an increasingly complex and rapidly changing market" (LaPointe, 2020).	Not available	In total, the deals would create a 34-hospital system in Louisiana.
2020—Four Chicago hospitals exploring a single system (LaPointe, 2020).	Report states that merger would help strengthen financials for all facilities while ensuring they can remain open for patients. They will have enhanced bargaining power for insurance con-tract negotiations and will be able to remove redundant expenses and services.	All four facilities are currently oper-ating in the red. Leaders cite both labor and nonlabor expenses as reason for their financial issues.	Leaders will try to create a system with one leadership team to service all four locations.

APPENDIX B

Past Mergers and Acquisitions That Were Questioned Regarding Possible Antitrust

Completed Mergers	Reason for Antitrust Investigation	Outcome of Trial
ProMedica Health System and St. Luke (a community health system) in Toledo, Ohio from 2010.	Merger resulted in more than 50% market share for ProMedica in primary and secondary services with more than 80% market share in obstetrical services (Kumar, 2019, para. 25).	The judge ordered ProMedica to divest St. Luke to an FTC-approved buyer within 180 days of judgment. After appeal by ProMedica, the decision was upheld (Kumar, 2019, para. 25).
St. Luke's Health System and Saltzer physician practice in 2015.	St. Luke's Health System (largest in Idaho), acquired Saltzer (largest physician-owned group in the area). St. Alphonsus Medical Center took them to court stating the merger violated the Clayton Act, so the FTC and state of Idaho filed a complaint.	Court found merger created a "substantial risk of anti-competitive price increases" (Kumar, 2019, para. 26). Divestiture was ordered as a result of the trial.
Partners Health-Care and South Shore Hospital in Boston in 2015.	Merger of three acute care hospitals and 800 physicians in the Greater Boston area would own too much of the market for other organizations to compete with them.	A previous state attorney general (AG) proposed a settlement with Partners HealthCare—a guarantee of no-price increase for a certain length of time was proposed. The district court rejected the agreement in 2015. The new AG threatened to sue Partners if it pursued the acquisition any further (Kumar, 2019, para. 27). Partners decided not to proceed with the acquisitions.
United and DaVita (a leading health services company and independent medical group) in 2017.	DaVita served 1.7 million patients through 300 clinics in six western states at the time of the merger. The FTC has requested more information under the Hart-Scott-Rodino Antitrust Improvements Act (Kumar, 2019, para. 28). Completion of merger would have left United holding 80% of the market in Las Vegas as well as a large share in other service areas (Kumar, 2019, para. 28).	Settlement reached, United agreed to partially divest DaVita to Intermountain Healthcare within 40 days of acquisition.

List of Lawsuits or Federal Trade Commission Antitrust Investigations of Past Mergers

Completed Mergers and Year of Lawsuit	Reason for Antitrust Investigation	Outcome of Trial
Hershey Medical Center and Pinnacle Health—investigated in 2015.	The two largest organizations in Harrisburg would bring postmerger market share to 76% (Capps et al., 2019).	District court denied FTC's request for preliminary injunction stating government's relevant market was "impermissibly narrow." Third Circuit determined that the district court's "analysis [was] economically unsound and not reflective of the commercial reality of the healthcare market" and that "the District Court committed legal error in failing to properly formulate and apply the hypothetical monopolist test" (Capps et al., 2019, p. 473). However, later having overturned the district court on market definition, competitive effects, and efficiencies, the Third Circuit directed the district court to issue a preliminary injunction; the parties abandoned the merger several weeks later. (Capps et al., 2019, p. 473).
Advocate Health Care's proposed acquisition of NorthShore University Health System.	FTC and the state of Illinois sued to halt this merger alleging a geographic market of that size would eliminate the competition. Market share would have been 60% after merger, according to the compliant. Based on a merger simulation, the FTC's expert predicted an average price increase of 8% among the parties' North Shore Area hospitals, which would increase payments to the combined system by approximately $45 million per year (Capps et al., 2019, p. 478).	On remand in March 2017, the district court ruled in favor of the government and granted the preliminary injunction (Capps et al., 2019, p. 482). FTC's expert had "persuasively demonstrated that the merger is likely to cause a significant price increase resulting in a loss to consumers" (Capps et al., 2019, p. 482). This ruling occurred in 2017. After the district court granted a preliminary injunction, Advocate and NorthShore called off the merger rather than proceed to an FTC administrative trial on the merits (Capps et al., 2019, p. 483).

Completed Mergers and Year of Lawsuit	Reason for Antitrust Investigation	Outcome of Trial
Saltzer Medical Group and St. Luke's Health System in 2013.	Complaint alleged the merger of the state's largest healthcare system and the state's largest independent, multispecialty physician practice would be anti-competitive (Brill, para. 5, 2015).	Federal district court held that the acquisition violated Section 7 of the Clayton Act and the Idaho Competition Act and ordered St. Luke's to fully divest itself of Saltzer's physician assets (Brill, 2015, para. 5).

CHAPTER 5

Consolidation in Healthcare
A Case Report on the U.S. Medical-Industrial Complex

BARBARA L. MCANENY, MD

Chapter 4 introduced the broader concept of the Medical-Industrial Complex (MIC), while this chapter provides a perspective on the MIC from someone directly impacted by it—an independent physician group trying to survive, offering high-quality and affordable care, in a world of healthcare providers that is becoming increasingly consolidated. Chapter 6 then introduces direct primary care as yet another alternative to obtaining (purchasing) healthcare from large MIC providers, with inflated prices.

Background

Healthcare in the United States is the most expensive in the world and the outcomes are far from the best (Sawyer & McDermott, 2019). Governments, insurers, and academics are publishing papers and instituting policies aimed at decreasing our cost of care, and none of it is working.

Independent physician practices are decreasing in number, not out of a great desire on the part of physicians for employment by a hospital, large group practice, or insurance company, but because the economic model of independent practice is becoming unsustainable. Practices are selling to large corporate systems as a strategy to survive (Rosenberg, 2018). Yet healthcare is now 18% of gross domestic product (GDP), and national health spending is projected to grow at an average rate of 5.5% per year and will reach nearly $6.0 trillion by 2027 (Centers for Medicare and Medicare Services [CMS], 2019b). This would consume all of the country's money, and that simply cannot happen.

How is it that independent physician practices go out of business when this much money is being spent on healthcare?

Medical costs in America are still the top contributor to personal bankruptcy in the United States, a risk factor in two-thirds of bankruptcies filed between 2013 and 2016 (Sarasohn-Kahn, 2019). Two-thirds of those

Barbara L. McAneny, MD, FASCO, MACP, is a board-certified medical oncologist/hematologist from Albuquerque, New Mexico and former president of the American Medical Association.

with bankruptcies resulting from healthcare costs have insurance (Himmelstein, Lawless, Thorne, Foohey, & Woolhandler, 2019). Employers are struggling to purchase health insurance for their employees. The ability of companies in America to compete globally is being hampered by the high cost of health insurance. State governments find their major budget challenge is the high cost of Medicaid, but Medicaid only pays about half of the costs of delivering care.

Despite the financial challenges affecting the delivery of healthcare, health plans routinely post annual profits of over $1 billion. In August 2017, the nation's top six health insurers combined reported $6 billion in adjusted profits in a single quarter (Coombs, 2017). Everywhere we look, there are new buildings being constructed for hospitals and health insurance companies. The volume of consultants advising some segment of the healthcare market, and the profits they generate, have never been higher. It seems the only way to *not* make money in healthcare is to actually take care of patients.

The fastest-growing segment of the healthcare workforce is administrators. From 1990 to 2012, the U.S. healthcare workforce grew by 75%. All but 5% of that job growth was in administrative staff, not doctors. It is estimated that there are 10 administrators for every one U.S. physician (Ross, 2013).

Figure 5.1 is over 10 years old, and administrative growth has only increased since then.

FIGURE 5.1 Growth in number of administrators outpaces that of physicians.

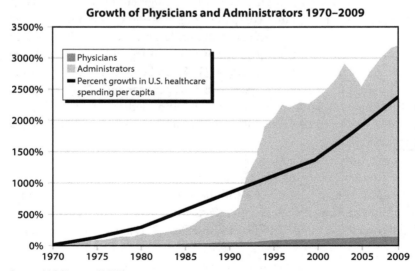

Source: MCOL.com (2018).

If I were to sell my practice to a hospital tomorrow and provide the same services to a patient in the same exam room with the same equipment and supplies that I provided yesterday, the payment from the healthcare system would be double for governmental payers, and the payment from commercial insurers would more than triple. That is a large part of the reason that more and more physicians are employed by hospitals. But burnout of physicians has never been higher, and patient frustration with the healthcare system is increasing.

How Did We Get to This Place? And More Important, How Do We Fix It?

When Medicare was first enacted in 1965, the average American retired at age 65 and died at 67. There were four working people, generally with good union jobs, supporting each of these retirees. Medicare Part A was designed to pay for hospital charges through the Hospital Insurance Trust Fund, which was funded by both employees and employers as a payroll tax. Back then, a retiree who got cancer might have an "open and close" surgery or a body part resected, but cancers usually came back and people died quickly.

Hospitals are paid by Part A for inpatient care and by Part B *Hospital Outpatient Prospective Payment System* (HOPPS) for hospital outpatient care (Medicare Learning Network, 2019). The *Physician Fee Schedule* (PFS) pays for outpatient care delivered in a physician office (CMS, 2019c).

Medicare Part B for outpatient care was an afterthought, as not much care was ever given outside of a hospital. So, in those early days, covering retirees was economically feasible because the existing care needed was relatively inexpensive. Medicare Part B was modeled on the most common insurance model of the time, where the insurer paid 80% and the patient paid 20% of the bill. The governmental insurance part of Medicare part B was funded through taxes from the general federal funds and from premiums paid by retirees, and that continues to be true.

Medicare additionally assumed that the profit margin for usual and customary charges was about 20%, so Medicare set an allowable amount of 80% of billed charges. Now, Medicare pays 80% of the 80% assumed to be the real cost of care (i.e., 64%), leaving 20% of the Medicare allowable to be paid by the patient. As more services became available in the outpatient arena and care became more expensive, Medigap insurance became available to pay the 20% expected from the retiree. However, as the cost of delivering care rose, the Medicare allowable became lower than the cost of delivering care in many instances. Medicare is counting on cost-shifting from the commercial insurers to bridge the gap of the cost to deliver care and what Medicare pays.

The above only applies to the PFS (CMS, 2019c). Care provided under HOPPS evolved out of a system where hospitals submitted their costs plus a margin for payment, which encouraged inflation of costs (CMS, 2019b). In reaction CMS created *ambulatory payment categories* to pay hospitals' outpatient Part B claims.

Over time the cost of delivering most services has grown faster than the Medicare allowable payment. Because balance billing, where physicians bill more than the Medicare allowable, is illegal under Medicare for physicians accepting assignment of the patients Medicare benefit, physicians are left having to make up the unpaid difference by cost-shifting from commercial insurance payments for non-Medicare patients.

Some states have higher payments for Medicare because of *geographic price cost indicators* (GPCIs) and are less affected, but Medicaid never covers its own costs, even for the states with higher GPCIs (National Academies of Sciences, 2011). As costs increased faster than payments, the amount paid by Medicare and Medicaid became less adequate.

In 2018 there were three people working for every retiree, the jobs were not as lucrative, and people lived on average to their mid-80s, including some cancer patients. Improved longevity came from improved surgery, radiation, chemotherapy, immunotherapy, and other expensive interventions, much of it in the outpatient arena.

Every year, CMS decides what changes in payment levels should occur. And every year the hospitals get a "market basket" increase based on the governmental estimate of the increasing cost of care, usually between 2.5% and 3.5%. During the years of the Medicare Sustainable Growth Rate, severe restrictions were imposed by the federal government on the PFS, holding them every year to nearly the same rate, but those restrictions were not imposed on the HOPPS (Medicare Sustainable Growth Rate, 2019).

So between 2002 and 2015 (see data from figure 5.2):

- Hospitals have seen an increase of 50% in payment.
- The cost of care has increased over 30%.
- The PFS has only increased by 6%.

This dramatic difference in payment is referred to as the *site of service differential* (Hayes et al., 2015). The lower payments to independent physician practices have decreased their viability and made them highly vulnerable to acquisition.

FIGURE 5.2 Cumulative Medicare payment updates since 2001: Physicians compared to hospitals.

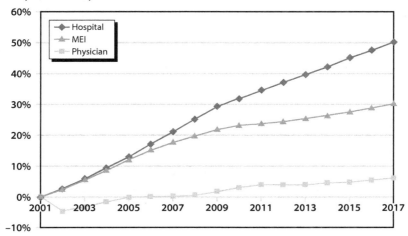

Source: Centers for Medicare & Medicaid Services (2019a).

Commercial Insurance

Commercial insurance evolved after World War II when salaries were capped and employers needed benefits to offer to desirable employees. The government encouraged this by defining the payment of health insurance premiums to be a business expense paid for with pretax dollars. Commercial insurers follow a Medicare-like system, paying facility fees and increased rates for hospital outpatient systems compared to physician offices. Commercial insurance networks must include the local hospitals, giving the hospitals more leverage in negotiation. Small physician practices generally do not have the ability to negotiate advantageous rates, leaving them no way to cover the shortfall of Medicare payments and contributing to the trend of acquisition of practices by hospitals.

The original health insurance companies were Blue Shield for hospitals and Blue Cross for outpatients. They were truly not for profit, not just tax exempt. The plans worked with communities and employers to cover employees. Over time, insurance companies found little resistance to rising premiums, but employers found that health insurance became a major expense. Companies competing globally found that the cost of health insurance made their products less affordable in overseas markets. Multiple mechanisms to shift costs to the patients, such as co-pays, coinsurance, and deductibles became prevalent. Employees could afford these costs when it was a short-term illness, such as needing gallbladder surgery, or when an illness did not interfere with work.

However, people too sick to work still have a difficult time. Payments under the Consolidated Omnibus Budget Reconciliation Act (COBRA) can extend coverage for 18 months, by which time the patient is expected to either die or recover and return to work (Consolidated Omnibus Budget Reconciliation Act of 1985, 2019). Since COBRA payments are often over $1,000/month, many chronically ill patients find themselves unable to maintain insurance.

Hospital Admissions and Revenue Growth Strategy

As healthcare practices became more sophisticated and medical science advanced to where it became safe to treat patients as outpatients, hospitals started to see their admission rates decline. There is a lot of overhead to a hospital, so this decline in income was first counteracted by higher prices and then by various machinations to sustain inpatient volumes. Physician groups were courted and services enhanced to promote referrals for inpatient care. Over time, that was not sufficient and hospitals began first developing outpatient services and eventually employing physicians. Since they could offer physicians higher salaries based on the site of service differential and more lucrative hospital contracts, it was easy to recruit primary care physicians. Because primary care physicians controlled the referral process to specialists, a loyal primary care doctor could generate downstream income—surgeries, lab tests, imaging, and admissions. Hospitals eventually realized that employing specialists meant that they could not only guarantee admissions but make revenue from providing the technical component of the physician service. Payments to the hospital for owning the operating room are much more than the payments to the surgeon doing the surgery, so the facility fees and operating room fees became a lucrative revenue stream for hospitals.

As a response to the hospital strategy that has resulted in increasing employment of physicians, some practices have also consolidated into larger physician groups. This has been effective in larger markets to protect the independence of the physician practice, but also contributes to the development of the Medical-Industrial Complex. It is not a strategy available in all markets, including mine.

Case Study: The New Mexico Cancer Center Experience and the Rise of Consolidation

My personal practice is an independent practice of mostly oncology, with medical oncologists, radiation oncologists, and rheumatologists. We started as a medical oncology practice, and at the beginning we admitted patients for chemotherapy. When better anti-nausea drugs were invented, we were able to move chemotherapy administration to our office. Infusion costs and other services like patient education or social services were supported by the margin we earned on the drugs, which worked well until drug prices began to skyrocket.

In my practice, as we treated patients in the office, we noticed that when cancer patients were admitted to a hospital, their quality of life typically did not return to the pre-admission level. So, we started working to keep patients out of the hospital by aggressively managing the side effects of cancer and its treatment. We added radiation and imaging to our practice, and at PFS rates, we soon figured out that the cost of treating a cancer patient in the office was significantly less expensive than in the hospital inpatient or hospital outpatient setting. Patients appreciated the convenience and the lower out-of-pocket costs.

These changes in our practice greatly improved patient satisfaction, outcomes, and costs, but adversely affected our hospitals' revenue streams. At that time, the local hospital followed national trends to become a hospital system, acquiring multiple hospitals around the state. Hospitals across the country figured out that if they merged into larger hospital systems they would have greater market power. Originally, the idea was promoted as quality improvement and as generating economies of scale in purchasing, but in reality the big money was in being able to generate better contracts from health insurers. If a hospital system included a hospital that was essential to an insurer's network, that system could charge higher prices for every hospital in the system and for all their outpatient services. There is published evidence that mergers result in higher prices, less choice, and no improvement in quality (Beaulieu et al., 2020).

Insurance companies, including most Blue Cross/Blue Shield (BCBS) plans, got rid of their *not-for-profit* tax status and began to merge as well. As they got increasingly large, most markets ended up with a dominant health insurer that could exercise market power. The consolidated insurance market fought back against the consolidated hospital market, and the independent physician practices found their leverage for negotiation declining, especially compared to the hospital-owned practices. Consolidation of physician practices also began, with management companies promising better negotiating positions and leaner management.

With consolidation on all sides, prices spiraled up and patients found their costs becoming unmanageable (Ginsburg, 2016). Hospitals became more interested in finding profitable "service lines" and, in response, health plans decided they were the arbiters of quality.

Health plans told the companies paying for their employees' health insurance that without their control of healthcare, costs would rise even more. Plans also were able to aggregate large amounts of premium dollars and make significant interest on money retained in their accounts. It clearly was to the plans' advantage to make the payment process slower by requiring prior authorizations and to keep less healthy patients out of their plans. Making it hard to get care meant that patients with a serious illness selected other plans. Having opaque processes for applications, renewals, quality measurements, and prior authorization have contributed to the generous bottom line of the health insurance plans, as all the interest payments on premiums accumulated.

All of this consolidation activity conspires to make it more and more difficult for independent physician groups to obtain payment rates that sustain the practice from payers and compete for patients with hospitals that control referrals.

The Genesis of an Antitrust Lawsuit and the 340B Pricing Scam

An interesting twist on the consolidation story presented above occurred in the market in which my clinical practice operates. The dominant hospital that we had always felt was our partner in patient care became a system of hospitals and then decided to vertically consolidate and acquire a health plan. In a small market, a dominant health plan paired with a dominant hospital controls the market. In 2005, the CEO of that hospital came to meet with our practice to announce that we could either become their employees or the hospital/health plan combination would pull $30 million out of reserves and put us out of business. At that time, the health plan was the majority of our business and supplied nearly all of the profit for our practice. The only other plan in town was a very minimal participant. This was a significant threat to our existence, but the doctors did not want to be employees of the hospital. Those with very small children would move, the ones with children in high school would stay until the children were in college, and those without parenting concerns would either retire or move. So, we decided to stay independent and compete on quality of care, customer service, and access.

We became the first *Commission on Cancer* and *National Committee for Quality Assurance* (NCQA)-certified Community Oncology Medical Home, aided by a $19.8 million award that I received from the Center for Medicare and Medicaid Innovation (CMMI), now called the CMS Innovation

Center (https://innovation.cms.gov/), for a project named COME HOME (www.comehomeprogram.com). The money was used to develop a carefully thought out triage system that promoted same-day office appointments over emergency department visits when appropriate and increased patient involvement and education in seven practices across the United States. Care was provided much more rapidly in the outpatient setting, hospitalization rates plummeted, complications were greatly reduced, and patient satisfaction was enormous. COME HOME saved over $600/patient and formed the basis for the Oncology Care Model that followed (CMS, 2020). This compares quite favorably with the accountable care organizations (ACOs) that have saved approximately $75/patient.

We tried to show the local health plans that our processes saved a lot of money. However, the health plan that was integrated with the dominant hospital was more concerned that our decreased admission rate to the hospital meant that revenue was not going to the hospital. By 2007, the hospital was building its own, new oncology practice, and by 2010, it was putting pressure on employed physicians to divert referrals away from us. Surgeons who had referred 80 patients a year to us were suddenly referring fewer than 10. The hospital then used the health insurer to put pressure on us so that we would agree to become employees of the hospital.

The hospital's renewed effort to acquire us failed, but it did not stop the hospital from trying to remove us from the market. In 2012, the hospital put in place an aggressive referral control plan. At the same time, the hospital's health insurer revised the benefit offered to cancer patients covered by its Medicare Advantage plans and forced those patients to purchase certain chemotherapy and chemotherapy support drugs from the hospital. Both of these events were devastating: We lost many commercially insured and Medicare Advantage patients as a result of the referral control efforts. The revenue that had always paid for the expensive services of infusion and patient support disappeared.

In addition to forcing our patients to purchase some of their drugs from the hospital, the hospital also planned to use this opportunity to harm us and to potentially earn significant profits under what is called the 340B program.

The Use and Abuse of the 340B Program

The 340B discount was originally created to require pharmaceutical manufacturers to give discounts of 30–50% to specific clinics and hospitals that provide significant amounts of charity care. The intent was that the discount on the drugs obtained for patients who are managed by the 340B eligible entity would create a revenue stream for relevant clinics (like Ryan White HIV clinics) and for the hospitals. Ideally, that would give the hospital or the relevant clinic funds to make up for the unpaid care. Many of the eligible entities receive federal grants, so the goal was to have these federal grants go further.

However, the 340B program became a way for many hospitals to increase their profits without having to commit to improving or expanding care. The 340B program does not require an entity receiving the discounts to use the profit to improve or expand care, and for many years there was extremely little oversight.

The hospital/health plan that forced our patients to purchase certain chemotherapy and chemotherapy support drugs from the hospital wanted to ship those drugs to our offices on a patient-by-patient basis. We could not accept these drugs for a number of obvious patient safety reasons, so the health plan sent our patients to the hospital's infusion center to have these drugs administered. This disrupted the care we provide to our patients and added extra burdens and costs on our patients.

When the hospital and health plan put this program into effect, they told consumers that this change was designed to lower drug costs and alluded to the 340B program. The hospital, however, could not lawfully sell drugs to the vast majority of our patients under the 340B program. We therefore tried first to convince the 340B Office of Pharmacy Affairs that the hospital should not be allowed to do this, because the discount rules require that the patients be managed by physicians employed by or contracted with the 340B entity (Health Resources and Services Administration, 2019). We have a contract with the insurance company but not with the 340B hospital, and we, not the hospital, managed the patients' care. We did convince the Office of Pharmacy Affairs to investigate the hospital.

Taking a Stand—the Antitrust Lawsuit

Given the hospital and health insurer's concerted, coordinated, and long-term plan to put us out of business, we filed suit asserting various antitrust claims against the hospital and health insurer. We alleged that the hospital and the health plan had monopoly power and were using that power to expand and protect that monopoly power. It takes a lot for physician groups to be willing to be plaintiffs, especially against a hospital where we admit patients. However, the willingness of the hospital/health plan to use its combined monopoly power to either acquire us or eliminate us, and its willingness to ignore the improved care processes we had created in order to further its control over the market, eliminated our reservations. The fact that it would take our most fragile patients, Medicare Advantage patients with cancer, and use them as pawns, angered all of us.

This Anticompetitive Behavior by Hospitals Is More Than an Isolated Incident

During my three years as the American Medical Association (AMA) president-elect, president, and past president, I traveled around the country visiting state and specialty medical societies and hospital systems and heard the stories of other physicians. It has become clear to me that we are fighting for more than the existence of our small New Mexico practice.

Physicians who are fighting the same fights, trying to provide care the way they feel is best for their patients, trying to remain independent, knowing their patients cannot afford the double co-pays of getting care from a HOPPS-based practice, need a legal precedent. I heard stories of physician practices that were slowly strangled until they were acquired. Many physicians, knowing that I believe that independent practice is the low-cost, high-quality alternative to the Medical-Industrial Complex that constitutes American healthcare, apologized to me for losing their own fights to stay independent. Young physicians, frequently advised by their academic mentors that private practice is dead, accept jobs with hospitals and cannot figure out why they are so dissatisfied with the way they are required to deliver care.

Speaking to oncology practices on my travels, I realized that hospitals that obtained chemotherapy drugs under the 340B program had an even greater and stronger incentive to purchase independent oncology practices. Acquiring an oncology practice is very lucrative for a hospital. The average oncologist orders $3 million of chemotherapy per year, and a hospital that is able to buy that for $1.5 million and charge commercial patients two to three times the rate paid to an office practice gets a windfall profit.

Today, over half of oncology practices in the United States have been acquired by hospitals and 70% of the acquiring hospitals are 340B hospitals (Avalere Health, 2015). Frequently, the hospital system acquires one hospital that meets the criteria for 340B purchasing and then extends that discount to its entire system. We are not seeing the increase in charitable care that was the original intention of 340B pricing. Instead, the affluence of these hospitals is used to increase market share, create facilities with lobbies like five-star hotels, and pay remarkable salaries to management.

The Growth of the Medical-Industrial Complex

Tools of Consolidation: Electronic Health Records and Referral Management

Larger hospital systems require larger management teams, making administration the fastest-growing segment of the healthcare workforce. Consulting groups specialized in maximizing payment on every patient charge earned lucrative fees in order to ensure that hospitals collect every last dime they can bill. Electronic health record (EHR) vendors recognized the opportunity to sell systems to hospital CFOs, claiming that their system can require physicians to document patient encounters in ways that will maximize payment. Once the electronic record is owned by the hospital, it is very hard for a physician to leave employment. Other consultants create processes to make sure that referrals remain within the system. The idea that a primary care physician might know which specialist is best suited to help her patient is swept by the wayside in favor of minimizing "leakage" out of the hospital.

The Role of Insurance Companies

The health insurance companies have fought back by convincing the employers who are purchasing insurance for their companies that insurance companies are the only barrier between them and exorbitant profiteering by the hospitals and other parts of the system. They convince employers that quality measures are rightly designed and enforced by insurance companies and that networks should be narrowed to keep patients from seeking care from more expensive providers. They promise that their prior authorization processes will protect employers from unnecessary care and quote statistics that about 30% of care is unnecessary. The more consolidated the health plan is, the easier this argument is to make. The administrative overhead of the insurance companies grows and prices rise again.

The Medical-Industrial Complex

Consolidation of hospitals and of insurance companies are the heart of the MIC and are responsible for the majority of the money spent in the health care delivery system, but they both blame the drug companies.

Pharma and Pharmacy Benefit Managers: The Exorbitantly Rising Cost of Drugs

It is no secret that drug prices have drastically increased and by some estimates account for about 16% of medical care costs (Watanabe et al., 2018).

In this era of rising drug costs, insurers developed pharmacy benefit managers (PBMs) to negotiate with the pharmaceutical companies. Over time this has evolved into a very profitable model for the payers. The PBMs negotiate discount percentages and quickly figured out that a percentage of a higher number is more profitable for them, so they encourage higher prices. Big Pharma (the pharmaceutical industry) is happy to oblige. The insurance company shares in that discount so there is no objection from the insurers. The PBMs also charge the insurer for their services, charge the pharmaceutical companies for access, charge a fee for every prescription written, charge the pharmacies that distribute the drugs to join the network, create and own specialty pharmacies, and then determine both what the pharmacist can charge and what the pharmacy must pay for the drug!

Then, to add just a bit more profit, the PBMs collect data on every prescription and every refill and sell that data both to the insurance companies and to the manufacturers. They put in pharmacies' contracts "gag clauses" that prohibit pharmacists from explaining to patients what the co-pay is and how it compares to the cash price. Some states are now passing laws forbidding this gag clause and pharmacists are able to point out that the total cash price of the drug is sometimes less than the co-pay. PBMs charge direct and indirect remuneration (DIR) fees months after the sale. These fees are opaque to pharmacies and removed from subsequent payments so that pharmacists have no way to know if they lost money on a specific prescription or not. When the pharmacies lose sufficient money, they receive an offer to be acquired by the PBM. Examples of this, and related problems in the pharmaceutical supply chain, are discussed in section 3 of this book.

Vertical Consolidation in the Pharmaceutical Supply Chain: CVS-Aetna

The PBMs administer the prior authorization process, and pharmaceutical companies pay significant money to have their drugs on a preferred formulary list with lower co-pays or coinsurance and easier authorizations. The leverage this gives the PBMs is enormous, and it is the patients and the employers who pay for their profits. As much as 42% of the cost of the drugs is from the processes that occur after the drug leaves the manufacturer and travels through the supply chain (Sood et al., 2017). The manufacturers are complicit in this process and have a significant lobby to help them keep profits high. There are now three PBMs that serve 85% of the insurance market and unfortunately one of them, Caremark (CVS), was allowed to purchase Aetna. The AMA opposed the merger and now will watch drug prices in Aetna products. But this consolidation of the PBMs helps merge the profit machinery of the pharmaceutical industry supply chain into the profit machinery of the insurance companies.

Do We Even Need PBMs?

The pharmacy benefit managers should not be allowed to profit seven different ways from every pharmacy transaction. These entities should not be allowed to engage in excessive profiteering. One might wonder if they even need to exist. The PBM market is currently highly concentrated, but in my opinion, PBMs do not need to be taken apart, they should simply be eliminated.

Hindered Access to Lower-Cost Generic Drugs

As biosimilars (i.e., generic versions of protein-based biologics drugs) and generics become available, the opportunity to lower drug prices becomes a threat to this part of the MIC. However, manufacturers pay generic firms to delay entry into the market ("pay for delay") and cut deals with insurance companies. For example, Amgen pays a rebate to United Health Group whenever its brand-name growth factor is used. The rebate makes the price equivalent to the biosimilar drug in the eyes of the insurance company. It is the patient who must pay the co-pay on the higher-priced drug and the oncologist who is prohibited from delivering the lower-cost drug to the patients.

A Vertically and Horizontally Integrated MIC

The U.S. healthcare system now consists of Big Hospital Systems, Big Insurance Companies, consolidated PBMs, Big Pharma manufacturers, massive armies of consultants, and consolidated electronic health record/electronic medical record (EHR/EMR) vendors. They are all merging into one vertically and horizontally integrated Medical-Industrial Complex. There is certainly no motivation to lower prices for patients or to deliver care to people currently unable to pay. There is no concern among these organizations about the imminent insolvency of the Medicare Part A Trust Fund and no concern about our country paying $6 trillion for healthcare. It all looks like profit to them.

To survive as a nation and give healthcare to all our people, we must dismantle the Medical-Industrial Complex. In some areas significant antitrust relief is imperative. In others, transparency in pricing is essential, as is more rigorous enforcement of consumer protection laws. Each component of the

MIC is making a lot of money and will fight hard to keep the system intact for as long as there are profits to be made.

Value-Based Care: ACOs, Bundled Payments, and EMRs

All the players in the MIC are thrilled about the idea of what is being called value-based care because it creates a distraction from the true causes of the high cost of healthcare, high prices, and a consolidated industry.

ACOs sounded like a great idea also: Link all the people delivering care to a population of patients into one organization with one EMR, hire nurses to coordinate care, and then put the entire organization at risk. There are two different kinds of risk:

- *Upside risk* is defined as being paid shared savings if the entire cost of care for the population is less than the target price and some quality measures are met.
- *Downside or two-sided risk* is defined as having to pay back the payer if the amount of money spent on care exceeds the target price by some predefined amount.

So far, these have been a disappointment. The ACOs that did not include a hospital saved money by avoiding hospitalizations. These ACOs, however, only saved about $75/person, the cost of one office visit and clearly not enough to make a difference in our trajectory toward insolvency. The ACOs developed by hospitals were a great mechanism to accelerate the acquisition of physician practices and did not save money.

The other value-based care model is the creation of bundled payments. Bundles tend to tie the physicians to the hospital for payment. Bundles for hip replacements saved a little money, but the cardiology bundles and the primary care bundles did not. Yet we continue to put all our hopes into these baskets. We need new programs that actually address the causes of the high cost of care.

CMS and commercial payers both assume that money can be saved if we put physicians or practices at risk for financial loss. The data to support this assumption is very meager, but that has not prevented it from becoming the accepted standard for all value-based care, to the exclusion of other options. The ACOs that saved money were the ones that were not taking two-sided risk.

The COME HOME program actually saved more money than either of these mechanisms. The Oncology Care Model (OCM), modeled after COME

HOME, pays medical enhanced oncology service payments to cover the unpaid services cancer patients need, but requires that oncologists are held to financial targets that are not clearly defined and that include drugs and the total cost of care. Presently, all participants who did not meet a target must either drop out or take two-sided risk. A surprising number of groups, about one-third according to the Community Oncology Alliance survey, are taking two-sided risk, and it will be interesting to see how they manage. Smaller practices do not have reserves to cover the payback in a year in which the target is exceeded. There is no report yet from CMMI on whether or not the OCM saved money. However, it did improve care by keeping patients out of the hospital.

Coordination of Care Is More Than EMRs and Employment

Coordination of healthcare has never been shown to be increased by having all physicians' paychecks signed by the same entity. Coordination of care is built on communication between the physician members of the care team coming up with a plan and then getting patient agreement and assembling the entire team to move forward. Our current EMRs have actually decreased communication while increasing the volume of computer entry. Physicians complain that they are well aware that the specialist to whom they referred a patient was able to justify the bill, but they have no idea what the specialist actually thinks or recommends. Yet currently our entire process of care coordination is based around EMRs and employment.

Solutions and New Ideas: We Need to Change the Economic Model of Healthcare and Move Away from the MIC

The Medical-Industrial Complex would prefer that we keep forming ACOs and bundled payments because ACOs accelerate the consolidation of the market and bundles are so opaque that it is easy to avoid accountability for prices. So, if the current iterations of value-based care are not saving money, what other options are there?

As a first step, we can stop paying double for services in order to support the ever-enlarging complex of buildings and hospital beds that far exceed what we need. Patients cannot afford to pay double and triple co-pays and deductibles for a service they could have obtained for far less from a physician office.

We must also protect independent physician groups and give physicians tools to resist integration into the Medical-Industrial Complex. That can be accomplished by increasing the Physician Fee Schedule to preserve independent practices and keeping patients out of the hospital where everything costs twice as much. While it may seem counterintuitive that we can decrease total costs by increasing the PFS payments, preserving the low-cost, high-quality alternative to the more expensive hospital-based services will result in significantly lower prices over the long run.

Independent practices can also deliver better care, particularly if they are given the necessary resources. In the United States, 90% of the healthcare dollar is spent managing chronic diseases like diabetes, hypertension, heart disease, and cancer. Effective chronic disease management requires a partnership between patients and doctors who know them well, support services that provide education about nutrition, and have time to develop caring relationships. Large hospitals were never intended to manage chronic disease, and literature has clearly demonstrated that small practices have far better long-term outcomes. We will not succeed at controlling costs until we control and dismantle the massive overhead built into hospital systems.

Keeping physicians in small towns is also necessary for the survival and economic development of communities. Businesses won't locate in a community if their employees can't get healthcare. Young families can't stay if they cannot have access to obstetricians and pediatricians. Older Americans can't retire in a community where they can't get healthcare.

Unraveling the hospital systems and returning hospitals to communities with a different payment structure could rebuild the medical infrastructure necessary for economic development. Rather than an economic system of paying hospitals that lowers choice and raises prices, a local hospital providing basic services could be linked by contracts and referrals with a system that offers more specialized services. We currently penalize small hospitals for taking patients back, closer to home, as their need for intensive care decreases, but we could fix that anomaly of the payment system. We must focus on paying appropriately for care delivered at the appropriate level.

Here are some specific ideas:

- Instead of philanthropists putting their names on new, large, very expensive hospital buildings, we could encourage wealthy donors to finance small clinics in population centers and small towns and offer primary care physicians the use of those buildings for $1/year rent. (The donors could still put their names on the walls!) Small communities could also build and offer low-rent clinic space.
- We could add payment for patient education services, which are currently not reimbursed.

- We could increase the fees for mental health providers if they work in these clinics and comanage patients. Literature shows that by addressing mental health needs, physical health also improves and costs go down.
- In small towns and underserved areas, we should allow the local medical communities to jointly invest in imaging centers and laboratories. Clinically integrated networks are local groups of physicians working together, collaborating to provide care, and would be a good structure to own and maintain the healthcare infrastructure. Imaging is a basic tool of modern healthcare, but imaging has been given a bad reputation because of alleged overuse. We need to enact guidelines for appropriate use and give the incentives back to the community of physicians.
- To that end, we should remove the profiteering from imaging. Hospitals have encouraged excess imaging on their own equipment for years to create a reliable revenue stream. If the imaging equipment is owned by a hospital, higher rates are negotiated, facility fees are charged, usage is encouraged, and the expense becomes an issue. Hospital-based usage of imaging might decrease: A lot of visits to an emergency department include imaging, sometimes needed, sometimes not.

Think of what this would accomplish: We would remove major financial barriers to the provision of drastically needed primary care. It would encourage primary care doctors to locate to smaller towns and underserved areas by giving them back control of their practices and a much-needed revenue stream. Hospitalists (doctors who take care of hospitalized patients) might find that if they leave the hospital and join one of these clinics, they can maintain their salaries but have more job satisfaction as they develop actual long-term relationships with patients.

Unraveling the Consolidated Health Insurance Industry

We must unravel the consolidation in the health insurance market, too. Highly profitable, publicly traded insurance companies are excellent for making money but not very good at making sure that patients get the care they need and that healthy people are kept healthy. Insurance is a necessary function: Few of us can afford the costs of a serious accident or acute leukemia, so we all put money into a common pot and hope that someone else will need it. That function could be done by a company that hires actuaries to determine what diseases the population is likely to see, calculating and collecting premiums, and paying claims. After all, that is exactly what insurance was designed to do: protect us from very expensive events.

If the profit for insurance companies were limited to levels more consistent with other industries, significant savings would occur. The enormous number of people who are currently employed in healthcare administration would be available to work in areas that actually provide patient care.

Decoupling Insurance From Employment

Employer-based insurance was originally designed to keep people at work, not to manage illness for the chronically ill, elderly, or disabled. Not-for-profit insurance companies were encouraged by the Affordable Care Act (ACA) and are a mainstay of the healthcare systems of other countries. Rather than having insurance provided by an employer, we could offer not-for-profit insurance that individuals could purchase for themselves and their families, subsidized so that it costs no more than 6% of their income, using tax credits advanced to people with income too low to afford insurance, such as people under 500% of the Federal Poverty Level. Tax credits could be claimed as part of the refund for families that can afford to pay up front. Employers would be out of the health insurance business, which would be a relief to them. People would not be trapped in a job they disliked because of the need to maintain insurance. (Incidentally, this is policy promoted by the American Medical Association.) People too sick to continue their employment would not find themselves with either unaffordable COBRA payments for 18 months and then no access to healthcare when they need it the most. Insurance companies would compete for business based on prices and the network of physicians and other providers they assemble. A company that paid big executive salaries or made it difficult to file and pay claims would lose out on customers in a competitive and consumer-driven insurance market.

The Need for Cost Transparency: Revamping the Site of Service Differential, Evidence-Based Cost Controls, and Tax Support

The site of service differential is the difference in prices for the same service delivered in different sites, such as hospital versus physician office. Prices should be set to cover the actual costs of delivering care in an optimal setting without the cost-shifting or lack of transparency that currently allows high prices. All businesses need a margin and the price should include a margin of about 6%. Of course, this would require that we repurpose some of the administrative employees' job descriptions from their current occupation into determining what constitutes a realistic price. Other industries know how much it costs to produce a product or service and we can apply cost accounting to healthcare as well.

Artificial mechanisms that have failed to control costs like budget neutrality for the Physician Fee Schedule must be removed. Under the current system, if one group of specialists comes up with a new treatment, the Medicare conversion factor used to determine payments is lowered for all physicians. Besides penalizing advances in medicine, this system has physician specialties competing with each other for the slice of the pie. Physicians should compete to provide high-quality services for a realistic price. If we had good benchmarks for cost, it would be easy for patients to compare prices.

Currently, physician practices carefully guard information on payment, because if our profitable procedures are paid less, we cannot backfill for all the processes that are underpaid. For example, when CMS decided in 2002 to implement drug purchasing under the Average Sales Price (ASP) +6% model we were told that the 6% would cover chemotherapy administration costs. When the sequester (across-the-board mandated spending reductions) was enacted, we were told that ASP +4.3% was enough to cover infusion costs. However, as more regulatory requirements like USP 800 were enacted, the payment for infusion of chemotherapy has fallen behind the actual cost. We carefully guard the drug margin from commercial payers to cover these costs and to pay for the Medicare shortfall, which is an example of cost-shifting. Every cost-shifting episode adds confusion to the system and opportunities for profiteering or for going out of business.

The Functions of Hospitals in Today's Healthcare System

Hospitals would all go under if they were paid by the PFS prices. Obviously, this cannot be allowed to occur. We need a rational system of deciding what functions hospitals must provide that only hospitals can provide and what functions would work more efficiently and less expensively in another system.

Emergency Services

As one example, communities need emergency departments (aka emergency rooms). People have heart attacks, babies, and car accidents at 2 A.M. All communities need a facility to provide emergency care. Now it is paid for by increasing prices for other services in the hospital, such as with overpriced imaging services, and by increasing premiums paid by all purchasers of insurance.

We should pay for emergency services with tax dollars, just as we do for other essential services such as fire and police departments. Having an emergency department (ED) staffed and available is a benefit to every member of the community. However, not all EDs need to be equipped to manage major trauma. Our current trauma system works well, so smaller EDs can stabilize and transport.

Centralized Care for Rare and Specialized Functions

Other functions that are expensive and needed infrequently like burn units need to be centralized. Not every hospital needs this kind of specialized function. There is time to stabilize and transport a patient. Those functions should also be tax supported and the unfortunate victims should not have huge medical bills and out-of-pocket expenses.

Minimizing ED Overuse

We need to have the ability to reschedule nonemergent patients to lower-cost sites of service. As soon as the ED physicians rule out an emergency, patients need to be referred out. The idea that the ED must work up chronic abdominal pain or a lung mass to avoid liability must be changed. A referral process that works should be all that is necessary.

Surgeries and Operating Rooms (ORs)

A major function of hospitals is to provide operating rooms and postoperative intensive care for people requiring complex surgeries. We should reserve hospital operating rooms for those surgeries that truly need them. Surgeries on stable patients and most elective surgeries can be performed in ambulatory surgery centers (ASCs).

One model of hip replacement performed in an ASC, with the patient staying for a few days in a nearby luxury hotel, with nursing and physical therapy performed in the hotel room with room service meals, had far better outcomes and patient satisfaction at about half the cost.

Hospitals complain that ASCs cherry-pick the lower-risk surgeries, but that is exactly what they should do. We would need fewer hospital-based ORs if we used them for only those procedures that require the postoperative care of a hospital. This would make more complex surgeries more expensive because there is no cost-shifting from the facility fees charged for less complex surgeries. However, it would be more than balanced by the lower cost of as many other surgeries as possible. Insurance coverage should be based on the actuarial likelihood of needing a complex surgery and would be more realistic. Hospitals would have the incentive to rightsize expensive OR space based on their capabilities and community needs and refer very complex cases to other centers. Currently our payment system penalizes hospitals that refer surgical cases and then take the patient back after recovery is under way. We must change that process to make sure each hospital and physician involved in the care is fairly paid for their work. We would also be able to look at the number of rare procedures done in the region and consolidate the resources to provide those services, in what are referred to as "Centers of Excellence." The country probably only needs one center that can perform face transplants and the rest of the country should just refer to that center. If there is any value to consolidation at all, it would be to consolidate expensive functions that do not require a patient to be close to home.

Delivery rooms are specialized operating rooms. If a woman selects a delivery at a different location such as a birthing center or home, we need to ensure that when complications occur the mechanism to transfer the patient is in place. Transportation of patients is a key part of healthcare at multiple levels.

Managing Patients With Multisystem Disease Who Are Very Unstable and Need a Team of Specialists

This is another major function of hospitals. Community-acquired pneumonia in a temporarily unstable patient should be managed in a local hospital until the patient is stable. The remainder of the course of antibiotics should be delivered in the outpatient setting. The patient may need to go to a clinic every day for IV antibiotics or have a home care nurse deliver them or even learn to self-administer the medicines. More seriously ill patients that require intensive care can be stabilized and either managed at the hospital where they presented, if it happens to be the right level, or transferred to a higher level of care. Our payment system should allow patients to be returned to the lower level when their medical condition allows, rather than being forced to stay at the referral hospital by the payment system.

Helping the Underserved and Vulnerable Populations

Hospitals also must be able to manage patients who have insufficient resources to manage their healthcare anywhere else. The homeless with even a mild illness may need hospitalization. Elderly patients without families cannot manage some parts of care at home. Patients who are unable or unwilling to actively participate in their care require inpatient care and possibly long-term care. Currently long-term care is often paid for by Medicaid, adding to the state budget issues. Long-term care insurance, privately purchased and subsidized, might be an alternative solution.

Academic Medical Centers and Research

Academic medical centers fill a different set of functions: treating patients, doing research, and training new doctors. They are the tertiary referral system as new treatments are developed, but they train their competition so that as more physicians are comfortable administering new treatments, patients can be treated closer to home at a less costly center. These centers must teach, but the people they teach will mostly be working in community settings and managing the burden of chronic disease that plagues our country. This does not need to be done in the inpatient setting but should be done in collaboration with outpatient physicians.

Our payment system forces medical schools to keep residents and students in the hospital. We must pay for the entire cost of medical education so that the site of the training can reflect the need. Training medical students is a service to the entire community and should be paid by taxes and not by fee-for-service payments to the hospitals.

Research is a public good. Academic centers should have collaborative agreements with the physician communities and design clinical trials that can be written by the academics but administered throughout the community to ensure that the data reflects the actual population. Now clinical trial requirements limit participation to people sufficiently affluent and healthy enough to travel to academic centers and do not reflect the majority of the population. Our current system of grants has prohibited younger investigators from getting grants for their research, and some multiyear grants have been canceled early, wasting years of research. Investing in medical research is investing in our future.

Pharmaceutical Companies, Research, Drug Prices, and the Need for Transparency

Perhaps rather than allowing pharmaceutical companies and device manufacturers to be the sole investors in new research, public funding mechanisms could be developed. For example, investment firms could specialize in biomedical research, and individual investors could buy stock in future companies. If the product is successful, all the investors benefit; if it fails, the risk is shared.

Drug prices are a major factor in the high cost of healthcare. Some of the cost is simple greed—venture capitalists acquiring sole rights to manufacture a drug and raising prices simply because they can. Competition in manufacturing would prevent this market consolidation. But as the 340B hospitals have increased in number from about 350 at the beginning of the program to over 4,000 now, pharmaceutical companies have seen their profits decline. So, prices go up to make up for the 340B discount, to the detriment of patients and to physician practices that must buy them at exorbitant prices. If the 340B discount followed the patient rather than the institution, it would help ensure that indigent patients could receive care wherever they chose. We would be focusing the discount on the people who need it and removing this rationale for price increases and practice acquisition.

Consolidation of pharmaceutical companies have made it possible to pay for delay of generic and biosimilar drugs entering the market and to team up with PBMs and insurance companies to keep prices high. A higher price with a discount leaves more money in PBM pockets. PBMs are thought to account for around 40% of the costs of drugs. As PBMs like Caremark/CVS purchase insurers like Aetna, the vertical consolidation will further increase drug prices.

The first step to lowering drug prices is to create transparency of the flow of money through the system. We must know how much is truly spent on research and development (R&D), but separately from marketing research. R&D cost is currently a proprietary closely held secret, but much of the early science is taxpayer-funded through the National Institutes of Health. The degree to which taxpayer-funded research is acquired by a pharmaceutical manufacturer should be able to determine maximum pricing. Pharmaceutical companies that put billions of dollars at risk to develop a new drug deserve a high rate of return on the successes to cover the losses on the failures, but if the research cost is taxpayer-funded the company should purchase the compound and the rights to develop it in a contract that limits list price. "Me too" drugs such as biosimilars and generics are not in that category and should have a lower rate.

The second step to lowering drug prices is to look at the post-manufacturing costs of the supply chain. In a rational transparent system, there would be no need for PBMs and the costs would drop.

Some old but essential therapeutics like sterile saline for injection or insulin do not generate sufficient profit to support the manufacturing facility. New ideas about not-for-profit manufacturing plants have been proposed to provide the nation with scarce but essential drugs at a low price. This is in the national interest and should be funded by either tax dollars or a tax-exempt, not-for-profit manufacturer as part of a contract to minimize prices. Allowing hospitals and physician groups to band together to create manufacturing companies to produce needed products at minimal cost would provide a secure supply stream and a modest revenue stream to the investors.

Insurance companies create co-pays and deductibles for drugs that have more to do with cost-shifting for insurance profits than to guide choices. Co-pays and deductibles have the effect of limiting needed care as much as unnecessary care and are especially difficult for poor people. We could replace the current system by removing co-pays and deductibles on all medically necessary drugs. Medical necessity should be defined by guidelines created by the specialty societies. To curb use of ineffective treatments, any guideline drug should have no co-pays or deductibles. The use of a drug not on the guidelines should have a deductible inversely related to the degree of effectiveness the drug possesses. For example, a cancer patient would pay no co-pays or deductibles for any curative therapy or any palliative therapy shown to increase disease-free survival. For palliative therapies that might prolong remissions or delay progression the co-pay would be inversely proportional to the outcome. If a drug delays progression for six months, the co-pays should be minimal, but if it delays progression by a week, the co-pay should be significant. For unproven therapy that patients want in desperation, the insurance system should not pay and those should be entirely out of pocket.

The process of determining the appropriate co-pay level, based on the medical literature, would be no more difficult and more rational than the current system.

Summary and Next Steps to Reform Healthcare

Enacting any of the remedies just presented would first require dismantling the Medical-Industrial Complex empires comprised of consolidated hospitals, consolidated health plans (including PBMs), consolidated pharmaceutical companies, and many vertically integrated systems. To do this, we need antitrust enforcement to prevent further market consolidation and to break up the current monopolies. Communities see no benefit from their local hospital being part of a system, as hospital systems are currently structured. Local control is lost and prices rise.

Under a system where these monopolies are broken up, local control can be regained and competition restored. Referral systems can be developed by contract and do not require ownership. For example, in the case study of Albuquerque described above, breaking up the vertical monopoly in favor of transparent pricing would have significant beneficial effects.

Independent practices would increase in number and stability. Surgeons would be able to build surgical centers and offer lower-cost outpatient procedures, significantly lowering the cost of care. Value-based payments such as those New Mexico Oncology Hematology Consultants has with Blue Cross of New Mexico could expand, showing better payments for care that keeps patients healthier and out of the hospital. We have shown both improved outcomes and lower cost. Any competent physician could obtain a contract with all the local insurance companies without worrying about competing with subsidized physicians owned by the hospital. Patients would be able to select insurance based on price and network. Physicians would be able to compete for patients based on quality, access, and cost.

We need to establish an antitrust legal precedent to enable communities to critically examine their local healthcare system and decide if they would be better off with more competition between hospitals within their community and independent physician practices competing for their business. Especially for tax-exempt hospitals, community input should be a requirement of their tax-exempt status. Legislation and lawsuits will play important roles in this reform process. Lawsuits, however, are very expensive and not realistic options for many adversely affected physicians and patients. Active involvement by the antitrust division of the Department of Justice and the Federal Trade Commission are critical.

As discussed previously, we must advocate for the end of PBMs, or at the very least, require them to be accountable and transparent. They are dominating the healthcare drug market, profiting wildly without providing substantial benefits except to themselves, and dramatically driving up costs.

Only by removing the parts of the Medical-Industrial Complex that do not add to patient outcomes, while extracting significant unjustified profit, will we be able to get healthcare costs under control and meet the quadruple aim of: better health, better healthcare, lower costs, and physician satisfaction.

CHAPTER 6

Direct Care
Empowering Patients

*DAVID BALAT, STEPHEN PICKETT, AND
ELIZABETH O'CONNOR*

Chapter 5 discussed the trend toward consolidation, resulting in the Medical-Industrial Complex (MIC) comprised of large hospitals and insurance companies, and how this is putting small physician practices out of business. At the other end of the spectrum from the MIC are the often very small physician and other practices that provide direct primary care. This chapter presents the growing trend toward direct care, where patient-consumers often pay out of pocket directly, rather than using insurance and relying on third parties to serve as their decision-making surrogates. This has the effect of consumerizing healthcare, strengthening the doctor-patient relationship, reducing the influence of intermediaries, and providing more transparency to the system. Ironically, relying on direct pay services is sometimes less expensive and yields better healthcare outcomes than using insurance and paying large co-pays and deductibles. In this way, high-deductible plans begin to act more as a safety net, for when more expensive procedures are needed.

My Grandmother—and the Dangers of Bypassing Her Primary Care Provider

Several years ago, over Thanksgiving, I had coffee with my grandmother before anyone else was up. As the caffeine started to do its work, we began talking about the family and how the children have grown. At one point she got up and lifted a tray from a kitchen drawer and meticulously sorted the 25 prescription medications she regularly took. I watched her carefully set aside the medications, in accordance with the instructions on the labels, as we continued to talk. Knowing that there can be bad interactions from taking that many drugs, I asked her what all the medicines were for. She told me about her specialists and the associated symptoms for which they had prescribed the medications.

David Balat is the director of the Right on Healthcare initiative with the Texas Public Policy Foundation. Stephen Pickett, Ph.D., is a healthcare economist. Elizabeth O'Connor is a legislative fellow also at the Texas Public Policy Foundation.

One specialist, a cardiologist, she visited because her friend Susie from water aerobics thought he was very cute. Cute as Dr. Cardiologist may be, I was naturally concerned and asked that she bundle all the bottles and show them to her internal medicine doctor. She excitedly called me after her next appointment to let me know that only four of the drugs were necessary for her conditions—four! I encouraged her to use her primary care doctor as a navigator moving forward so that he could guide her through the complexity of the system.

Patients are now self-directing to specialists for a number of reasons and many of them are symptomatic in nature. This potentially dangerous practice is enabled by third-party payment that creates an environment for little to no direct financial relationship between medical professional and patient, and it is not the only problem created through a third-party payment system. Instead, we have medical care focused on the needs of the third-party payer instead of the patient.

Impact of Third-Party Payers—Our Surrogates

In the United States, the healthcare industry has become increasingly dominated by third-party payers. An individual's health coverage, whether it is private, Medicare, or Medicaid, can significantly influence healthcare decision-making. A health plan can determine which medical professional is seen, which prescription drugs are filled, and even if a procedure can be done.

The United States healthcare system has not always been dominated by third-party payers, but recently it has become distorted by many years of government regulations (Balat et al., 2019). Third-party payers are any entity, other than the patient, that reimburses healthcare providers for their services. They include insurance companies, employers, the federal government, and state governments through Medicare and Medicaid. The current system, with heavy influence of third-party payers under government mandates, is the source of many frustrations. For most people, their health coverage is tied to their employer, making it more difficult to change jobs (Madrian, 1994). Prices for healthcare are typically unknown to patients (and sometimes even providers) before a procedure, leading to surprise bills after the procedure is done (Cooper & Morton, 2016).

Direct Care Practices—Putting the Patient Back in Charge

To address some of the frustrations caused by third-party payers, many patients and doctors have found it easier to bypass this system entirely.

Medical practices that do this are broadly referred to as "direct care." Direct care practices seek to resolve the flaws of recent years by providing transparent pricing and by strengthening the doctor-patient relationship. Direct care has gained momentum in primary care, surgery, pharmaceuticals, and dentistry. It functions differently in each setting, but the central idea is that third-party payers are not involved and prices are known *before* the patient sees the medical professional.

The current healthcare system as it stands is not working for many Americans. Awareness of direct care can limit the current dominance of third-party payers, encourage competition, and give patients more control of their healthcare. In this chapter, we will review several direct care models that put patients back in charge.

Direct Primary Care

Direct primary care (DPC) practices are a commonly used direct care model. These primary care practices require small periodic fees (typically monthly) and, in return, patients are not charged out of pocket for each individual appointment. Often, they have 24/7 access to their doctor. Patients are allowed to see their provider as often as they like for preventative, wellness, and chronic care, and certain medical tests are included in the membership fee depending on the agreement (American Academy of Family Physicians [AAFP], n.d.). Currently there are around 1,200 DPC practices in 48 states (DPC Frontier, n.d.b).

States have the ability to regulate DPC as they see fit, and more than two-thirds have crafted legislation to do so (DPC Frontier, n.d.a; Lucia et al., 2018). Texas, like many other states, has established in its laws that DPC does not fall under insurance and should not be regulated as such (Texas Occupation Code, n.d.). DPC is not a substitute for health insurance and frequently supplements traditional health insurance. It can be an option for people enrolled in high-deductible health plans (HDHPs), which have become more common in recent years (Cohen & Zammitti, 2018).

A common misconception about DPC is that it is concierge medicine by a different name. Concierge medicine—sometimes called "retainer," "luxury," or "boutique" healthcare—is primary care that is defined by having a supplemental fee for enhanced access to a primary care provider (Alexander et al., 2005), while still billing third-party payers.

Concierge medicine and DPC have similarities. For example, providers in these types of practices generally have fewer patients, compared to typical primary care providers, and they charge patients a regular fee. Patients are usually able to spend more time with their provider, and they typically can communicate with their provider after hours either by phone or email (and lately, through smartphone apps).

However, there are also major differences. First, pure DPC practices do not bill third-party payers, while concierge practices commonly bill third-party payers for the visits to supplement the membership fee. Second, concierge medicine generally requires fees to be paid annually or quarterly, while DPC practices typically require membership fees to be paid monthly. Finally, concierge practices have higher fees. One study found that DPC practices charge an average of $77 per month, while concierge practices charge an average of $182 per month (Eskew & Klink, 2015).

There are many benefits from DPC for both patients and providers, most notably the absence of requirements of third-party payers interfering with the doctor-patient relationship. For individuals enrolled in this type of care, the DPC provider can supply most medical care, and an HDHP can be purchased to cover unexpected, high-cost medical necessities. Employers looking to reduce healthcare costs for their employees can enroll their employees in DPC care memberships in conjunction with an HDHP, which can satisfy employees' needs as well as save money for the company. Companies that switch to membership agreements can have savings of 30% to 50% of their annual healthcare costs (Anderson, 2019).

Patients in Direct Primary Care

A significant benefit of DPC practices for patients is that they have a better opportunity to form a strong relationship with their providers. DPC practices generally have patient panels with between 600 and 800 patients, whereas a typical primary care provider who bills insurance will typically have patient panels with upwards of 2,000 patients (AAFP, 2014). Since DPC practices have fewer patients to care for, patients are able to spend an average of 35 minutes with their physician (Eskew & Klink, 2015) compared to an average of eight minutes for typical primary care providers (Schimpff, 2014).

Additionally, many DPC providers connect with their patients through an app that allows for texts and email, eliminating the need for in-person appointments in many instances. Physicians can meet virtually with their patients to diagnose illnesses and prescribe medications. Another benefit of DPC is flexibility and portability. If a patient has developed a strong relationship with a provider and the patient travels frequently or moves to a new city, the flexibility of emails and phone calls allows the patient to continue to receive care from the same DPC provider. According to a survey, 82% of DPC practices have physician email access and

76% allow patients to have 24-hour access to their DPC provider (Rowe et al., 2017).

Memberships can be purchased privately by individuals and families, or by employers as an alternative to traditional health insurance, or they can be bought in conjunction with fee-for-service health insurance plans. If one chooses to purchase this type of coverage, monthly fees typically cost between $50 and $100 per person (Thornton, 2019). Patients who switch can save 85% on out-of-pocket costs that are associated with fee-for-service models (Eskew & Klink, 2015).

Many minor procedures such as stitches, wart removals, and vaccinations are frequently included in the monthly fee. Other services, such as tests that cannot be done in-house or less common procedures will typically be provided to members at an additional cost, but in some cases the charges may be lower than what a patient would pay with insurance (Heartland Institute, 2019).

Price transparency is a welcomed feature for users of DPC. Prices are known up front, allowing patients to budget for their care. The extent of additional services varies by practice. One physician practicing in this model noted that paying an additional fee of $50 is still significantly cheaper than going to an emergency room for the same procedure with insurance, saving patients thousands of dollars (Rohal, 2015).

Because DPC only covers primary care, in the event of a more serious health need in which a patient needs to see a specialist, having an HDHP as a safety net is recommended. The American Academy of Family Physicians states that "because some services are not covered by a retainer, DPC practices often suggest that patients acquire a high-deductible wraparound policy to cover emergencies" (AAFP, n.d.b). Some members of cost-sharing plans participate in DPC as well.

There can be significant health benefits for patients who enroll in DPC practices. The DPC model is designed to foster more frequent and in-depth communication with primary care providers. Research has shown that primary care plays an important role in people's health. For example, one study found that higher utilization of primary care is related to lower rates of emergency department visits (see figure 6.1) (Primary Care Collaborative, 2019). Another study found that more access to primary care providers is associated with higher life expectancy (Basu et al., 2019). Since DPC promotes a closer relationship between doctors and patients, it has the potential to improve the long-term health of its users.

A recent study found that patients in a high-touch primary care model, which included more frequent visits to a primary care provider, have lower

FIGURE 6.1 Relationship between primary care spending and Emergency Department visits. R = -0.58. Circle size represents size of the population.

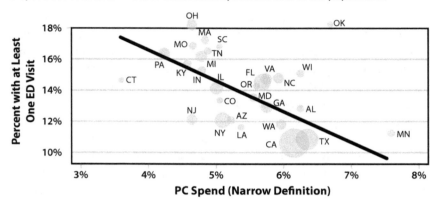

Source: Primary Care Collaborative (2019).

healthcare costs and fewer hospitalizations in the 12 months following the intervention, compared to patients in a standard course of treatment (Ghany et al., 2018). Though this study did not specifically study DPC, it suggests that the DPC model of encouraging more frequent primary care visits could potentially improve patient outcomes in the long run.

Physicians in Direct Primary Care

Increasingly, physicians are attracted to DPC because of the numerous benefits that it provides them. First, there is less administrative work involved when providers do not need to file claims or negotiate with insurance companies for inclusion in networks. The American College of Physicians states that "administrative tasks are keeping physicians from entering or remaining in primary care and may cause them to decline participation in certain insurance plans because of the excessive requirements. The increase in these tasks has been linked to greater stress and burnout among physicians" (Erickson et al., 2017). The DPC model may be an upgrade for providers frustrated by the traditional model.

With freedom from dealing with third-party payers, DPC providers can enroll fewer patients without sacrificing office space or income. Smaller patient panels for DPC providers allow them more time with each patient and will come with lower overhead for practices. One practice claims its overhead is about 40% to 60% lower compared to a typical practice (Forrest, 2007). DPC practices do not need the staff and other resources to process and carry out the responsibilities associated with third-party payers.

And insurance typically does not have a high compensation rate for small, outpatient appointments, which forces practices to bring in more patients with shorter appointments. By billing on a monthly basis, rather than on a per-claim basis, DPC providers have a more predictable revenue stream, which reduces uncertainty and can help them better manage their practices.

Other Direct Care Models

Other direct care models exist outside of direct primary care, allowing patients to find providers to meet their medical needs at affordable prices. For some, pharmaceuticals, surgeries, and specialty services may play a large part in their ongoing care for chronic conditions. Others may seek these services out as needed and see the benefit in not having paid a premium before knowing about their medical needs. The central idea of these other direct care models is that, like DPC, they do not involve third-party payers in the process. In the absence of the current third-party payer model, pricing becomes more transparent and patients are not limited by provider networks, giving patients more power to control their own healthcare decisions.

Surgical and Specialty Care

There is a growing market of surgical centers and specialty care practices that exclusively accept cash, bypassing third-party payers entirely. While different from the DPC model where a periodic fee pays for multiple medical services, these practices offer a fully transparent price list for patients in a pay-as-you-go model. Practices post their prices, which include the cost of the procedure(s), plus other associated fees, such as facility fees, anesthesiologist fees, overnight stay, and follow-up appointments. Although specifics vary by each practice, some providers will not charge additional fees if there are unforeseen complications before discharge from the facility (Surgery Center of Oklahoma, n.d.; Texas Free Market Surgery, n.d.).

Direct surgical centers will typically perform nonurgent procedures such as knee replacements, setting and casting broken bones, and procedures for carpal tunnel syndrome, as an alternative to inpatient care at a fee-for-service hospital. The Surgery Center of Oklahoma and the Texas Free Market Surgery are two prominent surgery centers of this style. Both centers have transparent pricing for every procedure on their websites. This level of price transparency gives patients not only one fixed price *before* the surgery is performed, but it also gives them the opportunity to decide if the cash prices are more affordable than if their procedure was processed through a third-party payer. In the current model of healthcare with third-party payers heavily involved, patients and doctors generally do not know the actual cost of their procedures until *after* the procedure is performed.

Cosmetic Procedures and Eye Surgery

Another model of direct care is common with cosmetic procedures, such as plastic surgery or LASIK eye surgery (Herrick, 2013). Because these types of procedures are not typically covered by health insurance, patients are required to pay out of pocket. Consequently, providers will frequently list prices on their website, so patients know the cost of the procedure. The benefits of this level of price transparency are clear. From 1992 to 2012, while the cost of medical care has increased by about 120%, cosmetic services have increased by only 30%. In fact, the cost of conventional LASIK eye surgery has *declined* by 25% from 1999 to 2011 (Herrick, 2013).

Direct Pharmaceutical Care

In direct pharmaceutical care, pharmacists and physicians are legally allowed to dispense prescription drugs to patients based on physician prescriptions without going through the patient's insurer to pay for the medications (DirectRX, n.d.). Direct pharmacies do not bill third-party payers and experience lower overhead costs by not relying on pharmacy benefit managers (PBMs). PBMs negotiate the cost of prescriptions for insurers, with their rebates from manufacturers potentially making up 40% of the price consumers pay (Seeley & Kesselheim, 2019). Under the PBM model, consumers are unable to see how much of a rebate they are paying back to manufacturers.

A poll released in 2019 found that three in 10 adults ages 50 to 64 have reported difficulty in affording their medications; 29% of adults reported that costs have caused them to not take their medications (Kirzinger et al., 2019). The expansion of direct pharmacies can help patients adhere to the medicinal directives of their physicians through ease of access and potentially lower costs.

Direct Dental Care

Similar to direct primary care, another growing direct care model is dental membership (Tuohy, 2017). Like DPC, dental memberships do not bill third-party payers but charge a regular fee (around $10 to $50 per month) (Raymond-Allbritten, 2019; Sadusky, 2018; Tuohy, 2017), which typically allows patients to receive two checkups, consisting of cleanings and X-rays, each year. Additionally, the dental professionals will give discounts on more extensive procedures such as extractions or dentures. Dental memberships typically replace dental insurance, in contrast to DPC, which will usually supplement health insurance.

While these dental memberships do not have unlimited access to the provider, they still benefit both patient and provider. These memberships bypass third-party payers entirely, providing transparent pricing and simplifying the doctor-patient relationship. With people increasingly citing financial barriers to dental care (Vujicic et al., 2016), these types of memberships may be a cost-effective method to increase access to dental care. Dental memberships are also beneficial for dental professionals by helping reduce overhead by eliminating the need to have the staff and infrastructure in place to bill third-party payers (Burger, 2018).

Conclusion

Access and affordability are some of the healthcare issues that matter most to average Americans. Physicians are innovating, and the healthcare markets in my state of Texas and across the United States are adapting to patients' needs by expanding direct care. We have seen direct care models prosper, particularly in primary care, surgery, pharmaceuticals, and dentistry.

These direct care models can vary quite a bit, but the central themes behind them are strengthening the doctor-patient relationship, reducing the influence of intermediaries, and providing more transparency to the system. DPC is a growing model that can have positive impacts on patients, particularly for their health and for their wallets. This innovative form of care allows patients to maintain a close relationship with their medical professional, with a membership fee that may be more affordable than paying the required premiums and co-payments necessary in a fee-for-service, third-party payer model. As the direct care model continues to grow, it can become another tool in developing a better doctor-patient relationship and could be a good supplement for people who face healthcare plans with higher and higher deductibles.

CHAPTER 7

Reforming Healthcare Licensure for the Twenty-First Century

MURRAY S. FELDSTEIN, MD

Chapter 6 described the growing importance of direct primary care. But for direct primary care to prosper, we will need more providers working on the frontlines delivering healthcare services. This chapter explores one solution to the high cost of healthcare from a supply-side perspective by rethinking the healthcare provider licensure process. More physicians, and other providers like physician assistants, nurse practitioners, and pharmacists, practicing at the top of their licenses, will increase the pool of frontline providers and ultimately lower healthcare costs. Licensure also needs to keep up with telehealth technology (e.g., chapters 1 and 2), which crosses state lines in a way that current state-based licensure cannot accommodate. One development that resulted from the 2020 coronavirus pandemic was the easing of regulations, for the first time, to allow physicians to provide medical care across state lines, which is a positive step forward to enable twenty-first-century medicine—via telemedicine.

Background

Most experts who write about healthcare policy agree that something is broken in the medical marketplace. There are as many explanations as there are proposals for fixing it. Factors commonly cited include lack of price transparency; third-party payer systems that impair consumers' market power; federal regulations and their underlying subsidies; the asymmetric knowledge between providers and patients; unnecessary expensive medical procedures; fee-for-service reimbursement; greedy doctors, greedy pharmacy companies, or greedy insurance companies. Some experts conclude that healthcare is a qualitatively different commodity that by its very nature cannot obey the normal market signals of supply and demand. Many people believe the government must either regulate medical care more rigorously, subsidize it further, or assume total responsibility for its provision.

Murray S. Feldstein, MD, is currently a Visiting Fellow for Health Care Policy at the Goldwater Institute in Phoenix.

Overview: Reforming Healthcare Licensure to Increase the Number of Competent Providers

In this chapter I shall recommend reforming our politicized, state-based system of healthcare licensure that restricts the supply of healthcare providers. These regulations historically preceded all of the other factors that policymakers discuss when they suggest possible reforms. In spite of good intentions, I believe these laws to do more to protect entrenched professionals from competent competition than protect patients from incompetent practitioners.

The aggregate supply of healthcare services struggles to meet the ever-increasing demand that results from scientific innovation, access to government programs, and an expanding, aging population. I have developed this opinion over my 50 years practicing medicine in a diversity of environments: in the military, in rural areas, in veterans' hospitals, on Native American reservations, in my own community in private practice, and as a faculty member at a prestigious medical institution. I have written elsewhere about how twenty-first-century technologies offer astounding opportunities for affordably curing disease and alleviating suffering for a greater number of people than ever before—opportunities that will either be delayed or squandered if our current system of assuring professional competence is not reformed (Feldstein, 2020).

A Brief History of Medical Licensure in the United States

It may surprise you to learn that there was a time when doctors' fees were too low and there were too many doctors—at least from the doctors' perspective. During the early republic there were essentially no effective state licensing laws. Various alternative practitioners such as eclectics, homeopaths, herbalists, osteopaths, Christian Scientists, optometrists, and chiropractors all practiced legally alongside allopathic medical doctors (MDs). The traditional profession looked down on these alternative sects. Each had a different theory of health and disease, but they were popular with the public because they often achieved similar (i.e., no) results without the harsh treatments such as purgatives, emetics, and blood-letting employed by MDs (Starr, 1982; Burrow, 1977).

As the country emerged from the Jacksonian era, physicians began to organize. The American Medical Association (AMA) was founded in 1847. Its avowed goal was to improve medical education and put medical practice on a scientific basis. From the very beginning, however, the AMA also had the clear objective of improving the economic status of physicians. The AMA felt there were too many doctors trained at too many substandard medical schools. Cut-throat competition was depressing medical fees (Goodman, 1980).

The Civil War focused the profession's thinking on the problem of poorly trained doctors. Poor hygiene led to epidemics of dysentery. Surgeons with little or no clinical experience performed mutilating procedures in military hospitals (Ludmerer, 1985, chap. 1). The AMA embarked on a decades-long effort to improve medical education. It inspected American medical schools several times, but the public was not initially receptive to the AMA's calls for reform. Many schools were small independent proprietary enterprises that granted a diploma after only two years of training. The medical curriculum may have consisted primarily of didactic lectures without laboratory, clinical, or surgical experience. Before the turn of the twentieth century, medical science was still in its infancy. There was no effective treatment for bacterial infection, and the need for sterility in surgery was still not widely disseminated among practicing physicians (Burrow, 1977).

Attitudes toward the government's role in regulating commerce changed in the Progressive Era. In 1910, a private school educator named Abraham Flexner was sponsored by the Carnegie Foundation to write a report about the state of American medical schools. He admitted knowing very little about medical education, but he was the brother of an influential physician in the AMA who headed the Rockefeller Foundation for Research. The AMA arranged a whirlwind inspection of each school and assisted writing his final recommendations (Starr, 1982; Burrow, 1977).

The sensational Flexner report raised a public outcry and had the desired effect. Flexner visited 155 medical schools out of the 168 in the United States and Canada over three months (Flexner, 1910). Two decades later only 97 remained, a 43% reduction (Hiatt & Stockton, 2003). The AMA was able to achieve its desired uniformity of the medical curriculum. Attendance at a college after high school was mandated as a prerequisite for acceptance. The medical school curriculum was expanded to four years and included more laboratory and clinical experience. The number of medical graduates fell precipitously.

The Flexner report has been both praised and damned. It did shine a light on poorly performing medical schools, many of which deserved to be put out of business. The leaders of the AMA were motivated to modernize and improve their profession—to put their own house in order. But there were significant trade-offs and associated harms. The drastic reduction of physicians graduating from medical schools led to shortages of doctors during an era when the demand for medical care was expanding rapidly from both immigration and the improved capability to diagnose and treat disease. Opportunities in medicine for white men in the working class and rural communities were diminished. Flexner was dismissive of the ability of African-Americans and women to practice medicine, reflecting the prevailing prejudices of the times. Almost all medical schools for both of these groups were shut down. Concerns about the cost and inequitable distribution of medical care began after Flexnerian reforms (Starr, 1982; Johnston, 1984).

In spite of this, the public continued to support alternative healthcare providers in the late nineteenth and early twentieth centuries. From its very founding the AMA realized it would have to do more than improve medical education. It would not be able to achieve control over competition it deemed unscientific without enacting legislation to bring the power of the state down on its rivals (Burrow, 1977).

The AMA's first political success was in Alabama. In 1873, a majority of legislators in both houses of the reconstructionist state legislature were doctors (Burrow, 1977). Subsequently, the AMA organized politically influential professional societies in one state after another. By the end of World War I, the AMA and its affiliated MD organizations had gained effective control of both medical education and licensure in every state. Only graduates of an AMA-approved medical school could qualify for a license to practice medicine or join the clinical staffs at hospitals. Schools for eclectics and homeopaths disappeared. The alternative professions that survived, like chiropractic, optometry, and osteopathy, found their practice restricted by the scope of practice regulations and hospital accreditation procedures. Government authority to control or criminalize MD competition had been effectively handed over to the AMA and its network of affiliated private organizations. While the names and acronyms of these organizations may have changed, they still regulate the number of medical school graduates as well as the number of postgraduate programs that train medical specialists.[1] As we shall see, organized MD groups wield significant political power whenever alternative providers attempt to compete against them.

---

1. It would be too complicated in a chapter like this to explain the interlocking relationships of MD-controlled private organizations that exert control of both numbers and types of physicians entitled to practice in the country. I will simply list them here: The American Association of Medical Colleges (AAMC) administers admissions tests and standards for entry to medical school; The Liaison Committee on Medical Education (LCME) accredits American (and Canadian) medical schools. The Accreditation Council for Graduate Education (ACMGE) accredits postgraduate residency (specialty) training programs. The Joint Commission accredits institutions that offer medical training programs; The Federation of State Medical Boards (FSMB) and the National Board of Medical Examiners (NBME) administer the United States Licensing Exam (USMLE). MDs make up the majority of medical boards in each state. These are the boards that issue licenses to physicians, investigate complaints, and punish when necessary.

This system has remained essentially the same for a century, in spite of the tremendous advances in medical knowledge and practice.

The Flexner report of 1910 was far from an "evidence-based" document. Modern medical academicians would scorn the report's methodology, sources of funding, and obvious biases. Yet its influence on medical education and practice cannot be overstated. Our current standards for admission to medical school, length of training, and qualifications for licensure remain empiric. They have not been objectively correlated with health outcomes or professional competence. It takes several years more after high school for American physicians to be licensed than equivalently trained physicians in Britain, France, Germany, and Italy (Global Knowledge Exchange Network, 2009). It can take 15 to 16 years after high school for subspecialists to enter medical practice.[2]

Do the Laws of Supply and Demand Apply to Healthcare Providers?

In a normally functioning marketplace, the price of goods or services reflects the ability of competing producers to meet the demands of individual consumers. A higher price attracts additional suppliers. Efficiency is theoretically rewarded. For as long as I have been in the profession, medical fees have not been market-determined. We have a system of legalized price-fixing dependent on negotiations between organized groups of providers, insurance companies, and governmental agencies. In general, physicians have argued that longer training programs merit higher fees. There is little impetus to gain efficiency by shortening programs. Advances in knowledge justify subspecialties and lengthening training times even further. The higher fees subspecialists are able to charge may be one reason for the shortage of primary care providers and a surplus of highly trained specialists. There is, however, a concern that an oversupply of specialists leads to performance of unnecessary procedures. Another concern is that some specialists are not doing a high enough volume of procedures to maintain their proficiency. All of this contributes to the high cost of healthcare without a corresponding improvement in outcomes (Scarberry et al., 2018; Lyu et al., 2017).

Organized medicine has mixed reactions when non-MDs attempt to make up for the shortage of medical services. The development of physician assistants (PAs) and nurse practitioners (NPs) has been welcomed when

---

2. The breakdown for my specialty of urology is as follows: four years of college, four years of medical school, four to five years of urology residency, and one to three years of surgical subspecialty training (fellowship).

they are employed or supervised by MDs. It may be a different story if there is a serious threat of competition.

How the Sausage Is Made: The Politics of Healthcare Licensure

Even though there is an acknowledged shortage of primary care providers, the licensing statutes in each state limit the ability of competent non-MD healthcare providers to make up the difference. Physicians, dentists, and, more recently, osteopaths are entitled to practice within a broad but vaguely defined standard of care for their profession. Potentially competing providers, such as nurses, pharmacists, optometrists, psychologists, dental therapists, physical therapists, and chiropractors are forced to practice within defined "scope of practice" statutes that specify what they legally are permitted to do. This gives MDs a competitive advantage even though they may not be "more competent" than another kind of provider in any particular skill.

For example, licensed physicians can prescribe medications whether or not they have ever used them before. However, an experienced certified nurse practitioner or pharmacist who is very familiar with a drug may not be able to independently prescribe it unless their state specifically grants their profession prescriptive authority. Legislated scope of practice regulations vary from state to state in an arbitrary manner. A nurse practitioner who has successfully performed minor surgical procedures and prescribed medication in one state cannot expect to practice in a state that forbids them.

Expanding Scope of Practice for Other Healthcare Providers

There is ample documentation accumulated over almost a half-century that nurse practitioners are capable of doing more than they are legally permitted to do (Altman et al., 2015). A recent White House report recommends reforming scope of practice regulations in healthcare (U.S. Department of Health and Human Services, 2018). Yet state lawmakers are slow to recognize the problems they created. Nurse practitioners, pharmacists, or optometrists are prevented from providing care they have been trained to do in areas with a shortage of physicians. These well-trained providers have two options: Apply to medical school or ask the legislature to change their profession's scope of practice. The first option is obviously impractical. The second option leads to a demeaning, prolonged, and expensive legislative "turf battle" that takes years to accomplish and may not be successful. The politicians who determine the outcome may either know little about the subject and depend on the arguments of lobbyists, or they are members of the medical profession themselves and therefore have a dog in the fight.

As a visiting fellow for the Goldwater Institute I have testified in a number of these turf battles in the Arizona legislature on behalf of nurse practitioners, nurse anesthetists, pharmacists, and optometrists. My experience in one battle that successfully licensed dental therapists after a multiyear effort is instructive in explaining how the sausage is made.

Case Study—Expanding Scope of Practice for Dental Practitioners

Dentists, like MDs, have an unlimited license to practice their profession and are not bound by scope of practice restrictions. Arizona, like many states, has a shortage of dentists, particularly in rural, Native American, and low-income areas. Many Arizonans travel across the border to Mexico to visit dentists who charge less. Each year, unlicensed dentists are arrested when they have been found practicing in immigrant communities. Dental therapists are mid-level providers who take several years of intensive training, often in dental schools, to become qualified to do some of the more common, painful, potentially serious but less complicated procedures. Dental therapists have successfully practiced in various countries for almost a century and have been licensed in a handful of states in the United States for over a decade. They have an excellent safety record (Nash, 2012).

Legislation to license dental therapists was introduced into the Arizona legislature in 2016. In public hearings in front of legislative committees, the dental association claimed dental therapists were unsafe and could threaten patient safety, even stating that some patients could die if they were permitted to pull infected or decayed teeth. The documentation introduced to support the safety of dental therapists was ignored, and no serious evidence was introduced to support the dentists' claims. The legislation died in committee and could not be even considered by the legislature because of the votes of only two influential legislators, one of whom was related to a dentist.

Two years later the legislation was reintroduced (SB1377) and ultimately overwhelmingly passed in both the Arizona house and senate. What had changed? The need for the therapists was no greater. Their training was no different. Only two things made it possible: One of the two committee members who previously blocked the legislation had retired from the legislature, and the dental association was able to limit dental therapists' practice to publicly funded community clinics and Native American reservations, thus insulating their private practices from competition for the time being (Roda, 2018).

State Medical Licensure

The common element of any turf battle is that the entrenched profession makes unsupported claims that potential competitors are incompetent and dangerous because they undergo less years of training. Ironically, states do not actually test MDs for specific competencies. They take for granted that applicants are competent if they have an MD diploma, complete one or two years of postgraduate training, and pass the U.S. Medical Licensing Exam under the authority of MD-directed private organizations. Once licensed, an MD is legally entitled to perform any acceptable medical procedure as long as it is not prohibited by law and falls within a vaguely defined standard of practice.

It may surprise you, therefore, that the state of Arizona never tested me for competence in my chosen specialty of urology. Nor does the state test me when I periodically renew my license online. I was granted an unrestricted license to practice medicine four years before I completed urological specialty training and went to work. I am legally entitled to open a psychiatry office and not be prosecuted by law. If patients or other doctors did not complain to the state, there would be no reason to investigate me or forbid me to do so.

The anachronism of licensing physicians before they even complete their training is a legacy of the situation that existed over a century ago when licensing statutes were first enacted. Most physicians went directly into general practice after four years of medical school and one year of a general internship. They treated heart attacks, delivered babies, set fractures, and removed the appendix. Today the first postgraduate year after being granted an MD degree is only the first year of a multiyear program of specialty training.

Beyond Licensure—What Ensures Competence of a Healthcare Provider?

So, what does actually ensure competence if not state licensure? My specialty board, the American Board of Urology, certified me for the skills I employ on a daily basis. While such certification is voluntary, it can be important for obtaining hospital privileges and getting accepted on insurance reimbursement panels. The threat of malpractice suits restrains poor medical practices. Branding and reputation are also very important. The

Mayo Clinic, Massachusetts General Hospital, and Sloan-Kettering Memorial Cancer Institute are brand names that connote quality to many people. All of these factors are important surrogates of professional competence, and none of these them are anticompetitive by nature. State licensing regulations mandate only minimum standards—standards that most physicians and facilities strive to exceed. State coercive power does have a role to play. It is needed to sanction practitioners once unethical or incompetent behavior is demonstrated, although the process is lengthy and lacks transparency (Svorny, 2008).

Competency-based Medical Provider Licensure for the Twenty-First Century

Imagine you have studied for your driver's license and successfully passed the written test and the eye exam. You go on a road test with the state examiner and do everything required of you perfectly. All that remains is for the state to issue your license. However, your state requires that all new drivers first get permission from the legislature. Politicians will vote to see if you deserve to be licensed. All it takes is one influential legislator on the Transportation Committee to block your application. It pays to stay on their good side!

Getting approved for a "scope of practice" for a healthcare provider should follow the same procedure as for getting a driver's license. Nothing more, nothing less, and nothing else but demonstrating competence.

Here are the three steps that applicants must go through to be granted a driver's license:

1. Learn the underlying fundamentals and practical skills during a period of supervised training.
2. Take a test to prove knowledge of the fundamentals (i.e., the rules of the road).
3. Pass a practical road test by a certified examiner.

No politician needed. The requirements for licensure are transparent and fair. Perhaps you believe this method cannot apply to healthcare because a high level of education and critical skills are required in diagnosing and caring for human lives. Proponents of the current system believe that only physicians can understand the complexity of medical care and cite an "asymmetry of knowledge" as one of the justifications for current licensing schemes. No one can possibly be as competent as physicians without their length of training.

A Model Competency-Based Licensure Approach in Another Field

Airline pilots are certified along the same principles as drivers. An airline pilot's competence is more critical to the immediate lives and safety of their customers than that of a dermatologist. The "asymmetry in knowledge" is just as large between passenger and pilot as it is between patient and physician. You may not know your pilot's name or catch a glimpse of her in the flight cabin, but you take for granted the pilot has the skill to fly you from Phoenix to London.

Anyone can be licensed to fly a plane if they go to a flight school, take a written exam, pass a physical exam, and, after a period of supervised training, pass a flight exam with a Federal Aviation Administration (FAA)-certified examiner. (My grandson earned his basic pilot's license six months before he was eligible to take his New York State driver's license.)

Unlike MDs, other airline professionals cannot limit the number of prospective pilots or flight schools. The flight school does not even have to be FAA-approved. Pilots have a much more efficient and equitable way to "specialize" in the marketplace and acquire additional skills to meet the public's ever-changing needs. A basic aviator must log more hours, take more written exams, undergo more supervised training, and take additional flight exams before being certified to fly by instruments a multi-engine aircraft. Even more training is required to be certified to fly for airlines. When new technology leads to new kinds of aircraft, pilots learn to fly them safely without asking permission from politicians to increase their scope of practice. Aeronautical training is modular: Pilots accumulate certifications without going back to square one the way nurse practitioners have to do if a state's scope of practice law forbids them from practicing at the top of their license and training.

Airlines seem to be able to meet the public's needs with less political interference. Policy experts are not needed to write papers guessing how many "specialists" are needed to fly 747s. That is because no politician holds hearings when 747 pilots grumble that there are too many pilots learning to fly their aircraft. A 747 pilot who insisted that potential competitors be barred from offering their services because it took less time to train them would be laughed out of the skies. Competitive market forces adjust the supply of appropriately trained pilots to meet the demands of the flying public. A politician, no matter how influential, has no right to limit the number of 747 pilots the airlines think they need, as long as they are proven competent.

The unscientific nature of medical practice a century ago arguably explains the prevailing system. Today there is general agreement as to what constitutes scientific medical practices. The process whereby the states grant exclusive licenses on the basis of a degree issued only an AMA-approved medical school is akin to the granting of monopoly charters to medieval guilds by the church or king. This legacy of the Middle Ages is inadequate for a modern healthcare system in a liberal democracy with a dynamic market economy. The various medical specialties of surgery, internal medicine, urology, and so on, are direct descendants of ancient guilds. Each practice in a separate silo, and the needs of the public, as reflected in the marketplace, often lag behind the priorities of the specialty. Competition would hopefully bust down the silos and put the patient in the driver's seat.

Keeping Up with Telehealth Technology—Licensure Needs to Cross State Lines

Twenty-first-century technologies are disrupting almost every industry, including medical care. Patients are increasingly using online consultation services to get immediate medical advice that is not conveniently available locally. Physicians in any part of the world can consult on—*and have already even robotically operated on*—patients in other part of the world over the internet (Marescaux et al., 2002). Body sensors on a smartphone or wristwatch, or implanted into the body or bloodstream, can continuously store vital information, such as blood pressure or blood sugar, and instantly transmit it to appropriate health care providers, often in another state, if emergencies arise. Special interests, working through state legislators, are trying to impede these developments, insisting that a patient's healthcare provider be licensed in the state where the patient lives. This makes no sense to me. When a patient traveled from another state to get advice from me, the encounter occurred where I was licensed. It should be no different if the consultation is done electronically. Physicians should not have to obtain a license in every state their patients reside (Svorny, 2017). Nurse practitioners should not be cut out of the electronic marketplace, either.

Uberizing Healthcare

The process whereby mobile or electronic technologies, like telemedicine, facilitate immediate and transparent transactions between individual consumers and providers of any desired service is called "Uberization" for an obvious reason. "Uberized" services have the potential to bypass bureaucratically regulated monopolies and result in better service for more customers at a lower price. Uberization disrupted the taxi industry, and it will ultimately disrupt the healthcare system as well.

To paraphrase James Madison, who spoke of governance: "If doctors were angels no licensure would be necessary. If angels were to govern doctors, no external or internal controls on licensing boards would be necessary."

The Government Has a Legitimate Role to Play

States should spend more time and money investigating the small minority of practitioners who are truly unethical or incompetent and far less worrying about which groups should be permitted to practice. Medical boards could be brought into the office of the secretary of state rather than having a quasi-independent organization comprised of professionals with a potential conflict of interest performing inquiries and recommending corrective action.

State-Based Innovation

One of the great strengths of federalism is that each state acts as a laboratory for public policy. If only one or two states can safely lower medical costs and improve the accessibility of healthcare by reforming their licensing regulations, others will follow suit. Every healthcare provider should be legally permitted to practice at the "top of their license"—that is, they should be allowed to do everything they have been trained and certified to do by their recognized and accredited professional board. In other words, competing healthcare providers should be assumed innocent of incompetence until proven guilty of it. Any organized professional group that objects to licensing a competing group on the grounds it will be unsafe should be made to produce the evidence supporting the contention.

Getting the ball rolling will not be easy. There are many possibilities. Model legislation for a system of fraud-protected private certification has been formulated (Schlomach et al., 2018) States could keep a registry of approved and accredited certifying organizations that would define the "scope of practice" for those they qualify for practice. A parallel track of such providers could coexist alongside the traditionally licensed professions without having to abolish a century's worth of legislation, except for the parts of the statutes that grant exclusivity and thus monopoly (Feldstein, 2020).

The Dangers of Complete Government Control of Essential Supplies of Anything

Why is it we argue about a right to healthcare but not a right to food or clothing? Surely these two items are more critical on a day-by-day basis for our survival than having a doctor examine a skin rash. Why don't presidential candidates clamor for a single payer for groceries? Of course, there is plenty of precedent on the dangers of state-based control of food supplies.

Countries such as North Korea and Venezuela do experience shortages of food. Cuba rations essentials. Millions died of famine in Russia and Ukraine last century when their government was the single payer of farmers. Complete government control of food supply led to rationing. One needs to ask if complete government control of healthcare could do the same.

We do not need a degree in economics to understand that the marketplaces for food and clothing work reasonably well in this country. There is no political impetus claiming a "right" to these essential commodities because we unthinkingly feed and clothe ourselves without the need for such rights. There is a social safety net for those experiencing difficulty paying for food, but they thankfully are a minority of the overall population. It is time to let a healthy, competitive, and functional healthcare marketplace flourish, and reforming medical licensure is an essential part of that task.

CHAPTER 8

Purchasing Healthcare as a Consumer
When Does It Make Sense, and How Do I Know If I'm Getting a Better Deal?

ERIC HABERICHTER

This chapter presents an overview of how pricing works, or does not work, in our healthcare system and how consumers can navigate this system and actually "shop" for healthcare value. Transparent pricing only works if prices are "accurate" numbers that bear some relationship to real cost and value and are not inflated "chargemaster" prices. Prices must also be easy to understand and reflect all aspects of what you need, in what are termed "bundled" prices (i.e., everything included). All of this is a necessary foundation if companies and individual consumers are going to be able to shop effectively as informed and empowered consumers, as is discussed more in chapter 9 (companies) and chapter 10 (individual consumers).

The Problem of Healthcare Costs

If you are like most people, you are concerned about the rising cost of healthcare. A recent Gallup poll showed that 55% of Americans chose healthcare costs as their greatest concern for the future. Given everything else that is going on in the world and people's lives, that might be surprising. But, unaffordable healthcare is a real threat to prosperity. The healthcare affordability crisis is very real, and it affects most of us on a monthly basis.

As a patient or consumer, there are tools or strategies you can use to lower costs, but understanding how healthcare costs are set and determined is important.

The first thing to understand is what makes up the cost of healthcare today. For most consumers, the most obvious cost of healthcare is the premium they pay with each pay period. The premium most of us pay is subsidized by our employer. In nearly all cases, our employer pays more than 50% of the premium. A 2019 Employer's Survey by Milliman showed that the average premium for a family of four was $1,634 per month for a plan

---

Eric Haberichter is CEO and cofounder of Access HealthNet.

that had a $2,500 deductible, 20% coinsurance, and a $6,500 out-of-pocket maximum. This is a pretty standard plan. Some employers offer plans with lower deductibles, but persons buying coverage from the marketplace likely have much higher deductibles and out-of-pocket amounts. An Affordable Care Act (ACA) "bronze" family plan can have a deductible as high as $11,300 and out-of-pocket amounts as high as $17,000.

The average amount that a family pays after the employer or government subsidies is less, about $684 per month for an annual total of $8,208, but that is only their share of premiums. The ACA expanded the amount of care that patients get at no additional cost, to include preventative care. But, any non-preventative medical care that the family needs will be paid for on a "cash basis" until the deductible (the first dollars paid before insurance coverage kicks in) is met. Once the deductible has been met, coinsurance costs remain until the out-of-pocket maximum is met. Understanding your plan's specific details and their effect on your portion of medical bills is important, not only so you can choose the right plan for your family and budget, but also so you can make well-informed financial decisions when you need care.

Premiums Are Bankrupting American Families and Affecting Care Choices

With the average family paying more than $8,000 in premiums, it is easy to see why so many struggle. Household income averages are around $60,000, which makes premiums alone more than 13% of a family's earnings. Add in out-of-pocket costs and the amount can be 20% or more of total family gross income, likely 40% or more of net pay (after taxes and benefits) for the average family. For those making less, the impact is even greater. The result is that healthcare expenses contribute to more than 60% of bankruptcies and people are avoiding medical care for fear of the cost, resulting in poorer diagnoses, treatment, and outcomes. The cost of healthcare deductibles has increased eight times faster than wages (figure 8.1) and is causing consumers to postpone early detection and treatment of medical problems. Delaying diagnosis and treatment can have a tremendous impact on the eventual cost of care and quality of life. Simple infections and communicable diseases that have low-cost, highly effective cures can evolve into expensive life-threatening medical emergencies when left untreated. An infectious disease such as Lyme's is a good example. If you see your doctor or visit the urgent care soon after being infected, the disease can be treated with oral medications that cost around $250. The total for an urgent care visit, a Lyme disease test, and the antibiotics would typically be

FIGURE 8.1 General annual deductibles for covered workers have increased eight times as fast as wages.

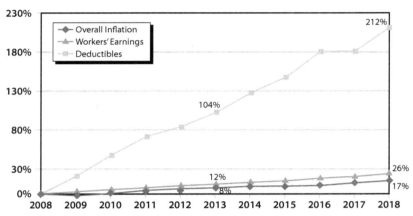

Source: Kaiser Family Foundation (2019).

less than $1,000. Left untreated, Lyme disease can progress into heart disease, paralysis, or blindness. Any of these could cost tens or even hundreds of thousands of dollars to treat. A patient trying to avoid the short-term cost of an urgent care visit can unknowingly cost themselves tremendously more. For many families, however, the cost of an urgent care visit can be the difference between having or not having money for food. This is not an easy choice to make (Kirzinger et al., 2019; Carter, 2018; Kaiser Family Foundation [KFF], 2019).

Cost of the Healthcare Itself, in a Fee-for-Service World

The cost of premiums is one component of the cost of healthcare. The cost of the medical care you need is the other. Controlling your healthcare cost requires a willingness and a desire to be a medical consumer. The prospect of making decisions about when and where to seek care to control costs is even more daunting than not seeking care for many patients. The medical world is deeply complex and almost intentionally convoluted and clouded when it comes to prices. Providers and insurance companies have spent decades growing the current model, which is known as fee-for-service. This model is one where providers get paid, or not, for each thing that they do. It is like "piecework" for healthcare. Essentially the more work they do the more they get paid (see chapter 1). That is not inherently flawed, except that it has the potential to motivate doctors and hospitals to provide more services than the patient requires.

Opposing Sides: Providers and the Insurers That Reimburse

To combat the potential of providers charging for unwarranted services, insurance companies review every bill for accuracy and compliance with standard care paths. Again, this is not inherently wrong. A system of checks and balances is valuable, especially when it comes to something as important as our health. The system of "opposing sides," however, has grown to the point where it consumes a huge percentage of healthcare costs. As noted in chapter 5 (figure 5.1), the increasing spending on administrative staff to oversee this bureaucracy far outpaces the increasing spending on the physicians who administer the healthcare services themselves.

Birth of the Chargemaster

Neither side started this way. Fees were standardized for years with every patient and insurance company paying pretty much the same. Medicine at that time was pretty limited. Most major surgeries and advanced treatments we use today had yet to be invented, and offering health insurance to workers was not a standard practice. As medicine advanced and more and more employers started offering medical plans, health insurance companies were formed and profits were to be made. Being a successful insurance company required a competitive advantage. Insurers went to hospitals looking for discounts from the standard rates everyone paid. Most hospitals and physicians of the time charged "fair" prices that were affordable for most patients and employers, so offering a greater discount was not possible. Insurers wanted discounts anyway, so they came up with the idea of "the chargemaster"—a list of prices that were inflated from the standardized rates (see chapter 1). This allowed hospitals to offer a discount to insurers, who could then market that they had the "best prices." Insurers and providers quickly got on board and the conditions that drive our current lack of affordability (at least in part) were born.

The Reimbursement Wars

For a long time, things rolled on with care remaining relatively affordable, but the business of healthcare got bigger and more expensive as previously untreatable diseases became treatable and therefore required insurers to cover them. New drugs and surgical options were being invented at a pace that was unimaginable in the past. A system of checks and balances came into play. Insurance companies started to limit access to new drugs and procedures by either requiring patients get permission to have them or by retrospectively looking at medical bills and refusing to pay all or a portion due to lack of "medical necessity." The stage was set for a new way for insurance companies to make money—by not paying for care.

If insurance companies refused to pay all or part of a bill because it was an error or unwarranted, it would save money and have the potential to reduce what you and your employer pay, but it does not necessarily work that way. Instead, insurers charge employers to control costs and take a portion of the charges they do not pay in fees. Insurers getting paid to not pay providers has driven as much healthcare inflation as anything else, because it caused providers to raise prices (for fear of not getting paid). This dynamic grows every year and will continue to increase prices until a fundamental change is made in how we pay for healthcare and whom we allow to profit from our medical system.

Your Role, as a Healthcare Consumer

Understanding that your healthcare costs have two components (premiums and your portion of the actual cost of care) allows you to start to think about your role in finding value. Your employer or the marketplace decided what your insurance offering and premiums look like. You decide the level of coverage you want (can afford) and how much risk you are willing to take in terms of potential out-of-pocket costs beyond your premium. Once you are locked into a plan, what is left to control is the actual cost of care. You will need to become a consumer for that to happen.

As a patient, being a consumer of healthcare is much like being a consumer of anything else. How much you pay is based on (a) what services you obtain, (b) who performs those services and where they perform them, and (c) the contracted rate (discount) applied to services rendered. Each of these factors has the potential for tremendous impact on your cost as a patient.

What services you consume (or are charged for) is a factor that you have some control over in one manner and no control over in the other. You do have the ability to choose to go to the urgent care or stay home; you can have the recommended MRI or not. Those are difficult choices you control and it is easy to see the immediate impact on your pocketbook. They may not be good choices, but they are your choices. Doctors, hospitals, and your insurance company control the rest. When you go to the hospital, you do so with trust, believing that they are there to help and that any care they offer is warranted. That may or may not be the case. Offering more care than the standard or than circumstances demand may be an unfair business practice or fraud, or it could be driven by fear of litigation from patients that did not receive that level of care and had a rare but bad outcome. It may also be the result of erroneous billing. In this case, the services were never performed but they were billed for anyway. Again, fraud is possible, but human and/ or machine error is an even more likely cause. In either case, few patients feel comfortable or competent to direct their care clinically or to review a complicated medical bill. We need to be able to trust doctors to do the right thing and insurance companies to get the payments right.

Shopping for Where You Get Healthcare Services— Realizing That Hospitals Charge More

Where you get services is important and can drastically lower your costs while maintaining or improving service and quality. Here is an example of how where you get care impacts your cost (see table 8.1). Most hospitals offer knee surgery at the main hospital and at surgery centers they own. Overhead at surgery centers is lower than at hospitals.

Table 8.1 presents a typical example of the price difference between a hospital and a surgery center. The savings for the patient would be around $1,600. The surgery performed would be the same, the surgeon could be the same, even the anesthesiologist and nurses might be the same. The difference is that outpatient surgery centers charge 30–40% less for the same procedure as the hospital systems that own them charge in their hospitals.

Not only do outpatient surgery centers charge less, but they often have better outcomes as well. Why? Because outpatient facilities typically have lower infection and complication rates. Hospitals see the sickest patients and therefore have germs from the sickest patients that can infect other patients no matter how careful the hospital and surgeons are. The savings could go far beyond the initial amount. Not having to go back to the hospital to treat complications eliminates those costs as well.

The ability to lower costs does not only apply to major events like surgery. The greatest savings as a percentage are often on tests and procedures that are less serious or complicated. Lab work and imaging tests are two good examples. The prices for medical tests can vary by 500% with little to no

TABLE **8.1** Typical Charges for a Prototypical Knee Surgery

Knee Surgery Hospital		Knee Surgery Hospital-Owned Surgery Center	
Total Cost	$25,000	Total Cost	$17,000
Deductible	–$2,500	Deductible	–$2,500
Coinsurance (20%)	–$4,500	Coinsurance (20%)	–$2,900
Employee Portion	$7,000	Employee Portion	$5,400

Source: KFF (2019).

difference in quality. Lab work is relatively standardized. Where you have lab work done has as much to do with the cost as which test(s) you have. Tests performed in-office with "quick labs" (small automated lab machines that some offices own) can be nearly equivalent to the lab work performed at hospitals, but only for a limited number of tests. In-office lab work should be less expensive than services performed in a centralized lab, but that may not always be the case. Many hospitals and medical centers send lab work via courier to a central lab that is often owned by an outside company. These outside companies also work with other facilities and usually run their own outpatient locations. In this case, the product that is the lab test is the same (except who collected the sample) but the price patients pay for the same product can be highly varied.

Imaging tests like MRIs or CT scans are another area where the service location has a tremendous effect on how much tests cost. These exams are less standardized than lab work. There are differences in the quality of the equipment that is used and the training of the physicians that interpret the tests. That variability means that patients need to make an informed choice regarding where tests are performed.

How to Comparison-Shop for Healthcare Services

Making an informed choice can start by asking your doctor about the exam, how it is done, and if there is any special equipment needed for the test they are ordering. Your doctor or a member of the care team should be able to answer these questions in some level of detail. In most cases, these tests are ordered in advance and you will have time to do a little online research as well. These tests are very common and the specifics around which equipment and training are required for each test are readily available with near consensus. Knowing these details allows you to comparison-shop and save hundreds or even thousands of dollars.

Lab work and imaging tests are not as expensive as surgery, but the financial impact of cost can still be enormous. Unlike surgery where patients are likely to meet and exceed their deductible, these tests typically fall within one's deductible. If you pay $500 for a lab test instead of $1,500 for the same test, the $1,000 is direct savings for you. It raises the question, Why pay more for the same thing? More and more patients are doing the research and asking themselves just that.

Price Transparency

Many insurance companies and other parties offer information to their members or online consumers regarding price and quality. In healthcare, they call this transparency. This can make shopping for care easier than doing the work on your own, but it is important to know how transparency works and what version of transparency you are using. Insurance companies have contracts with providers and they can tell you either the exact or average amount they pay a particular provider for a particular service. For less complicated medical tests and procedures, these sites typically offer an "exact" price because there are minimal or no variables. As procedures increase in complexity and variability the information becomes an estimate instead of an exact amount.

Medical services have a uniform system of description for charging or billing purposes. The American Medical Association and Medicare define the details of these charges or codes and Medicare establishes a price for each code. The variability in the cost of a medical service is determined by the number of possible codes that can be assigned (fee-for-service). In the case of lab work and imaging, there may be only one code. Something as complex as cardiac surgery, the hospital stay, and the recovery that comes with it could have hundreds of codes assigned or even more.

Insurance company transparency sites are a good place to find out how much your insurance typically pays a provider for a particular service. Other transparency sites tell you how much services cost the average patient. Different insurance companies pay providers different rates for the same services. Public transparency sites either average those rates or estimate what a "good" rate might be. Either way, the accuracy of this information is subject to the same variability or more.

Even with variability, the information on these sites is valuable. Insurance company sites give you a relative comparison of the costs that providers charge because they are sharing a comparative discount, and the public sites give you some insight as to how good that discount is. If an insurance company website indicates that provider "A" charges $550 for a CT scan and provider "B" charges $1,500, then you will pay less at provider "A." The charge of $550 may, or may not be a "good price" for a CT scan, and even if it is a good price, what about quality? A poor-quality scan is not a good deal at any price if it could lead to a misdiagnosis.

Value Considers Quality Also, Not Just Price

It is probably not that difficult to imagine making an informed choice about a test where you can personally save hundreds or thousands of dollars, especially if you can feel confident that quality will be relatively the same. But quality in healthcare is not always easily defined. The more standardized and technological something is, the easier it is to determine quality. The more dependent on human skill and decision-making, the more difficult.

All medical professionals are required to have a specific level of education, training, certification, licensure, and in most cases accreditation from a professional body to perform a specific role in your care (as discussed in chapter 7). Medical facilities (hospitals, surgery centers, imaging centers, physical therapy centers, labs, etc.) also have licensure and accreditation requirements. Providers that have all the right certifications and accreditations are more than happy to share that information with you and your insurance company. Medicare and your state play a role in this as well. Medicare collects information on every participating doctor and facility and much of this information is shared with insurance companies and other vendors that summarize and publish these data for use by doctors, insurance companies, and consumers.

Having the right credentials is one part of the equation. Outcomes are the other. Medicare is currently the most universally used outcomes reporting standard because Medicare has access to the largest patient sample and keeps at least limited quality information on every participating provider and patient served. With trillions of data points, Medicare has been able to provide objective measurements of physician and facility quality. The number and complexity of data points being collected are increasing and the dataset is getting better. Medicare measures outcomes based on complications, readmissions, and patient responses to standard questions. Insurance companies and many other vendors combine all of this information: cost, training, and outcomes. Combining this is the information needed to make an informed choice to pay less with confidence. It is what consumers need to "shop" effectively.

After Comparing Price, Then You Have to Take Control, and Actually "Shop"

Knowing I can pay less is just the first step. *How do I take control?*

Being an energized and informed medical consumer is great, but the next step is to assert your freedom to choose to pay less. It does not sound like something that should be that difficult, but it can be. It requires change in mindset for us as consumers, and a shift away from a paternalistic history in healthcare where we were overly passive about our healthcare.

Several practical factors that influence a patient's ability to take control and lower their costs.

- The contracts their insurance company has with providers
- The contract their employer has with the insurance company
- The business of healthcare systems
- The lack of financial and health business training in the medical field

Negotiated Contracts With Insurance Companies and the Secret Chargemaster

The contracts that insurance companies have with providers are "secret" and the hospital chargemaster rates (the inflated prices that hospitals discount from) are generally not published. The result is that only your insurance company can disclose contractual information. In many states, laws require providers to tell you how much services cost. Provider contracts with insurance companies specifically ban providers from sharing contracted rates with anyone because their "discount" is the insurance company's advantage in the market. Providers are left charging patients the average prices that patients with private insurance pay, which are inflated prices.

Insurance company contracts often have other provisions that might limit your access to lower prices as patient-consumers. Most insurance company contracts disallow a provider from charging you less than their contracted rates, even if they offer cash rates that are lower than the contracted rates. The insurance company gets the discount they do because they can bring many patients to their door. People with insurance have deductibles and other out-of-pocket costs. Not everyone pays those bills. In fact, providers only collect about 30% of patient's out-of-pocket expenses. The result is that providers need to charge insured patients more because they rarely get all of the money they are contracted for.

Restrictions From the Insurance You Get From Your Employer

The contract your employer has with the insurance company may also limit your choices. Patients rarely have any say in the details of insurance contracts. Employers may unwittingly limit your choices by signing prohibitive agreements that limit your choices. Most commonly this restriction is in the form of a limited list of providers or provider systems being allowed. This is referred to as *in-network versus out-of-network*. Providers that are out-of-network are treated differently than those in-network. Specifically, you pay more out of pocket with out-of-network providers than with in-network providers. Out-of-network providers may offer the lowest price, but you pay a penalty for using them because what you pay to them does not satisfy your in-network deductible. Matters become more confusing when a hospital is in-network but some of the doctors working there are not in-network. In many of these cases, it is actually much cheaper for you to not use your insurance and instead pay out of pocket in cash (see chapters 6 and 10) to avoid these penalties and inflated chargemaster prices.

The lack of influence and power that patients have over who controls their network and the secret agreements between providers and insurers (leading to the chargemasters) are factors that individual patients really cannot change. Nearly all traditional insurance works this way. Using transparency websites and being generally informed, however, will afford you the ability to reduce their impact and find savings. This is what the grassroots consumerization revolution is all about—putting power and decision-making back in the hands the consumer. Often though, a bigger hurdle is the way healthcare systems work.

Healthcare Systems

In most markets, healthcare systems employ doctors, physician assistants, and nurse practitioners (the healthcare providers discussed in chapter 7). Employed physicians and other allied health professionals are like any other employee. They are strongly encouraged to support their employer. What that means is that medical services are referred in-house rather than to competitors. There are clinical and financial reasons for this practice (discussed also in chapters 4 and 5). One clinical reason is integration. An integrated health system can share records in near real time across geography. The promise of integration is a reduction in the overutilization of tests and a team approach to treatment. This can be very real and have significant advantages, or it can be a goal more than a promise with limited advantages in care or cost reduction. It is not a one-size-fits-all solution. The financial reasons are less conceptual and more practical. Hospitals pay the overhead of the doctor and their staff. They provide a safety net and support for healthcare professionals versus independent practice by taking care of the business aspects of care, allowing health professionals to focus on care instead of billing. All of that sounds great! Who wouldn't want their doctor focusing on their health instead of money? This practice can, however, drive patient costs up. If an employed physician refers you for a test in-house where charges are two times what they might be elsewhere, that provider is referring you to overpriced care.

Innocent Frontline Participants in the Medical-Industrial Complex

It is highly unlikely that your doctor or nurse is knowingly referring you for overpriced care unless they own the facility and would get some of the money themselves. Sadly, few allied health professionals have any idea of what the hospital or facility they work for charges. They are either blissfully ignorant or simply so far removed from the process as not to care. Nurses are not thinking about how much an IV costs when they hook you up to it.

They are thinking that (1) the doctor told them to do it, and (2) you need it. Similarly, physicians order treatments you need with little concern for cost. Their goal is to help you get or remain well.

The vast majority of healthcare providers live under the assumption that people with insurance or government coverage can pay and that "insurance" will pay the majority of the cost. This may be entirely true, but it does not relieve patients of their out-of-pocket burden. Medical schools and nursing schools do not require students to have any financial literacy around insurance or medical costs. Instead, they teach a focus on doing "what is medically correct, supportive of the community, and inclusive." The business of healthcare is left to administrators and the billing department.

These obstacles are real, but if you as healthcare consumers use the transparency tools that are available, the obstacles can be overcome with some effort. Patients have certain rights that give them the power to take control of offsetting these limitations. Patients need to realize they have these rights, exercise them, and become empowered.

Know your rights.

- *I have the right to choose where I get healthcare*: Your insurance company can tell you what is in-network, but it cannot stop you from buying outside of your network. The insurance company can only refuse to apply it to your in-network deductible.
- *I have the right to take physician referrals wherever I want*: When a doctor employed by a healthcare system gives you a referral they typically have their staff assist you in scheduling the service. You have a right to take that referral anywhere you want.
- *I have the right to pay the lowest price available*: You cannot be forced to pay more. If you can negotiate a lower rate or shop for a lower rate you are allowed to pay that rate. Keep in mind that once you give a provider your insurance card, you are agreeing to the contracted rates your insurance company agreed to. The time to shop is *before* you get services. Healthcare cannot be returned or exchanged.
- *I have the right to question my insurance company*: If you think you are paying too much you have the right to question your insurance company and to get a detailed and complete answer. You may not get the answer you want, but persistence can pay off.

Using This Knowledge to Find *Value*

A common definition of value in healthcare is an equation where Value = Quality + Service + Price. Using both insurance company and private transparency online tools, you can find the quality rankings of many providers and the prices they typically charge for a given service (see the examples in chapters 1, 6, and 10). Shopping for less complex services like an MRI can be quite easy and nearly every insurance company's site can direct you to a value choice. It gets a bit more complicated when it comes to surgery.

Unlike simple procedures like an MRI, surgery has many components that collectively make up patient charges. These components may or may not bill under the same contract and may charge wildly variable prices versus their competition or even relative to the other providers involved in the care team. Let us explore a common procedure, a hip replacement surgery. Multiple services come together when a patient has a hip replacement surgery. The hospital or surgery center has charges for use of the surgical suite, for the recovery room, and for your hospital room. They charge for skilled nursing and the efforts of every other person who comes into your room or offers you any care. There will be charges from the surgeon and most often an assistant surgeon. There will be anesthesia charges, pathology charges, lab charges, charges for X-rays, and other imaging. There will be drug charges, charges for physical therapy, follow-up care, and a myriad of other possibilities.

In the case of a surgery, the information on most transparency sites and the provision of that care is done under the fee-for-service model, and there are a range of prices that could be charged. It is almost impossible to know what things will cost until you get the bill and it is too late. These are great examples of the very frustrating "surprise bills."

Remember, in fee-for-service, the providers get paid for every line of code they charge (see chapters 1 and 4). If the surgery takes longer they make more. If you need to spend more time in the recovery room, they get more. If you need or want to stay at the hospital another day, they make more. If you need 25 physical therapy appointments instead of the typical 12, they get more and so on. If the hospital and surgeon do their best, but you have a complication or need to be readmitted, they get more. In healthcare, you pay more when you get less. Patients want great outcomes, but the structure of fee-for-service rewards poorer results with more money.

There Is a Methodology That Flips the Equation—It's Called "Bundling"

Bundling is a payment methodology where providers get paid one fee for every aspect of an exam or procedure. That fee is determined in advance and "locked in." Bundling is not new. Medicare has been paying by its version of bundles for decades, so most providers are comfortable with the idea of offering an all-inclusive price. Locking in the price in advance eliminates the problems (e.g., opaque pricing, bad incentives) driven by fee-for-service and makes confidently shopping for healthcare truly possible. It is also what will enable the consumerization of healthcare and the subsequent control of costs.

Bundling is transparency taken to the next level. Consider hip replacement surgery. Each of the services provided (hospital charges, physician charges, anesthesia, etc.) are variable. Not only are the amount and exact type of services provided variable, but the potential outcomes are variable as well. Knowing what a hospital might charge or usually charges is helpful, but it is not a quote for services: instead, it is just an estimate. The accuracy of that estimate varies wildly, and patients won't know how accurate the estimate is until they get the bill weeks or months later.

An Illustrative Example

Imagine this pricing and billing scenario in another more familiar area of consumerism, let's say auto repair. It would look something like this. I take my car to the shop because my brakes are not working like they should. My mechanic tells me it will cost $300. That sounds reasonable, so I leave my car and come back later. When I pick it up, the mechanic says he will send me the bill in a week. I get the bill and instead of $300, it is $1,800. After regaining composure, I carefully review the bill and it shows that the mechanic did not just do the work quoted but also replaced a bunch of parts that I did not know needed replacing. I call the mechanic and he says that the brake job did not go as planned. The initial assessment that it was a partial brake job was wrong and more parts needed to be replaced than he thought. I think we can all accept that happening. Then he tells me the rest of the story. They have master mechanics and junior mechanics. A junior mechanic worked on my car and when removing one of the parts, he broke another, which then needed to be replaced. Replacing that part took several hours and that part was expensive. It would leave me questioning why I had to pay for the junior mechanic's mistake! Most of us would not only refuse to pay this bill, but we would also tell everyone we know the mechanic was a crook.

While it is not a direct parallel, this is nearly exactly how healthcare works when you do not have a bundled price. Back to the hip replacement surgery. I use my insurance company's transparency site and it states that a hip surgery at "Hospital A" costs $30,000. Hospital A has a reputation for excellence and is an academic medical center where the best doctors are trained by the area's leading experts. I feel very confident and schedule my surgery with one of their most skilled and experienced surgeons. My surgery goes pretty much as planned, and I am fine. The next day I wake up with a fever. They do blood work and realize I have an infection. My surgical site is inflamed and oozing. They treat me with antibiotics and I don't respond. Turns out the surgeon in training that assisted in my surgery made an error. Eventually, they need to take me back to surgery to clear out the infected tissue. I end up staying at the hospital for several extra days. The good news is that I make a full recovery. The bad news is that my bill just went up to $120,000. In a fee-for-service arrangement, my insurance company (and me) are stuck paying that entire bill.

How Price Bundling Is Better for You

Bundling is different. In a bundling arrangement, Hospital A quotes the price of $30,000 and is held to it. The all-inclusive bundle includes a "warranty" that covers any unexpected complications, like my infection, so if it were to occur I would still pay only $30,000.

In a fee-for-service arrangement, the mistake (my infection) drives additional revenue for the hospital. In a bundled arrangement, it costs the hospital tens of thousands of dollars. Bundling changes provider behavior. Normal market principles favor the highest quality and the most efficient providers when prices are fixed. Hospitals and surgeons that have the lowest complication rates, the shortest surgical durations, and the best outcomes inherently can charge less and "win" business. Facilities with less rigorous quality controls and less experienced or efficient surgeons are not interested in fixed prices because they will lose money. That is actually how free and competitive markets work (chapters 1 and 19). It is very simple. Setting a fixed rate increases quality. In its current state (i.e., not a free and transparent market with informed and empowered consumers), healthcare is unlike most consumer products where you get more when you pay more. With healthcare, you typically get more when you pay less. It is counterintuitive but true.

So How Do I Get the Best Deal?

Getting the best deal means finding value. Finding value requires that you be a medical consumer, which means that you need to do a little homework. You need to be an informed (use transparency tools) and empowered (learn and exercise your rights) healthcare consumer. Your health and finances are linked and influence every aspect of your life. Insurance companies and public transparency sites are a great place to get information on what procedures should cost and what a great price is. Providers of all types will consider cash prices, and you may be better off paying cash than using insurance (see chapters 1 and 10). There is no single correct answer, but new ways of thinking about healthcare like bundling can lower your risk and make comparison-shopping possible. Taking control means being informed and feeling empowered. Knowing your rights and asserting them when you need to will go a long way toward reducing your costs and keeping more of your money in your pocket. Lowering your cost has benefits for you, your employer, and the patient community as a whole. If we do not stand up as medical consumers, we all face the same threats (runaway inflation, lack of access to information, etc.) that has driven us to unaffordability. We all have a stake in the future of healthcare. We need to become part of a grassroots healthcare revolution, as informed and empowered consumers who take ownership and control of our own healthcare. These are the topics of chapters 9 and 10.

CHAPTER 9

Lessons from the Grassroots for National Healthcare Reform

JOHN TORINUS

This chapter continues the discussion presented in chapter 8 on transparent pricing and shopping for bundled healthcare services. It also provides a company perspective on healthcare reform, which is crucial since companies provide more than half of the healthcare insurance coverage in the United States. High costs are a heavy burden for companies, just like they are for us as the end-consumers of healthcare services. Examples from a Wisconsin company, Serigraph, are used to illustrate how companies have been able to constrain healthcare costs while providing better care. The concept of a healthcare navigator is also presented, as a resource to help find the best medical service values in this complicated marketplace.

Background—and the Need for Healthcare Navigators

One of the tools that begs to be injected into the messy, somewhat superficial national debate on the delivery of healthcare in America is that of a healthcare navigator. Those are the professionals who help patients to make good decisions on treatment options and on keeping the cost of those treatments under some level of control. At Serigraph, that person is Robin in our human resources department. No coworker in the company would think about navigating the Medical-Industrial Complex (MIC) for a major procedure without consulting Robin. She is the major reason our company delivers first-rate care at about $7,000 per person, compared to a national average of $11,000, according Amadeo (2020).

Other astute companies in the private sector provide high-quality care at the same cost level. Note to the big thinkers on healthcare at the national level: Best practice private payers spend about 40% less than the national average. That is a huge difference, out of which flows several major conclusions:

1. About 8.5% of the U.S. population still goes without healthcare coverage, according to the U.S. Census Bureau (Berchick et al., 2019). Obviously,

---

John Torinus is former CEO and now chairman of Serigraph Inc., a manufacturing company with about 550 employees.

if all payers had a Robin and followed best practices, the 40% savings would be way more than enough to cover the uninsured—without raising taxes.

2. Controlling health costs, the number-one political and economic issue in the country, is mostly about management science, not political science. Costs can be managed.

3. The main reason, in my assessment, that healthcare inflation has dropped from double digits in the late 1970s and early 1980s, according to Hartman et al. (2019), to about 4.6% in 2019 is the collective efforts of private employers to clamp down on outrageous medical and drug prices. (In contrast, according to the administrator of the Centers for Medicare and Medicaid Services, Seema Verma, the Affordable Care Act, otherwise known as Obamacare, drove premiums up, not down.)

4. The main beneficiaries from taming out-of-control costs are American citizens, who are bearing an ever-increasing share of the healthcare burden through higher premiums, coinsurance, and deductibles. That share is now more than 40% by some estimates, including Kaiser (2019). Furthermore, outrageous bills are aggressively pursued by some hospital corporations, to the point of driving families into bankruptcy.

There are other tools in the war against soaring health costs, but creating smarter consumers at the ground level is the most powerful. That is where the healthcare navigators enter the battle.

Navigating the Healthcare Pricing Fog

It was long thought that more transparent pricing would empower consumers. But even the publishing of prices, which President Donald Trump has been pushing for, has not removed obstacles, leaving the intended goal still unachieved. Even when "transparent," healthcare pricing remains in a fog. It is just too complicated for the average American to sort out, in its current state.

Bundled Prices to Clear the Fog

Bills usually come as an unpleasant surprise. Only providers that collect their charges into one bundled bill can be understood by individual consumers. Example: $28,000 all-in for a joint replacement (market average is about $50,000 without a fixed price). One price, that's all. Unfortunately, only a few providers, and almost no major health systems, offer transparent pricing. They love the fog.

Healthcare Navigators to Clear the Fog

The navigators have access to many prices. Robin first checks to see if our company has negotiated directly for a fixed price. Then she compares it to discounted prices through our health insurance. She also uses whatever quality data we can access. She presents the hospital comparisons to the coworker in need of that medical procedure, who then makes an informed decision. Robin has become a real consumer. As a result, high-priced, low-quality providers lose our business to high-value shops. That is as it should be. It is that navigator assistance through the healthcare maze that makes the difference.

The sound bite here is that politicians running for high office could do something real by insisting on the availability of an objective healthcare navigator for every American who needs to make a costly healthcare choice.

Note that the healthcare systems that have adopted in a serious way the lean disciplines that have transformed the manufacturing world are often the winners. They have learned to eliminate defects and waste in partnership with engaged healthcare workers. Their costs come down as their quality rises. There is an inverse correlation between quality and price. If you need a heart bypass, select the cheapest one you can find (I am serious about that, even if it is counterintuitive).

To find those best-in-class providers, policymakers need to make sure that every health plan makes a Robin available.

Other Strategies to Control Healthcare Costs for Employers

Beyond navigation to value-based decisions in a world where treatment decisions are largely blind to price and quality, what are other levers that private payers are bringing to bear on healthcare inflation? Let's take them one at a time.

Proactive primary care delivered at company on-site or near-site clinics ranks near the top. They can be full-time clinics with doctors on the employer campuses or part-time using nurse practitioners or physician assistants. Company size dictates the model.

Telehealth is also often used to provide coverage during nonwork hours when the physical clinic is closed. Again, cost savings result. We pay $55 for a telehealth visit at Serigraph.

On-site Clinic and Relationship-Based Care Benefits

Many benefits and savings result from this kind of relationship-based care offered in a convenient setting like a company's on-site clinic:

- The on-site team really gets to know each employee and their families. It is high-touch medicine.
- The on-site team delivers annual health risk assessments, either mandatory or voluntary. Medical trouble is spotted early when it is less expensive to treat.
- Lesser issues can be managed instantly at less cost.
- The medical team works with the care navigator to steer to value providers. Our company saves about 10% of its annual bill through channeling procedures.
- Expensive tests are purchased through the clinic at prices far below charges in the Medical-Industrial Complex.
- In the case of Serigraph, each adult family member is given a health report card that is delivered in a mandatory face-to-face meeting. It includes the development of a three-year mutually developed health plan for each person.
- Chronic diseases such as diabetes and hypertension are addressed aggressively and continuously. Huge savings result from heading off major consequences from the chronic conditions. By example, one member reduced her dangerously high blood sugar count from more than 200 to below 100. It is a team effort. Our pharmacy benefit manager alerts the on-site team if a diabetic member misses an insulin prescription, a telephone call, or a meeting.
- Some employer clinics treat mental health issues with the same energetic attention as physical issues. They work to remove the stigma of mental health problems. A simple annual questionnaire can reveal depression. Treatment is often outsourced. A more productive workforce is one outcome.
- The cost-effectiveness of wellness plans is widely debated, but most employer clinics offer a variety of programs through their clinics, such as diet classes for weight reduction, exercise regimens, and even financial planning to address stressful money matters. Note that outrageous health bills can be a major cause of family financial torment.

Self-Insurance for Employers

Another major device in the toolbox that companies can use for health cost containment is self-insurance. Four of five private companies with more than 500 employees are self-insured, meaning they are underwriting their own risks. That monumental development has largely escaped the big thinkers in healthcare. The big insurers like United HealthCare and Blue Cross have been pushed out of the risk business at larger employers and many medium-sized companies. They have also been left out of the network business in which they offer discounts off sticker prices. Most savvy buyers of healthcare know that discounts are a shell game, so payers are moving fast to contract directly with providers and skip the middlemen, the insurers.

General Motors in Detroit now buys services for salaried employees directly from the Henry Ford Health System. For those members, its former network provider, Blue Cross, is left with the relatively mundane business of processing claims.

These major changes in the supply chain for healthcare make total sense once it is understood that when companies take on the healthcare economic risk, they move quickly to manage that risk, just like they do with any other risk in their businesses. In the old model, healthcare savings went into an insured pool of many companies. Now, the savings go directly to each self-insured company. They and their employees, who share the company's healthcare burden, keep the savings. They show up in lower premiums. Boeing, Walmart, Lowe's, Whole Foods, Disney, and Intel have also gone around the insurers to direct contracting.

Cost-Sharing with Employees—as Skin in the Game

Educated employees know that they share health costs with their employers, to the tune of 30% to more than 40%. Best practice plans save each employee several thousand dollars per year. That new dynamic provides huge incentives for both employers and workers to battle soaring health costs. Unbeknownst to the presidential candidates of both parties, employers and employees are the ones bending the curve on health cost inflation across the country.

Drug Prices

Despite promises by leaders of both political parties, drug prices have been the nemesis of employer health plans, of taxpayer-supported plans in the public sector, and of family budgets. Hard-won savings in other medical areas have been chewed up by steep price increases jammed at consumers and their health plans by drug companies. Employers and employees stuck with the bills feel helpless, partly because many of the drugs work well on various afflictions and people rely on them to just live or to live with an acceptable quality of life.

One cancer drug for a Serigraph employee billed out at $7,400 per month when it was prescribed. The drug worked wonders, but who can afford that? To help the company, the employee, an older person, made the decision to leave the company plan and go onto Medicare instead. He shifted the burden to the taxpayers.

After rigorous research, he also found he could buy the same drug, Abiraterone, for about $3,100 from a Walgreens specialty pharmacy. His coinsurance dropped sharply, and he saved U.S. taxpayers $4,300 per month. This is not chump change. The employee was still stuck with $5,900 per year in co-payments and the taxpayers ate the balance—more than $34,000. This was just one example that is repeated day in, day out across America. Our company's drug costs ran about 10% of our total healthcare expense 10 years ago. Now they are running at 16%. We did find one tourniquet on the drug price hemorrhage. An innovative pharmacy benefit manager (PBM) offered us complete transparency on the rebates they received from the drug companies. Furthermore, it passes along 100% of the "kickbacks"—my description of the incentives to favor their drugs—to our health plan.

We also win the rebates to consumers. If the "coupon" from the drug company for the consumer to offset the drug cost is $100, we set our co-pay at $100. If it is $5,000, we set the co-pay at $5,000. Our employee wins with no co-pay, and the company wins by offsetting a drug price that can be $40,000 or more, even with the co-pay rebate. With the capture of the rebates, our pharmacy billings dropped from about $1.2 million per year to around $800,000. An incredible reduction!

We are still searching for additional innovative ways to lower the horrendous charges for specialty drugs, including infused and injected treatments. These drugs really work for afflictions like rheumatoid arthritis but are killer-priced. We have only nine people on those drugs, but they account for a $400,000 spend, half of our drug costs.

Congress Should Learn from the Grassroots Revolution, in Companies Like Serigraph

So far, Congress and the Trump administration have been of little help on drug costs. Some bills in Congress would eliminate the rebates, aka kickbacks. Some would install price controls. None have passed.

At Serigraph, like most companies, we incent generic drug substitutes for branded drugs. And we use preauthorization of expensive drugs to make sure they are the most cost-effective answer.

The purpose of making public these grassroots solutions for taming the health cost beast is to make the case that costs must be managed from the top down and bottom up simultaneously. Smart decisions by managers and by individual employees in tandem are what works. That is what our leaders need to learn and incorporate before they adopt another arrogant master plan for healthcare for the country. They need to be humble and talk to and listen to the people on the frontlines, not the lobbyists and middlemen who created the health cost crisis in the first place.

Finally, members of Congress are going to have to use their pragmatic smarts to implement workable solutions and turn their backs on big donations from the pharma industry that lobbies ferociously for ever-higher prices.

Bottom-up reform always works better than top-down reform. It has the virtue of positive pragmatic results and the resulting buy-in.

CHAPTER 10

A Retail Revolution
Consumerizing Healthcare in America's Drugstores

DANIEL SEM

Chapter 9 discussed how companies and consumers can navigate a direct pay and (for companies) a self-insurance world, using transparent and bundled (i.e., all in) pricing for healthcare. This chapter extends that concept from companies to individual consumers shopping for the best healthcare value. This topic was also discussed in chapters 6 and 8, but now is focused on consumers like you getting their care from a very new setting—drugstores that offer on-site clinics, which serve as a kind of medical home for neighborhoods. They can typically accept insurance but will also offer very transparent prices for routine procedures and medical problems that are low cost and highly transparent. This retail store venue offers an alternative to, for example, getting direct primary care from small clinics or physician groups, or concierge medicine—both of which are also good options for consumerized healthcare. It is just one more way to empower us as consumers and give us more choices. The 2020 coronavirus pandemic has placed retail pharmacies in the limelight as places to get tested for Covid-19, thereby accelerating a revolution that was already underway, where consumers increasingly look to retail pharmacies for community-based healthcare, including for diagnostic tests.

Background

Companies like John Torinus's Serigraph are finding ways to shop for better healthcare at lower cost for their employees, avoiding expensive insurance and inflated chargemaster prices. By self-insuring and shopping for the best bundled price for medical procedures, they are saving a lot of money and finding good quality healthcare. But what are the options for individual consumers like you and me who want to find solutions for their healthcare needs directly, whether or not they have or use employer-sponsored healthcare plans?

Chapters 1 and 6 discussed the increasing number of direct primary care options that are available and will become available for healthcare consumers, including concierge medicine where you can get 24/7 access to a physician for around $100/month. This is a trend that is growing and will increasingly empower consumers to take control of their healthcare. Going beyond the growth in direct primary care, there is another exciting trend in healthcare: the increasing availability of low-cost direct pay options (i.e., out of pocket, with no insurance) in retail settings like drugstores, including Walgreens, Walmart, and CVS (Japsen, 2019a). This trend is creating even more options for us as healthcare consumers.

If you need healthcare now, you typically make an appointment with your primary care physician and you struggle to make sure everything you do is covered by your insurance, if you have insurance. Typically, you wait a week or so to get in with your doctor or (maybe after calling an online nurse) you decide to go to urgent care and, in more serious cases, an emergency room (ER). The latter two options are a bit frightening because you are never quite sure if the condition you have warrants such an extreme measure and what the downstream expense will be, and whether you will get one of those surprise $1,000-plus bills because you did something wrong or because you just need to pay toward your large deductible. What if you could avoid all of this angst—except of course when you are sure you need to go to the ER (and for God's sake, go then!)—simply by stopping by your local Walmart, CVS, or Walgreens, which is probably open 24/7? They are everywhere, open always, and have a clinical—pharmacy—focus. Why not get our healthcare at Walgreens, for example? That appears to be what the leadership at Walgreens has been thinking.

Walgreens as a Case Study: The Frontlines of a Healthcare Consumerization Revolution

It seems like there is a Walgreens on every other street corner. Wouldn't it be convenient if we could get routine primary care at any Walgreens, wherever we traveled across the country, 24/7, and at reasonable out-of-pocket prices that we are told up front? That is a vision for Walgreens and other pharmacies like Walmart and CVS. Right now, we as consumers have too few options for buying our healthcare, and the choices we do have are constrained by our insurance. What Walgreens and others are finally doing is addressing healthcare economics on the supply side of things by providing more consumer choices. More options are good for us as consumers, and it means there is new competition that will likely drive down inflated prices. Plus, as anyone who has been through an Economics 101 class should know, if you increase supply of anything, prices come down.

Retail pharmacies are entering the broader world of healthcare delivery in a bold way. The motivation and plan for Walgreens to deliver healthcare in its stores was presented at the 2019 *Healthcare Economics Summit* by

Chet Robson, DO, MHCDS, FAAFP, and chief medical officer of Walgreens (Robson, 2019). Dr. Robson noted that high-deductible plans are putting increasing burdens on consumers and that Walgreens is looking to address this problem directly. He said, "In retail health, we generally start with the consumer—start with the patient and ask, what's most important to them?" It turns out that high-deductible plans are driving consumer interest in retail healthcare and that is what is driving Walgreens' interest in moving into this area. "The average annual out-of-pocket expense per patient rose almost 230% between 2006 and 2016." Furthermore, he noted that there are now more outpatient services and more drugs that are over the counter (OTC), which puts more decision-making responsibility in the hands of patient-consumers, which further drives this trend toward consumerization of healthcare.

Another concern in healthcare is that it needs to do a better job of factoring in our individual life situations as part of our treatment plans. Healthcare delivery should consider what we as individual and unique patients are experiencing in our own neighborhoods, communities, and families. This would be something the family doctor of 50 to 100 years ago did well but has been lost to history in this new era of corporate medicine. Dr. Robson noted how these social determinants of health are increasingly being viewed as important, and he argues that because the neighborhood Walgreens is physically located close to where we live, work, and play, it is ideally situated to be our community-based medical home and provide care that better addresses these social determinants of health.

Connecting with consumers where they live can also transcend physical location. More and more telemedicine is being used, and consumers want more digital convenience for finding or using their healthcare. The easing of interstate medical licensure restrictions, resulting from the 2020 coronavirus pandemic, will only increase the availability and usage of telemedicine. Thus, both physical location and digital healthcare tools are a focus for Walgreens, to connect with consumers where they live. What Walgreens is trying to create is "customer-centered, pharmacy-integrated healthcare services and connected solutions."

Walgreens has 9,800 locations and 78% of Americans are within five miles of a Walgreens. The company also employs 85,000 healthcare providers, so it is arguably the world's largest healthcare provider already and poised to now deploy its resources more broadly (Remedium eXchange, 2019). This is evident in the company's central involvement in providing Covid-19 tests as part of the Trump administration's response to the 2020 coronavirus pandemic (Walgreens, 2020). To this end, Walgreens now has clinics in many locations and its "strategy is to partner those [clinical services] out with health systems," which "creates a front door for the health system," according to Dr. Robson. Thus, Walgreens is not intending to acquire and own everything but rather is looking to be a portal to existing healthcare services (figure 10.1). For example, in the Wisconsin-Illinois area, the company has partnered with Advocate-Aurora, the largest provider in those states, to provide primary care. Walgreens may also offer optical, hearing, and dental services provided through partnerships. For clinical lab work, it has "a partnership now with LabCorp." Dr. Robson commented that based on that, Walgreens is "in the process of opening up at least 600 patient service centers in our stores over the next three years." The company has even experimented with urgent care in nine locations with United HealthCare, in places that do not normally have access to urgent care. In effect, Walgreens is acting like a portal to a wide range of services for healthcare consumers. This is in contrast to the other possible business strategy of acquiring or merging with all these ancillary service providers, which would produce

FIGURE 10.1 The suite of partnerships and services for which Walgreens provides a portal. Robson (2019).

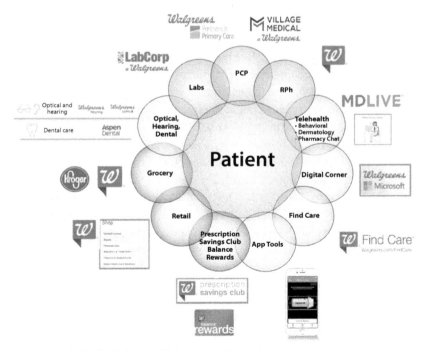

Source: Provided by Dr. Robson of Walgreens, with permission.

large vertically integrated structures that are arguably anticompetitive (as discussed in chapters 4 and 5) and not conducive to free and competitive markets.

Software and telemedicine are other ways to provide healthcare anywhere. To that end, Walgreens has developed an app that geolocates and tells patients about all the Walgreens resources near them and what the cash price would be to purchase those services (figure 10.2). The company is working to integrate this resource with insurance providers too, for consumers that do not want to use direct pay and prefer to use their insurance. This way Walgreens would provide cost estimates (e.g., co-pays) for those with insurance, similar to what was described for the price transparency software front ends being developed by providers (see chapter 1). This app will connect with telemedicine providers like MDLIVE (www.mdlive.com) and Heal (heal.com), which enables on-demand doctor house calls. With all of this, Walgreens' stated goal is "healthcare in the flow of [your] life, where you live and where you work." And it will do this not entirely on its own but through a wide range of strategic connections with partners that are both traditional providers and direct pay providers. Walgreens appears to be democratizing and consumerizing healthcare in a way that could be revolutionary, as long as consumers do not let themselves remain hostage to insurance plans and large providers that overly restrict and dis-empower them. This could be a consumer-led revolution in healthcare, if consumers embrace it, and if other forces, like government regulations or the Medical-Industrial Complex (chapters 4 and 5), don't block it.

After listening to Walgreens' consumers, Dr. Robson observed that "what patients want is more information, more integration, and more understanding of what something is going to cost." Putting it all together, these are the elements that could be made available in the pharmacy retail setting: pharmacy, medication therapy management (MTM), chronic disease management, lab services, digital health services (MDLIVE, Pharmacy Chat, Heal, and healthcare services locator Find Care), medical supplies, along with optical, hearing, and dental services. What Walgreens envisions offering is one integrated healthcare delivery experience, which is consistent and available wherever you live, work, or play. Besides the physical availability, the company also hopes to offer a wide range of digital resources so that you will be able to access everything in one digital space (summarized in figure 10.2). According to Dr. Robson, what Walgreens is working to create is a "Healthcare Neighborhood with all these services . . . this would be

FIGURE 10.2 Digital and telehealth solutions offered by Walgreens. Robson (2019).

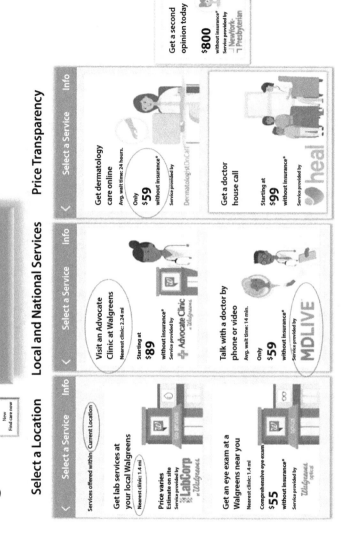

Source: Provided by Dr. Robson of Walgreens, with permission.

FIGURE 10.3 Integrated physical and digital services platform as part of the Walgreens vision for community-based delivery of healthcare. The suite of partnerships and services to which Walgreens provides a portal.

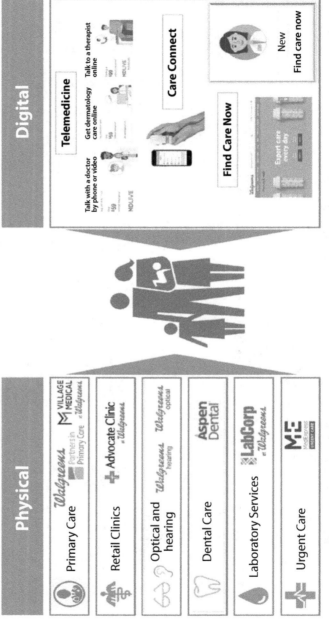

Healthcare Neighborhood: *in the flow of people's lives*

Source: Robson (2019). Provided by Dr. Robson of Walgreens, with permission.

an integrated, transparent, convenient, personalized service that's available wherever you go" (figures 10.1 and 10.3).

This looks like a revolution in how we could get our healthcare, by providing new options for consumers to get healthcare with or without insurance, and as a refuge from the increasingly painful deductibles and co-pays, such as in the high-deductible bronze plans under the Affordable Care Act (ACA). But Walgreens is not alone in this healthcare consumerization and patient empowerment revolution.

Walmart as a Case Study: The Front Lines of a Healthcare Consumerization Revolution

Another pioneering effort at consumerizing healthcare within drugstores is occurring at Walmart, a ubiquitous brand and store that is also in nearly every neighborhood across America. Currently, Walmart is looking to add a wide range of healthcare services in its stores, initially focusing on certain test locations. I learned more about details of the Walmart vision in an interview with Amanda Deegan Winters (Deegan Winters, 2019), director of Healthcare Public Policy at Walmart. Walmart is a natural venue to provide healthcare services, for the same reasons that Walgreens is considering a similar move, since 90% of people live within 10 miles of a Walmart, including in rural areas where healthcare options are sometimes very limited. Walmart is creating healthcare "Super Centers" (Japsen, 2019b) for basic services, which the company is calling "Walmart Health." These centers could someday provide a wide range of services that include primary care, dental, optometry, lab tests, X-rays, hearing care, wellness education, and even behavioral health. The idea, according to Deegan, is to be able to have consumers just walk into Walmart and ask their questions and take control of their healthcare needs on the spot. Other creative ideas being explored are partnerships with Centers for Excellence to get high-quality primary and even specialty care. Patients needing care from a premier provider at a respected Center for Excellence, like Geisinger Health, for example, could be flown out to the center to get their care. And routine lab tests could be done on-site at Walmart through strategic partnerships, such as with Quest Diagnostics. Physicians and nurse practitioners, within the Walmart umbrella, might also be on-site providing services. What is being proposed and at some level already offered is holistic, so that you can get a large fraction of your healthcare needs addressed all at one location, and perhaps in one visit, at transparently posted affordable prices—teeth cleanings for $25, as an example, or behavioral health counselor sessions at

$1/min. Procedures that often require multiple appointments could be done all at once, so if you show up for a doctor visit and the doctor decides you need an X-ray, you would go right to the next room and get the X-ray, or lab test, or whatever is needed. Deegan views this as being consistent with the Walmart tagline of "Save money. Live better." This would be affordable and convenient healthcare, and an alternative to the high deductibles and co-pays consumers are increasingly burdened with in our current system. And if we ever adopt a universal public healthcare plan, it could provide an alternative to the occasional long waits or excluded services that inevitably would happen in such a system.

What Is Needed for the Healthcare Consumerization Revolution to Occur

These trends are moving us away from the corporate practice of medicine, consumerizing healthcare by putting power and control in the hands of us—the patient-consumers who are purchasing it directly and making our own decisions. This is an exciting development that could have a positive impact on healthcare delivery in America by providing more options. But, for it to happen, there may need to be regulatory changes or allowances at the federal or state level that include:

- Allowing other practitioners besides doctors—namely, nurse practitioners, pharmacists, and physician assistants—to practice at the top of their licenses (see chapter 7).
- Modernization of telemedicine laws to keep up with technology, including a reexamination of state law restrictions when your doctor or other provider may be physically in a different state than you are in; but the 2020 coronavirus pandemic may have just forced this regulatory change as one positive outcome of a tragic situation.
- Making patient electronic health record (EHR)/electronic medical record (EMR) data more portable so that you, as a patient, can see more providers more easily, even if they are not part of the provider network required by your insurance. Our EHR data should be under our control and go where we want to it go, without current regulations under the Health Insurance Portability and Accountability Act (HIPAA), which were intended to protect us, blocking or hindering this mobility (Collins, 2014) to the benefit of large corporate medicine.
- Addressing the shortage of certain healthcare providers, such as nurse practitioners.

Regarding the last point, Walmart has created a program that provides college education to its employees for $1/day (Friedman, 2019), and this could include training to become nurses. Thus, Walmart would be addressing the national nursing shortage internally through its existing extensive workforce.

Disruptive Innovation—Haven, Amazon, and More

The large Medical-Industrial Complex will not easily change, since it wields significant political and economic power and changes with glacial speed. To go against this is like Don Quixote attacking windmills. But disruptive innovation, famously described and promoted by the late Harvard professor Clay Christensen (Christensen et al., 2015), is what America excels at (remember Kodak and Blockbuster?). It is this disruptive innovation that could and will change how we deliver healthcare in America, even against the resistance of corporate medicine and government regulations. Such an undertaking would be hubris for any small healthcare tech startup, even if it has hundreds of millions of dollars of venture capital behind it and a better way to deliver healthcare. The only hope to change what we have in place now is a consumer-led revolution, such as we saw with Uber, where hordes of consumers were suddenly empowered and demanded this new and better service. Government regulators and the existing industry had to yield against such a powerful and organic grassroots force. The route to change is for new and powerful market entrants to come into the field with a disruptive healthcare delivery model that, hopefully, is not itself anticompetitive. That is why there was so much hope and anticipation when Amazon, Berkshire Hathaway, and JPMorgan spoke of reshaping healthcare in their venture that is now called Haven (havenhealthcare.com). But while we wait to see how Haven materializes, it looks like the large retail pharmacies that have a significant physical footprint across America are stepping in to quietly reshape healthcare delivery. In an interesting domino effect phenomenon, one wonders if their motivation to do this came from Amazon's threat to step in and reshape the role of pharmacies through Amazon's proposed offering of mail-order pharmacy services (Kokosky & Hall, 2018), which is now available as "PillPack" (Pifer, 2019). If the only purpose of a drugstore is to hand us our medicines, then drugstores will soon go away, thanks to Amazon. No matter what, capitalism is at work here, and we may soon be getting affordable healthcare at our local pharmacies and our drugs from Amazon—and possibly those from Canada. Of course, with a properly supported telemedicine and remote medicine technological revolution, we may end up doing almost everything from our homes anyhow using virtual tools—and Covid19 will likely accelerate this transition. In this regard, the Walgreens and Microsoft partnership suggests that a pivot from brick-and-mortar clinics to telehealth may be under way, with that playing field expanding to also include Rite Aid, Publix, and Target (Wicklund, 2019). It will be interesting to see how this all evolves. I only hope it reaches a point where we the consumers are in charge of and own our healthcare—maybe managed from our iPhones or Androids and wearable devices. I would defy the cynics and fans of paternalistic medicine and predict that the American consumer is up to this challenge.

CHAPTER 11

Purple Solutions to Decrease Healthcare Costs and Increase Patient Empowerment

DANIEL SEM

The previous chapters in section 2 of this book provided an overview of our current healthcare delivery system, from large hospital providers to small physician groups to neighborhood retail or on-site clinics in companies and drugstores. Emphasis was on current trends in healthcare delivery, the role of insurance (reimbursement) models, current and proposed government regulations, and the role of transparent pricing, bundles, and consumerization to empower consumers and introduce market forces. This chapter attempts to summarize some of what was presented in those earlier chapters while also discussing potential bipartisan solutions that could result in better, more accessible and more affordable healthcare for everyone. Given the emphasis on the importance of free markets and competition in establishing and controlling prices (see also chapter 19) and empowering consumers over big government or large corporations, this section might be viewed as being somewhat on the Red side of the political spectrum. But, be patient, because the last section of this book also discusses the need for some sort of broad healthcare safety net (albeit not exclusively government controlled), which is often viewed as being more on the Blue end of the political spectrum.

Government or Physician-led Decision-Making

Government regulations were intended to improve the quality of healthcare delivery, but they actually created unintended negative consequences—because of one-size-fits-all regulations. Regulations made in and enforced from our nation's capital, no matter how well intentioned and intelligently crafted by experts, are never as effective as locally developed and enforced procedures that allow more flexibility to deal with the unique situations and needs of a given patient. That is not to say there should not be some regulatory guidelines and constraints, only that they should not be so restrictive that they force providers (e.g., physicians) to focus more on compliance with regulations than on providing the care that they think their patients really need. Dr. Watchmaker (chapter 3) gives a number of examples of how providers ignored medical best practice for the sole purpose of complying with regulations, and/or they simply were not thinking of medical best practice since they were just doing what the regulations and internally developed procedures (established to be compliant with regulations) required of them. The data support Dr. Watchmaker's conclusion that quality outcomes are not better when regulations are put in place to try to force those healthcare quality outcomes. It is better to provide broader regulations that allow more flexibility and autonomous decision-making at the frontlines of healthcare delivery. Indeed, the field of "continuous improvement" (Lean Six Sigma) actually requires empowered decision-making at the frontlines.

Creation of the Medical-Industrial Complex

One unintended consequence of overregulating the delivery of healthcare is that it has catalyzed a massive consolidation trend in the healthcare industry, as providers struggle with the larger complexity and administrative expense required to remain compliant with government regulations (see chapters 4 and 5). Whatever the exact cause, there is no denying that there is a trend toward consolidation in healthcare, not only with horizontal integrations that create large provider networks, but also vertical integrations that have hospitals merging with insurers or health plans. These larger healthcare entities, sometimes called the Medical-Industrial Complex (MIC), are wielding increasing economic and political power and are considered by many to be anticompetitive. For example, small physician practices are being merged or sometimes aggressively acquired or forced out of business by larger provider networks. A case study of the latter scenario, with discussion of broader implication in healthcare, was presented by the former president of the American Medical Association, in chapter 5.

The large healthcare providers typically charge more for services, since their internal pricelist (the "chargemaster") has inflated prices that were negotiated with the insurance companies that reimburse them at that level (see chapters 1 and 8). The large providers also participate in something called *cost-shifting*, where they cover losses in some areas (e.g., under-reimbursement by the government for Medicaid; use of emergency rooms by those who cannot pay). It is for this reason that you might pay $2,000 for an MRI in a large hospital, whereas if you go to another location, you might pay $700. But you cannot easily learn that you are allowed to go out of network for these less expensive and better healthcare options because of certain anticompetitive and dysfunctional incentives in the current MIC system.

There needs to be more carefully thought out and implemented oversight of this kind of anticompetitive behavior by, for example, the Federal Trade Commission (FTC) to ensure that smaller practices can still exist—and that we are not left only with one large provider or an oligopoly of a few large providers. That would not be much different or better than a single universal government-run plan. Too much concentration of power and decision-making, whether in government or corporations, is never in the best interests of individual consumers.

Bad Incentives in the Current System

In the large hospital systems, primary care providers—typically physicians—are rewarded financially to provide as many services internally as possible, optimizing what are called relative value units (RVUs) in a fee-for-service reimbursement model (see chapters 1 and 4). Physicians are also not encouraged to refer outside of the hospital network, even though better or more affordable care options might be obtained outside the network. The proprietary electronic health record (EHR) systems they use also make it difficult for patients, who are supposed to own their medical record data, to go out of network. Finally, primary care providers are not aware of prices and co-pays, and neither are their patients; and yet it is becoming increasingly common for us to get large surprise bills after the fact that are often financially debilitating for us. So, we should be interested in knowing up front what we will someday be paying.

Empowering Patient-Consumers to Shop

Informed patient-consumers actually do have ways to shop for their care, using some of the direct pay resources presented in chapter 1 and making use of the direct care options discussed in chapter 6. The industry and/or government needs to (1) make these options more available by requiring transparent pricing, as new regulations from the Centers for Medicare and Medicaid Services (CMS) are attempting to do; (2) encourage patient-consumers to research these provider options; and (3) increase the number of direct primary care providers, perhaps by rethinking how we do medical licensure (chapter 7). For this to happen, we as patient-consumers need to take more ownership and control of our healthcare, moving away from the old paternalistic model of healthcare where we are passive bystanders and do what we are told. That passivity is not consistent with any other aspect of American culture or behavior.

This kind of empowerment and change in mindset is possible only if we are given information, like the transparent and bundled pricing options presented in chapters 8 and 9. If this seems too intimidating for the average consumer, maybe they can make use of a new kind of person in the healthcare world—the "healthcare navigator." The healthcare navigator's job is to help us navigate our various provider and service and payment options, for a small and transparent fee that they charge us (see chapters 1 and 9). In the simplest possible world of empowering us as consumers, even without the aid of a healthcare navigator, we could also get some of our routine healthcare needs met at the local Walmart or Walgreens, either in a physical location or using telehealth, with easy to view and understand prices and options (see chapter 10). All of this "shopping" is made possible only if we can easily see prices, what we get for that price, and if we can have our medical records easily travel with us where and when we want. Finally, we also need to be incentivized to shop for healthcare value. But, with the large co-pays and deductibles most of us now have, we are already incentivized—we just do not have the information or the power to make those decisions about our own healthcare.

A Good Role for Government: Facilitate Patient Empowerment

Big government or big corporations (the MIC) should not be unilaterally controlling our healthcare. It should be us, the patient-consumers. Government, working with industry, should if anything create needed infrastructure—the tools and resources to help make this patient-empowerment and consumerization vision a reality. It would be the healthcare equivalent of creating highways and fiber optic lines. One key infrastructure need is to give us as consumers mobile and secure access to our medical record data.

As suggested by Dr. Watchmaker in chapter 3, it should be a goal to place the patient-consumer at the center of healthcare reform. But, as he noted, "asking patients to be active, responsible advocates for their own health will require education and engagement from all stakeholders. Taking 'ownership' of one's health is innate for some but will require significant messaging for others." He suggests that government can play an important role by "establishing a healthcare data 'bill of rights' whereby providers in all settings are required to electronically transmit patient clinical data such as lab results, office visit notes, hospitalization reports to a patient controlled, patient-centered repository." He proposed that "providers transmit data to a secure, HIPAA-compliant repository of the patient's choosing within

48 hours of the encounter." This repository, with patient permission, could then be shared with future providers. In this way, patients could more easily move from provider to provider, shopping for what is best for them, and not be held captive to one provider network by an anticompetitive usage of their EHR systems. CMS is already taking positive steps in this direction with its newly developed MyHealthEData and Blue Button 2.0 initiatives. The MyHealthEData initiative is an example of the government serving as a central data repository for Medicare beneficiaries. Dr. Watchmaker envisions this helping to put patients at the center of their own healthcare advocacy, by allowing a secure flow of information (HIPAA-compliant) between providers, no matter the setting. And it puts us, as patient-consumers, in charge.

Price Transparency and Competition: The Need for Market Forces

A clear goal that emerged from the earlier chapters is to empower and inform us as patient-consumers so that we can shop for our healthcare needs (chapter 8). Of course, if you knew you could save $1,300 on your MRI by going somewhere else, you would, right? But there are a few reasons why you wouldn't:

- Our current healthcare system in the MIC discourages you from going out of network, even if better value exists out of network.
- Doctors—employed by the MIC—are rewarded based on the number of procedures offered; this is a bad incentive that inherently makes them less helpful if you want to shop.
- Your medical record data, in the EHR software database, which in theory you own, is not mobile. That makes it hard for you to easily go to outside providers. It is, in effect, a tool being used in an anticompetitive way that restricts you.
- You do not know how to find prices anyhow, and when you are given prices, it is hard for you to interpret what they mean. CMS rules are changing this situation, hopefully.
- You do not care about price anyhow, because either your insurance pays or you (wrongly) believe that you have to use your insurance no matter what, even if the co-pay and deductibles (which are never disclosed up front) would be financially devastating for you. Then, you get the surprise bill and feel (wrongly) you had no choice in the matter—and now you are mad.

How to Get to Better Healthcare: The Foundation for Purple Solutions

Because most of us now have large deductibles and co-pays, we should be incentivized to find better healthcare options to avoid these expenses (see chapter 19 and the discussion of Milton Friedman's Category I). In theory, this is a market force that would lead us to shop for better healthcare value, but for reasons explained later (in this book's last section) we do not. Nonetheless, if we did, then the market forces that would come into play would eventually drive down costs and increase quality and—perhaps more important to you—put you in a more empowered decision-making position of deciding where and how and what kind of healthcare to get, instead of being helplessly and passively tethered to what your insurance tells you that you can do (i.e., what is reimbursed and at what level). How do we get to this better healthcare delivery world, and how would you pay for it, if you did not use your insurance? Below are presented some *Purple solutions*, drawing on this discussion and the previous chapters.

Purple Solution Requirements: From You, the Healthcare Industry, and Government

Some changes are needed to get to better healthcare in America. Here is a listing of what we want from government, the industry, and from you as consumers.

- Do not overregulate healthcare quality from afar. Rather, let physicians do what they do best and empower them to make their own diagnostic and therapeutic decisions, within reasonable boundaries (chapter 3).
- Rein in anticompetitive behavior of the MIC; the FTC should better enforce existing antitrust laws (chapters 4 and 5).
- Increase the supply of frontline healthcare providers; allow healthcare practitioners (e.g., pharmacists, nurse practitioners) to practice at the top of their license (chapters 6 and 7).
- Allow consumers to take ownership, responsibility, and control of their healthcare, to shop for the best care and go outside of the restrictions that our insurance plans impose on us, by using direct pay and direct primary care options (chapters 6 and 8).
- Grow the profession of "healthcare navigators," so that we as consumers can use them as non-conflicted agents to guide us to find the best healthcare value (chapters 8 and 9).

- Increase the number of direct pay options—small physician groups, retail clinics, and on-site clinics (chapters 8–10)—and lower barriers to their usage. We as consumers should begin using these options, too, breaking away from the control of our restrictive insurance policies.
- Require transparent and easy-to-understand and easy-to-find bundled prices for medical procedures, with or without insurance, so empowered patient-consumers can shop. This is something CMS is trying to force, with new regulations.
- Remove dysfunctional incentives for our providers—incentives that discourage us from going out of network and encourage getting too many procedures. Our primary care providers should have a fiduciary duty to put our interests (medical and financial) first. Empower physicians and other providers to help us shop; remove gag laws.
- Let us shop for our care by giving us more control of our medical records. This could present a positive role for government.
- Provide standards (another positive role for government) to facilitate patient HIPAA-compliant ownership of mobile EHR data; create a Patient Bill of Rights; create an EHR repository (chapter 3).

Purple Solutions in Summary

All of the above proposals would work best if, as discussed in chapter 1, we as patient-consumers were using insurance like insurance was intended. Insurance should only be used for more rare/expensive events, and we should pay for our own routine healthcare needs ourselves directly, out of pocket (see chapter 19). In this way, we are the ones making our own healthcare decisions, not our surrogates (in government or in insurance companies). Does this sound too radical of a change for you? Well, we sort of already have it. We already have high-deductible plans, like the bronze plan under the Affordable Care Act, so we are already incentivized to save money for routine care. High-deductible plans should ideally not be used for routine medical care—but rather for emergencies, like open-heart surgery, cancer treatment, or end-of-life care. For over 90% of what we use the healthcare system for—annual checkups, cuts and broken bones, medication dosing (cholesterol, high blood pressure), worrying symptoms that we need an opinion on, dermatological problems, behavioral therapy, and so on—we could pay out of pocket, with the direct pay options that were discussed in earlier chapters of section 2. The prices are much lower, quality outcomes are as good or better, service and time spent with your provider is better. The cost to us is often less than our co-pay or deductibles anyhow. This would introduce market forces that would lower price and increase quality. We just need to begin using these options. We need a consumer-driven grassroots healthcare revolution.

Perhaps you argue that this is no solution—that I am just asking you to pay for your healthcare out of pocket (only using insurance for catastrophic events). You say that is no solution. You maybe also worry about how you can even pay for these routine expenses. Of course, right now you possibly have no way to pay with your high-deductible plan that already makes you pay full price, although it makes you pay inflated chargemaster prices that you could avoid with direct pay options.

One solution to finance these out-of-pocket expenses is for you to have a health savings account (HSA) that you can use to pay for these various direct pay options, and that HSA account could accrue money each year. This would only be for healthcare (including direct pay options), and if there is money left at the end of our lives, it could go toward our estate, like a life insurance policy (or perhaps a retirement account). Thus, it is our money to spend wisely (see chapters 19 and 23 for more on this topic). The country of Singapore has excellent health outcomes but spends only 2.5% of gross domestic product (GDP) on care, and it makes use of HSAs. This is essentially what David Goldhill proposed in his book *Catastrophic Care* (discussed in chapter 1).

I would argue that this healthcare model should be considered bipartisan and Purple so far, at least until we get to the part about how to fund it. The one question that remains then is how to finance this HSA account. Those on the Blue side might say the government should finance it, while those on the Red side might say we should fund it personally, with some tax breaks perhaps. Those in the middle might find compromise solutions, maybe even suggesting partial funding with a payroll tax that our employers pay, in lieu of (and the exact same amount as) what they are paying for overpriced insurance premiums now. No matter how we finance the HSA, though, my point is that it is a far better solution than what we have now—because even if it were government funded, it at least puts buying decisions in the hands of us, the consumers, which introduces market forces that we have never had in healthcare to date. If government funded, though, it is important that the money feel like it is our money, so that we have incentives to spend it wisely (chapter 19). A benefit is that we—the patient-consumers—are put in charge of our own healthcare decision-making, instead of relying on a paternalistic system that, frankly, has either government bureaucrats or insurance executives deciding what healthcare we should or shouldn't get. In the extreme, that is what Canada has, but not what most other countries, like Singapore or even Germany and Switzerland, have. Most countries, even those with universal healthcare, do not completely restrict everyone to using only the government-run program. They typically also offer private options (see chapter 1).

A Hybrid Healthcare System Is Needed—With Both Public and Private Options

In and for our American culture, we need to recognize that we like to have power, autonomy, and decision-making authority in our hands. If some sort of universal healthcare is ever adopted in America, even if just as a baseline or safety net (see section 4 of this book for that discussion), we should be sure to have a hybrid system that also offers private options and direct primary care options, where we as patient-consumers can purchase whatever healthcare we want out of pocket, perhaps with the help of an HSA/retirement plan. We should make sure that we never destroy free markets entirely, because if we do, there will be no constraint on price and there will inevitably be some type of rationing that we cannot escape from. Whenever there is complete government control of essential resources, there is eventually rationing—that was the lesson from the former USSR, which Boris Yeltsin illustrated so dramatically when he visited a grocery store in the United States for the first time. Overjoyed, he noted with awe the large selection of items on the shelves, something that the USSR simply did not have. One could imagine his reaction to the wide array of healthcare choices available as well, due to free markets (fig. 11.1)

FIGURE 11.1 From scarcity to abundance: Boris goes shopping. Boris Yeltsin was famously in awe of the wide range of choices at American grocery stores (Lights on Econ, 2015) and perhaps would be just as impressed with the diversity of healthcare choices in a free market system.

Source: Art by John Alberti, reproduced with permission.

This is not to say that some sort of hybrid system, with some government control of healthcare, could not work. It is only to say that there should always remain some place for competitive and free markets. Democrats and Republicans will of course disagree on the relative roles and importance of government versus free markets (note that I did not say corporations, especially the MIC). I am simply saying we should avoid complete government control of healthcare, at the exclusion of some sort of complementary private and free market option. No matter where we end up on the political spectrum, my hope is that we somehow keep private insurance and private providers of healthcare that can compete for our healthcare dollars in a free and open market. That will ensure that public options stay current and feel some market pressure to continually improve quality, occasionally reaping the benefits of innovations from the private sector. Indeed, that is how we handle education in the United States—we have both public and private options, and for those that opt out of using the public option we provide vouchers. Perhaps we could do that for healthcare as well.

SECTION 3

Drug Prices

CHAPTER 12

Should Drugs Ever Be Expensive?
Drug Discovery and Development, Pricing, and Market Forces

CATHERINE BODNAR AND DANIEL SEM

Section 2 of this book focused on the delivery and high cost of healthcare, including especially primary care. This section has a very different theme, focusing specifically on high drug prices. And this chapter begins that exploration by first considering the process of making a new drug, including research and development (R&D), clinical trials, and the regulatory requirements. The chapter looks at what the true cost and value of a drug should be and the role of patents in encouraging the innovation and R&D that leads to new lifesaving therapeutics. It also considers the occasional abuses of the pricing power that patents give companies and how these matters should be policed.

Background

Drugs appear to be getting increasingly expensive for us as consumers, although on average they have long represented only 10% of total healthcare spending, with much higher spending on hospital care (33%) and on physician and clinical services (20%) (Centers for Medicare and Medicaid Services, 2019). Some would argue that this spending on medicines, overall, saves money in healthcare (Pope, 2019). But the United States does pay more for drugs than other countries (American Academy of Actuaries, 2018), a topic of much political and public frustration with sometimes bipartisan calls for action:

> Bernie Sanders: "The greed of the pharmaceutical industry is a public hazard to the American people" (Sanders, 2015)

> Donald Trump: "Prescription drug prices are out of control. The drug prices have gone through the roof" (Kim, 2017)

Catherine Bodnar is an MBA student at Concordia University–Wisconsin and a medical student at Medical College of Wisconsin.

Unusually high-priced and sometimes truly unaffordable new cancer therapeutics, gene and cell therapies, and infusible drugs (biologics) seem the most likely culprits causing this public outrage. Prices are often in the tens to hundreds of thousands of dollars. Daraprim, Actimmune, and Myalept fall on the high end of that spectrum, costing $40,000 per month (Marsh, 2019b). Deraprim is the drug that Martin Shkreli—referred to as "Pharma Bro" (and now serving time in federal prison for fraud)—infamously increased in price by 5,000% (Mangan, 2019).

In some cases, though, the medicines that are priced so high truly are lifesaving and truly were expensive to develop. But how can a consumer (or even a payer, like your employer) be expected to pay these high costs? The 10 most expensive drugs in the United States ranged in cost, per year, from $573,820 to $2,125,000 (Marsh, 2019a). Since these drugs are often used to treat rare diseases that afflict fewer than 200,000 people, they are priced high because the number of people purchasing them is too low for the company to recoup its drug discovery and development expenses. So how can these high drug prices be paid? Do the drugs cost that much to discover, develop, and distribute? Even if they do cost that much (barring fraud or price gauging), are they worth that much money? How much money is a human life worth, if a drug truly is lifesaving and no other treatment is available? And even if we believe the drugs are worth that much money (in the truly lifesaving cases), how should they be paid for? While these are really important questions, they often get little attention in our typically superficial political debates. Some of the key issues are bioethical, touching on how to deal with the harsh reality that all societies—even those with a single-payer healthcare system—have limited resources to spend (the United States already spends 18% of gross domestic product on healthcare). Indeed, countries like Canada that do have universal single-payer government-sponsored systems limit coverage through regulatory decision-making bodies (in Canada it is the CDR—Common Drug Review), such that over 30% of drugs for rare diseases are rejected for reimbursement (Davio, 2018); outside of Germany and France, in the European Union (EU) reimbursements are rejected 40–70% of the time (and 50% in England) (Zamora et al., 2019). So while universal coverage does exist, access is necessarily limited because resources are inherently limited.

High drug prices in the United States, however, are not limited only to those that are used to treat rare diseases, but rather include more common therapies like insulin (Tsai, 2016) and the EpiPen (Willingham, 2016). So while on average the U.S. may not spend too much for drugs (10% of healthcare), these spikes in prices for certain drugs are problematic, leading to public outrage. This chapter addresses why drugs are expensive to make, why prices are sometimes justifiably high, and why sometimes they are unjustifiably high (also covered in chapter 13). Subsequent chapters will explore solutions to these problems.

Why Are Drugs Expensive to Make, and Why Are Prices So High?

Let us begin with a discussion of the economics of pharmaceuticals and why drugs are sometimes justifiably expensive in the first place. We will attempt to better define the drug development process in general, considering it from the perspective of economic principles and market forces and exploring cost and demand factors that may affect the price of a drug. Chapter 13 will then explore factors beyond this baseline of cost that consider downstream effects on drug prices in the "supply chain," from the pharmaceutical manufacturer/developer to the wholesaler/distributer, the pharmacy benefit manager (an intermediary), and ultimately the pharmacy. Some of these expenses are justified, some are not, and some are outright abuses or fraud. In many cases, these expensive drugs are essential means of treating life-threatening conditions, so there is a real need to find ways to make them accessible within whatever bioethical boundaries society sets (e.g., do we spend $1 million to extend a life six months at the expense of spending that same money on other medical needs?). Later chapters discuss potential solutions to some of the problems associated with high drug prices, including some current proposals from the federal government, patients, scholars, the industry, and trade organizations.

Cost Factors

Fixed and variable costs go into producing any commercial product—in this case, a drug. These costs include manufacturing and distribution expenses. Estimates suggest that production costs represent 15–30% of total cost, marketing and distribution 20–30%, and R&D along with licensing 20–40%, with margins ranging 20–35% (Parexel Pharmaceutical, 2002). These numbers, however, ignore much of the expense of what came before the creation of the new product (in this case a drug) as part of the drug discovery process; indeed, such expenses often get chalked up to mere sunk cost (DiMasi et al., 2003). In the case of developing a new drug, these discovery expenses are nontrivial, proving a major reason for that ultimately high price. Without this up-front R&D expense, there would be no more new drugs—no more new lifesaving medical interventions. The cost and time spent on all these clinical trials is also significant, being anywhere from eight to 13 years (Gassmann & Zedtzitz, 2004). Since patents last only 20 years, this means companies have only about 10 years left to recover their R&D expenses before the drug goes generic. Based on an analysis provided by Tufts University, the widely cited cost of taking one drug to market, all expenses considered, is estimated to be $2.6 billion (DiMasi et al., 2016). This includes all capital expenses as well as variable costs, and it considers the many failures that occur as part of the drug discovery and development process. This estimate also includes consideration of the fact that, on average, 80% of drugs that enter clinical trials fail during one of the three phases never making it to market (Willingham, 2016).

Some (DiMasi et al., 2003) have made an argument that this cost estimate is misleading because it includes sunk costs that should not influence drug pricing; having said that, DiMasi acknowledges that the large profits offered by monopoly power for newly approved drugs entice companies to spend that much up-front money and take on the risk of 80% failure in expensive clinical trials. At a minimum, companies need to at least be able recover the money they spent developing the drug (considering drug failures), which is on average in excess of $2 billion. Unfortunately, if the drug is to treat a rare disease (fewer than 200,000 patients), that means that the cost per patient will necessarily be unusually high.

Patents may be partially to blame for higher drug prices, rewarding biomedical innovators with 20-year monopolies. Nonetheless, these very same patents provide the impetus for innovation, incentivizing companies to pursue the development of what is the most expensive-to-develop innovative product in society. This purpose for patents, by the way, was a concept thought up by our founding fathers who created the U.S. patent office. George Washington approved the first patent (U.S. Patent and Trademark Office, 2001) and included the concept of patents and copyrights in our Constitution, in Article I, Section 1, Clause 8:

> To promote the progress of sciences and useful arts, by securing for limited times to authors and inventors the exclusive right to their respective writings and discoveries.

So, by design of our founding fathers, patents allow invented products (drugs in this case) to be priced higher (due to a government-granted monopoly), because these higher prices encourage the innovation that leads to better products, drives the economy, and in the long run lifts the prosperity of the country, in many ways defining our American entrepreneurial culture. Patents are why U.S. companies develop the majority (57%) of drugs (Lyman, 2014), which some conclude means that America finances the bulk of new medicine development for the world (Boustany, 2018). Thus any excessive price controls could certainly have the effect of decreasing the creation of new lifesaving medicines.

The large expense of developing drugs has led to a model in the pharmaceutical industry (pharma) whereby companies tend not to pursue drugs that have a market of much less than $1 billion a year (this defines a "blockbuster") and certainly not less than $200 million a year, because it is hard for them to justify taking on the financial risk associated with drug discovery that costs over $2 billion, unless of course the reward of a blockbuster awaits at the end. In 2002, 58 drugs were categorized as blockbusters, generating $120 billion in sales, or one-third of the world market (Gassmann & Zedtzitz, 2004). The top-10 blockbusters contained two drugs for lowering cholesterol and three for central nervous system (CNS) conditions (e.g., depression and schizophrenia). This focus on blockbuster drugs had been a controversy in the field, and one industry expert (Parks, 2009) suggested to me in a phone interview that a balanced portfolio might be better. Whether a drug is a blockbuster or not, pharmaceutical companies make the bulk of their money only while their patents are active, which creates a barrier to market entry by enabling monopoly market power. Patents expire in 20 years, and since it takes approximately 10 years to get a drug to market, that leaves only 10 years of high profitability to recover R&D expenses (sunk costs) and also make a profit. When a drug does go off patent, revenues can decrease up to 80% (Gassmann & Zedtzitz, 2004) as the generic version (a substitute good, in the language of economics) enters the market. The generic market is itself large—50% of pharmaceutical sales and rising (Gassmann & Zedtzitz, 2004)—but generic companies have small profit margins, so they also tend to pursue only very large markets (Parks, 2009). These small profit margins come with significant challenges; in order to keep costs as low as possible, generic companies cannot have excessive production capacity. This means that if anything in their process fails (e.g., a chemical reactor goes down), problematic and debilitating drug shortages result—a familiar challenge that all pharmacies must deal with (U.S. Food and Drug Administration [FDA], 2020). The FDA director views these drug supply shortages as a kind of market failure (Kacik, 2019). Generic drug prices may be too low and there may be too few manufacturers, meaning the drugs have become commoditized products (*The Economist*, 2019; Ventola, 2011), but the true problem lies in the dire public health implications that result when shortages in these "commodity products" do occur. So while one could argue that brand name patented drugs are *sometimes* too expensive (remembering that often the high drug price is what financed the very expensive medical innovation), one could also argue that generic drug pricing has sometimes become too low with too few suppliers, resulting now in drug shortages and occasional spikes in drug prices.

Demand Factors

Take a deep breath and get ready for a flashback to your high school or college economics class and demand curves. One can imagine that demand curves for drugs would depend heavily on the seriousness of the disease being treated. For example, the demand curve for a drug to treat cancer would be very inelastic (a person would spend a large fraction of their income to buy that drug; they will pay for it no matter the price), whereas the demand curve for a drug for smoking cessation, or perhaps even Viagra, would be more elastic (figure 12.1). But there are multiple drugs to treat most cancers on the market, so depending on the extent to which the drugs are substitutes for each other, this variety of available substitute drugs increases the elasticity of the demand curve for even vitally important medications.

The concept of substitute products has relevance even for patented drugs, where patents are supposed to confer brief (approximately 10-year)

FIGURE 12.1 Price elasticity for drugs. If a drug is life-saving and there are no other options, you would pay anything for that drug. Should you have to?

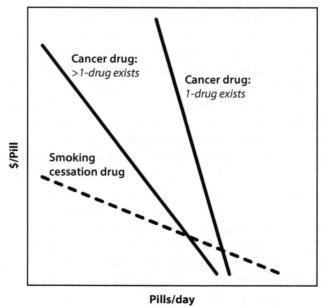

monopoly power to the company. Consider the cholesterol-lowering drug Lipitor—a $6 billion/year drug from Pfizer (Njardarson, 2009)—and the various competing statin drugs. Does the world need so many statin drugs? While these drugs are in many ways equivalent (substitute) goods with only small differences, there is some value in having more than one drug in a class on the market to create competition and provide slightly different benefits. In the process, this $20 billion cholesterol-lowering market pie has been divided between multiple competing companies with what are sometimes referred to as "me too" (i.e., similar, copycat) drugs, and the monopoly has evolved into an oligopoly where each new player's level of innovation is increasingly of marginal value. One hopes no price fixing will occur, and the government—via the Federal Trade Commission (FTC)—tries to ensure this won't happen (Federal Trade Commission, 2020). But the danger of price fixing always exists as an unintended consequence of price transparency when a market has very few competitors (see chapter 14). In ideal situations, having multiple drugs in a class (like the statins) tends to drive price down. This is good for the consumer and good for the "me too" companies, but not so good for the first company to market, which has just lost some of the large profit associated with the monopoly power it previously enjoyed. In practice, price still stays somewhat elevated, perhaps because of the lack of free and open competition or because the implicit price fixing does not rise to the level of FTC intervention. This division of large markets occurs for other diseases as well. For example, when surveying the top-200 selling drugs, three of them, all chemically similar in their inclusion of a "thiazolidinedione" ring (figure 12.2), were legally/patentably distinct (each had a patent). Again, an original monopoly has transitioned to an oligopoly. Does the consumer benefit? Yes, in two ways: The competition from the "me too" drugs could drive price down somewhat, and perhaps some "me too" drugs could have fewer side effects. Indeed, in the case of the three aforementioned drugs, Avandia and Actos possess different risk profiles (Turner, 2019).

Anti-infectives are one drug category of particular interest with regard to effects of substitute products. While the emergence of drug-resistant strains of bacteria (e.g., methicillin-resistant *Staphylococcus aureus*, or MRSA) necessitates new antibiotics, these new drugs are typically prescribed only after a frontline broad-spectrum antibiotic (e.g., penicillin) is used. Therefore, the MRSA market is doomed to be a small subset of the overall antibiotic market. But if pharma waits until that market grows bigger (e.g., drug-resistant strains become dominant), public health crises could result, as there is over a 10-year lead time for developing and taking a new drug to market.

FIGURE 12.2 Diabetes me-too drugs.

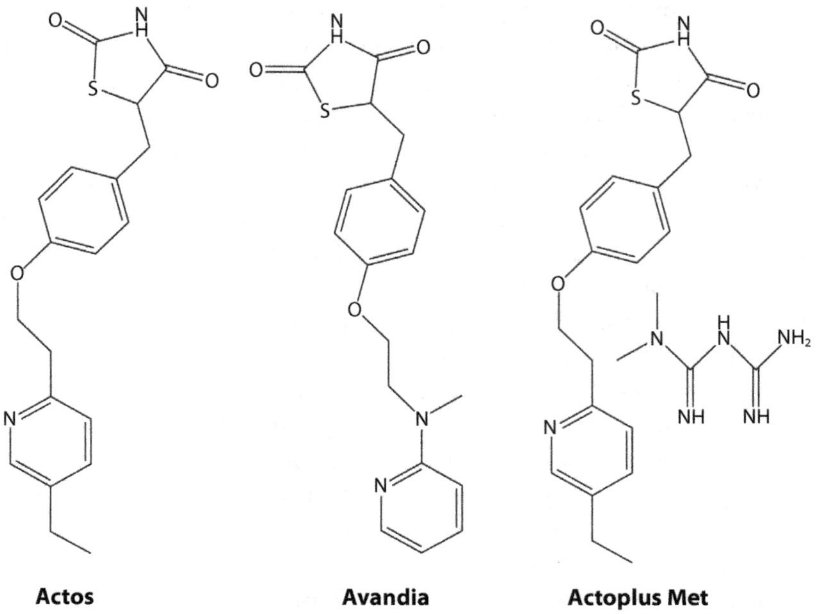

Actos   Avandia   Actoplus Met

Another public-health-related issue is whether companies should make, and physicians should prescribe, "narrow spectrum" antibiotics that only kill the infecting bacterial organism (e.g., *Staphylococcus aureus*) or use a broad spectrum that will kill both it and any other related bacteria (e.g., broad-spectrum penicillin). If a company sells a narrow-spectrum antibiotic, by design it chooses a subset of a larger market where the present product can do what yours can and more. The only downside is that such a choice leads to the unintended effect of promoting drug resistance in other bacteria, due to unnecessary exposure to the drug. Such drug resistance proves a negative externality for society but has little effect on the patient being treated. One solution might be to place an excise tax on the broad-spectrum antibiotic and/or subsidize the narrow spectrum.

A final point with regard to demand, especially for anti-infectives, is that Third World countries promise a huge potential market for drugs to treat tuberculosis (2 billion people infected; 3 million die/year), but these countries have much lower income: 60% of the world makes less than $1,000/year, and this 60% is predominantly the group affected by both tuberculosis and AIDS (DiMasi, 2003). These countries' demand for anti-infectives would be high, but the people who need the drug have little financial means. Their demand curve might be better represented if the Y-axis (price) in figure 12.1 were scaled by gross domestic product (GDP) or gross national product (GNP), which is a better representation of personal income in these countries, as it would then reflect what fraction of total income they were willing to spend, since the average income in sub-Saharan Africa is $762/year. This is a measure of social need. Demand might then be considered high even with far less money spent (money spent as a percent of total income still being high). It is for this reason that companies do sell at lower prices to some countries, even for the goal of profit-maximizing. Companies routinely practice such price discrimination: often Third World countries are sold drugs at 20% the rate charged in developed economies like the United States (DiMasi, 2003).

Pricing of Drugs

Recalling your economics, you perhaps know that supply and demand should determine price in a free market with competition and freely available information. You might reasonably argue, however, that this does not apply to drug prices in the United States for a number of reasons, including the fact that you as the consumer have no say in purchases. Rather, you simply hope that the drug your doctor tells you to take (or the purple pill you saw on a commercial that you ask for) is reimbursed by your insurance or the government (Medicare in the U.S. and Canada, or the National Health Service in the U.K.). You hardly have perfect information to ask for medicines, since drug commercials are never informative in any useful way, and consumers are not used to thinking they have any input into the process anyhow. Hopefully this will change. Currently, the "buyer" or consumer deciding whether to purchase a drug and at what price is typically a person or committee employed by the insurance company (or the government) that reimburses your claim and/or decides which drugs are put on the "formulary" of approved drugs that an insurance company or government allows you to take. The point is, in all cases, the decision is not made by you, or for that matter, by your physician. Your physician only makes a recommendation while someone else decides which specific drug in a class or category gets reimbursed, and therefore which drug you are allowed to get in your insurance- or government-sponsored plan. Despite these challenges, changes in regulations are starting to allow consumers to shop for alternative therapies (e.g., check out GoodRx.com), while new laws now allow pharmacists to recommend equally good generic versions of branded drugs. Little by little, such changes allow you as a healthcare consumer to get the treatment that both you and your doctor think you need and that you know you can also afford whether with a co-pay or direct out-of-pocket pay (Caffrey & Inserro, 2018). Typically, your prescribing doctor probably neither is aware of or cares about the cost of drugs for you, so that you may get a $300 prescription co-pay or deductible that could have been $25 if physicians had given some thought to the real need for the branded or out-of-formulary drug versus the equally good generic drug. If physicians did this, the U.S. health care industry could save $325 billion per year in prescription drug costs (American College of Physicians, 2015).

How Then Are Drug Prices Determined, if Not by Market Forces?

The United States has been characterized as "the last of the free pricing" countries (Agrawal, 1999), since the rest of the world largely exercises some sort of price control. (Although, as just noted, we do not have consumer-driven markets and price controls.) But now, it seems that both Democrats and Republicans are advocating for some sort of price controls. President Donald Trump's administration recently proposed price controls by benchmarking against other countries in the American Patients First blueprint proposal (U.S. Department of Health and Human Services, 2020).

Until these price controls (with reference pricing) occur—and they may not happen—what system do we have in place for setting drug prices in the U.S. and internationally? To address this question, I researched industry best practices and also interviewed someone at the frontlines of drug pricing, Joshua Parks (2009), who at the time was director of international pricing at Schering Plough (later purchased by Merck). Parks's job was to determine the differential pricing that was to be used for different countries in Europe and to determine how price "referencing" was to be done—for example, many countries reference what France and a collection of other EU countries pay (Rémuzat et al., 2015). Parks described how a pharmaceutical company must attempt to get on *the reimbursement list* in each country, and this involves offering discounts to one country or another for various reasons. A classic example of price discrimination to maximize profits, this action satisfies the minister for health (or other government regulatory agent) in a given country, rather than serving as a direct response to a market with free and unhindered competition. The drug that makes it on the reimbursement list then has a competitive advantage (just as a drug that makes it on a formulary does in the United States), effectively creating a regulatory barrier to entry. For newly developed drugs that are more expensive, these are sometimes (as noted above, as high as 50%) not available in countries that can't afford what is—in some cases—a justifiable price based on value and cost of drug development.

When asked about changes coming in the United States, Parks suggested that transitioning to a single-payer system will lead to a *de facto* formulary that is analogous to the EU reimbursement lists, which means some drugs will not be available anymore unless we have a supplementary private system. Some committee will decide what drugs get sold preferentially, rather than the patient and consumer-driven market. Furthermore, some countries like Italy do not even allow a drug to be sold off-formulary without government permission, even if the drug had been approved by the European Medicines Agency (EMA), which is the EU's version of the FDA. He noted that countries might negotiate prices based on prices offered to "reference countries," but also that those prices are not necessarily publicly known or discoverable. In short, the system is plagued by multiple market failures, including an absence of complete information, but most important, an absence of free competition because of government regulation through the restrictive reimbursement system. If this is what lies ahead for the United States, it is important to ask: *What will determine which drug makes it on the formulary, and how will it be decided?* And, if a drug does not make it on the approved formulary, will there be some mechanism (or market) in which a patient could obtain the drug at a higher price, or through a supplemental insurance policy that provided broader access to drugs?

Parks also commented further on how the industry determines drug pricing in practice (for branded and patented drugs, not generics—which typically do respond better to market forces). He said that while in theory one might use more sophisticated methods like a van Westendorp analysis to determine optimal price point (Martin & Raynor, 2008), ultimately executive decisions determine final prices based on information at hand and past experience. Such decisions, however, still apply the basic concept of trying to determine at what point companies "break the trust" of their customers by asking too much: They are feeling their way down the demand curve. In terms of ranges, Parks said one might charge 15 to 20 times the generic competition (assuming, of course, the new drug is significantly more efficacious) but possibly as high as 75 times the cost. He also notes that in the EU, companies can decrease—but not increase—price.

But Who Is the Customer That Responds to Price?

For example, let us imagine that a physician—say, a cardiologist—must go to the person in charge of the pharmacy, who may be constrained by the pharmacy benefit manager (PBM) (Frank, 2001), and *lobby* for the more expensive and "better" drug. While you as the patient may think your physician is calling the shots, there is more going on behind the scenes. That is, by acting as the agent for you, the patient, your cardiologist necessarily becomes the customer/demander for the drug, but is in turn also constrained by the insurance company, the PBM, and the formulary. Again, the market forces working here are rather indirect. Is the market listening to and responding to the physician (in this case the cardiologist), allowing the doctor to justifiably lobby for the higher price? Not really. The goal of those selling drugs is to convince those in charge of the formulary to permit this new drug. Right now, the market power resides in the insurance company and the PBM that decides which drugs get reimbursed and end up on the formulary. In the EU, a government body executes a similar decision-making process. It is too bad that the power cannot somehow rest in the hands of consumers—the patients—in simple conversation with their physicians. Later, the dangers of having surrogates making funding and coverage decisions for patients and providers is presented, along with possible solutions.

Do Customer-Driven Market Forces Exist That Can Drive Prices Down?

The above discussion makes clear that there is no unhindered competition between pharmaceutical companies and their supply chain for selling their medical products to us, as their customers. Rather, we have empowered surrogates (typically insurance companies or the government) to act on our behalf and in our interest. If we had an actual free market, we the customers would have an agent acting on our behalf, our physicians or other healthcare navigators, who would be more able to interpret differences between competing drug products for us, empowering us to make or at least affect the buying decision. But even in this system, physicians are not paying, so they are not responsive to—and most often not even aware of—drug prices and/or their patients' co-pays. One current strategy being considered gives physicians a financial stake (DiMasi, 2003) or at least a fiduciary duty to patients. Moreover, restrictive gag laws that favor the interests of PBMs have even prevented pharmacists from recommending equally efficacious but less expensive generic versions of branded drugs. These restrictions are, thankfully, being removed by new legislation (Clark & Breslauer, 2018; Coppock, 2018; Jaffe, 2018).

Interestingly, patients are more likely to not pick up their prescriptions if the co-pay is higher. Drugs costing them over $30 are twice as likely to be left behind as drugs with a lower co-pay. While co-pays are a small fraction of the total price of a drug, this phenomenon does indicate that co-pays can be used as a surrogate for a real market force in order to create a consumer demand curve. Indeed, they are used at present to discourage out-of-formulary drug usage. This is highly relevant in the United States, as third-party providers that use a formulary pay over 70% of prescriptions. And 70% of the time, private health plan prescriptions are managed using a PBM firm to oversee the prescription drug pricing (Frank, 2001). Challenges and market dysfunctions caused by a lack of price transparency from PBMs are discussed in chapter 13.

Another frustration consumers face occurs when their medicines are not covered by their insurance. Increasingly, and as high as 30% of the time, consumers are finding that drugs prescribed by their doctors are not covered by their insurance (NPR, 2020). The reasons are not very clear, but it seems only reasonable that, whether insurance companies or government (e.g., in Medicare, Medicaid, or "Medicare for All") reject the use of a medicine that both patient and physician feel is necessary, we need to provide some pathway for consumers to get access to those medicines and bypass that roadblock. This could be achieved either through a reasonably priced direct pay option (Seal et al., 2016), or through access to a supplemental insurance policy that can be purchased (in the case of Medicare, something like Medicare Advantage and Medicare Part D), such that some market and path exist to obtain these desirable, useful, but uncovered medicines. It is simply an illusion and even a lie to claim that government-sponsored universal care will not also have this problem, since resources are always limited and current universal care (e.g., in Canada and the U.K.) will not and does not cover everything. As noted earlier, countries like Canada and those in the EU that have universal single-payer government-sponsored systems limit coverage, and patients are rejected for rare disease therapies 30–70% of the time (50% in England) (Zamora et al., 2019). So while these countries have universal coverage, access is necessarily limited because *resources are always inherently limited*. That concept, and the notion that proper incentives (typically communicated via price) are essential, is what the field of economics is founded on.

Conclusion

In summary, we need a way to provide consumers and patients with access to medicines not reimbursed or covered in a formulary. This especially includes the very expensive but sometimes lifesaving new drugs for rare diseases, or gene therapy, infusion, biologics and cell-based therapies, that may cost as much as $40,000/month (sometimes justified and sometimes not). We also need a way to ensure that pharmaceutical companies still develop justifiably expensive drugs, even if those companies spend on average over $2 billion and 10 years to bring one drug to market. Companies may not engage in such risky endeavors if price controls are imposed—and especially if they are imposed recklessly in a broad way that does not recognize how higher drug prices, enabled through our patent system, lead to pharmaceutical innovation that has resulted in the United States producing the majority of the new medicines brought to market every year. Having said that, it is fair to say that the U.S. consumer, paying more for patented drugs than any other country, should not be financing medical innovation for the rest of the world (Goldman & Lakdawalla, 2018; Pitts, 2017). That is to say, U.S. consumers should not have to pay more for drugs made by U.S companies than do consumers in other countries that have imposed price controls. Finally, we need to better police our drug discovery, development, and distribution system to prevent abuses like spread pricing (price gauging), anticompetitive behavior (including price fixing), and the abuse of the pricing power granted by patented (legal monopolies), when in fact the level of innovation and R&D spending by a company was only marginal. Those who abuse the pricing power of patents cause the public to mistrust the patent system and dislike patented drugs, so that when a higher drug price actually is justified, the public protests it and demands across-the-board price controls that would stifle innovation. A reasonable middle road does exist, as do Purple solutions. What are these solutions? They are discussed in two chapters—so be patient and read on right now!

CHAPTER 13

Problems in the Pharmaceutical Supply Chain
From Pharma to PBM to Pharmacy— Who Is to Blame, and Where Is the Money Going?

DANIEL SEM

Chapter 12 looked at what the true cost and value of a drug should be, focusing on the actual drug development process and the role of industry and of government in monitoring pricing abuses. This chapter looks at the pharmaceutical supply chain, from the pharmaceutical company to the pharmacy, and explores if there are steps in this process that lead to unreasonably inflated prices and to a lack of free and competitive markets. While this chapter presents a case for the value of price transparency in the supply chain to avoid pricing arbitrage and other abuses, chapter 14 by Robert Graboyes considers the dangers of price transparency in some situations (oligopoly with barriers to entry) that can lead to implicit price fixing and collusion.

Background

Chapter 12 discussed why some drugs might justifiably need to be expensive—especially completely new drugs or classes of drugs—to at least cover the cost of the research and development (R&D) that went into making that drug, assuming, in fact, the drug provides real clinical benefit. The high price for new classes of drugs is a result of patents, which give the pharmaceutical company a limited and legal monopoly that allows for charging a higher price. But this is necessary since the average drug costs over $2 billion to discover, develop, and bring to market (DiMasi et al., 2016). While the exact cost to develop a drug has been disputed (Feldman, 2019), it is indisputable that developing a drug is extremely expensive and certainly in the hundreds of millions of dollars, in large part because of the cost of conducting human clinical trials that are compliant with Food and Drug Administration (FDA) regulations. Therefore, drugs often are justifiably very expensive.

Having said that, there are at times abuses of the monopoly power that patents provide, and there are market dysfunctions that need to be addressed. A summary of some of the market dysfunctions that lead to unjustifiably high drug prices are presented below and are a focus of this chapter:

a. Abuses of patent-based monopoly power that go beyond rewarding innovation, paying for real clinical value, and recovering R&D costs. Companies should not be able to overprice a drug merely because they have a patent, if they did not do significant innovation to develop the drug and obtain the patent, and if the drug does not provide real clinical benefits. How we avoid this scenario depends on one's political persuasion. Some would argue the government should police these abuses, perhaps through the U.S. Patent and Trademark Office (www.uspto.gov) or the FDA (www.fda.gov), to better flag marginal innovations that do not warrant a new patent or approved drug. Others would argue that the industry should self-police, such as through Pharmaceutical Research and Manufacturers of America (www.phrma.org) or BIO (www.bio.org), the biotechnology trade organization for the industry.

b. Cases where new drugs are developed at significant cost but with only incremental medical benefit to patients. This should be minimized, while also recognizing that it is good to have more than one drug in a class (e.g., more than one statin drug). How we avoid this scenario again depends on one's political persuasion again.

c. Lack of price transparency in the supply chain that gets drugs from the manufacturer to the patient, which can lead to non-value-added intermediaries adding unjustified cost. Again, the industry could self-regulate or the government could intervene by creating new regulations or enforcing existing laws, such as by state attorneys general.

d. The case of drugs that treat small numbers of people (fewer than 200,000). The so-called orphan drugs for treating rare diseases are often extremely expensive since the high cost of developing them cannot be spread over a large population. Some would say the government should finance these, and others would say there is a way to spread this risk and expense using private insurance and the free market.

In all of the above scenarios, I think we can largely agree on the problems and agree that they need to be addressed. Certainly, people will disagree on how to address them based on their political viewpoint. But a good first step would be to acknowledge that a problem does exist. If we can at least do that, perhaps we can then have a respectful discussion about potential solutions and perhaps even find compromises that work.

Drug Price Considerations in the Supply Chain to the Pharmacy

What happens downstream of the pharmaceutical company that discovered and/or manufactured the drug that the doctor prescribes for you? This path—from drug manufacturer to patient—is called the pharmaceutical supply chain. Are there pricing problems that arise in the supply chain, and what is the relative role of the pharmaceutical company and/or manufacturer versus the pharmacy versus the distributors/intermediaries, including the pharmacy benefit managers (PBMs)? These questions were addressed at the 2019 Rx Think Tank Healthcare Economics Summit (Remedium eXchange, 2019) by experts Robert Popovian, Pfizer VP of U.S. Government Relations; Antonio Ciaccia, the Ohio Pharmacists Association Director of Government Relations and Public Affairs; and Senior Director, Industry Relations and Contracting Jim Van Lieshout, with Navitus Health Solution, a PBM. Videos of their talks, which are a foundation for this chapter, can be viewed at http://rxthinktank.org/the-2019-healthcare-economics-summit-in-review. In addition to bringing together the views of these various stakeholders and thought leaders, this chapter is supplemented with reference to the scholarly and public policy literature. The perspectives presented herein represent the three industries that make up the pharmaceutical supply chain.

The Pharmaceutical Perspective

Robert Popovian of Pfizer commented that it is good that we as a society are finally having a candid and critical discussion about drug prices. It is perhaps long overdue. Certainly the public is frustrated with the high cost of some drugs, especially the specialty drugs like injectable/infusible drugs, biologics, and drugs to treat rare diseases. But, as Popovian noted, this issue is not just about the pharmaceutical companies. "A lot of people make money off of drugs, it's not just the pharmaceutical industry . . . the lion's share, about 60%, goes to the drug companies, but the other 40% goes to entities such as wholesalers, pharmacies, hospitals, physicians, PBMs, . . . and other entities in the supply chain." It is important to also track and understand what happens to that other $40 out of every $100 we spend on drugs. Are we getting value for that, or is it non-value-added intermediaries acting as a "tapeworm" on the economy, as Warren Buffett famously referred to healthcare, more broadly (Marketplace, 2018)? Popovian observed that if you look at how much we spend in the United States each year, "We spend about $450 billion annually on drugs, both retail and pharmacy, and out of that, $160 billion goes back into the system" to what he calls the "Bermuda Triangle of the healthcare system"—including rebates, fees, 340B, and the like.

What are rebates, and what is 340B? The 340B system was created in 1992 to provide eligible organizations, especially those serving vulnerable populations, drugs at significantly lower prices (Health Resources and Services Administration, 2020). Savings can be as much as 25–50% (Office of Population Affairs, 2016). And the program is growing since the number of 340B-covered healthcare entities increased under the Patient Protection and Affordable Care Act (2010). But this is a potential concern since a recent study by the Pacific Research Institute (Winegarden, 2017) reported a number of abuses of and problems with the 340B system, including encouraging the use of higher-priced drugs, cost-shifting, and the creation of pressures leading to consolidations (see chapters 4 and 5 on the adverse impacts of hospital consolidations). Rebates have also been suggested to be a tremendous source of fraud and abuse that can be gamed and that remove transparency of pricing from the pharmaceutical supply chain (see chapter 5). This is why President Donald Trump's administration proposed eliminating them on January 31, 2019 (Faget & Waltz, 2019; U.S. Department of Health and Human Services, Office of Inspector General, 2019) as part of the larger initiative to address high drug prices in the America Patients First blueprint (U.S. Department of Health and Human Services, 2018.) Most of these proposed changes, including reference-based pricing and price controls, have not yet come to fruition. The Congressional Budget Office (CBO) killed the rule from the Centers for Medicare and Medicaid Services (CMS) that would have done away with rebates because the CBO felt that the roughly 15% discounts they would have provided would no longer be available; but, according to Popovian, that is not likely to be true since the PBMs would simply have negotiated a lower price on their own without using rebates. In his view, rebates were simply a negotiation tool.

What about the price of drugs set by the pharmaceutical companies, before the rebates—the 60% of the price that we pay? Is that excessive, at least in some cases? And how does the industry decide what those prices should be? Chapter 12 discussed at length why some drugs might need to be priced high to recover the significant R&D investment (upwards of $2 billion per drug) that leads to creation of new lifesaving medicines. But sometimes there are what appear to be abuses, as were also discussed in chapter 12: drugs that can cost up to $40,000/month, as well as cases where prices were increased by as much as 5,000%. Abuses may occur and need to be addressed, but we also need to support the innovation that leads to new lifesaving medicines. Popovian noted that 75% of new FDA-approved drugs from 2008 to 2017 were funded by R&D at private companies, with only 25% benefiting from some sort of public support (Popovian, 2019). Thus, the pharmaceutical industry does play a central role in discovering and developing new medicines, but do the pharmaceutical companies over-charge and are they good stewards of the money we pay for drugs?

Many have criticized the industry for seemingly useless advertisements to consumers, suggesting they spend too much on marketing (Ventola, 2011). Indeed, the pharmaceutical industry has dramatically increased its spending on marketing in the 1997–2006 time frame, especially "direct-to-consumer advertising" (32% of the advertising budget in 2016), leading some critics to call for more regulatory oversight (Schwartz & Woloshin, 2019). There remains much controversy about the relative levels of R&D versus marketing spending in the pharmaceutical industry: By one account the industry spends somewhat more on R&D than advertising and on average invests 21% of sales into R&D (Dunn, 2018); however, a peer-reviewed study indicated that the industry spends, on average, roughly the same on each ($29.6 billion on R&D versus $27.7 billion for promotional activities in 2004) (Gagnon & Lexchin, 2008). Given the questionable value of the direct-to-consumer advertising (in its current form), which is typically not that infor-mative, it is reasonable to ask if that level of marketing spend is too high. But the question is, then, what can or should be done about it? That is the realm of politics. Should government regulate it? Or, if we truly had consumer-driven care and free markets with *useful* information about drugs, maybe the advertising could actually be made to be productive and of value.

Market Distortions That Have Us Buying the More Expensive Branded Drugs

What about the biologics-based drugs (monoclonal antibodies, cell-based therapies, infusibles) that are quite expensive? You can dispute whether they are overpriced or if they are priced properly and we just need to find a better way (via insurance?) to cover the expense. But no matter what, we can agree that when drugs go off patent to become generic they should become more affordable and prices should come down. Popovian noted that there is a market distortion that employs rebates to prevent this from happening so that the more expensive branded drug can still be sold. This happened with the anti-inflammatory, anti-arthritic drug REMICADE (generic: Infliximab), which is an infusion-delivered biologic. The generic is 30% cheaper, but because of the rebates that the insurers got from the PBMs, they still used the more expensive branded drug. The PBMs kept their fees but passed on the rebates in a selective way, so that pharmacies still chose the more expensive drug. So it is a market distortion that ends up making more money for the PBM and costing the patient more in the end. As a consequence, the generic option only has approximately 6% market share.

Consistent with this, Popovian also cited a *Journal of the American Medical Association* article (Socal et al., 2019) that reported how more expensive branded drugs are sometimes getting more favorable placement on formularies of allowable drugs, due to rebates, with 72% of the Medicare Part D formularies having at least one branded drug that got more favorable placement than the less expensive generic equivalent. "That just doesn't smell right," he said, and agreed that it is likely because the rebates are causing these market distortions and discouraging use of the more economical generic versions of drugs.

In summary, there are cases when drugs need to be priced high by the pharmaceutical industry, when the value justifies that high price based on the medical benefit they provide and the R&D costs that went into making the drug. But there are also clear cases of pricing abuses by the pharmaceutical industry and by the PBMs downstream in the supply chain that abuse the rebate and 340B process and take advantage of the lack of price transparency. Potential solutions to these problems are discussed in chapter 14.

Next in Line, the Wholesalers and the Pharmacy Benefit Managers

After a pharmaceutical company discovers, develops, and manufactures a drug, they move on to the wholesalers and PBMs. The wholesalers are in charge of distribution and include predominantly three companies: McKesson Corporation, AmerisourceBergen Corp., and Cardinal Health, Inc., of which each had 2017 revenues of $114 billion to $161 billion (Fein, n.d.). The PBMs act as agents in the middle of the supply chain that oversee prescription drug benefits for employers, healthcare insurers, Medicare Part D, and other payers. The top three PBMs in the United States by market share are CVS Caremark (CVS Health)/Aetna at 30%, OptumRx (UnitedHealth) at 23%, and Express Scripts at 23%, with three other PBMs at 6–7% each: Humana Pharmacy Solutions, Prime Therapeutics, and MedImpact Healthcare Systems (Paavola, 2019b). Furthermore, most insurers now have their own PBMs, sometimes obtained through strategic mergers: UnitedHealth Group (OptumRx), Anthem (IngenioRx), Humana (Humana Pharmacy Solutions), Aetna (merged with CVS Health), and Cigna (merged with Express Scripts) (Paavola, 2019a).

Potential anticompetitive concerns with vertical integrations, such as of insurers and PBMs, were discussed in earlier chapters. And as noted earlier, PBMs have, in some cases, used the rebate system in ways that can create market dysfunctions by encouraging purchasing of more expensive branded drugs over generics. As will be discussed later in this chapter, the lack of price transparency by PBMs has also been abused in what is called "spread pricing," where discounts (rebates; 340B) are not fully passed on downstream in the supply chain, with the PBM taking excessive profits. It is for this reason that the Trump administration had proposed to eliminate rebates and to introduce more price transparency as part of the American Patients First blueprint (U.S. Department of Health and Human Services, 2019). It is also for this reason that companies like Navitus Health Solutions, a PBM, are making price transparency a central part of their business model as well, according to Jim Van Lieshout, Navitus's senior director of industry relations and contracting, who spoke at the 2019 Healthcare Economics Summit. The approach at Navitus is to completely pass through discounts (e.g., rebates) from the pharmaceutical company. The PBM negotiates with pharma on price, which typically results in rebates that the company can then pass on to healthcare plan sponsors so they have zero spread pricing. The other three major PBMs are now beginning to talk about price transparency, but not at this level. So while one approach is government regulation to enforce price transparency, another is to have the market somehow adjust by providing price transparency on its own because consumers demand it. With regard to the former approach, according to Van Lieshout in 2019 there were 49 states considering 500 bills relating to PBMs, such as by requiring the reporting of rebates to the state insurance commissioner. Some proposed legislation also required licensing and registration of PBMs with audits or annual reports. Other proposed legislation prohibited claw backs so that patient co-pays could not be more than the cost of the drug to the insurer or the PBM.

In general, there is government (state and federal) pressure, and now an industry trend toward introducing more price transparency in the pharmaceutical supply chain. While this may introduce some danger of implicit price collusion (see chapter 14 by Robert Graboyes), it is important to know if rebates are being used to manipulate the market or if PBMs are using spread pricing to obtain excessive and unjustified profits. It seems only reasonable to have PBMs disclose their fees to begin to get at where in the supply chain the other 40% of spending on medicines is actually going.

Van Lieshout felt that one positive trend in the industry is "value-based pricing," where drugs are only paid for if they work (Kaltenboeck & Bach,

2018), and he felt we could use legislation to help get biosimilars (generics of expensive branded biologics) to market faster. Popovian agreed at some level but added that he felt value-based pricing would only work in a practical sense for drugs such as oncology therapeutics, where one could know outcomes of drug treatment in a short period of time (versus chronic treatments over many years). He also added that PBMs are not involved in the biologics and specialty medications world, since those are dealt with directly by hospitals and insurance companies in a buy-and-bill process that has its own unique challenges (Fein, 2016; McCain, 2012).

Next in Line, From the PBM to the Pharmacy

Pharmacies, whether chain or hospital pharmacies, populate their drug formularies (i.e., collections of drugs they offer, often dictated by what insurers reimburse) by negotiating with the PBMs. Thus, they experience price (cost) of the drug from the "market" through the PBM, with the hope that the PBM is negotiating the best price possible from the pharmaceutical manufacturer. But this assumption and this trust has been severely breached in the last few years, which is what has led to the onslaught of proposed state and federal regulations to introduce price transparency into the pharmaceutical supply chain—focused especially on the PBMs. At the frontlines of this battle, shining a light on some pricing abuses and how they affect pharmacies, has been Antonio Ciaccia, director of government relations and public affairs for the Ohio Pharmacists Association. Ciaccia also spoke at the 2019 Healthcare Economics Summit, and what he discovered in the pharmaceutical supply chain in Ohio was the result of a great piece of detective work on his part and was nothing short of shocking.

According to Ciaccia, the Ohio Medicaid managed care plan in 2016 was working with two PBMs: CVS Caremark and OptumRx. He was noticing in 2017 that pharmacies were reporting huge decreases in reimbursements and that profits were "cut in half overnight" because of pressure somewhere upstream in the supply chain and/or from Medicaid, a system that had no transparency. When Ciaccia investigated, the managed care plans (insurers that help manage the Medicaid benefits for Ohio) and Medicaid itself said nothing changed dramatically. The question remained: Where was the money going? He noted that lawmakers and Medicaid officials were of little help in resolving this problem, simply saying they had looked into it.

Over a two-year period, pharmacies saw a cut in gross margins of 60–80%. At the end of 2017, on average they were losing money on all Medicaid prescriptions. Ciaccia said that "pharmacies were dropping like flies . . . with a loss of 165 pharmacies." In an interesting and ironic twist, CVS Caremark later offered to buy the pharmacies as a solution to the challenge of lower margins because of lower reimbursements (an attempt at vertical integration). The bottom line was that because the state was paying high prices for Medicaid-reimbursed drugs while pharmacies were suffering, Ciaccia suspected spread pricing by the PBMs; they were "paying low, billing high, and pocketing the difference."

As part of his investigation into this situation, Ciaccia said the Ohio Assembly's Joint Medicaid Oversight Committee (2020) was reviewing spending for Medicaid-financed generic drugs and said it was actually increasing 1%, while at the same time pharmacies were seeing a 60–80% decrease in profits. This indicated to Ciaccia that there was indeed a spread pricing issue. Frustrated at the inaction by those he talked to, Ciaccia brought this information to *The Columbus Dispatch*, a local newspaper, in early 2018 (Candisky & Sullivan, 2018). This small story turned into 100 stories, editorials, and podcasts across the country and ultimately led to the Ohio Department of Medicaid doing a state audit under the guidance of State Auditor David Yost. The auditor found significant spread pricing that was going on with the PBMs, with generic drug spread pricing at 31% of gross generic drug spending for the Medicaid managed care system in Ohio. Specifically, the state identified $244 million in spread pricing from the second quarter of 2017 to the first quarter of 2018 (one year), and of that, $208 million of the spread was from generic drugs. This was a serious problem, but was it unique to Ohio?

Ciaccia began doing more extensive research and compared two very useful CMS databases: the National Average Drug Acquisition Cost (NADAC), which is the average pharmacy invoice price to acquire drugs (Centers for Medicare and Medicaid Services, 2020), and the State Drug Utilization Data (SDUD), which is what state Medicaid programs are being charged for the same drugs (Centers for Medicare and Medicaid Services, n.d.). Comparing these databases allowed for identification of likely cases of spread pricing for states across the country. Ciaccia also created a nonprofit, 46brooklyn (2019), to share his data and findings toward the broader goal of making drug pricing more understandable to the public. In short, the spread pricing by PBMs that he discovered in Ohio was actually happening in other states in a significant way. This was a broader phenomenon and market dysfunction because of a lack of transparency in the pharmaceutical supply chain at the level of the PBMs. What he uncovered in Ohio has now been covered broadly in the national media, including in *Bloomberg* and *The Wall Street Journal*. According to Ciaccia, other states that have found significant spread pricing include New York, which has the largest Medicaid managed care system in the United States, with 32% markups.

Then Ohio State Auditor Yost is now the attorney general in Ohio and is suing OptumRx for $16 million for overcharges in the Ohio Bureau of Workers' Compensation program (Candisky, 2019). Ciaccia noted that other attorneys general across the country are also considering legal action as significant spread pricing is being discovered in other states.

Conclusion

In summary, drug prices are a source of great public concern, especially for the very expensive biologics, specialty medicines, orphan drugs (for rare diseases), and infusibles. In some cases, these high prices may be justified, and we as a society have to figure out how to pay for them through some sort of insurance, whether private or based on Medicare Part D. In other cases, they reflect outright abuses, such as the abuse of pricing power enabled by patents or regulatory barriers, like FDA approval requirements. A classic example of this abuse might be the 5,000% markup of the drug Daraprim by Martin Shkreli of Turing Pharmaceuticals, which most feel was not justified based on value or on R&D spending (Beck, 2015). Abuses could also include the non-value-added activities of intermediaries that participate in price gauging or arbitrage using the rebate system, which is easily done when a system like the pharmaceutical supply chain lacks transparency. In the end, if 40% of the "cost" of drugs is occurring downstream of the pharmaceutical company that made the drug, those so-called Bermuda Triangle supply chain costs need to be addressed just as much as the high prices that pharmaceutical companies are charging.

Finally, while Democrats and Republicans alike consider some sort of price controls on drugs, we need to balance those considerations with their potential impact on funding the expensive drug development process that produces new medicines, as well as the access issues that could arise if expensive lifesaving drugs are no longer included on insurance- or government-based formularies. Possible ways of solving this are discussed in chapter 17.

CHAPTER 14

Pitfalls of Price Transparency in Healthcare—Especially for Pharmaceuticals

ROBERT GRABOYES

While other chapters of this book discuss the advantages of price transparency, this one points out that, while price transparency may be useful in some cases, such as where there are competitive markets, in other cases it can lead to price increases because of "tacit collusion." This happens when three conditions are met: (1) There are small numbers of providers, (2) there are large barriers to market entry (e.g., regulations), and (3) information about competitors' pricing is available. This scenario occurs in several places in the healthcare industry, including and especially for pharmaceuticals.

Background and Overview

Opaque healthcare prices rightfully frustrate Americans. Go to a hospital for some procedure, and total costs may drift into your mailbox piecemeal over a period of weeks or months. Even the most astute shoppers will have difficulty learning in advance the price of a common procedure, such as delivering a baby (Harris, 2016). "Surprise billing" means a patient may discover after-the-fact that a visit to the emergency room cost many times more than was anticipated beforehand.

Price opaqueness is commonly perceived as a key reason for the rapid rise of healthcare spending over the past generation or two. (We won't attempt to determine the veracity of that observation here.) From this angst arises a bipartisan notion of how to improve this situation: Require healthcare providers to publicly reveal prices. By this logic, informed consumers can do comparison shopping, as with automobiles or apples. Newly empowered purchasers will, the story goes, drive prices down. For this reason, price transparency in healthcare and the desirability of mandating it enjoys broad bipartisan support.

Robert Graboyes is a senior research fellow and healthcare scholar at the Mercatus Center at George Mason University.

However, under certain conditions—relatively common in American healthcare—mandatory price transparency and even voluntary price transparency can harm consumers and patients by pushing prices upward and leading to reduced supply of healthcare goods and services. The implications for public policy are profoundly important. It suggests applying transparency mandates with great caution and selectivity.

Following is the logical structure of this chapter:

- In a highly competitive market (many buyers and sellers, with easy entry for new sellers), transparent prices give sellers the incentive to lower prices to the point that profits are at the minimal level necessary to sustain the market. This is good for consumers and produces the maximum benefits to society ("total surplus" in economics lingo).
- In a market characterized by oligopoly (a small number of providers and high barriers preventing entry by new competitors), as is the case for pharmaceutical benefit managers (PBMs) and many pharmaceuticals, providers have an incentive to collude to increase prices and decrease output, thereby harming buyers and reducing total surplus. Explicit collusion is often illegal under antitrust laws.
- In an oligopolistic market (few sellers and high barriers to entry), price transparency can have the opposite effect of that seen in competitive markets. If the small number of sellers know the prices their competitors are charging, they can act as if they are colluding without actually doing so explicitly. In this process, called "tacit collusions" by economists and "conscious parallelism" by attorneys, the competitors will raise prices and reduce output without any need to communicate directly with one another. In this case, transparent prices effectively communicate the mutually beneficial strategy to the small number of sellers. In general, tacit collusion, unlike active collusion, does not violate antitrust laws.
- Tacit collusion works only if no seller has to guess its competitors' prices. Therefore, there is less motive to undercut one's competitors. Each seller knows that any attempt to undercut competitors to gain market share will provoke those competitors to respond with their own round of undercutting. Hence, the motive for each competitor is to keep prices high and stable.
- In a famous example, prices in Denmark's oligopolistic cement market rose after antitrust authorities began publishing the sellers' prices. In the United States, antitrust authorities have sometimes prohibited

sellers from posting their prices publicly, treating such transparency as at least bordering on active (illegal) collusion.

■ The healthcare sector in America is a mix of competitive and oligopolistic markets. While there are many drug companies, for example, specific therapeutic markets (specific conditions to be treated) often feature no more than two or three sellers. The same is true in the medical device space, as exemplified by news stories on epinephrine devices. In many communities, the markets for hospitals, insurers, specialty physicians, and in some cases, primary care physicians are highly concentrated. PBM companies are sweeping in breadth and impact and few in number.

■ Many or most federal laws mandating price transparency take broad-brush approaches—applying mandates to all firms in a sector. Such laws, then, are likely to push prices downward in competitive markets but upward in the oligopolistic markets. So, for example, a sweeping hospital price transparency law might lead to lower prices and greater output in an urban market with lots of hospitals but higher prices and lower output in a rural market with few hospitals.

■ Tacit collusion is not the only problem with mandatory price transparency. There is also the risk of "regulatory capture." Large, powerful sellers may influence policymakers to craft transparency regulations that disadvantage smaller rivals or aspiring market entrants. An example might be weighty paperwork requirements for which larger institutions, but not smaller competitors, are well suited.

■ In competitive markets, price transparency is unlikely to generate the price-increasing, output-decreasing dynamic seen in oligopolistic markets. Nevertheless, in competitive markets, transparency mandates may be disappointingly ineffective at lowering prices and increasing outputs. First, buyers may be relatively price-insensitive, either because they focus on other dimensions of care (familiarity with a particular doctor or hospital, for example) or because buyers do not actually feel the benefits of shopping around because someone else (e.g., an insurer or employer) ultimately pays the bill. Second, transparency will be relatively ineffective at prompting price-reduction if sellers' profit margins are already slim.

■ None of this means that price transparency is everywhere and anywhere a bad thing. In many circumstances, voluntary or mandatory transparency may, indeed, lead to the desired outcome—lower prices and higher output. The arguments presented here do suggest that policymakers should be highly selective in applying transparency—for example, crafting regulations whose effects are maximal on competitive markets and minimal on oligopolistic markets.

- Nor does this mean that policymakers need be passive or nihilistic in the face of excessively high prices and profits in specific markets. I do suggest here that, rather than mandating price transparency, more effective strategies might be found in public policies that lower barriers to entry into oligopolistic markets.

At this point, let us examine these issues in greater detail.

What Is Tacit Collusion, and Why Is It Important?

Price transparency need not lead to lower prices and/or happier consumers. This chapter focuses mostly on "tacit collusion"—competitors using publicly available price information to act as if they were conspiring together to raise prices—without actually doing so. Tacit collusion requires three ingredients: (1) a small number of competing producers, (2) substantial barriers to entry for aspiring producers wanting to enter the market, and (3) the capacity for producers to know their competitors' prices. In many healthcare markets, such as a wide variety of therapeutic markets for pharmaceuticals, the first two ingredients are already present. Often, the only thing missing for this undesirable phenomenon is mutual knowledge of competitors' prices.

Consider an American city with three competing hospitals. If the three CEOs agreed to share and coordinate prices, they would likely run afoul of antitrust laws. If the government required those same hospitals to publish prices publicly, the CEOs would not have to reach such an agreement. They would naturally move toward a collusive pricing arrangement without actually colluding.

In economics textbooks, the ideal situation—perfect competition—features many sellers, many buyers, highly standardized products, and publicly available prices. With perfect competition, market interactions reduce prices and expand output until the benefits to society reach their maximum feasible levels. In contrast, with monopoly, the lone seller can raise prices and constrict output to maximize profits. The resulting reduction in society's benefits is called "deadweight loss."

An intermediate case is oligopoly, where the number of producers is small but more than one. If oligopolists undercut one another, they could in the extreme drive prices down and output up to the levels that would hold under perfect competition. In contrast, oligopolists who form an effective cartel can, in theory, replicate or nearly replicate the prices and outputs that would prevail under monopoly, with deadweight loss equal or close to that under monopoly. Enforcing cartel agreements is difficult, however. Some producers secretly underbid competitors and sell more output than agreed-on levels. Then, prices, outputs, and deadweight loss fall somewhere between the perfect competition and monopoly situations. American antitrust law generally treats active collusion between competitors as a conspiracy against the public because of this negative impact on consumers and the economy.

If producers can act as if they were conspiring but without communicating with one another, they can replicate the collusive case and obtain the financial benefits of price fixing, without violating antitrust laws. This is tacit collusion. While the law may treat active and tacit collusion differently, economics, for the most part, does not. Where one draws the line between active and tacit collusion is often the subject of litigation.

Collusion—active or tacit—is difficult to maintain once the number of sellers grows beyond a handful. With larger numbers, it becomes likely that some competitors will undercut others. Low barriers to entry also hamper collusion because if profits are unusually high, outsiders will seek to enter the market. High barriers to entry, like the extensive Food and Drug Administration (FDA) regulations that control drug approval, make collusion easier. Collusion is also difficult to maintain if producers cannot carefully monitor the prices charged by competitors.

As Stühmeier (2014) notes, the commonsense logic that price transparency allows consumers to push prices downward is not wrong in the case of tacit collusion. The problem is that consumers' downward pressure can be overwhelmed by the colluding producers' upward pressure.

More complete explanations of the economics of competition, monopoly, and oligopoly can be found in almost any microeconomics textbook, such as Mankiw (2018). The classic presentation of oligopoly is found in Stigler (1964).

What Are Some Real-World Examples of Tacit Collusion?

A frequently cited example of tacit collusion is the 1990s Danish concrete manufacturers. The number of manufacturers was small and the barriers to entry were high. In 1993, Denmark's Competition Council (antitrust agency) began collecting price data and posting them publicly—ostensibly to increase competition by encouraging comparative shopping. After the data became public, concrete prices rose by 15–20%. In the classic study of this case, Albaek et al. (2015) could find no causal factors for these price increases other than tacit collusion. They concluded that the Competition Council "unwittingly" reduced competition by mandating price transparency. According to Schultz (2002), the Danish government eventually acknowledged that price transparency can underlie such perverse results.

In the United States, a commonly cited example is the federal court case of *White v. R. M. Packer Co., Inc.* (2011). This case revolved around gasoline pricing on Martha's Vineyard, Massachusetts. The court determined that gas prices on the island averaged $0.56 more than on the mainland—$0.21 from the added costs of transporting fuel to the island and $0.35 apparently deriving from oligopoly power. Plaintiffs argued that this premium resulted from collusion, but the court ruled that this premium resulted from tacit collusion rather than active conspiracy, with no violation of antitrust laws.

Martha's Vineyard had a few gas station operators, strict regulatory barriers against new operators, and perfect mutual knowledge of competitors' pricing behavior (since gas prices are listed in large numbers on marquees). Each operator knows that if they attempt to lower prices, competitors will instantly respond. Thus, station operators can adhere to an unwritten, unspoken agreement to restrict output and raise prices—to the detriment of consumers. Byrne and De Roos (2019) examined similar circumstances among gasoline stations in Western Australia. While they could not rule out explicit collusion, it appeared more likely that tacit collusion prevailed over many years.

What Does All of This Have to Do With Healthcare?

Garthwaite (2019) uses the Martha's Vineyard case to explain tacit collusion in pharmaceutical markets. While there are quite a few drug manufacturers, he notes, specific therapeutic markets often have few producers and substantial barriers to entry. But, he says, "The pharmaceutical market . . . currently lacks the third important market condition for tacit collusion— publicly posted and verifiable prices. Instead, prices in this market are kept deliberately confidential. This likely increases competition because it makes it hard for firms to monitor secret deviations from tacit collusion." The third condition, Garthwaite argues, could be provided by a law or regulation mandating public disclosure of discounts agreed on in contracts between drug manufacturers and PBMs—say, prohibiting the private rebates common to such contracts. The U.S. Department of Health and Human Services (2019) proposed such a mandate.

A U.S. Federal Trade Commission blog (Koslov & Jex, 2015) posed the question as "Price Transparency or TMI?"—TMI reflecting the popular expression "too much information." The post asked, "Is more information about prices always a good thing for consumers and competition?" The report's reply was, "Too much transparency can harm competition in any market, including in health care markets."

How Much of Healthcare Is Characterized by Oligopoly and Barriers to Entry?

Medical Professions

Fulton (2017) wrote, "In 2016, 90 percent of Metropolitan Statistical Areas (MSAs) were highly concentrated for hospitals, 65 percent for specialist physicians, 39 percent for primary care physicians, and 57 percent for insurers." Pauly (2019) notes that many markets for medical specialists are highly concentrated. In their comprehensive overview of healthcare staffing, Flier and Rhoads (2018) discuss barriers to entry in the medical professions, including restrictive medical licensure and specific barriers for foreign medical graduates. Barriers include the academic requirements for admission to medical school and the costs of medical education (National Center for Education Statistics, 2018). Other barriers include state controls over the number of medical school slots and the difficulties in obtaining residencies (Association of American Medical Colleges, 2018). These barriers, and possible solutions, are discussed further in chapter 7 of this book.

Hospitals

Hospital markets, too, are often characterized by small numbers of institutions. One reason is the presence of certificate of need (CON) laws, whose history Mitchell and Koopman (2016) reviewed. Pauly (2019) writes that the Hirschman-Herfindahl Index (HHI) for hospital markets in the United State rose from 2,340 in 1987 to 3,161 in 2006. An HHI above 2,500 triggers concerns at the U.S Department of Justice's antitrust division.

Pharmaceuticals

In pharmaceutical markets, the biggest barrier to entry is likely the enormous cost of gaining approval from the FDA. DiMasi, Grabowski, and Hansen (2016) write that this process can take more than a decade and can cost nearly $2.56 billion ($2.87 billion with post-approval R&D costs). Musgrave (2006) wrote that in many therapeutic markets (e.g., cardiovascular treatments, antibiotics, diabetic therapy, psychostimulants), market concentration is high. For most Americans, drug benefits are managed by PBMs. According to Werble (2017), "In 2014 the top three PBMs managed pharmacy benefits for over 180 million lives—about 80 percent of the total number covered by PBMs."

Insurance

In the Affordable Care Act (ACA) insurance marketplaces, the Commonwealth Fund reports that five states had only one insurance issuer; 20 states had two to three issuers; and 26 states had four or more issuers (Gabel et al., 2018).

Summing up, many American healthcare markets have the first two ingredients for tacit collusion—small numbers of suppliers and significant barriers to entry. In such markets, price transparency, mandatory or voluntary, can potentially provide that third ingredient.

What Are Other Potential Problems With Mandatory Transparency?

The focus of this chapter has been tacit collusion, but there are other reasons why mandatory price transparency might be ineffective in or counterproductive to lowering healthcare prices.

First, transparency may have little effect on consumer behavior. Capretta (2019) explores why consumers may not be inclined or able to engage in price shopping. Desai et al. (2016) found online healthcare price transparency tools had little effect at two large employers. Jenkins (2019) noted the indecipherability of mandated data and sharp disconnect between reported prices and patients' out-of-pocket expenses. Gorke (2019) writes that "standard" prices rendered transparent are relatively useless for consumers to make meaningful comparisons but may engender tacit collusion.

Second, laws and regulations designed to make data more comprehensible to consumers may force producers into inefficient business models. Emanuel et al. (2012) proposed "full transparency" as a way to rein in prices. Their idea would have mandated standardized bundled prices that could become de facto tying arrangements (multiple goods and services that can only be sold as a package). Goldhill (2013), in contrast, explains the virtues of ever-changing provider-determined bundles. Bryant (2017), a Texas anesthesiologist, addressed this problem in testimony before the state's Senate Health and Human Services Committee.

Third, in some areas of healthcare, risk-adjusted profit margins are thinner than commonly perceived, leaving less room for downward pressure on prices than is commonly perceived. For example, Danzon (2000) writes, "There is the general belief that drug prices are simply 'too high'—that the pharmaceutical industry is making excessive profits. . . . These bits of conventional wisdom may be conventional but they are not wisdom." If Danzon's assertion is correct—that drug prices reflect actual underlying costs and not excess profits—then transparency will be relatively powerless to exert downward pressure on prices.

Fourth, there is the problem of regulatory capture. Someone has to write the rules for transparency, and there is the risk or likelihood that large, established providers will steer lawmakers toward rules that put potential market entrants at a disadvantage. (An example might be heavy paperwork requirements that are manageable for large institutions but not for small ones.)

What Should Policymakers Do?

Nothing here implies that healthcare prices are what they ought to be or that consumers have adequate knowledge of prices. Nothing here implies that policymakers cannot take positive steps that will result in lower prices. The message here is simply that troweling transparency laws and regulations over the healthcare sector may not be particularly effective at accomplishing that goal and, quite often, may result in the exact opposite—higher prices.

One can do well by recalling the words of H. L. Mencken in 1917: "There is always a well-known solution to every human problem—neat, plausible, and wrong," and of Hippocrates: "First, do no harm" (Rentoul, 2016).

In a memo on its website, the Federal Trade Commission advised the state of Minnesota that then-recent transparency legislation could "chill competition" by facilitating or increasing the likelihood of unlawful collusion, and may also undermine "the effectiveness of selective contracting by health plans," which serve to reduce health care costs and improve overall value in the delivery of health care services in Minnesota (Koslov & Jex, 2015).

The Martha's Vineyard example offers valuable lessons for policymakers, and we can frame the options in terms of the three ingredients for tacit collusion—small numbers of providers, high barriers to entry, and mutual knowledge of competitors' pricing strategies. In this case, mandating transparency is not a valuable option, such prices are already posted in large numbers on every gas station marquee. Antitrust law sometimes *prohibits* transparency. Cutler and Dafny (2011) cite a case from the 1960s and 1970s in which competitors in the turbine market published "price books." The

Justice Department viewed this as a tacit attempt to raise prices, and the books were abandoned as part of a deal with the antitrust authorities. But prohibiting gas stations from posting their prices is obviously not a viable solution.

Rather than focusing on the third ingredient, Martha's Vineyard authorities might instead focus on the second ingredient—lowering barriers to entry. Island regulations made it nearly impossible for new entrants to open stations on the island. Without such barriers, the high profitability of island stations would attract new entrants, thereby increasing the number of competitors.

In healthcare, too, lowering barriers to entry can be a highly productive way of reducing the price of care. Mandating transparency in contracts between insurers and drug manufacturers may result in higher prices through tacit collusion. (No need to bid low when you already know what your competitor charges.) Lower barriers to entry may be a better response. In the case of pharmaceuticals, that can mean lightening the burden involved in obtaining approval for new drugs from the FDA. Van Norman (2016) writes that "new drug and device approval in the United States take an average of 12 and 7 years, respectively, from pre-clinical testing to approval." DiMasi et al. (2016) estimated that the cost of this process for drugs averages between $2.6 billion and $2.9 billion. Furthermore, "today, the United States has among the most stringent regulations regarding medical drug and device development and marketing" (Van Norman, 2016). Rather than mandating price transparency, policymakers might wish to focus on reducing the time period, costs, and uncertainty involved in the FDA approval process.

America's healthcare sector is chock-full of barriers to entry. This galaxy of barriers can provide policymakers with innumerable opportunities to help drive prices down without compromising the quality of care. Possibilities include the following:

- Making it easier to gain approval for new drugs or devices from the FDA
- Making it easier for physicians and other healthcare professionals to obtain licenses in individual states
- Making it easier for immigrants and Americans with degrees from foreign universities to obtain licenses
- Increasing the number of slots in medical schools and allied health professional programs

- Increasing the number of medical school residencies
- Altering the compensation schemes enshrined under the Medicare reimbursement methodologies
- Allowing physician assistants, nurse practitioners, nurse anesthetists, optometrists, opticians, pharmacists, dental hygienists, addiction counselors, psychologists, midwives, licensed professional counselors, and other allied health professionals to practice autonomously and up to the limits of their training
- Lowering restrictions on alternative business models, such as direct primary care
- Enabling public and private insurers to reimburse patients who choose to receive care outside of the United States
- Reducing special taxes on providers of care
- Allowing greater use of telemedicine, telepsychiatry, telepsychology, teleoptometry, online prescribing, and other technologies for providing care at a distance
- Eliminating CON requirements for hospitals and other providers
- Allowing greater use of specialty hospitals, ambulatory surgical centers, and freestanding emergency rooms
- Enabling drones (unmanned aerial vehicles) to transport blood supplies, drugs, defibrillators, and other medical goods
- Developing more portable and therapy-driven electronic health records
- Enabling providers to adopt lean manufacturing methods
- Eliminating corporate practice of medicine (CPOM) laws that restrict providers' business models

And, no doubt, there are roles to play for greater price transparency. Cutler and Dafny (2011), who provide ample warning of excessive faith in transparency initiatives, are not nihilists in this regard. They recommend, for example, mandatory disclosure of broad price data, such as plan-specific patient co-payments and *average* reimbursement rates across all payers—while shrouding certain information on low prices. The latter limitation would make it more difficult for competitors to see exactly what sort of price negotiations a specific firm is undertaking. In this way, consumers gain greater information while leaving producers with motives to undercut one another.

It should be noted that "price transparency" is a somewhat amorphous term whose meaning depends on whom you ask. One can see this by surveying the dozens of transparency bills offered in the 116th Congress

(2019–2020), many or most of which had bipartisan cosponsorship. Among the most expansive is H.R.1409 (Perlmutter, 2019), which specifies:

> Any and all individuals or business entities, including hospitals, physicians, nurses, pharmacies, pharmaceutical manufacturers, dentists, and the insurance entities . . . and any other healthcare related providers or issuers that offer or furnish healthcare related items, products, services, or procedures (as defined by the Secretary of Health and Human Services) for sale to the public shall publicly disclose, on a continuous basis, all prices for such items, products, services, or procedures in accordance with this section.

Other bills are more narrowly focused. For example, S.474 (Wyden, 2019) is limited to drug prices, S.1895 (Alexander, 2019) to surprise billing, and H.R. 3965 (Lipinski, 2019) to hospital price. State laws also vary widely on what they mean by "price transparency" (National Conference of State Legislature, 2019).

In summary, mandatory price transparency may have its place in the policymaker's tool kit, but it is wisely applied surgically, to highly specific markets and datasets, rather than slathered on broadly on the assumption that all transparency is good. And policymakers would do well to look at lowering entry barriers to healthcare markets, rather than focusing so heavily on price transparency.

CHAPTER 15

The Orphan Drug Act
A 30-Year Perspective on Lifesaving FDA Regulations

ANNE MARIE FINLEY

Orphan drugs are drugs developed and used to treat rare diseases. This chapter presents how the Orphan Drug Act, and subsequent regulations and initiatives of the Food and Drug Administration (FDA), have led to a dramatic increase in the number of new drugs developed to treat rare diseases. While in some cases the cost of these drugs is quite high, because the populations of patients treated are relatively small (< 200,000 and sometimes only in the hundreds), often this cost is mitigated because treatments are acute and cost can be spread out. Earlier chapters in section 3 discussed the causes of high drug prices for orphan drugs, including cases where high cost may be justified (chapter 12). Chapter 16 provides additional perspective and a discussion of the impact of FDA regulations on getting lifesaving drugs to patients.

Background

In 1983, at the urging of thousands of rare disease patients, the United States Congress passed the Orphan Drug Act (ODA), a landmark piece of legislation designed to foster development of drugs for rare diseases, defined in statute as affecting fewer than 200,000 patients in the United States.

Congress identified the enormous public health problem of rare diseases and their lack of treatments because of patent expirations on potential therapies, lack of pharmaceutical company interest in development of drugs with perceived small markets, and lack of knowledge about most rare diseases by clinicians. The ODA provided seven years of market exclusivity as well as research and development tax credits to spur pharmaceutical development for rare disease therapies. While there may be fewer than 200,000 patients with a given rare disease, there are a large number of rare diseases, and it had become a common frustration among patients with these diseases that

Anne Marie Finley, MS, RAC, is a former policymaker with 25 years of experience at the Food and Drug Administration, the Department of Health and Human Services, and Congress.

the pharmaceutical industry was not prioritizing the development of new drugs to treat them. The ODA was passed to address this problem.

Approval Rates for Orphan Drugs in the United States Have Greatly Improved Since 1983

In the decade before the passage of the Orphan Drug Act, fewer than 10 therapies were approved for rare diseases by the FDA (Lanthier, 2017). Since then, the agency has approved over 770 drugs for rare disease indications (PhRMA, n.d.). Specific FDA programs combined have facilitated development of many new treatments for unmet medical needs, including (a) the FDA orphan products development grants, (b) FDA user fee waivers for orphan drugs, (c) specific rare disease therapy development guidance, and (d) the protocol assistance offered by the Office of Orphan Products Development (OOPD).

In 2019, 21 of the FDA's 48 new molecular entity (i.e., new drug) approvals were for orphan drugs to treat rare diseases, nearly 44% of the total numbers of drugs approved by the agency last year. FDA approved more than twice as many novel orphan drugs from 2012 to 2019 than in the previous eight-year period from 2004 to 2011—142 versus 63, a 125% increase (Woodcock, 2020). The ODA, and subsequent FDA programs, seem to have had their desired effect of increasing the development of new treatments for rare diseases.

The Public Health Impact of Rare Diseases Remains Vast, Unmet, and Poorly Understood, but Better Quantified and Addressed Now Than in Previous Decades

The science of rare disease research is not static and the public health impact of rare diseases is staggering. When I started my career in orphan drug development in 1988, the federal government estimated 20 million Americans had rare diseases. Now we know that the actual numbers are much higher at 25 million to 30 million Americans, approximately 1 in 10 (FAQs About Rare Diseases, 2017).

The Department of Health and Human Services (HHS) then estimated the number of rare diseases at 5,000 (National Institutes of Health, 1990). Now, the number is estimated at closer to 7,000 rare diseases, with an estimated 80% recognized as having a genetic cause (FAQs About Rare Diseases, 2017).

In additional to orphan drug eligibility, accurate prevalence numbers determine recognition of the impact of the unmet medical needs on patients with rare diseases and spur patient advocacy, public policy incentives, clinical interest, and drug development efforts.

Similar advances in rare disease etiology and natural history, formerly unknown in many rare disease indications and often supported by the National Institutes of Health (NIH) National Center for Advancing Translational Sciences (NCATS), have advanced successful development of orphan drugs.

Industry Progress Is Impressive but Outmatched by Medical Need

For millions of American patients with poorly treated or untreatable diseases, the pharmaceutical industry holds the key to their future. Currently, there are more than 560 medicines in development for rare diseases (PhRMA, 2016). That is an encouraging number from an industry whose trade association opposed the passage of the Orphan Drug Act (ODA) in 1983 (Mikami, 2019). Regrettably, only 5% of rare diseases have even one treatment today (Global Genes, n.d.).

The incentives of the ODA have led directly to the establishment of numerous drug companies including Alexion, Amgen, BioMarin, Celgene, Genentech, Genzyme, and Ultragenyx, which were founded to develop new therapies for rare diseases and have successfully brought many orphan drugs to market. In addition, many larger pharmaceutical companies such as Pfizer, Novartis, and Johnson & Johnson have established rare disease research programs and divisions (Statista, 2019). The resulting economic boon in therapeutic development, employment, and economic development has been of incalculable benefit to patients, shareholders, employees, and local, state, and federal governments alike and can be directly attributed to the ODA.

Myopic Focus on Drug Pricing Obscures the Unique Orphan Drug Challenges

The inclusion of orphan drugs in the drug pricing debate has often been disingenuous and inaccurate. Certainly, expensive drugs for some rare disease patients (exceeding $100,000 per patient per year) have been concerns for decades, starting with the price controversies of the late 1980s and early 1990s surrounding human growth hormone, EPO, and Gaucher enzyme replacement therapy.

However, the challenges and related expenses in research and development of rare disease therapies are often poorly described. The Tufts University Center for Drug Development cited the following orphan drug research and development challenges as responsible for significant development delays: "variability in expression, severity, and/or course of the disease; geographically dispersed population; small population; selecting among multiple pathways; lack of endpoints and outcome measures; required flexibility in regulatory decision making; biology of disease not understood; natural history of disease not well known; and translating new knowledge into useful knowledge" (Redfearn, 2018).

Tufts concluded that "orphan drug development takes 15.1 years to go from first patent filing to product launch, 18 percent longer than the average time required for all new drugs, . . . And development time for drugs to treat ultra-orphan diseases—which affect only a few hundred patients in the U.S.—is even longer: 17.2 years" (Redfearn, 2018).

Spreading the Cost of Expensive Orphan Drugs

Unlike many drugs for more common conditions, the chronicity of rare diseases, and the fewer number of patients over whom the development costs may be spread, often renders the treatment more expensive. This, of course, has raised public concern over high drug prices. However, a few patients taking a more expensive drug can have minimal impact on the overall drug spend of a health plan, in comparison to expensive therapies that are used by more patients for more common diseases, such as hepatitis C drugs.

Minimal Abuse of Orphan Drug Pricing

The National Organization for Rare Disorders (NORD), an umbrella organization of 280 member patient advocacy organizations, stated in a 2018 report on orphan drug pricing, "Some recent media stories have questioned whether drug makers may be manipulating the ODA to benefit in ways that were not originally intended. NORD appreciates the important watchdog role of the press and supports ongoing vigilance against misuse of the ODA. Based on data available to date, NORD believes the ODA has generally been used appropriately—and to the benefit of patients—over the years" (National Organization for Rare Disorders, 2018).

Patients Are Now Significant Players in Drug Development and Product Review

Helpful Government Regulations and Laws

As a congressional oversight investigator at HHS in the late 1990s, I frequently worked on facilitating patient interaction with federal agencies, which included supporting roles for patients and patient organizations on

FDA, NIH, and HHS advisory committees and advancing NIH research in critical rare disease areas.

In the last decade, very effective rare disease patient lobbying has prompted Congress to use legislation to effect changes in rare disease research and orphan drug decision-making at HHS. The 21st Century Cures Act, signed into law in 2016, and the reauthorization of the Prescription Drug User Fee Act, notably PDUFA V in 2012, have provided important platforms for patient issues to be recognized by the federal government.

In 2012, the FDA announced the Patient-Focused Drug Development (PFDD) initiative to "more systematically obtain the patient perspective on specific diseases and their currently available treatments. PFDD meetings are unique among FDA public meetings, with a format designed to engage patients and elicit their perspectives on two topic areas: (1) the most significant symptoms of their condition and the impact of the condition on daily life, and (2) their current approaches to treatment" (FDA, 2020). The FDA held several workshops and over 30 meetings with individual patient organizations to identify key endpoints and data of value to patients to include in clinical trials, and it continues to develop regulatory plans to use real-world data (RWD) and real-world evidence (RWE) provided by patients in clinical trial designs (FDA, 2020).

Grassroots Patient Advocacy and Entrepreneurialism

Unable to wait for academic and pharmaceutical company interest in their diseases, patients and their families have also launched research networks in Castleman disease, Duchenne muscular dystrophy, hereditary hemorrhagic telangiectasia, and Phelan-McDermid syndrome, among many others. In addition to raising funds for studies, patients have led organizations to develop patient registries, conduct natural history studies, and establish tissue registries to advance further knowledge and study of their diseases.

In the past 20 years, rare disease patients and family members have even founded pharmaceutical companies to develop promising orphan drugs. Akashi Therapeutics, Amicus Therapeutics, Envoy Therapeutics, Exigence Neurosciences, Intellimedix, and Lysogene were founded by patient families for the purposes of advancing therapies in Duchenne muscular dystrophy, Pompe disease, ataxia-telangiectasia, Dravet syndrome, and Sanfilippo syndrome.

Nicole Boice, founder of Global Genes, said, "People with rare diseases are an impatient group because they have to be. Time is a luxury patients and families can't afford, and 10 years is sadly more than a lifetime for many.

As such, even the dizzying pace at which scientific advances are being made today can still seem plodding to the thousands of rare disease communities without approved treatments" (Global Genes, 2019).

Conclusion

This is without doubt the "golden age" of rare disease research and orphan drug development, at least in comparison to the three previous decades since passage of the ODA in 1983. There have never been more drugs in development for unmet medical needs and more coordination and commitment between patients, pharmaceutical companies, policymakers, academics, and government researchers and regulators. There is an old ad campaign sponsored by the pharmaceutical industry with the tagline "The Patient Is Waiting." For some fortunate patients, the wait may be over, but for the remaining 95% of rare disease patients without a single treatment, the wait may be interminable. The Orphan Drug Act, and various government programs within and outside of the FDA, has played an important role in these exciting and lifesaving advances.

In the next 30 years, I hope we all work harder to achieve more collaborative research, successful clinical trials, flexible regulation, and appropriate reimbursement of therapies for as many of the 7,000 rare diseases as we can.

CHAPTER 16

How Outdated FDA Overregulation Is Limiting Patient Access to the Next Generation of Treatments

NAOMI LOPEZ-BAUMAN AND CHRISTINA SANDEFUR

Chapter 15 presented how the Orphan Drug Act and subsequent Food and Drug Administration (FDA) regulations and programs had the beneficial effect of increasing the number of new drugs in the physician's toolbox for treating rare diseases. This chapter presents the other side of the regulatory coin, where well-intentioned regulations actually get in the way of delivering lifesaving therapies. In truth, since the Orphan Drug Act worked to simplify regulatory approval for orphan drugs, there is a common theme in both chapters of adjusting regulations to fit the science and medical needs, simplifying them when it makes sense. FDA regulations exist to ensure drugs are safe and efficacious, and that is good. But overregulation also has unintended bad consequences, as this chapter presents. As observed in chapter 3, well-intentioned regulations (in that case, on quality) can sometimes cause more harm than good. An additional lesson from the 2020 coronavirus pandemic is that, in unusual circumstances, there need to be faster routes to drug approvals—balanced against safety concerns. This chapter presents an argument for expanding "Right to Try" legislation to permit more ready access to personalized medicine therapeutics, like gene-targeted therapies tailored to individual patients.

A Story to Illustrate the Problem

Identical twin sisters Alex and Jaci Hermstad both developed symptoms from a rare form of amyotrophic lateral sclerosis (ALS), but at different times in their young lives. Alex first developed symptoms at the young age of 11 and died in 2011 at age 17. Last year Jaci, 25 years old and facing significant deterioration as a result of the disease, obtained an "n-of-1" treatment (i.e., she is the only patient in the treatment trial) that targets the gene mutation that causes her ALS.

Naomi Lopez-Bauman is the director of Healthcare Policy at the Goldwater Institute. Christina Sandefur is the executive vice president of the Goldwater Institute.

The treatment is a custom-designed antisense oligonucleotide (ASO) therapy made specifically for Jaci and is based on her individual genetic profile. Many would argue that if it weren't for the help of the congressional representative from her district, Steve King, other lawmakers in Congress from both sides of the political aisle, and national media attention, the FDA might not have expedited and approved her appeal to access this treatment that was not yet under Phase 1 FDA clinical review. FDA approval of a new drug treatment is normally a long and expensive process.

For Americans like the several thousand diagnosed and currently living with ALS, the drug approval system is broken. It blocks Americans from potentially lifesaving medicines and treatments until those treatments receive final FDA approval. But it takes an average of 14 years and $1.4 billion (with some estimates higher) for a drug to make its way through the clinical trial process and obtain FDA approval (President's Council of Advisors on Science and Technology, 2012; Tufts Center for the Study of Drug Development, 2014). This is time that dying patients do not have. Patients suffer in limbo, with no say in their own destinies. All of this occurs even though one of the foundational principles of medical ethics is patient autonomy: decisions about healthcare are ultimately for the *patient* to make.

Fortunately, a new law called Right to Try is starting to change things. Another ALS patient, former U.S. Navy pilot Matt Bellina, used the federal Right to Try law last year to access a treatment, NurOwn, that is currently in Phase 3 FDA-regulated clinical trials. Note that drugs cannot normally be used broadly in the clinic until after they have been through Phase 3 clinical trials and subsequently approved by the FDA.

Signed into federal law in 2018, Right to Try protects the right of terminally ill patients to try a medicine that has received basic safety approval (Phase 1) from the FDA—and that is being given to patients in ongoing clinical trials (typically Phases 2 and 3)—but that has not yet received final New Drug Application (NDA) approval for sale. Right to Try is saving lives and allowing people to have a say in their own destinies. It is a declaration that people should be able to decide for themselves—in consultation with their doctors—whether to try medicines that could prolong or even save their lives. It is a basic human right to fight for one's life.

Today, however, many of the newest treatments are personalized for the individual patient. A small handful of individualized treatments are now in FDA clinical trials. While there are a growing number of personalized treatments that target a specific genetic mutation, for example, personalized treatments are custom-designed for the individual patient. In addition to

ASO therapies, other "n of 1" therapies include some stem cell therapies and neoantigen-directed therapies. These are challenging, because FDA regulations were originally designed for clinical trials with hundreds or even thousands of patients (especially Phase 3), not for single patient trials.

Right to Try—which is available to patients only after a treatment has passed the FDA's basic safety testing in Phase 1 and remains in clinical review but has not received final FDA approval—would not generally apply to today's newer, individual treatments because only a small handful have even reached Phase 1 trials. Furthermore, the current clinical trial system for these individual treatments by definition lacks a separate, stand-alone safety threshold. Because no two patients receive the same exact treatment, safety and efficacy are "tested" simultaneously—and only on that individual patient.

But patients seeking personalized treatments are no less in need of prompt access to lifesaving medicines. At the same time, establishing that a personalized treatment is safe primarily has consequences for that individual, rather than for a broader population. Therefore, extending Right to Try to individualized patient treatments in the extreme case of what is called "personalized medicine" is both imperative and sensible, and it should be on the policy agendas of every state and federal lawmaker.

Decades-Old Regulatory Bureaucracy

At their inception, federal drug regulations focused on ensuring that drug products marketed to the public at large were safe and correctly labeled (Pure Food and Drug Act, 1906) so that patients had truthful information to make informed decisions about the medicines they were going to take. The law did not require manufacturers to submit information to the FDA as a prerequisite to marketing. Then, in 1938, Congress passed the Federal Food, Drug, and Cosmetic Act, requiring manufacturers to prove that a drug was safe *before* marketing (21 U.S.C. § 301). Still, the law did not require federal evaluation of *efficacy*, only of safety.

Gradually, however, federal law shifted from a focus on empowering patients to a more paternalistic approach—one that in practice is often preoccupied with erecting roadblocks. This reached fruition in the 1962 Kefauver-Harris Drug Amendments to the Federal Food, Drug, and Cosmetic Act, which required manufacturers to provide "substantial evidence" that the drug is effective for its intended use (Drug Amendments Act, 1962). These amendments were passed in reaction to the infamous incident involving thalidomide, a sleep aid sometimes prescribed to pregnant women as a treatment for morning sickness that was found to cause birth defects.

Kefauver-Harris imposed new rules for preapproval of medicines, including new standards for investigating new drugs for both safety and efficacy.

* * *

Yet that law was not matched to the concerns raised by the thalidomide incident. Thalidomide posed a *safety* problem, not an efficacy problem, and thalidomide had not been approved in the United States because of lingering safety concerns (Madara, 2009). Only 17 of the more than 10,000 worldwide cases of children with thalidomide-related birth defects occurred in the United States (Bren, 2001), and American consumers had been protected under the safety rules that were already on the books.

Nevertheless, thanks to the 1962 Drug Amendments, today's FDA tests are not just for safety but also for efficacy (21 U.S.C. § 355(d) (2012)). And these two things are quite different, both scientifically and ethically. Nobody wants to take an unsafe medicine, but many patients are willing to try one that has not yet been proved to work—that is, to show "efficacy," which is normally established in the large Phase 3 clinical trials.

It is not even entirely true that nobody wants to take unsafe drugs. Chemotherapy, after all, is not *safe*, in the sense that it is technically poison. Even acetaminophen kills hundreds of people per year. In some states, terminal patients have the option of ending their lives with a physician's help, if they choose. The fact that these patients have the right to *end* their lives but *not* to take medicines that might *cure* them or alleviate their suffering, presuming they are told and they understand the risks, is just one of the many tragic paradoxes of our overly bureaucratic drug-regulation system.

The FDA evaluates potential drugs and treatments under a multistep process that—after basic research and animal testing have been completed—consists of three phases and sometimes more. To simplify what is often a complicated system, Phase 1 consists of basic safety evaluations in a clinical trial consisting of about 100 people (U.S. Food and Drug Administration, 2018). Only about 70% of drugs pass this phase. Phase 2, which can take up to two years, assesses efficacy in addition to safety and involves about 100 to 300 people. Again, only about a third of medicines survive this stage. Phase 3 tests the drug predominantly for efficacy against placebos as well as the currently available treatments, and these trials generally consist of 300 to 3,000 test subjects. These tests can take up to four years, and only about a quarter of drugs survive this round of testing due to financial constraints, safety, or efficacy. For some drugs, there is yet another phase of clinical trials (Congressional Budget Office, 2006). Of course, in one sense the testing is never completed because the FDA continues to monitor drugs for safety as long as they are available on the market, and sometimes withdraws them years after final approval. As the FDA admits, "There is never 100% certainty when determining reasonable assurance of safety and effectiveness" (U.S. Food and Drug Administration, 2015).

Nevertheless, until the multistage testing process is completed—until the FDA approves a drug for sale—pharmaceutical manufacturers may not sell it. And because these stages of approval can take so long, patients often find themselves blocked from using medicines that had not only passed basic safety but were being administered to other patients in Phase 3 or Phase 4 clinical trials. As a result, countless patients would suffer and die, unable to access medicines that could help them and that the FDA considers safe enough to administer to those patients fortunate enough to be allowed into clinical trials.

Recognizing the inhumanity of this system, the FDA has made exceptions to its own rules. Under the so-called compassionate use or Expanded Access program, it has allowed people to obtain preapproval access to medications outside of a clinical trial. But these exceptions are applied inequitably, on a case-by-case basis, and the process is extremely cumbersome and time-consuming. The paperwork required to seek Expanded Access can take dozens of hours to complete and requires doctors to obtain information that is often inaccessible, such as technical or proprietary data on the drug, which may not be available to the doctor. And to administer the treatment under Expanded Access, the doctor must abide by burdensome protocols and data-reporting requirements, essentially making the doctor responsible for overseeing (and often funding) a miniature clinical trial for a single patient. Additionally, a separate committee at a hospital or medical clinic, called an Institutional Review Board (IRB), must weigh the ethical considerations associated with the patient's use of the treatment. Because there are no requirements on how often IRBs must meet or how quickly they must respond to these requests, people in rural areas or without a major university hospital nearby can have few IRB options, which adds more time and delay to the process. These and other complications mean that only about 1,200 patients per year are even able to submit compassionate use requests to the FDA (Flatten, 2016)—even though over half a million Americans die annually of cancer alone (American Cancer Society, 2015). This regulatory labyrinth clashes with the principle of patient autonomy. Often, in the name of helping the patient with well-intentioned regulations, the system undermines individual choice and personal dignity, cedes deeply personal decisions to bureaucrats, and leaves patients to suffer.

A New Way: The Right to Try

Decades of trying to change this system from within met with little success. That changed in 2014 when the Goldwater Institute—a free market public policy and litigation organization—partnered with patients, doctors, and activists to take the movement to protect patient autonomy to the states. The Right to Try movement blossomed—a genuine grassroots reform that was ultimately passed by 41 states in only four years. Then, in 2018, what seemed impossible became reality when President Donald Trump signed the federal Right to Try Act (formally known as the Trickett Wendler, Frank Mongiello, Jordan McLinn, and Matthew Bellina Right to Try Act of 2018).

In one sense, Right to Try is a conservative reform. It simply extends to all terminal patients the same option of trying investigational treatments that the FDA already allows to the fortunate few who are accepted into clinical trials or who are granted Expanded Access. Right to Try applies only to terminally ill patients and only to medicines that have passed the FDA's Phase 1 clinical trial safety testing and that are being administered to patients in later FDA-approved clinical trials as part of the subsequent phases of testing. If a treatment is withdrawn from FDA-approved clinical trials, it also becomes unavailable under Right to Try. And if a treatment has not received initial safety approval, it is not eligible.

But in another sense, Right to Try represents a major change. Before it was enacted, the federal system barred dying patients from potentially lifesaving treatments unless they were able to contribute to a scientific research study-experiment on terms set by the FDA. Under that system, patients matter, not as individuals in their own right, but only if they can contribute to bureaucratically approved testing protocols. Right to Try, by contrast, is premised on the principle that each person owns their own life and can make their own autonomous decisions. It respects the principle of medical autonomy—which is not just a cornerstone of medical ethics, but one of the basic principles of freedom guaranteed by state and federal constitutions. It is unethical and unconstitutional for government to violate that right—especially when patients are facing certain death. In short, Right to Try reflects the belief that compassionate use should be the rule, not the exception, for terminal patients.

A New Hope

Right to Try has given patients new hope by allowing them to seek potentially lifesaving treatments without a government permission slip—and it has saved lives. Houston-based oncologist Dr. Ebrahim Delpassand successfully treated nearly 200 terminally ill neuroendocrine cancer patients using LU-177 (or Lutetium Dototate), a drug that is now approved but at the time had not yet received final FDA approval for sale. Dr. Delpassand administered a successful clinical trial for LU-177 therapy for five years. In 2015, after the final trial phase was completed, the FDA refused to allow Dr. Delpassand to treat additional patients until the drug received final agency approval. One patient, Marc Hayutin, was in the midst of treatment when the FDA halted the trial. Marc—who before receiving treatment was told he only had months to live—was desperate and out of options.

But a few months later, Texas lawmakers adopted a Right to Try bill, giving patients a new avenue to access this safe and effective therapy. Invoking his rights under the new law, Dr. Delpassand continued administering LU-177 to patients suffering from neuroendocrine cancer. Many of these patients were only given three to six months to live, but years later, many of them—including Marc—are still alive.

Matt Bellina, mentioned earlier, had been an advocate for the Right to Try ever since he was diagnosed with amyotrophic lateral sclerosis in 2014. His illness had progressed too far for one FDA-approved treatment and not far enough for the other, so before Right to Try, he was out of options—and out of hope. He could barely stand or speak. But after Right to Try became federal law, Matt was given access to an investigational drug, and after the first round of treatment, he could speak and swallow, pull himself up to a standing position, and no longer needed to sleep with a breathing machine. Of course, nobody can know what the future has in store, but these dramatic improvements mean he has been able to better enjoy time with his wife and three sons. Most importantly to Matt, he was able to make that treatment decision himself, rather than being at the mercy of a federal bureaucrat.

The Next Step: A Personal Right to Individualized Medicine

As the availability and accessibility of next-generation genetic sequencing increases, more patients, especially those with rare and ultra-rare terminal illnesses, will be pursuing these "individualized medicine" treatments leading to an influx of patients.

But patients seeking personalized treatments still face the same regulatory obstacles that patients like Marc Hayutin and Matt Bellina faced before Right to Try became law. That is because individualized treatments are essentially required to undergo mini clinical trials that test a specially designed drug or treatment on the single patient for whom it was created (Fiore, 2019).

Requiring patients receiving individualized treatments to undergo clinical trials is a regulatory mismatch—a square peg in a round hole. After all, the goal of a clinical trial is to learn something about the treatment that will be generally applicable to a group of patients and move the treatment closer to FDA approval for sale. Any benefit to patients participating in a clinical trial is secondary. But in clinical *care*, the primary goal is treating the individual patient (Kravitz & Duan, 2014). The current regulatory system for personalized medicine subjects patients seeking individual care to a system designed for general study. As such, as with other lifesaving treatments before Right to Try, it forces patients to undergo lengthy processes and beg the federal government for permission before they can receive treatment.

Right to Try has removed a key regulatory barrier that had been standing in the way of terminally ill patients' access to treatments. But Right to Try cannot be applied to personalized treatments since there is no "Phase 1" safety threshold—safety and efficacy are simultaneously "tested" on the individual patient in the "trial." Thus, Right to Try must be taken to the next level, expanded so that the growing number of patients seeking individualized treatments are not caught in needless bureaucratic red tape.

The concept of Right to Try for personalized medicine parallels that of the original Right to Try: Once the FDA ensures basic safety, a terminally ill patient can work directly with their doctor to seek treatment—without having to first get government permission. In the personalized medicine context, the safety component would not be Phase 1 of a clinical trial, but could be, for example, a set of standardized safety protocols that the manufacturer and doctor must follow when providing the treatment or IRB approval once toxicology and animal studies are conducted.

Consider how the FDA regulates the production and sale of food (except meat and poultry, which are regulated by the U.S. Department of Agriculture). The agency does not require every individual food item to undergo testing before it can be sold to the public. Such a process would make little sense, given that each unit of produce is unique. Instead, the FDA sets basic safety standards and protocols for food producers to follow, such as levels of acceptable additives, safe tolerances for unavoidable poisonous substances in food, tamper-resistant and other packaging requirements, cleanliness and sanitation standards for food production establishments and warehouses, and general quality benchmarks. Indeed, Congress eliminated many of the FDA premarket-approval requirements for food packaging and distribution, replacing them with processes manufacturers can follow to self-determine safety (Food and Drug Administration Modernization Act, 1997). A Right to Try for personalized medicine could replace the current, unfair, and unworkable clinical trial approach with a set of standards for the manufacture and administration of treatments that, if followed by the manufacturer and doctor, would allow patients to receive personalized treatment without waiting on a government permission slip.

A Path to Success—Legal Arguments

The original Right to Try movement was so successful because it started close to the people—in the states. As California's Right to Try sponsor, Assembly Member Ian Calderon, declared: "The only way you can get change from the FDA is pressure from the states" (White, 2015). Once again, state lawmakers have an opportunity to employ state law to protect individual rights—this time, with a Right to Try for personalized medicine.

Under our federalist system, the Constitution provides a floor of protection for individual rights, not a ceiling, leaving states free to enact laws that protect those rights more broadly than the federal Constitution does. According to Kelo v. City of New London (2005): "Nothing . . . precludes any State from placing further restrictions on its exercise of . . . power . . . that are stricter than the federal baseline." And states have always had the primary responsibility for regulating the practice of medicine (Metropolitan Life Insurance Co. v. Massachusetts, 1985; *see also* Rush Prudential HMO, Inc. v. Moran, 2002) (see chapter 7). Indeed, the FDA is not empowered to regulate medical practice at all (21 U.S.C. § 396 (2012)). But through its prohibition on medical access and the unduly complex process for compassionate use, it does something very much like that. Rather than focusing on ensuring that physicians and patients have the information they need to make their own decisions, the FDA has become the decision-maker, prohibiting doctors from treating patients to the best of their ability and to the full extent of their medical knowledge. When states adopted Right to Try laws, they provided greater protections for a fundamental right than are provided by the federal system.

The right to try to save one's own life is deeply rooted in the nation's history and tradition and is among the crucial rights protected by the principle of due process of law. The U.S. Supreme Court has acknowledged that the individual has a constitutionally protected liberty interest in *refusing* life-saving medical treatment when it is not wanted (Cruzan v. Dir., Mo. Dep't of Health, 1990), and that unjustified intrusions into the body violate due process (Rochin v. California, 1952). The right to medical privacy and the right "to care for one's health and person and to seek out a physician of one's own choice" (Doe v. Bolton, 1973) are also rooted in the law's basic respect for patients' fundamental right to decide for themselves what medical procedures to undergo. The Constitution even protects one's right to cut or not cut their own hair (Griffin v. Tatum, 1970). The most basic of all rights is the right to one's own body. And there is no stronger liberty interest than a person's right to choose actions in an effort to save one's own life—even if that attempt is ultimately unsuccessful.

True, the U.S. Supreme Court has said that a right is not without limits. Terminally ill patients do not have the right to take *unsafe* medicines (United States v. Rutherford, 1979). But Right to Try does not involve unsafe panaceas; it applies solely to drugs and procedures that have already passed FDA safety testing. So, too, with a Right to Try for personalized medicine. Indeed, the entire concept of an individual Right to Try could be designed around ensuring all individualized treatments are tailored through a standard FDA-prescribed process that maximizes safety or where an IRB can approve the use of these treatments for an individual patient before the completion of a Phase 1 trial.

The Right Treatment

Right to Try is not a call to ignore research or undermine science, or for doctors to abandon obligations to patients, or for drug companies to disregard complex ethical questions such as how to distribute limited supplies of drugs. And obviously Right to Try is not a guarantee that investigational medications will work, or that patients and doctors will have perfect information to inform their decisions. But the FDA's "permission first" system is none of these things, either. As the FDA admits, no system will ensure against all risks. The question is, who should ultimately decide what level of risk is acceptable to a patient—federal officials or patients themselves, in consultation with their doctors? Terminally ill patients have a basic human right to try to save their own lives by using promising medicines.

Right to Try was an important step in the right direction. But modern medicine requires us to go further to ensure that the right treatment, for the right patient, and at the right time is available when a life hangs in the balance. Terminal patients have enough on their hands fighting for their lives. They should not have to fight the government, too.

CHAPTER 17

Purple Solutions for Controlling Drug Prices

DANIEL SEM

The previous chapters in section 3 provided an overview of factors that go into drug pricing, considering everything from the pharmaceutical research and development (R&D) to manufacturing to the entire pharmaceutical supply chain, including the role of pharmacy benefit managers (PBMs), wholesalers, and pharmacies. There was also discussion of the role of Food and Drug Administration (FDA) regulations in determining drug safety and efficacy, and conversely in making it more challenging to get lifesaving drugs approved for rare diseases or for personalized medicine. This chapter attempts to summarize those various discussions, and present possible Purple solutions (or at least considerations) to address high drug prices.

Chapter 12 specifically discussed the issue of high drug prices in the United States and attempted to identify a series of problems or abuses that contributed to these high prices. Of particular concern to the average American healthcare consumer are:

a. The high prices for certain categories of drugs (e.g., specialty pharmaceuticals, infusibles, orphan drugs), especially when they are not adequately covered by insurance.
b. The fact that we Americans have to pay more for our drugs than those outside of the United States, such as in Canada.

While the average Canadian spent $772 per year on prescription drugs in 2014, the average American spent $1,112, so 44% more (Miller, 2018; Organization for Economic Development [OECD], 2014).

The particular challenges, abuses, or market dysfunctions identified in chapter 12 that lead to overly high prices for drugs include:

- Monopoly-based price gouging. There are abuses of patent-based monopoly power to overprice, when the drug pricing goes beyond simply rewarding innovation, paying for real clinical-therapeutic benefit, and recovering R&D costs.

- R&D waste, unjustified overspending. There are cases where new drugs are developed with R&D at significant cost, and yet there is only incrementally better medical benefit to patients compared to existing drugs on the market (e.g., "me too" drugs) (Young, 2015).
- Supply chain waste, spread pricing, arbitrage. Lack of price transparency in the pharmaceutical supply chain that gets drugs from the manufacturer to the patient can lead to non-value-added intermediaries adding unjustified cost.
- The rare disease dilemma. Drugs that treat small numbers of people (fewer than 200,000), the so-called orphan drugs for treating rare diseases, are often extremely expensive since the high cost of developing them cannot be spread over a large population.

The ongoing public outrage over drug prices is not so much about whether the above items are the source(s) of the pricing problems. Rather, it is more about how to address these problems. The public generally perceives there is some unfairness in how drugs are priced, and they want it rectified, if not by the industry and market forces then by government. Both Democrats and Republicans want these problems addressed as well, and both want Americans to have good-quality and affordable medicines that can be readily accessed at hospitals or pharmacies. Politicians will differ on how they think this should be done and how heavily we should rely on the government versus the private sector, on regulations versus market forces. Let us start from the premise that we all want to address the problems and that (indulge me) both sides of the political aisle present some value to the debate on how these problems should be addressed. That is, that there is value to both government and the private sector, and that we need both market forces and regulations. In other words, we need political compromise *and* we need politicians to work across the aisle to find solutions. The main question should be: How far do we shift that balance between market forces and regulations, between industry and government control?

The reality is that any healthcare reform will require compromise, and that, for the most part, compromise is what the general public wants. The current political debate on high drug prices, though, is full of hyperbole and not much compromise, even though both parties agree that—in their opinions—drug prices are too high.

Before delving into proposed solutions to high drug prices, let us discuss what is currently being done or being proposed by our politicians to address the first cause of high drug prices, as mentioned at the start of this chapter—unjustified overpricing, or price gouging. To start with, based on the discussion in chapters 15 and 16, let us accept that at least some drugs need to be expensive and that the high prices are in some cases justified because it costs a lot of money and R&D to make them, and they provide real clinical and therapeutic value to patients.

Price Controls and Purchasing Drugs from Canada

Indirect Price Controls—Purchasing from Canada

Currently, one unusual and popular solution being proposed, and indeed practiced, is the purchase of drugs from countries, like Canada, that have price controls. Based on these price controls, these countries have negotiated with pharmaceutical companies on price and to determine if that company's drugs get added to the country's formulary. But Americans buying their drugs from Canada is not addressing the real issue head-on and is probably not a long-term solution. For example, if this were done on a larger scale, companies that sell drugs to Canada would simply limit their supply to what they estimate the Canadian population needs. So, not surprisingly, Canada generally opposes this strategy of indirectly supplying the United States market, as proposed by the current administration, because it endangers the supply of medicines for Canadians (Erman & O'Donnell, 2019). Nonetheless, the current administration under President Donald Trump initiated a federal rulemaking process in December of 2019 to allow importation of drugs from Canada (U.S. Department of Health and Human Services, 2019c).

Price Controls

Importing drugs from Canada is just a roundabout way to implement Canada's price controls in the United States, so why not just address that question head-on? This gets to the recent proposal, by both Democrats and Republicans, to impose price controls on drug sales in the United States (Wynne & Llamas, 2019), although the parties differ in their approaches. It is somewhat surprising that Republicans are proposing some price controls, although, even they are divided on the issue (Davis, 2019). What is more surprising is that given this unique and new stance the two parties still have not agreed on legislation to implement them (Huetteman, 2019), setting aside the issue for now as to whether price controls should or should not be implemented.

What has been proposed? The current administration has proposed drug price limits within the American Patients First blueprint (Assistant Secretary for Public Affairs, 2018) that would limit U.S. drug prices by pegging them to an International Price Index (Nathan-Kazis, 2019), which is basically an index created by compiling drug prices from a preselected group of countries, such as Canada and various countries in the European Union (EU), with this pricing strategy being applied first to Medicare Part B drug reimbursements (Centers for Medicare and Medicaid Services, 2018). This proposal is not popular with the pharmaceutical industry and has raised concerns that it would ultimately decrease the level of R&D spending and innovation leading to new drugs (Pipes, 2019). Other features of the American Patients First blueprint are:

- Removing "gag clauses" at pharmacies to allow pharmacists to recommend lower-cost and equally effective alternative drugs.
- Introducing steps to improve competition, such as through the Biosimilar Action Plan to get faster access to generic versions of expensive biologics drugs.
- Giving states and Medicare Advantage the tools they need to negotiate lower drug prices.
- Publishing drug prices in CMS's drug dashboard database to increase transparency and competition.

The Democrats have passed their version of a drug price control bill as well, in December 2019 (Sullivan, 2019). Thus, the two parties are pursuing their own parallel tracks, suggesting there will be no compromise on an issue that they almost—strangely—agree on.

Price controls are not generally considered favorable by Republicans and certainly not by those that favor free markets. Of course, monopolies (which patents grant and which permit high pricing) are a unique deviation from free markets that are justified by the U.S. Constitution based on the innovation they foster. So perhaps there is a middle road that is warranted—a balance. Arguably, the Trump administration is trying to level the playing field on drug pricing so that the United States does not end up financing a disproportionately large amount of worldwide drug innovation by having Americans paying much more than other countries for the same patented drugs. There is an apparent injustice in the fact that other countries get to pay lower prices than Americans do, even in situations where high prices are justified. Thus, these price benchmarks from the International Price Index might be viewed as a way to not just pull down the prices in the United States but to encourage pharmaceutical companies to lift prices to what they should be in other countries (the countries that are in the basket used to benchmark) by negotiating more fairly with them versus the United States. Differential pricing is not unusual in business and makes sense in many cases, but it breaks down if there is leakage between seg-mented markets (World Health Organization, 2003), such as if drugs from a country with strong price controls and low prices are imported into the United States, which has high prices. Certainly if a country's gross domestic product (GDP) and income per capita is low it makes sense for a company to charge a lower price there. But one could certainly argue that the price differential between the United States and Canada or the EU is not for that reason but is only because those countries have price controls and we do not—therefore, Americans gets stuck with the larger bill to finance drug development for the world. That, of course, is not fair. So some variation of the American Patients First blueprint could be viewed as a Bluish-Purple solution, as long as it does not cap the price so much for truly innovative drugs that were expensive to develop and where the high price was justi-fied based on cost and value. That latter point is, of course, the challenge—free market advocates would say that government is not qualified to make those judgment calls and the market is much better at deciding how to price. Of course, that also goes back to the original concern that we do not have a free market, at least not on the global scale, where we are selling to cus-tomers that have price controls. Furthermore, here in the United States we are selling "products" (drugs) that are patented, which are limited and legal monopolies where companies can charge high prices with few constraints. If a drug is lifesaving, patented, expensive, and there are no other options, you, as a consumer, would sell your house and even go into bankruptcy to buy it for yourself or a loved one if you had to. Against that backdrop, and in situa-tions like this (lifesaving drugs, patented, expensive, no other options), some variation of the American Patients First blueprint might be a reasonable and uniquely Purple solution that likely will not be offered by future Republi-cans, so it behooves the Democrats to work toward some sort of reasonable compromise around this while the window of opportunity is open. Mean-while, there is also a proposal from the administration to the Department of Health and Human Services to go even one step further on limiting price and give the United States a "most favored nation" status for drug pricing, so the United States would effectively get the lowest price for drugs sold to developed countries (Kaiser Health News, 2019). With that, we are firmly on the Blue end of possible Purple solutions.

Alternatives to Price Controls: Government Regulations

Do we or should we even want these price controls? Are there additional options? It would be bad for the pharmaceutical market to have overly aggressive price controls, and yet the unique market situation of drugs (sometimes justifiably high prices enabled by patents, a market that is not a level playing field globally) justifies something be done, *unless the pharmaceutical industry can self-regulate*, avoiding the watchful eye and enforcement threat of government regulators like the FDA, Federal Trade Commission (FTC), and Patent and Trademark Office (PTO) that police abuses, keeping them honest when they overstep reasonable pricing and related boundaries—or else more and stronger regulations will be created. This is the history of government regulations in America: When bad things happen, and the industry does not step in to self-regulate, the public gets outraged and asks the government to step in. That is how we got the Securities and Exchange Commission regulations after the Great Depression during the 1930s (U.S. Securities and Exchange Commission, 2013); the Dodd-Frank Wall Street Reform and Consumer Protection regulations after the 2008 Great Recession and subprime mortgage crisis (Guynn, 2010); and even a wide range of FDA regulations, including those governing clinical trials that were created in 1938, created after the death of 100 patients in a reckless drug test (Junod, n.d.). This pattern teaches us that industry functioning in a free market needs to step up to the plate and self-regulate or the public will demand that our politicians impose regulations on them—such as the Trump drug price controls or the even stricter price controls being proposed by the Democrats. That brings us next to a discussion of industry oversight options and what regulations or market oversights already exist.

Alternatives to Price Controls: Industry Self-regulation

PhRMA is the Pharmaceutical Research and Manufacturers of America trade organization, and BIO is the trade organization for the biotechnology and pharmaceutical industry, both of which could play some role in monitoring and policing their industries. At the 2019 BIO conference in Philadelphia, it is not surprising that the industry was generally opposed to price controls and price indexing, but there was room for some balanced discussion. At the meeting, the issue was addressed by session speaker Duane Schulthess, who serves as managing director of Vital Transformation, a consultancy dealing with healthcare policy and regulations. Schulthess (2019) discussed how the proposed price indexing for Medicare Part B drugs would cap price at 1.25 times the basket of prices from other countries (versus 1.8 times now), and this would likely lead to less innovation and fewer new drugs. Later, speakers at the BIO conference, like John Doyle from Pfizer (Vital Transformation, 2019), discussed how one promising industry response (perhaps responding to the threat of price controls) is to pursue value-based pricing. That is to say, drug pricing would be based on some estimate of the actual value of the drug, considering factors such as clinical benefit, economics, and humanistic and social concerns. If an honest and transparent attempt were made to do such value-based pricing by the industry, this could be presented as a justification for the prices that a company charges in a world where monopoly power normally allows almost unconstrained pricing. If this were done, then an independent industry auditing body could assess this justification, and it could ultimately be up to government regulatory bodies to assess whether the pricing case seems reasonable or is an extreme overstep— at which they could step in, just as the FTC steps in when a merger flags anti-competitive concerns. I am not proposing requiring government approval for pricing, only oversight of the value-based case that is made by an independent auditing body. In other discussions at the conference by BIO leadership, including BIO CEO Jim Greenwood and others, some interesting points were made that companies should ". . . call out bad actors in our industry . . . who taint us all . . ." and ". . . fulfill our covenant with the patient and our covenant with society . . ." Some concerning trends were (a) the consolidation of hospital and payer systems, (b) the increasingly opaque reimbursement system, and (c) the few bad actors that raise prices unreasonably because they can, violating the industry's trust with patients. These are accurate and heartening comments that suggest the industry is beginning to take long-overdue steps to self-regulate and monitor abuses. Time will tell if they act quickly and substantively enough, because if they do not, then surely the public will demand regulations that will likely include some sort of price controls or imposed leakage from markets that have price controls, like Canada (i.e., a *de facto* price control in the United States).

One final point of discussion at the BIO conference of relevance was a suggestion that in addition to value-based pricing there could be capitation of payments and installment plans. And, it was suggested, of course, to look more at the PBMs and the role of rebates, as discussed previously in this book.

In summary, it seems reasonable, then, that before the government steps in and overregulates or imposes price controls, the industry itself should:

a. Oversee its pricing strategy and ensure there are not serious abuses, and that pricing is to some extent based on true value. They should call out abuses in some substantive way.

b. Recognize the true challenges associated with consumers needing to pay for lifesaving yet expensive specialty pharmaceuticals and orphan drugs, and propose and advocate for solutions. It is not enough to charge such a price, even when justified, and then leave it in the hands of the market to figure out how to finance something of that magnitude.

With regard to the first point, the industry could assess the following factors:

- How much it costs to develop the drug
- How much innovation went into developing it
- If there are good treatments currently
- How serious the disease is that is being treated
- The medical benefit, which could be categorized as follows: (a) first new class for a disease that has no treatment; (b) safety of the drug; (c) efficacy of the drug, relative to existing therapies; (d) critical scenarios with and without the drug (the incremental medical benefit)

The industry (e.g., BIO or a new objective entity) could assess the proposed pricing based on the above and other factors. It could act like a nongovernmental agency, like Moody's for credit ratings or the International Standards Organization (ISO), which sets standards while others ensure compliance with ISO, or for those inclined to more government involvement even create a quasi-governmental body with arm's-length independence, like the Federal Reserve, or a fully federal administrative body, like the FTC, but for drug pricing. We could call either of these the Pharmaceutical Pricing Auditor (PPA). From a minimal government intrusion perspective, the last option is the least desirable—it just depends where you stand on the Red-Blue spectrum.

Alternatives to Price Controls: Industry Self-regulation Combined with the Threat of Government Regulation

If clear pricing abuses are occurring based on the above metrics to guide value-based pricing, then agencies like the FTC, PTO, or FDA—or the newly created PPA—could intervene. Although the FTC already addresses anticompetitive activities that are *illegal*, it could in theory also address when a legal monopoly is abusing its monopoly pricing power, too. This approach needs to be balanced against government over-intrusion by still recognizing the legitimate value of patents and associated monopolies that can and should be allowed to reward innovation and pay back the invested R&D dollars and create products of great value to consumers.

Are there situations when a company invests significant R&D dollars in a new drug that gets approved by the FDA, but the level of innovation and medical benefit is not that significant? This situation describes the second cause of high drug prices, mentioned at the start of this chapter, and refers to what are sometimes called "me too" drugs that offer minimal changes to existing patented drugs but allow the company to capture a fraction of a rather significant market and price the drug at the high levels that a patent allows. Sometimes this may be justified, but sometimes it may be an abuse and a market dysfunction. The FDA is another body that could intervene more aggressively in situations like this if the clinical or medical benefit (safety, efficacy relative to existing drugs) is not deemed adequate to justify putting another patented drug on the market. This government oversight needs to be balanced so that it also is not an over-intrusion that makes it too hard to get new drugs approved or that limits the availability of at least several drugs in a class. There is value, certainly, in having more than one patented drug on the market in a class, such as the statins, so that—even in this world of legally allowed monopolies—there is some competition to constrain price and give clinicians options based on price and slightly different clinical features. As a point of reference, the Japanese regulatory system has a high level of government regulation, but it still allows and rewards, at increasingly lower levels, additional drugs added to a class on a formulary. The Japanese system of pricing is also unique in that it takes a systematic, almost algorithmic approach to assessing value and calculating drug price based on value-based factors with great precision (although, accuracy is another question) (Ministry of Health, Labour, and Welfare Insurance Bureau, 2016; Ministry of Health, Labour, and Welfare, Economic Affairs Division, Health Policy Bureau, n.d.). The Japanese approach could be used as a partial guide for U.S. companies or government bodies that decide which drugs to add to formularies, to assign a valid value-based price to a new drug.

Finally, the PTO decides which patents are granted and which are not, and a significant aspect of that process is deciding if there is sufficient novelty (35 U.S.C. § 102) and nonobviousness (§ 103) of the new invention relative to prior discoveries and inventions. Specifically, for example, the PTO would ask if a new statin drug is chemically different enough from prior statins and does it provide sufficiently better clinical outcomes, though this latter point is more under the realm of the FDA. In principle, we could "ask" the PTO to be stricter in its interpretation of novelty and obviousness requirements for drugs when there are multiple similar drugs in a class. This would be a matter of looking for a stricter interpretation of existing law (35 U.S.C. §§102, 103) or considering drafting new law specific to pharmaceuticals. Or we could challenge such patents for new and of questionable value drugs before the PTO administrative courts. Of course, such regulatory activism needs to be constrained so that it does not make it too difficult to obtain new patents on truly innovative new drug classes or useful variations of drugs within a class. The point in all of these regulatory constraint options is that if government intervenes more it cannot be black-and-white and needs to be with some intelligent restraint. Politicians paint a picture that is black-and-white: Patents are evil or a panacea; free markets and companies are evil or a panacea; government is the source of all solutions or the source of all problems. The reality is somewhere in between. But one thing is for certain: If the pharmaceutical and biotechnology industry does not step up and begin to self-regulate, critique, and police itself more, the public—listening only to the simple one-dimensional and polarized arguments of politicians—will someday demand that the government solve this problem through excessive regulations that are not balanced. Rather than oscillate between these dangerous extremes, we need a more nuanced solution that involves compromise between these two extremes.

Beyond Pharma: Supply Chain Waste, Spread Pricing, and Arbitrage

The third drug pricing issue presented at the beginning of this chapter was the spread pricing and arbitrage that occurs because of the lack of transparency in the supply chain. This problem includes the abuse of rebates and the 340B process discussed in chapters 5 and 13, but it is made possible in large part because of the lack of transparency of pricing in the pharmaceutical supply chain, involving drug wholesalers and PBMs.

A Trump proposal had been put forth to end the rebates to PBMs (U.S. Department of Health and Human Services, 2019a), and the administration also issued a guidance to address the spread pricing problem of the PBMs (Centers for Medicare and Medicaid Services, 2019). But, later in 2019, a proposed rebate rule was withdrawn—so it appears that for now rebates remain intact (Dearment, 2019). Nonetheless, the administration is continuing to push for price transparency for pharmaceutical drugs and, more generally, healthcare (U.S. Department of Health and Human Services, 2019b). Indeed, healthcare price transparency in general is one of the few areas that both Democrats and Republicans embrace (Frakt & Mehrotra, 2019), although they probably still will not vote for each other's bills because, well, they never do when it comes to healthcare. Who knows? Since some—like Robert Graboyes (chapter 14)—see dangers in price transparency for drugs, maybe there are advantages of them being in a perpetual stalemate. And it is always possible that the industry will self-regulate and the market will correct. PBMs like Navitus that prioritize transparency are emerging now that a light has been shined on the previous pricing abuses in the supply chain.

Current Federal Proposals

Various Trump administration proposals try to address the issue of waste in the supply chain. The work of Antonio Ciaccia, noted in chapter 13, shines a light on pricing abuses by PBMs so that now government regulators and attorneys general can step in and stop the abuses. In the case of spread pricing, it is a matter of enforcing existing antifraud laws once there is enough transparency to identify the abuse. To that end, there may be some value in eliminating rebates, since they are a tool that has been used by the PBMs to make the system less transparent, which tempts price gaming and arbitrage, for example, where they encourage overuse of more expensive branded drugs in pharmacies. We also need to empower patients with price and value data and allow those discussions to occur with pharmacists, now possible with the removal of "gag clauses" that restrict those discussions. This was made possible by the Patient Right to Know Prices Act, S.2554, and the Know the Lowest Price Act, S.2553 (American Pharmacists Association, 2018). These are seemingly good developments that should now be acted on at the pharmacist-patient interface. Finally, we should let patient-consumers have more ready access to price, safety, and efficacy data instead of "protecting them" from "complicated" information that we, somewhat condescendingly (a holdover in part from the early paternalistic days of medicine), feel that patient-consumers won't know how to use. Patient-consumers are now more incentivized than ever before to shop for their best healthcare and medicine options, now that they have large co-pays and deductibles, or if they pay directly from savings or health savings accounts (HSAs) without using insurance. So for better or worse, patient-consumers are motivated. We just need to provide them with help making informed decisions, with the pharmacist, physician, physician assistant, nurse practitioner, or even a "healthcare navigator" at their side to consult and advise them on their healthcare journey (Heath, 2017).

Healthcare Navigators

The idea of healthcare navigators (HNs) grew out of the Affordable Care Act (ACA). A healthcare navigator is defined as an "individual or organization that's trained and able to help consumers, small businesses, and their employees as they look for health coverage options through the Marketplace" and "these individuals and organizations are required to be unbiased" (HealthCare.gov, n.d.). This model, and the concept of healthcare navigators, could be expanded as we look to further consumerize healthcare in private markets, putting power and decision-making increasingly in the hands of patients working with their various providers. The HNs can also help as we let patient-consumers have more direct pay options for purchasing their medicines, like GoodRx, to supplement what is covered in a more limited way by their insurance or Medicare. As a society, we "Uberized" transportation, and we order most of our consumer products and sometimes even groceries now on Amazon.com, and we buy homes and cars online and make travel arrangements online, all without the help of expensive agents and surrogates. In all of these cases, consumers are fully empowered and using information they have at their fingertips to make their own decisions, in markets where we once argued that consumers needed intermediaries and infrastructure to help navigate worlds that were far too complicated for average people. Many will say healthcare is different because it is too complex and consumers are not educated enough to figure it out and make smart decisions. I say this underestimates consumers in America—and, besides, we can provide them with access to HNs that they pay a fee for (or can be subsidized by government or paid from their employer's HSA program, if needed) as objective advisers to navigate the system of providers. The HNs could have both legal fiduciary and clinical duties to ensure that they always put the financial and medical interests of their patient-clients first. The day may come where patient-consumers feel they can do without the HNs, but until then this eliminates the argument that patient-consumers cannot figure out the healthcare system and cannot interpret the medical information needed to make informed decisions within the scope of their doctor's recommendations. But at least THEY (the patient-consumer) would be making the ultimate important decisions, not government panels or insurance reimbursement experts or other surrogates who do not have their interests in mind.

The Grassroots Healthcare Revolution in America

It seems like the time is right to empower us, the patients and consumers, in what John Torinus (chapter 9) calls a grassroots healthcare revolution, with the healthcare consumer and payer put in charge in a free and transparent healthcare marketplace (Torinus, n.d.). It should also be noted that this approach to consumerizing healthcare fits very well with our American culture, which typically emphasizes empowerment of individuals. The cultural fit for any healthcare solution, for a given country, is something that often gets ignored in political discussions. We in America want to do and control everything, which is why HMOs did not last long (Enthoven, 2005). Now we even want to do and control everything on our iPhones or Androids. And we loathe powerful outside forces, such as the government or corporations, forcing their decisions on us, whether it be what medicines we can take, what procedures are covered, what doctors we can use, or what parts of our medical information we have access to and how much input we have into our physician's treatment plan for us. With regard to the latter point, the fact that 38% of adults in America use complementary and alternative medicine, which they hide from their doctors because they are sure their doctors will not help at best and more likely will resist, indicates we as a society want to take control of our health and wellness, but we are doing it in a fragmented, disconnected (from the traditional healthcare system), and dysfunctional way at present. Why do we not stand up and put ourselves in charge in a true patient-centered care model (Heath, 2017), with us serving as the CEO of our health, wellness, and treatment plans? This actually is the trending path we are on, and a goal we hopefully and likely will reach before 2030. It will disrupt the current healthcare system and infrastructure and put the patient at the center with all financial and decision-making power, decreasing the need for most healthcare going through large centralized hospitals and insurance companies or their government equivalent. The Medical-Industrial Complex and/or trends toward pure socialized medicine will yield to a more balanced consumer-driven and patient-centered care model, where we are all CEOs of our health, treatment, and wellness plans, with the help of our personal HNs (and with advances in AI, maybe Siri or Alexa can adopt that role someday, too). I once shared some of these lofty ideas with a senior strategist at a top healthcare provider who said I should stop talking about disruption—because leadership does not like that word. I will not because it is coming in the same way that Amazon came and blindsided the retail industry. And it is all for the benefit of us, the consumers.

The Rare Disease Dilemma

The fourth and final issue related to drug pricing, presented at the start of this chapter, is the rare disease dilemma. What do you do when a drug costs over $2 billion (or even say $300 million) to develop, and yet there are not enough people with the disease to even recoup this investment in R&D? Of course, there are cases where orphan drugs are overpriced and there is price gouging, but that would be addressed by the proposals in the previous chapters in this section on either industry or regulatory oversight. I am asking now, quite simply, how do we finance this very real situation (even if government pays), where there is actual verifiable and justified expense that needs to be recouped, and there is real value to people (e.g., without this drug, the patient would die; with it, they are cured or their life is dramatically extended). In cases like this where the expense and subsequent high price is justified, it seems the only viable solution is to design insurance policies that better address these scenarios, whether they be public/government, private, or some combination—a more Purple solution. In any of those insurance funding scenarios, we as a society need to address the simple fact that you may have a less than 0.05% chance of getting a particular rare disease (that afflicts one in 200,000 people), but you would like to protect yourself against the risk of that happening. If and when it does happen, because it afflicts a small population, the cost of the drug is often over $100,000/year and often exceeds the limits covered by insurance. So you should be able to insure against that risk with an appropriate kind of insurance. Another perspective on addressing the high cost of orphan drugs is to decrease their cost by simplifying the regulatory approval process so that the cost to develop them would be less. Although, it should be noted that the government has already taken large steps to make regulatory approval of orphan drugs easier and less expensive (U.S. Food and Drug Administration, 2018). How much is reasonable to spend on drugs like this, ultimately, is a question of bioethics.

Bioethical Considerations in the Rare Disease Dilemma

How much can we spend on a drug even if it is lifesaving? Is money really no object? Let me carry this to the extreme so you see my point. What if we could spend the entire United States federal budget of $4.7 trillion (Amadeo, 2019) to create a drug to save the life of a 10-year-old who would die without the drug but would live a full life with it? There is no money left for anything else in the country—no education, no new roads, no Medicare or Medicaid, no social security, no defense, no nothing. This is a silly example, I know, but my point is that resources are limited, and we do not acknowledge that as a society, especially when we discuss healthcare—where we often say money is no object. Perhaps a more realistic example involves expensive cancer treatments, with drugs like Tykerb, Avastin, and Tarceva, that cost as much as $100,000 per year but often only extend a life several months (Thoma, 2007). Indeed, in the case of Avastin (late-stage breast cancer), the FDA eventually pulled it from the market in 2011 because of questionable benefits to patients—and yet this led to outrage from some cancer survivors and clinicians who believed the benefits of the drug were real and significant, in spite of data suggesting minimal value (Vitry et al., 2015). If we as a society spend $300,000 to extend a life several months, we have to consider what healthcare priorities we will not fund because of that if the budget is fixed, as it would be. Of course, we will not have that discussion, and what will end up happening is that someone else who oversees reimbursement processes will decide for us. We need to have those discussions and discuss those priorities.

Some Sort of Rationing and Spending Limits Will Occur

It is not true that money is no object in healthcare. The unfortunate reality, and the underlying principle of economics, is that resources are always limited. So we need to confront these bioethical issues of when and where to limit coverage more candidly as a society. If we ignore them, what will happen is that limits will eventually need to be set for us (e.g., fewer drugs on the formulary), and the bar where those limits will be set will not always have been thought through as we like in some cases, and it will be decided by reimbursement committees working for the government. As it is right now, in the EU there is a centralized authority for approving drugs, but the reimbursement process, and decisions about what drugs to include on formularies, varies from country to country. In Germany, it is the Federal Joint Committee (G-BA) and the GKV-SV that negotiates prices and formulary inclusion with the pharmaceutical companies based on reference pricing from other countries. Reimbursement committees determine reimbursement status (inclusion on the formulary) and reimbursement price, typically looking at therapeutic value (relative to alternatives), medical necessity, safety, cost-effectiveness, and effect on budget (IGES Institute GmbH, 2019). They will decide, and that process is necessary in that system. The decisions are especially difficult in the case of expensive orphan drugs to treat rare diseases. Hopefully the process is fair, but when you have a cancer that needs to be treated and the drug is not on the formulary—and that will happen—you will feel it is unfair. So we need to discuss more openly the limits to what we as a society will fund, instead of perpetuating the illusion and the lie that everything will be available no matter the cost. To partially address this problem, if we implement some government-funded program, because resources are always limited, we should, as most countries do, also have some supplemental private insurance option like Medicare Advantage or supplemental private insurance that can be purchased so that consumers are not stuck with limited choices and no solution. Most countries that offer public option insurance also offer private supplemental options (voluntary health insurance) as well, representing 61% of private healthcare spending in France, 39% in Germany, and 20% in the United Kingdom (Sagan & Thomson, 2016). The political hyperbole around public-only options in the United States is misplaced, since most countries do not have only public-only options—they recognized that they also needed to offer supplemental or complementary private options to address gaps in the public options (Kliff, 2019; The Commonwealth Fund, n.d.).

Not Having Consumer Choice Is Not an Option for Us in America

Politicians use their rhetoric. It is either (a) death panels or (b) corporate greed and cold free markets that will limit our access to healthcare and medicines. They polarize the public but ignoring the reality that it is actually not so extreme. If we ever have universal government-sponsored plans, we will also need a private market as well, to ensure some access to all medicines, as nearly all countries provide. We will also need direct pay options, for purchasing through venues like GoodRx.com, with the help of our pharmacist who can now guide us in our comparison-shopping for the best medicine for our ailments, after our physician makes the prescription. Finally, even if we have some free and competitive private markets, we need to recognize that we also have a moral obligation as a society to protect the poor and underserved, to ensure a baseline of good care for everyone. How that might be accomplished is the topic of the last section of this book.

A Healthcare Safety Net

CHAPTER 18

America Already Offers Universal Healthcare, the Most Expensive Way Possible

DANIEL SEM

Section 3 of this book focused on the high cost of drugs, and section 2 focused on the high cost of healthcare generally, especially primary care. This final section discusses a decidedly Blue topic: Whether there should be some sort of universal healthcare safety net for everyone and especially for vulnerable populations. Before diving into that broad topic, this chapter considers the notion that America already has a kind of universal healthcare, by offering anyone who needs it access to emergency rooms, irrespective of whether they can pay. This is required by law. An argument could be made that we merely need to replace this current offering with something that provides a better baseline of healthcare for everyone more humanely, efficiently, and at lower cost.

Background

The political debate over universal healthcare is heated and polarized. It is also moot in at least one respect. We already have universal healthcare in America; we just do it the most expensive and cumbersome way imaginable. Under President Ronald Reagan's administration in 1986, Congress passed the *Emergency Medical Treatment and Active Labor Act* (EMTALA) (Centers for Medicare and Medicaid Services, 2012). EMTALA is legislation that permits anyone to get medical care in emergency rooms (ERs), whether or not they can afford to pay. A hospital that does not provide this care faces fines of $50,000 per incident. It is an unfunded government mandate that requires hospitals to provide ER services but does not offer or suggest any way for them to pay for it. Because of this EMTALA law, an emergency department (ED) cannot turn away anyone that enters its doors looking for care, even if they cannot pay or do not have insurance. According to the American College of Emergency Physicians, that makes

---

This chapter is adapted from a law review article by Sem, Gou, & Aljabban (2018).

this "the *de facto* national health care policy for the uninsured" in America, delivering healthcare to the underserved the most expensive way possible (Caldwell et al., 2013). The uninsured and poor use this ER service, and yet since they often cannot pay, other healthcare consumers or taxpayers end up paying. One way that others pay is through inflated chargemaster prices and through "cost-shifting" that hospitals must do to cover unreimbursed expenses (see chapter 1). The cost of providing these unreimbursed and unpaid services was estimated to be $46 billion in 2013 (Pope, 2015).

Since EMTALA can already be considered a form of universal healthcare, implemented in a Republican administration, a bipartisan argument could be made that we should simply replace it with something that provides a better, more appropriate, and more cost-effective baseline of healthcare to the underserved and (more boldly, from the Democratic perspective) general population. From a private-sector perspective, perhaps retail clinics (see chapter 10) or smaller urgent care clinics could be located in proximity to ERs, and there could also be telemedicine access from a private booth, at the entrance to the ER, providing a first round of triage care that would likely address most of the needs for people going to the ER unnecessarily. Some hospitals are exploring solutions just like this, to decrease ER overuse and abuse (New England Healthcare Institute, 2010). This free market approach, coupled with some reasonable sort of public safety net like those to be discussed in the following chapters, would avoid the expensive and unnecessary overuse of ERs, saving hospitals significant money and providing better care to underserved populations. While the broader concept of a safety net or universal healthcare is discussed in the next chapters, it is worth considering now how to address the more pressing issue of helping the uninsured and decreasing their overreliance on ERs.

The pressure on hospitals to find better ways to serve the uninsured and those on Medicaid is only increasing. Besides the fact that hospitals must bear the cost burden of ER use by the uninsured, they also must bear the cost of the Medicaid population that uses their services, when in fact hospitals are not reimbursed enough by Medicaid to cover their expenses. This invariably must lead to some form of cost-shifting, even if only in the form of hospital overhead costs that paying customers are charged in some indirect manner. This financial challenge will only get worse as states, which must pay for Medicaid, move to a block grant system of reimbursement for Medicaid expenses, where states receive a fixed amount of federal money to cover their Medicaid expenses. That means that their state-level Medicaid budgets will be set to a limited and fixed amount, and it is up to each state to figure out how to make it work (Luthra, 2017). State-level control of resources probably makes more sense than federal control, for something like Medicaid, but the challenge remains how to do what is needed within the limited budget that is given. In any case, this adds even more pressure on hospitals to address the ER overuse and Medicaid reimbursement funding gap problems. Some solution is needed.

These financial pressures are forcing hospitals to find better ways to serve the uninsured and Medicaid populations. Hospitals are required to serve them under EMTALA, even though they are not reimbursed to do so. One creative solution being pursued by Chicago-area hospitals and providers suggests a possible solution that could be pursued more broadly across America, whether implemented in the public or private sector. Several of the major hospitals and providers in the greater Chicago area joined forces to form an *accountable care organization* (ACO), using a nonprofit called *Medical Home Network* (www.medicalhomenetwork.org). Medical Home Network uses cutting-edge telehealth software solutions and *healthcare coordinators* (real people) to assist the uninsured that they have flagged as being frequent users or abusers of ERs, to monitor their healthcare needs more closely, and to ensure they get chronic and other medical conditions taken care of before they need to go to the ER. While normally one might expect competing hospitals and providers to not collaborate on healthcare coordination services, and not to make transfer of electronic medical record (EMR) data between their systems fluid, they have come together for this exact purpose in a limited scope because they have a common desire to help the uninsured avoid using and abusing their ERs. This is both noble, to help the poor, and financially justified, avoiding significant unreimbursed expenses. To repeat that second point, they save money with this collaborative approach—so the motivation is also financially driven. They paid for the Medical Home Network solution that saves them money and provides better care for the uninsured in the greater Chicago area. Medical Home Network uses a telehealth software solution created by a HealthTech start-up company called Texture Health (Texture Health, 2020), which provides healthcare coordination using a software tool called *MHN Connect*. Behind the software is a healthcare coordinator. This person serves as a healthcare navigator or social worker and is agnostic to providers and their financial incentives, acting as an agent or consultant for the patient. Healthcare coordinators have access to a coordinated EMR, and it is their job to look out for their patients—ensuring they take their medicines for chronic conditions like diabetes, electronically tracking when they have gone to an ER, and investigating what could be done to help them avoid letting their condition get to that point in the future. The healthcare navigator builds a personal relationship and connection with the patient via the telehealth tool. This is similar to the healthcare navigator concept presented in chapters 1 and 9, but now for underserved and uninsured populations. Medical Home Network's goal is to help navigate and find good quality, cost-effective care for this underserved population, in a network of normally competing primary care providers and hospital systems. Is all this purely philanthropic, charitable, mission-driven kindness on their part? Maybe somewhat, but it is also revenue and financially driven. In a two-year period, Medical Home Network saved providers $11 million and provided care for 1,189,195 Medicaid participants (Pipes, 2017). That's a positive financial impact and a positive social impact, done by the private sector to deal with an unfunded federal mandate.

The example of the Medical Home Network initiative indicates that some sort of safety net program—where the uninsured are helped using a healthcare navigator, coupled to an open and shared EMR that still protects patient privacy (via HIPAA regulations)—can be used to save money and decrease the financial drain from a Republican-initiated *de facto* universal healthcare plan, under EMTALA. Many without insurance have learned that they can get their healthcare at the ER, and this is costing paying healthcare consumers and hospitals too much money, while at the same time not providing a decent baseline level of healthcare to the underserved. This is not the right or humane way to provide healthcare to vulnerable populations. It seems that a purple solution would at least find a creative replacement for the EMTALA-enabled delivery of primary healthcare to uninsured in America's ERs. It is not clear how a safety net should be structured, but it seems that it should at least address this significant problem in how we currently care for the poor and uninsured in America. It is simply not right to provide the poor with no access to a baseline of care, or to create incentives that force them to (over) use emergency rooms which are high priced and often have long waits (see figure 18.1). It could be done in a financially neutral manner, if modeled after what the Medical Home Network has done in the greater Chicago area—in that case through the private sector.

The final chapters of this book present a wide range of safety net options that could provide healthcare for vulnerable and underserved populations, or in some cases the general population. The more universal, monolithic, and controlled-by-government, the more the plans appeal to the political left. The more reliant on capitalism and free markets, with minimal centralized government control, the more they appeal to those on the political right. We will hear a range of such perspectives and options in the coming chapters, and then discuss what are possible hybrid or purple solutions. For the

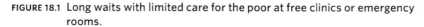

FIGURE 18.1 Long waits with limited care for the poor at free clinics or emergency rooms.

Source: Art by John Alberti, reproduced with permission.

die-hard free market fans, please keep an open mind here, and remember the words of the father of free market thinking, Friedrich Hayek, that some sort of safety net may be warranted (see chapter 1). He would, though, also want a role for free and competitive markets, I would think.

CHAPTER 19

The Economist Perspective on a Healthcare Safety Net

TYLER WATTS

Chapter 18 presented the notion that, at some level, America already offers healthcare to everyone as a safety net, by virtue of requiring emergency rooms to never turn away anyone. This is an expensive and inefficient way to offer a baseline of healthcare to everyone, so it may make sense to provide a better alternative as a safety net. But, any safety net should be sustainable and feasible and therefore consistent with sound economic principles. That is the purpose of this chapter, to provide an economic foundation for the analysis of possible structures for a healthcare safety net. Subsequent chapters then propose different versions of what a safety net might look like, from the perspectives of government policymakers (chapters 20 and 21) as well as payers and consumers (chapter 22).

"There are no solutions, only trade-offs"

—THOMAS SOWELL

Opportunity Costs

Lesson number one in economics is the ever-present fact of scarcity: You can't have it all. Whenever my children get excessive in asking for toys or treats, I make them recite the economist's mantra: "Wants are unlimited, but means are scarce." Children and politicians might view economists as perennial party poopers for our nagging insistence on considering costs, but the sooner we orient ourselves to reality, the better off we will be. There is no such thing as a free lunch—all of our choices involve costs. Precisely speaking, these are *opportunity costs*: what we give up when we choose a particular option. Opportunity costs loom very large in government, because government programs spend huge sums of money. President Dwight Eisenhower was a rare politician who both recognized and cared

---

Tyler Watts is an assistant professor of economics at Ferris State University and an adjunct faculty member at Concordia University Wisconsin.

about the large opportunity costs of government spending, which he spelled out in the context of the cold war arms race:

> The cost of one modern heavy bomber is this: a modern brick school in more than 30 cities. It is two electric power plants, each serving a town of 60,000 population. It is two fine, fully equipped hospitals. It is some 50 miles of concrete pavement. We pay for a single fighter plane with a half million bushels of wheat. We pay for a single destroyer with new homes that could have housed more than 8,000 people (Eisenhower, 1953).

The opportunity cost of any government program consists of a) another program that could have used the allocated resources, and b) any number of individual "programs" taxpaying citizens could have pursued on their own—a mix of consumer spending, business investment, and charity—in the absence of the increased taxes required by government activity. Realizing that these opportunity costs exist, however, is not enough to inform our decision-making. We need a mechanism for assessing and comparing the costs of specific activities, a mechanism that can reveal what might be the most useful of several possible options. In market-based economies the *price system* has served this function quite well, helping us optimize scarce means across competing ends and achieve ever-increasing levels of economic growth and prosperity.

To see how the price system works to help us discover opportunity costs, optimize production and consumption decisions, and achieve consistent economic growth, let us examine an industry that is more important than even healthcare for the maintenance of human life: food. Food markets illustrate the price system at its finest, accurately revealing opportunity costs and providing incentives for consumers and businesses to spend and produce efficiently. Food represents about 13% of consumer spending, behind housing (33%) and transportation (16%) (U.S. Department of Agriculture, 2019). There is a vast array of consumer food tastes and preferences. The average grocery store in the United States carries over 33,000 food items (FMI—The Food Industry Association, 2020), and there are over 1 million restaurants in the nation—one for every 330 people (Resendes, 2020). No other industry offers close to the same startling array of choices regarding product variety, quality, and mode of delivery than does the food sector. We tend to take the operation of the food economy for granted because it functions so smoothly, almost in the background of our daily lives.

Food is an extremely competitive, fluid market where millions of entrepreneurs offer a vast array of products for all possible consumer tastes, from organic vegan to gluten-free to deep-fried. These food providers operate on the basis of profit and loss in a harshly competitive market environment with no government directives regarding who can produce what, when, and where.[1] Because the food industry is staunchly competitive, food producers survive and grow only when the value they offer to consumers is higher than the value of the resources they use up. In other words, food companies' measure of success is given by the equation: Revenue – Expenses = Profit (Loss). Because consumer tastes can be fickle and food inputs—especially at the agricultural commodity level—can be very volatile on account of weather patterns, geopolitical disturbances, and so on, food businesses' revenues and expenses are subject to constant fluctuations. These changes are partly responsible for business failure and success; most important, they keep entrepreneurs on their toes and encourage them to adapt to the changing market conditions revealed through ongoing price fluctuations.

For example, when bad weather reduced African cocoa harvests in 2018, some analysts predicted rampant chocolate shortages. As principles of economics students know, this did not happen—cocoa and chocolate prices merely rose to reflect a new equilibrium, and high prices induced consumers to cut back on chocolates and switch to other treats. High prices likewise encouraged farmers to ratchet up production of the crop, ensuring ongoing availability of confections. The increased efforts of cocoa farmers—incentivized by the high prices—led to larger crops that eventually pulled prices back down (Maltais, 2019). Although most price changes go unnoticed by the public, pricing dynamics are the centerpiece of an unseen, albeit seamless, mechanism that aligns producers with consumers to ensure supply will be there to meet consumer demands.

The food industry in the United States features what I like to call "full-spectrum competition," with basically no price controls or legal barriers to entry at the product or input level. This system is reliable and resilient because it is competitive: It is built entirely on the basis of consumer and producer *choice*. While tastes change and individual products and businesses come and go, the food market thrives and offers an ever-expanding array of ever-more affordable food products. This is because the price system functions very well for food products, food markets are highly competitive, and government regulations over the food industry are relatively stable and equally applicable to all producers—in other words, regulations are not

---

1. While the government does subsidize certain input producers at the farm commodity level, retail food markets are free of producer subsidies and price controls.

designed to help one food segment at the expense of others. Food is essential for life, yet few if any advocates for the poor have called for government provision of food or government intrusions into food markets beyond basic, general regulations of product safety. Perhaps this is because they realize that food markets function in a healthy, reliable manner. What many politicians and policy wonks might not realize is that the benefits of market pricing and robust competition could deliver some of the same amazing results in the provision of healthcare services—if only we would let them.

Incentives: Spending

Economists like to describe prices as "information wrapped in incentives." Price differences indicate the relative value and scarcity of different products. Prices tell me that I can have a Timex, but not a Rolex—at least not yet. Once we realize that all human beings operate under what economists call "rational self-interest"—that is, they are trying to improve their own situations—we can see that the price system relays quite powerful incentives that can get people to do wonderful things for each other. Prices are not the only incentive, but we might say prices are the star at the center of the economic universe. We choose our jobs and careers, for instance, based in no small part on what they pay. We choose all consumer goods based on what we can afford. Entrepreneurs strive for profits[2] by inventing new and better products and applying more efficient modes of production. Incentives to consume goods carefully and to produce goods efficiently stem from the prices each of us face daily in our various economic roles. But what happens when someone else pays the price for our choices?

Economist Milton Friedman noted that spending always involves either our own money or other people's money, and that we can spend that money on ourselves or on other people. Two sources of funds, multiplied by two objects of spending, means there are four categories of spending, as laid out in table 19.1. Friedman explains how incentives differ across these categories:

> Category I refers to your spending your own money on yourself. You shop in a supermarket, for example. You clearly have a strong incentive both to economize [minimize spending] and to get as much value as you can for each dollar you do spend.

---

2. Profit is best understood as a price differential: the difference between a product's price and the sum of the prices of the land, labor, and capital required to produce it. Thus, without prices, entrepreneurs lack the ability to assess profits and adjust product features and/or the production process in the pursuit of efficiency.

TABLE 19.1 Friedman's Spending Matrix

	On Whom Spent?	
Whose Money?	Yourself	Other People
Your Own Money	I	II
Other People's Money	III	IV

Source: Adapted from Friedman & Friedman (1981).

Category II refers to your spending your own money on someone else. You shop for Christmas or birthday presents. You have the same incentive to economize as in Category I but not the same incentive to get full value for your money, at least as judged by the tastes of the recipient.

Category III refers to your spending someone else's money on yourself—lunching on an expense account, for instance. You have no strong incentive to keep down the cost of the lunch, but you do have a strong incentive to get your money's worth.

Category IV refers to your spending someone else's money on still another person. You are paying for someone else's lunch out of an expense account. You have little incentive either to economize or to try to get your guest the lunch that he will value most highly. (Friedman & Friedman, 1981)

The incentive structure mapped out by Friedman (table 19.2) applies to all spending in all markets, healthcare services included. When we are considering a particular model of healthcare delivery, it is important to realize what kind of spending it involves and what kind of incentives are at work. Healthcare spending incentives are more complex than for most other products, as healthcare spending typically involves some combination of payment by individuals (self-pay), insurance companies, and government.

Self-pay for healthcare services, which represents Category I spending, is the least prevalent way of purchasing healthcare in the United States. Consumer "out of pocket" expenditures totaled just 10% of U.S. healthcare spending in 2017 (Wilson, 2019). Consumers who are directly financing their own care have strong incentives to search out the lowest cost for a given level of care and to ensure that they are getting their money's worth. As is always the case, consumers are loathe to overspend their own funds, as

TABLE 19.2 Comparison of Spending Categories

	Incentive to:	
Spending Category	Minimize Amount Spent?	Maximize Value Received?
I	Strong	Strong
II	Strong	Weak
III	Weak	Strong
IV	Weak	Weak

doing so limits alternative consumption or investment opportunities. Put another way, we spend frugally when we personally face the full opportunity costs of our spending.

Insurance providers are responsible for a substantial amount of total healthcare spending; private insurance payments totaled 34% of U.S. healthcare spending in 2017 (Wilson, 2019). Unlike food, healthcare needs are unpredictable, and healthcare costs can become crushingly large in the event of catastrophic injury or illness. Thus, most people prefer to carry some form of health insurance to avoid large shocks to their income and savings. Spending for insurance *coverage* itself is Category I for people buying their own individual plans, [3] so incentives exist to keep premium costs low, provided consumers have choices among different coverage options in a competitive insurance marketplace. Once patients incur insurer-covered medical bills, however, they are in a Category III situation—spending other people's (i.e., the insurance company's) money on themselves. There is a strong incentive to focus on the quality of care provided but little regard for minimizing total spending. For this reason insurers take steps, through tools such as co-payments, coinsurance, and deductibles, to put at least some fraction of healthcare spending for consumers into Category I and thus retain some incentives to limit spending.

Insurance is unique and troublesome because of the third-party complications it always involves. As noted, covered patients are always operating under Category III with respect to medical services once they reach a certain out-of-pocket threshold and thus have no concern over the total

---

3. Only 5% of health insurance plans are purchased directly by consumers in the individual market (Wilson, 2019); 49% of Americans receive health insurance through their employers (Kaiser Family Foundation, 2018a).

amount spent. The fact that another entity, whether an employer or the government, is paying for the insurance *coverage* itself introduces another layer of third-party effects. Employer purchases of health insurance are Category II spending. Employers seek to keep insurance premium costs down in order to save themselves money, but they won't be able to attain the same degree of individualized satisfaction with plan coverage as people would when shopping for themselves. Government-provided coverage is Category IV spending. Bureaucrats in charge have little to no incentive to keep costs down and minimal incentives to tailor plans to consumers' unique preferences over coverage levels. Category IV spending is a red alarm for those interested in cost containment and/or consumer satisfaction. In Category IV, healthcare providers are in control, knowing that consumers will assent to any proposed treatments (whether effective or not) and that maximum payments can be extracted from the government.[4] Because government healthcare programs typically operate under a fee-for-service model, in which providers simply bill the government for all indicated tests and treatments, these safety net programs are essentially designed to ensure maximum spending and maximum growth in spending.

Government is the single largest healthcare spender. In 2017, the U.S. government funded more than 45% of total healthcare spending, mostly through Medicare and Medicaid (Wilson, 2019). Again, this government spending falls into Categories III and IV. Medicare and Medicaid allow consumers to obtain coverage from among a pool of participating private providers, and the government then foots the bill. To the extent that Category III consumers are spending "government" money, they have no incentive to minimize costs. To the extent that consumers have choices of service providers and/or treatment plans, they at least have some ability to achieve the best possible care, as judged by their own perceptions of quality. When government both pays for and provides the healthcare services we are dealing with Category IV spending; spending tends to be maximized while attention to quality and patient satisfaction often suffers.

Veterans' Health Administration (VHA) hospitals and clinics exemplify this kind of pure Category IV spending. In early 2014, major news outlets began reporting shockingly long wait times and delays in treatment for VHA patients, which potentially led to dozens of premature deaths of

---

4. Indeed, the only remedies that government has for upward-spiraling costs in this case are price controls and/or rationing of services. Price controls are ineffective for reasons discussed above—when prices cannot move to reach their equilibrium levels, they cease to relay information about changing scarcity conditions and thus also fail to relay appropriate incentives for consumers and producers. The rigidities and uncertainties of rationing make it a poor substitute for market-based allocation of resources.

patients waiting as long as 115 days to see a doctor. Chronic wait times went unreported to VHA higher-ups because of widespread fraud and systemic misreporting by VHA staffers (Farenthold, 2014). Outrage over the scandal prompted a slew of official investigations and the resignation of the Secretary of the Department of Veterans Affairs.

As we all realize when in line at the DMV or when applying for a passport, inefficiency in government-provided services is to be expected. While this inefficiency can cause tragic consequences, as with VHA delays, it is not at all surprising in light of an economic understanding of incentives. VHA bureaucrats—most of whom are likely good people and good citizens— are spending other people's money on other people. They just do not have the same strong incentives to seek out high-quality service as people do when spending their own money on themselves. Business-wise, they are not subject to the "market test" of profit and loss that private businesses always face in a competitive environment. They lack incentives to keep costs down and develop innovative ways to control spending while ensuring or even improving quality of service.[5]

Private healthcare charities at first blush appear to parallel government provision: Those in charge of healthcare charities are spending other people's money on other people. Operating in Category IV, they face weak incentives both to economize and to provide excellent quality. But charities also must compete for donations in an environment where donors' perception of quality matters; to achieve ongoing fundraising success, charities do face pressures to demonstrate effective care and efficient operation. Take St. Jude Children's Research Hospital, for example. St. Jude has a strong incentive to minimize administrative costs so it can maximize patient care and build up a reputation as an effective healthcare provider. St. Jude's promotional materials cite improvements it has achieved in child cancer survival and individual patients whose lives are being saved by its work. This is compelling evidence of St. Jude's effectiveness, and it helps the hospital bring in nearly $1 billion per year as the nation's third-largest healthcare charity (Jones, 2012).

Most consumer spending—food, clothing, entertainment—is Category I. Total spending on these categories may rise as consumer populations grow and businesses offer a larger variety of quality products, but consumers

---

5. Economists refer to the owner(s) of a private, profit-oriented business as the "residual claimant"— that is, the person entitled to the funds left over after the business has paid all expenses. Because these funds (net income) are the property of the owner(s), owners and the managers they hire have powerful incentives to keep costs low for a given level of operations and thereby maximize their own takeaway from the enterprise. From the owner's and entrepreneur's perspective, business spending fits into Category I.

can be more or less sure of getting their money's worth and not over-spending. In the United States, the vast majority of healthcare spending, on the other hand, is paid by government or insurers, making it Category III or IV (see figure 19.1). It is thus no surprise at all that healthcare spending grows at a faster rate than any other goods or services, and healthcare quality is inconsistent—especially in Category IV situations.

Healthcare providers, more often than not, are spending other people's money on other people. This is a recipe for inefficiency and dissatisfaction—which is today's healthcare marketplace. When dealing with other people's money, consumers no longer have any interest in limiting spending but only in maximizing quality of care. They are perfectly willing to allow third parties to absorb higher healthcare spending, even if higher spending does not ultimately translate into better results.

When it comes to designing and implementing a healthcare safety net, we must be aware of the radically different incentive structures formed by different spending regimes. Category IV spending is bound to be less efficient and effective than Category III, and both of these pale in comparison with Category I. Thus, the big question is, can we push healthcare spending, even for a healthcare safety net, away from the problems associated with spending other people's money and make it more like spending your own money on yourself?

FIGURE 19.1 Health spending distribution by payer in the United States in 2017.

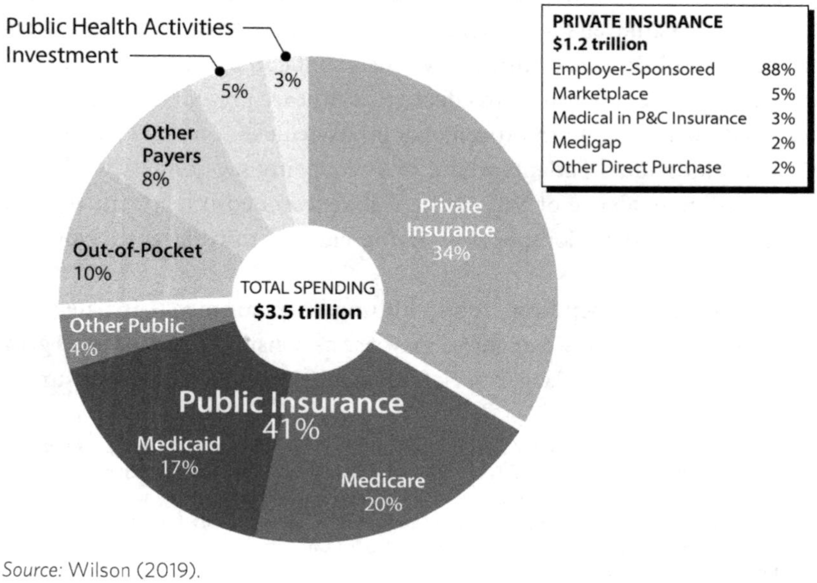

Source: Wilson (2019).

Safety Net or Sofa?

In addition to the perverse incentives generated by spending other people's money, government safety net programs can generate perverse incentives regarding work and income. Aid for the poor is, by definition, subject to income requirements. The more generous that aid is, people may become less enthusiastic about achieving higher incomes, as doing so might disqualify them for government assistance. When looked at this way, income gains for the poor can be seen as subject to two forms of taxation: (1) regular payroll and income taxes, the latter of which is of course progressive and hits higher incomes at higher rates; (2) taxation in the form of losing access to government benefits, such as food stamps, housing subsidies, Medicaid, etc.—a phenomenon labeled the "welfare cliff."[6] According to a 2014 study by the Illinois Policy Institute, a single parent of two children who earned $12 per hour would be worse off after receiving a pay raise to $15 per hour. While this person's after-tax pay would rise by $5,451, they would lose eligibility for $8,336 worth of federal and state government benefits, including the earned income tax credit, food assistance, housing assistance, child care assistance, and medical assistance (Randolph, 2104). Some analysts downplay the relevance of the welfare cliff due to the fact that most people on various forms of welfare are either not working or, if working, are not near the cliff threshold (Adolphsen & Ingram, 2018). For this reason, economists recommend that eligibility for safety net aid be gradually phased out as incomes rise.

Advocates of a safety net must also think very carefully about which people constitute the truly needy. As the public choice school of economics has pointed out, most income transfer programs are not aimed at the poor but rather have as their beneficiaries politically powerful interest groups that can effectively lobby the government for programs and policies that benefit their members (Kreuger, 1974). Medicare is a classic example of a "safety net" that overwhelmingly benefits the nonpoor. According to data from the Kaiser Family Foundation, in 2018 a mere 12% of Medicare recipients were at or below 100% of the federal poverty level (income of $12,100 for a single person), while 37% of Medicaid recipients were at or below 100% of this mark (Kaiser Family Foundation, 2018b; 2018c). There may be good reasons for expanding safety net eligibility above the official poverty level, but the line for a true safety net must be drawn somewhere in the neighborhood

---

6. The term arises from the fact that a line graph of total income—wages plus government benefits—for those with low incomes initially rises with increases in pay, but at some point drops off, in some cases substantially, because the person then crosses the income-based eligibility threshold. See Randolph (2014) for a detailed analysis with graphs.

of actual poverty. In 2018, 35% of Medicare and 8% of Medicaid recipients had incomes at 400% of poverty level ($48,400 for a single person) or higher (Kaiser Family Foundation, 2018b; 2018c). This economist is not aware of any economic rationale for government paying for basic goods for people who can afford them. Government coverage for middle-class households cannot be fairly described as a safety net but merely an income transfer to the politically favored. Tremendous savings could be obtained by paring back aid to those who do not need it. Perhaps the most obvious healthcare safety net reform is making it into an actual safety net, rather than a mere cushion for the middle class.

Principles for an Efficient, Effective Healthcare Safety Net

The United States has the most cutting-edge healthcare in the world, but our healthcare system is plagued by waste, inefficiency, and rising costs. Detailed explanations of these symptoms are provided elsewhere in this book, but the overall problem is a rather simple matter of basic economics: lack of market pricing mechanisms, lack of full consumer choice, lack of robust competition, and an incentive structure that encourages maximal spending, even for minimal or no results (see chapters 1, 3, and 4 for more on this topic). Any efforts to improve healthcare efficiency must address these issues. Likewise, efforts to improve our healthcare safety net must be based on sound economics. Successful reforms to the healthcare safety net will rely on incentive structures generated by the price system, consumer choice, and provider competition.

Food Stamps for Healthcare?

So, what is the solution to inefficiencies and overspending in our healthcare safety net and our healthcare system in general? Trick question: There are no solutions, only trade-offs. But there may be some trade-offs worth making, especially if the benefit of realigning consumer and producer incentives to promote efficiency can be achieved at the cost of simply restructuring how government doles out healthcare aid to the needy.

To begin, let us examine how a safety net can be layered over top of a functional price system, allowing government to support the poor without stifling the market process. As discussed above, the food economy works marvelously well because market prices and a consumer-oriented payment system align producers' incentives with consumers' interests and desires. When it comes to a food safety net, we do not expect government intrusion into food production, allocation, or payment decisions, as is done so often with healthcare. We simply provide the targeted population (the poor) with additional funds—food stamps—that can only be used for food purchases. In this way, the food safety net can provide whatever level of support society, through the political process, deems appropriate for helping the poor in meeting this basic need. This safety net, moreover, can be easily adjusted by changing eligibility rules and benefit levels without fundamentally altering a production and delivery system that works well—the competitive free market in food.

Could the healthcare safety net function more like the food safety net? Possibly. All that is required is to put consumers in the driver's seat and, to the extent possible, give consumers additional exposure to the opportunity costs of their own healthcare spending—that is, provide consumers with maximum choice and incentives to economize. This is not all that radical an idea. As noted, this is how food stamps operate at the federal level; at the state and local level school voucher programs also function in a similar manner. School vouchers are intended to both increase consumer choices and discipline education providers by forcing them into competition for students' (parents') business. Controversy surrounding vouchers arises at least in part because of the voucher program's potential to disrupt local education monopolies. Success of vouchers can be seen in the rising popularity of voucher programs,[7] particularly among education consumers in low-income communities that are often served by low-quality public schools.

Health savings accounts (HSAs) could be used as a tool to "voucherize" the healthcare safety net, thereby shifting at least some welfare spending away from Category III/IV and toward Category I. Michael Cannon and Michael Tanner, in their healthcare reform book *Healthy Competition*, provide a concise overview of HSAs and their benefits:

An HSA is much like a 401(k) dedicated for medical expenses. As with a 401(k), eligible individuals and their employers can make tax-free contributions. Earnings are also tax-free. Funds withdrawn before age 65 are generally taxed as income, plus a 10 percent penalty. After age 65, withdrawals are taxed as income with no penalty. However, in contrast to 401(k)s, *withdrawals for medical expenses are never taxed.* This is true

7. A recent poll conducted by Harvard's Graduate School of Education finds that "public support for vouchers targeted to low-income families has jumped 12 percentage points since 2016, to 49% (41% opposed) from 37% (48% opposed). Republican support has jumped 13 percentage points to 44%, while opposition has fallen to 50% during the same time period. Democratic support has increased to 52% support today from 42% in 2016" (Education Next, 2019).

before and after age 65. For this reason, HSAs have been described as a "401(k) on steroids." . . . To be eligible for an HSA, individuals must be covered by a qualified high-deductible health plan. . . . HSAs are a milestone in health care policy. By reducing government encouragement of excessive private coverage, HSAs will restore much of the consumer sovereignty, product choice, and producer competition that have been eroded by government. HSAs reestablish the freedom to choose one's doctor, to own one's health insurance, and to self-insure for future medical needs without bureaucratic interference or being penalized by government. HSAs can help change the culture of health care in the United States by reorienting providers to enhance quality and contain costs. . . . Unlike other forms of health coverage, whatever patients do not spend from their HSAs, they keep in their accounts, which follow them from job to job (Cannon & Tanner, 2007).

Because funds deposited into an HSA become the personal assets of the consumer, spending out of an HSA is always Category I spending, even if the funds are provided by an employer or the government. Furthermore, because HSAs are typically tied to high-deductible health insurance plans, HSA consumers tend to have more skin in the game when it comes to healthcare spending decisions. Consumers face at least part of the opportunity costs of healthcare spending as dollars they spend out of their HSAs are dollars they cannot then invest for themselves. HSA-based health coverage helps to place consumers in greater control of healthcare spending decisions, and this "consumerization" of the market can bring about an incentive environment for producers to respond to consumer desires.

Implementing HSAs into the healthcare safety net could be accomplished in a relatively straightforward manner. Safety net enrollees on Medicaid or Medicare would be provided with HSAs, into which the government would make an initial deposit of funds. Coverage could then be modeled on high-deductible, HSA-based private insurance coverage as described above. Beneficiaries would be directly responsible for a substantial portion of their healthcare expenses, particularly routine health services; with HSA funds in hand they would be able to pay "out of pocket" for some non-negligible fraction of their total healthcare bills (see various direct pay options in chapters 6 and 8 through 10). Policy wonks would need to work out important details regarding eligibility criteria (e.g., income thresholds and phase-outs), annual and lifetime caps on HSA contributions, and so on. A federalized program, in which states could experiment with different funding formulas, eligibility rules, deductible levels, and so forth, would facilitate the discovery of an optimal rules framework and allow local values and priorities to govern safety net policy.

Health policy analyst John Goodman aptly summarizes many economists' views regarding what is wrong with healthcare in the United States: "The problem with our health care system is not that it is market-based. To the contrary, we have so suppressed the market that no one ever sees a real price for anything. The answer to that is to liberate the market. Buyers and sellers should see real prices for every service" (Goodman, 2020). He is right about the lack of real prices; what is also needed to complement a true market price system is to minimize as much as possible the perverse incentives attached to third-party payers spending other people's money. General reforms that increase price transparency and remove price controls over healthcare products and services can help bring a true price system to healthcare. Implementing more Category I spending models into the healthcare safety net through consumer-centered delivery options (such as HSAs) might accomplish the other goal of improving spending incentives.

My suggestions here should not be taken as a complete or exhaustive enumeration of optimal reforms for the healthcare safety net. Ongoing political discussions are needed to discover both how generous Americans want their healthcare safety net to be and how it might be delivered in a cost-effective way. The goal here has been to motivate these discussions with some foundational economic considerations. If our aim as a society is to create a healthcare safety net that works well and does not waste too many resources, we must, as much as possible, rely on the price system to reveal the true opportunity costs of different actions and guide people in optimal decision-making. We must recognize that incentives matter, and people do not spend other people's money with the same care as they spend their own money. Finally, we should be aware of the perverse incentives of overgenerous, improperly phased aid, which can promote dependency and stifle personal responsibility and growth.

CHAPTER 20

A Safety Net Health Insurance Proposal
Back to the Future With the Wisconsin Health Plan of 2005—a Review

CURT GIELOW

Chapter 19 presented the economist's perspective on a healthcare safety net, requiring those receiving safety net aid to be in a situation where they feel as though they are spending their own money and where there are some sort of market forces at play. This chapter presents an overview of actual draft bipartisan legislation, proposed by Democratic and Republican legislators, to provide universal healthcare in Wisconsin—but using both health savings accounts (HSAs), and private insurance marketplaces that attempt to keep market forces at play. This proposal never passed and was not favored by Republicans in Wisconsin, but it is an example of a version of universal healthcare that tries to at least maintain market forces and ensure that Milton Friedman's "Category I" spending is occurring. Chapter 21 presents the related YoungMedicare proposal by policymaker David Riemer, who also worked with Curt Gielow to draft the legislation presented in this chapter.

Background

During the 2005–2006 legislative session of the Wisconsin State Assembly, I introduced, along with Representative Jon Richards (D), a bipartisan health insurance proposal we called the Wisconsin Health Plan (WHP). A major element of the proposed WHP was that it would extend health insurance coverage to all Wisconsin residents at a time (2005) when a Wisconsin Family Health Survey reported about 9% of all Wisconsin residents under the age of 65 were uninsured.

In a June 2007 report by the Lewin Group, commissioned by the Wisconsin Health Project, a joint developer of our WHP, the authors stated that "the WHP is potentially a landmark piece of legislation that would provide

---

Curt Gielow is the founding dean of the Concordia University School of Pharmacy and served 13 years in elected office in Wisconsin.

health insurance for all state residents not otherwise covered by Medicare, Medicaid, Badger Care or TRICARE (i.e., military dependents and retirees)" (Lewin Group, 2007).

The Lewin Group also projected that by 2007 there would be about 476,000 uninsured people in Wisconsin. Surely, this was a rally cry for a need to provide a "safety net" program of health insurance for these nearly half million residents.

The Wisconsin Health Plan was summarized in a State of Health Care supplement to the *Small Business Times* on August 5, 2005, as follows:

The Wisconsin Health Plan seeks to address Wisconsin's triple crisis in health care: the skyrocketing cost of health care, increasing numbers of uninsured, and the ever-present deficit in the state's Medicaid program.

Wisconsin-specific data show that employers now spend an average of 15 percent of payroll for health care premiums of their employees. Health care costs are rising 10–25 percent per year, and the result is an adverse economic effect on wages, profits, job creation, and new investment in Wisconsin.

Wisconsin has been a national leader in having low rates of uninsured in our state. Yet, at some point over the course of the year, up to 500,000 Wisconsinites have no insurance coverage. Conservative estimates suggest that 6 percent of our population is not covered on any given day. Lack of insurance is a significant factor in premature death, unnecessary illness, and bankruptcy; and the trends in this area are getting worse, not better.

Wisconsin's Medicaid program is facing a structural deficit because costs and caseloads are rising much faster than state revenues. The state has relied on short-term fixes to get by thus far, but the ongoing structural deficit in this $4 billion program continues to undermine other state priorities.

The Wisconsin Health Plan provides a new way to pay for health care in Wisconsin. This proposal creates an effective purchasing pool and incorporates "consumer driven" incentives to promote health care quality and use market forces to drive down health care costs. The proposal has three simple components:

- ◆ All Wisconsin employers pay a fair assessment
- ◆ All Wisconsin residents (under age 65) own a Health Insurance Purchasing Account
- ◆ All participants have an annual choice for healthcare plan and providers

The plan is structured in a way that would free up nearly $1 billion in the state's biennial budget. This revenue could be used to cut taxes or make needed investments.

—SMALL BUSINESS TIMES, 2005

The Wisconsin Health Plan was introduced in the Wisconsin Assembly on March 21, 2006 by Representatives Gielow (R) and Richards (D) and referred to the Committee on Insurance and the Joint Survey Committee on Tax Exemptions. It did not receive a hearing in either committee and failed to pass the legislature subject to Senate Joint Resolution 1 on May 11, 2006. Wisconsin 2005 Assembly Bill (AB) 1140 is included here as appendix A for the reader's review.

This bill would have established a private health insurance purchasing arrangement (PHIPA) to provide health insurance coverage for state residents by asking private insurance companies to bid on an array of three tiers of coverages they would offer and make available to all residents. The lowest tier of coverage (minimum coverage benefits) would be defined by the PHIPA and all private insurance companies could bid to "win" the right to offer the lowest tier to any and all takers. Two additional tiers with slightly better benefits would also be offered by the private companies for residents to choose, should they wish to pay a bit higher premium than the cost of the basic tier.

The WHP also proposed to offer a $500 HSA to each Wisconsin resident under age 65 and a $100 HSA to those under age 18. That money would be available to use as discretionary spending to pay any coinsurance (co-pays) or deductibles required.

Funding provided to the PHIPA would come from a payroll tax to employers, a limited portion of which could be allocated to the employees. This funding source would then pay insurance companies for the coverage tier selected by the resident at the lowest (Tier 1) rate. Premiums above the Tier 1 choice (the difference between Tier 1 and the tier chosen) would be paid by residents, who were free to choose better coverages and benefits if they wish. Notwithstanding the required deductibles and co-pays, an eligible resident who is age 18 or older would not be required to pay more than $2,000 per year in total cost-sharing and a family of two or more would have a $3,000 per year cap on their cost-sharing.

The WHP would have required an annual enrollment in the program and the HSA accounts would be increased annually at the U.S. consumer price index.

The introduction of the Wisconsin Health Plan in 2005 was intended to stimulate a discussion on the critical issues facing the provision of healthcare services to Wisconsin residents. Although not all details were fine-tuned, at the time an estimated 4.0 million people (Lewin Group, 2007) would have been enrolled in a program that would have begun to address realignment of the incentives in a health insurance coverage environment that did not provide a "safety net."

Representative Richards and I sought a compromise that by its nature would not make all people and certainly politicians happy. We attempted to stimulate a discussion of what today might be called a *purple solution* to incorporate some free market principles with limited government participation that was necessary in order to make this work. Unfortunately, we got the rancor but not the results.

I offer this review of the thinking of 15 years ago on a subject that still is arguably the most significant domestic problem of our day.

APPENDIX A

State of Wisconsin
2005 - 2006 LEGISLATURE

LRB-2922/3
PJK/RAC/MES:lmk:rs

2005 ASSEMBLY BILL 1140

March 21, 2006 – Introduced by Representatives GIELOW and RICHARDS. Referred
to Committee on Insurance. Referred to Joint Survey Committee on Tax
Exemptions.

1   AN ACT *to amend* 40.51 (1), 111.70 (1) (dm), 632.755 (1g) (a) and 632.755 (1g) (b);

2   and *to create* 13.94 (1s) (c) 5., 20.855 (8m), 25.17 (1) (gd), 25.775, 71.83 (1) (ce),

3   subchapter XVI of chapter 71 [precedes 71.98], 111.91 (2) (pm), 149.12 (2) (g) 7.

4   and chapter 260 of the statutes; **relating to:** creating the Private Health

5   Insurance Purchasing Corporation of Wisconsin, establishing a health

6   insurance purchasing arrangement through the use of private accounts for all

7   state residents, adopting federal law as it relates to health savings accounts for

8   state income and franchise tax purposes, making appropriations, and

9   providing a penalty.

Analysis by the Legislative Reference Bureau

Health insurance purchasing arrangement; corporation

This bill establishes a private health insurance purchasing arrangement
(PHIPA) to provide health insurance coverage for state residents, and creates a
private, nonstock corporation, called the Private Health Insurance Purchasing
Corporation of Wisconsin (corporation), to facilitate and administer PHIPA. The
eight members of the corporation's board of directors are designated by the governor
and various business organizations and labor unions. The corporation's meetings

2005 – 2006 Legislature   – 2 –   LRB-2922/3
                                                        PJK/RAC/MES:lmk:rs

ASSEMBLY BILL 1140

must be open to the public, and it must keep its records open to inspection by the
governor, the secretary of administration, any committee of the legislature, the
Legislative Fiscal Bureau, and the Legislative Audit Bureau, which must conduct
both a financial audit of the corporation and a performance evaluation audit of
PHIPA at least once every two years. The corporation must keep its hiring practices
and its procedures for soliciting bids or proposals in writing and open to public
inspection, as well as all of its requests for bids or proposals and its analyses of, and
final decisions on, bids and proposals received. The corporation must annually
report to the governor and the legislature on its activities.

Eligibility; establishing accounts

Every eligible resident is eligible for PHIPA. An eligible resident is defined in
the bill as an individual who is under 65 years of age; who has been domiciled in the
state for at least six months or, if under six months old, whose parent or guardian
has been domiciled in the state for at least six months; who maintains a substantial
presence in the state; and who is not an inmate of a penal facility, not a resident of
an institution for the mentally ill or developmentally disabled, not eligible for health
care coverage from the federal government, and not eligible for Medical Assistance
or Badger Care unless a waiver from the federal secretary of health and human
services is granted that allows individuals who are eligible for Medical Assistance
or Badger Care to be covered under PHIPA.

Beginning in 2008, the corporation must establish for every eligible resident,
except for one who objects for religious reasons, a private health insurance
purchasing account (account). The account of every eligible resident who is at least
18 years of age will include a health savings account (HSA).

Insurers; health care plans

The corporation must solicit bids from, and contract with, insurers to offer
health care plans under PHIPA. There must be at least two health care plans offered
by at least two insurers in each county of the state. The corporation must rank, on
a countywide basis, each of the health care plans offered, assign each plan to one of
three tiers, and determine the premium for each. Plans that the corporation
determines provide high quality care at a low risk–adjusted cost will be assigned to
Tier 1; plans that the corporation determines provide care at a higher risk–adjusted
cost will be assigned to Tier 2; and plans that the corporation determines provide care
at the highest risk–adjusted cost will be assigned to Tier 3. Every year there will be
an open enrollment period during which each eligible resident may select a health
care plan from among those offered. An eligible resident who does not select a plan
will be randomly assigned to a Tier 1 plan.

Funding and uses of accounts

Although the bill does not provide a funding source or mechanism, the accounts
and HSAs are to be funded beginning in 2009, which is also when coverage under
PHIPA begins. The amount that is to be credited to each eligible resident's account
is the full premium amount for coverage under a Tier 1 plan in the county in which
the eligible resident resides, actuarially adjusted for the eligible resident's age, sex,
and other appropriate risk factors. The corporation pays this amount to the health
care plan selected by the eligible resident. Only if an eligible resident has selected

a Tier 2 or Tier 3 plan must he or she pay any additional, out–of–pocket amount for the premium. The bill provides that the amount credited to an eligible resident's HSA will be $500 in 2009, and adjusted to reflect changes in the U.S. consumer price index for years after that. The amount credited to an HSA, however, may be increased or decreased for various reasons, such as whether the eligible resident follows a healthy lifestyle protocol and whether the corporation estimates that revenues will exceed expenses or expenses will exceed revenues in a given year. Federal law requires that amounts credited to an HSA must be used to pay for medical care.

Benefits; cost–sharing; preexisting condition exclusion

Every health care plan offered will provide the same benefits and, except for premiums, will require the same cost–sharing. Benefits under PHIPA include medical and hospital care coverage and related health care services, prescription drug coverage, and limited dental care. Cost–sharing, including deductibles, coinsurance, and copayments, will not apply to certain types of care, including emergency care, prenatal care, medically indicated immunizations for children, and other specified types of preventive care. However, benefits may be reduced, under a procedure outlined in the bill, if the corporation determines that expenses will exceed revenues for a given year or years.

Except for those services to which cost–sharing does not apply, each eligible resident who is at least 18 years old on January 1 must pay a deductible of $1,200 in that year, and each eligible resident who is less than 18 years old on January 1 must pay a deductible of $100 in that year. After the deductible has been satisfied, an eligible resident must pay coinsurance of between 10 and 20 percent, as determined by the corporation, for prescription drugs and covered services, except for those services to which cost–sharing does not apply. Prescription drugs are subject to additional coinsurance or copayments, as determined by the corporation. The additional coinsurance or copayments must be higher for prescription drugs that are not on a preferred list determined by the corporation.

Notwithstanding the required deductible, coinsurance, and copayment amounts, an eligible resident who is at least 18 years old on January 1 may not be required to pay more than $2,000 per year in total cost–sharing; an eligible resident who is less than 18 years old on January 1 may not be required to pay more than $500 per year in total cost–sharing; and a family of two or more eligible residents may not be required to pay more than $3,000 per year in total cost–sharing. In addition, the corporation must reduce one or more of the cost–sharing amounts for low–income eligible residents, and the deductible and maximum cost–sharing amounts are to be adjusted annually to reflect changes in the U.S. consumer price index.

There is a coverage exclusion for any preexisting condition of an eligible resident who, at any time during the 18 months before becoming an eligible resident, resided outside of Wisconsin and did not have health insurance coverage substantially similar to the coverage under PHIPA. However, the preexisting condition exclusion may not extend beyond the date on which the eligible resident has been continuously covered under PHIPA for a total of 18 months.

2005 – 2006 Legislature   – 4 –   LRB-2922/3
                                                PJK/RAC/MES:lmk:rs
ASSEMBLY BILL 1140

Health care advisory committee

The corporation is required to establish a health care advisory committee to advise it on specified health-related issues. The corporation must consult with the health care advisory committee and other experts on various health-related issues, such as creating incentives for eligible residents to adopt healthier lifestyles and increasing transparency of health care cost and quality information, and must adopt policies that further these goals.

Waiver of federal requirements; proposed legislation

Under the bill, the corporation and the Department of Health and Family Services (DHFS) must develop a plan for providing coverage under PHIPA for individuals who would be eligible residents except that they are eligible for Badger Care or for Medical Assistance under what DHFS determines is the low-income families category. DHFS must submit the plan to the legislature, along with its recommendations on the desirability of requesting waivers that would allow implementation of the plan and the use of federal financial participation to fund health care coverage for those individuals under PHIPA. If DHFS requests waivers upon the authorization of the legislature, and if the waivers are granted, DHFS must submit proposed legislation implementing the provisions approved under the waivers. In addition, to facilitate the provision of coverage under PHIPA for individuals who are eligible for Badger Care or for Medical Assistance under what DHFS determines is the low-income families category, DHFS and the Legislative Fiscal Bureau must submit proposed legislation that separates the Medical Assistance provisions of the statutes, including related appropriations, into two eligibility categories, one for low-income families and one for elderly and disabled persons.

Adoption of federal law for health savings accounts

The bill adopts, for state income and franchise tax purposes, section 1201 of Public Law 108-173 as it relates to claiming a deduction for an amount that a person pays into a health savings account.

This bill will be referred to the Joint Survey Committee on Tax Exemptions for a detailed analysis, which will be printed as an appendix to this bill.

For further information see the *state* fiscal estimate, which will be printed as an appendix to this bill.

The people of the state of Wisconsin, represented in senate and assembly, do enact as follows:

1   SECTION 1. 13.94 (1s) (c) 5. of the statutes is created to read:

2   13.94 **(1s)** (c) 5. The Private Health Insurance Purchasing Corporation of

3   Wisconsin for the cost of the audits under s. 260.05 (4).

1   SECTION 2. 20.855 (8m) of the statutes is created to read:

2   20.855 **(8m)** PRIVATE HEALTH INSURANCE PURCHASING CORPORATION OF

3   WISCONSIN. (r) *Health insurance purchasing accounts and administration.* After

4   deducting the amounts appropriated for the state's share of benefits and

5   administrative costs under the Medical Assistance program that are attributable to

6   the low-income families category, as determined under 2005 Wisconsin Act .... (this

7   act), section 14 (1) (b) and the amounts appropriated for the state's share of benefits

8   and administrative costs under the Badger Care health care program under s.

9   49.665, the balance of the moneys in the health insurance purchasing trust fund to

10   be paid to the Private Health Insurance Purchasing Corporation of Wisconsin for

11   establishing, funding, managing, and assisting individuals with the use of, the

12   health insurance purchasing accounts established under ch. 260.

13   SECTION 3. 25.17 (1) (gd) of the statutes is created to read:

14   25.17 **(1)** (gd) Health insurance purchasing trust fund (s. 25.775);

15   SECTION 4. 25.775 of the statutes is created to read:

16   **25.775 Health insurance purchasing trust fund.** There is established a

17   separate, nonlapsible trust fund designated as the health insurance purchasing

18   trust fund, consisting of all moneys appropriated or transferred to or deposited in the

19   fund.

20   SECTION 5. 40.51 (1) of the statutes is amended to read:

21   40.51 **(1)** The procedures and provisions pertaining to enrollment, premium

22   transmitted and coverage of eligible employees for health care benefits shall be

23   established by contract or rule except as otherwise specifically provided by this

24   chapter. Health care benefits provided under this subchapter shall be in addition to

25   health care benefits provided eligible employees under ch. 260.

1   **SECTION 6.** 71.83 (1) (ce) of the statutes is created to read:

2   71.83 **(1)** (ce) *Health savings accounts.* Any person who is liable for a penalty

3   for federal income tax purposes under section 223 (f) (4) of the Internal Revenue Code

4   is liable for a penalty equal to 33 percent of that penalty. The department of revenue

5   shall assess, levy, and collect the penalty under this paragraph as it assesses, levies,

6   and collects taxes under this chapter.

7   **SECTION 7.** Subchapter XVI of chapter 71 [precedes 71.98] of the statutes is

8   created to read:

9   **CHAPTER 71**

10   SUBCHAPTER XVI

11   INTERNAL REVENUE CODE UPDATE

12   **71.98 Internal Revenue Code update.** The following federal laws, to the

13   extent that they apply to the Internal Revenue Code, apply to this chapter:

14   **(1)** HEALTH SAVINGS ACCOUNTS. Section 1201 of P.L. 108–173, relating to health

15   savings accounts.

16   **SECTION 8.** 111.70 (1) (dm) of the statutes is amended to read:

17   111.70 **(1)** (dm) "Economic issue" means salaries, overtime pay, sick leave,

18   payments in lieu of sick leave usage, vacations, clothing allowances in excess of the

19   actual cost of clothing, length–of–service credit, continuing education credit, shift

20   premium pay, longevity pay, extra duty pay, performance bonuses, health insurance

21   coverage of benefits not provided under ch. 260, life insurance, dental insurance,

22   disability insurance, vision insurance, long–term care insurance, worker's

23   compensation and unemployment insurance, social security benefits, vacation pay,

24   holiday pay, lead worker pay, temporary assignment pay, retirement contributions,

25   supplemental retirement benefits, severance or other separation pay, hazardous

1   duty pay, certification or license payment, limitations on layoffs that create a new or

2   increased financial liability on the employer and contracting or subcontracting of

3   work that would otherwise be performed by municipal employees in the collective

4   bargaining unit with which there is a labor dispute.

5   SECTION 9. 111.91 (2) (pm) of the statutes is created to read:

6   111.91 **(2)** (pm) Health care coverage of employees under ch. 260.

7   SECTION 10. 149.12 (2) (g) 7. of the statutes is created to read:

8   149.12 **(2)** (g) 7. Health care coverage under the health insurance purchasing

9   arrangement under ch. 260.

10   SECTION 11. Chapter 260 of the statutes is created to read:

11   **CHAPTER 260**

12   **HEALTH INSURANCE PURCHASING ACCOUNTS**

13   **260.01 Definitions.** In this chapter:

14   **(1)** "Board" means the board of directors of the corporation.

15   **(2)**   "Corporation" means the Private Health Insurance Purchasing

16   Corporation of Wisconsin.

17   **(3)** (a) "Eligible resident" means an individual who satisfies all of the following

18   criteria:

19   1. The individual has been domiciled, as defined by the corporation, in this state

20   for at least 6 months, except that, if a child is under 6 months of age, the child is an

21   "eligible resident" if the child lives in this state and at least one of the child's parents

22   or the child's guardian has been domiciled, as defined by the corporation, in this state

23   for at least 6 months.

24   2. The individual maintains a substantial presence in this state, as defined by

25   the corporation. In defining what constitutes a substantial presence in this state, the

1   corporation shall consider such factors as the amount of time per year that an

2   individual is actually present in the state and the amount of taxes that an individual

3   pays in this state, except that if the individual attends school outside of this state and

4   is under 23 years of age, the factors shall include the amount of time that the

5   individual's parent or guardian is actually present in the state and the amount of

6   taxes that the individual's parent or guardian pays in this state, and if the individual

7   is in active service with the U.S. armed forces outside of this state, the factors shall

8   include the amount of time that the individual's parent, guardian, or spouse is

9   actually present in the state and the amount of taxes that the individual's parent,

10   guardian, or spouse pays in this state.

11   3. The individual is under 65 years of age.

12   4. The individual is not eligible for health care coverage from the federal

13   government, is not an inmate of a penal facility, as defined in s. 19.32 (1e), and is not

14   placed or confined in, or committed to, an institution for the mentally ill or

15   developmentally disabled.

16   5. Unless a waiver is requested under s. 260.60 and granted and in effect, the

17   individual is not eligible for medical assistance under subch. IV of ch. 49 or for health

18   care coverage under the Badger Care health care program under s. 49.665.

19   (b) Notwithstanding par. (a), an individual who satisfies par. (a) 1. to 5. and who

20   receives health care coverage under a collective bargaining agreement that is in

21   effect on January 1, 2009, is not an "eligible individual" until the day on which the

22   collective bargaining agreement expires.

23   **260.05   Private Health Insurance Purchasing Corporation of**

24   **Wisconsin. (1)** INCORPORATION. The secretary of administration shall do all of the

25   following:

2005 – 2006 Legislature   – 9 –   LRB-2922/3
                                                            PJK/RAC/MES:lmk:rs
ASSEMBLY BILL 1140   SECTION 11

1   (a) Draft and file articles of incorporation for a nonstock corporation under ch.

2   181 and take all actions necessary to exempt the corporation from federal taxation

3   under section 501 (c) (3) of the Internal Revenue Code.

4   (b) Provide in the articles of incorporation filed under par. (a) all of the

5   following:

6   1. That the name of the corporation is the "Private Health Insurance

7   Purchasing Corporation of Wisconsin."

8   2. That the board shall consist of 8 directors who, except for the initial directors,

9   shall be designated or appointed as follows:

10   a. One designated by Wisconsin Manufacturers and Commerce.

11   b. One designated by the Wisconsin State American Federation of Labor and

12   Congress of Industrial Organizations.

13   c. One designated by the Metropolitan Milwaukee Association of Commerce.

14   d. One designated by the Wisconsin office of the National Federation of

15   Independent Business.

16   e. One designated by the Wisconsin Farm Bureau Federation.

17   f. One designated by the SEIU Wisconsin State Council.

18   g. Two designated by the governor to represent consumers.

19   3. That the term of a director shall be 4 years, except that the term of an initial

20   director shall be one year.

21   4. The names and addresses of the initial directors.

22   5. That 7 votes shall be necessary for adoption of any decision of the board,

23   except for those designated categories of decisions, if any, that the board agrees to

24   adopt by a simple majority of the votes.

1   (c) In consultation with the persons charged with designating the directors

2   under par. (b) 2. a. to g., designate the initial directors.

3   (d) Draft bylaws for adoption by the board.

4   **(2)** DUTIES. As a condition for the release of funds under s. 20.855 (8m) (r), the

5   corporation shall do all of the following:

6   (a) Establish, fund, and manage health insurance purchasing accounts in the

7   manner provided in this chapter; assist eligible residents in using their accounts to

8   purchase health care coverage; and perform all other functions required of the

9   corporation under this chapter.

10   (b) Establish an independent and binding appeals process for resolving

11   disputes over eligibility and other determinations made by the corporation.

12   (c) Keep its records open at all times to inspection and examination by the

13   governor, the secretary of administration, any committee of either or both houses of

14   the legislature, the legislative fiscal bureau, and the legislative audit bureau.

15   (d) Keep its meetings open to the public to the extent required of governmental

16   bodies under subch. V of ch. 19.

17   (e) Cooperate with the legislative audit bureau in the performance of the audits

18   under sub. (4).

19   (f) Submit on each October 1 an annual report to the legislature under s. 13.172

20   (2) and to the governor regarding its activities and including any recommendations

21   of the health care advisory committee under s. 260.40 (1) (d).

22   **(3)** CONTRACTS AND HIRING. (a) The corporation may contract with other

23   organizations, entities, or individuals for the performance of any of its functions.

24   With respect to contracts under this subsection, the corporation shall do all of the

25   following:

1   1. Use generally accepted procedures, which shall be in writing and open to

2   public inspection, for soliciting bids or proposals and for awarding contracts to the

3   lowest–bidding, qualified person or to the most qualified person submitting a

4   proposal.

5   2. Make open to public inspection all of its requests for bids or proposals, all of

6   its analyses of bids or proposals received, and all of its final decisions on bids or

7   proposals received.

8   (b) The corporation shall use generally accepted hiring practices, which shall

9   be in writing and open to public inspection, for hiring any staff.

10   **(4)** AUDITS. At least once every 2 years, the legislative audit bureau shall

11   conduct a financial audit of the corporation and a performance evaluation audit of

12   the health insurance purchasing arrangement under this chapter that includes an

13   audit of the corporation's policies and management practices. The legislative audit

14   bureau shall distribute a copy of each audit report under this subsection to the

15   legislature under s. 13.172 (2) and to the governor. The corporation shall reimburse

16   the legislative audit bureau for the cost of the audits and reports required under this

17   subsection.

18   **260.10 Health insurance purchasing accounts. (1)** ESTABLISHMENT AND

19   FUNDING. (a) Beginning in January 2008, the corporation shall establish a private

20   health insurance purchasing account for each eligible resident, except for an eligible

21   resident who notifies the corporation that, for religious reasons, he or she does not

22   wish to have an account. Beginning in 2009, the corporation annually shall credit

23   to each account a dollar amount that is the full premium, as determined by the

24   corporation under s. 260.15 (2) (b), of any of the Tier 1 health care plans offered in

25   the county in which the eligible resident resides and that has been actuarially

2005 – 2006 Legislature   – 12 –   LRB–2922/3
                                                              PJK/RAC/MES:lmk:rs
ASSEMBLY BILL 1140   SECTION 11

1   adjusted for the eligible resident based on age, sex, and other appropriate risk factors

2   determined by the board. Subject to sub. (2) and s. 260.20 (3), the corporation shall

3   pay the amount credited under this paragraph to the health care plan selected by the

4   eligible resident, or to which the eligible resident has been assigned, under s. 260.15

5   (3).

6   (b) 1. The health insurance purchasing account of an eligible resident who is

7   at least 18 years of age shall also include a health savings account, as described in

8   26 USC 223. For an eligible resident who is under 18 years of age when his or her

9   health insurance purchasing account is established, his or her health insurance

10   purchasing account shall include a health savings account beginning in the year in

11   which the eligible resident is 18 years of age on January 1.

12   2. Beginning in 2009, the corporation annually shall deposit an amount into

13   each health savings account. Subject to s. 260.20 (5), the amount deposited in 2009

14   shall be $500 and the amount deposited in each year thereafter shall be adjusted to

15   reflect the annual percentage change in the U.S. consumer price index for all urban

16   consumers, U.S. city average, as determined by the U.S. department of labor, for the

17   12–month period ending on December 31 of the preceding year.

18   3. If the corporation estimates that revenues will exceed costs in a year, the

19   corporation may deposit into each health savings account an amount in addition to

20   the amount deposited under subd. 2.

21   4. In addition to amounts deposited under subds. 2. and 3., the corporation may

22   deposit into the health savings account of an eligible resident who successfully

23   follows a healthy lifestyle protocol certified by the corporation under s. 260.40 (2) (a),

24   an amount determined by the corporation to be equal to the average reduction in

25   health care costs per eligible resident who adopts a healthy lifestyle protocol.

2005 – 2006 Legislature   – 13 –   LRB-2922/3
                                                          PJK/RAC/MES:lmk:rs
ASSEMBLY BILL 1140   SECTION 11

1   5. Notwithstanding subds. 2., 3., and 4., the total amount deposited in an

2   eligible resident's health savings account may not exceed the maximum amount

3   allowed under federal law.

4   **(2)** ADDITIONAL PAYMENT FOR DISPROPORTIONATE RISK. The corporation may retain

5   a percentage of the amounts credited under sub. (1) (a) to pay to health care plans

6   that have incurred disproportionate risk not fully compensated for by the actuarial

7   adjustment in the amount credited to each account under sub. (1) (a). Any payment

8   to a health care plan under this subsection shall reflect the disproportionate risk

9   incurred by the health care plan.

10   **260.15 Health care plans. (1)** PARTICIPATION OF INSURERS. (a) Subject to par.

11   (c), the corporation shall solicit bids from, and enter into contracts with, insurers for

12   offering coverage to eligible residents. Any insurer that is authorized to do business

13   in this state in one or more lines of insurance that includes health insurance is

14   eligible to submit a bid.

15   (b) In determining which insurers qualify to offer coverage, the corporation

16   shall use financial, coverage, and disclosure standards that are comparable to those

17   that the department of employee trust funds has used in qualifying insurers for

18   offering coverage under the state employee health plan under s. 40.51 (6).

19   (c) The corporation shall ensure that in each county at least 2 health care plans

20   are offered by at least 2 different insurers.

21   **(2)** TIER ASSIGNMENT AND PREMIUM DETERMINATION. (a) The corporation shall

22   rank the health care plans offered in each county and assign each health care plan

23   to one of 3 tiers, on a countywide basis, based on the health care plan's risk–adjusted

24   cost and quality. The corporation shall assign to "Tier 1" health care plans that it

25   determines provide high quality care at a low risk–adjusted cost, assign to "Tier 2"

2005 – 2006 Legislature   – 14 –   LRB-2922/3
                                                            PJK/RAC/MES:lmk:rs
ASSEMBLY BILL 1140   SECTION 11

1   health care plans that it determines provide care at a higher risk–adjusted cost, and

2   assign to "Tier 3" health care plans that it determines provide care at the highest

3   risk–adjusted cost.

4   (b) The corporation shall determine the monthly premium amount for each

5   health care plan, including the out–of–pocket monthly premium amounts that

6   eligible residents must pay to enroll in Tier 2 health care plans and Tier 3 health care

7   plans. The out–of–pocket monthly premium amounts shall be based on the actual

8   differences in risk–adjusted cost between Tier 1 and Tier 2 health care plans, and

9   between Tier 1 and Tier 3 health care plans.

10   (3) PLAN SELECTION. Beginning in 2008, the corporation shall offer an annual

11   open enrollment period during which each eligible resident may select a health care

12   plan from among those offered. Coverage under the health care plan that an eligible

13   resident selects during an annual open enrollment period shall be effective on the

14   following January 1. An eligible resident who does not select a health care plan will

15   be randomly assigned to a Tier 1 health care plan. An eligible resident who selects

16   a Tier 2 or Tier 3 health care plan but who fails, as defined by the corporation, to pay

17   the out–of–pocket monthly premium amount will be randomly assigned to a Tier 1

18   health care plan.

19   **260.20 Benefits.** (1) GENERALLY. Coverage under this chapter shall begin on

20   January 1, 2009, and shall include medical and hospital care coverage and related

21   health care services as determined by the corporation, prescription drug coverage,

22   and limited dental care coverage, as provided in sub. (4).

23   (2) BENEFITS WITHOUT CERTAIN COST SHARING. Deductibles, coinsurance, and

24   copayments shall not apply to coverage of any of the following health care services,

25   as defined by the corporation:

2005 – 2006 Legislature   – 15 –   LRB-2922/3
                                                    PJK/RAC/MES:lmk:rs
ASSEMBLY BILL 1140   SECTION 11

1   (a) Emergency care.

2   (b) Prenatal care for pregnant women.

3   (c) Well–baby care.

4   (d) Annual medical examinations for children up to 18 years of age.

5   (e) Medically indicated immunizations for children up to 18 years of age.

6   (f) Annual gynecological examinations for older girls and women.

7   (g) Medically indicated Papanicolaou tests and mammograms.

8   (h) Annual medical examinations for older men.

9   (i) Medically indicated colonoscopies.

10   (j) The limited dental care specified in sub. (4).

11   (k) Other preventive services or procedures, as determined by the corporation,

12   for which there is scientific evidence that exemption from cost sharing is likely to

13   reduce health care costs or avoid health risks.

14   **(3)** PHARMACY BENEFIT. (a) Except as provided in par. (b), the corporation shall

15   assume the risk for, and pay for, prescription drugs provided to eligible residents.

16   For this purpose, the corporation shall retain the portion of the amount credited

17   under s. 260.10 (1) (a) that is actuarially allocated for prescription drug coverage.

18   (b) If the corporation determines that the method of providing prescription

19   drug coverage under par. (a) is not cost–effective, the corporation may require the

20   health care plans to provide prescription drug coverage to eligible residents and shall

21   pay the portion of the amount credited under s. 260.10 (1) (a) that is actuarially

22   allocated for prescription drug coverage to the eligible residents' health care plans.

23   **(4)** DENTAL BENEFIT. Every health care plan shall provide coverage of dental

24   examinations and the application of varnishes and sealants, as determined by the

2005 – 2006 Legislature   – 16 –   LRB-2922/3
                                                                PJK/RAC/MES:lmk:rs
ASSEMBLY BILL 1140   SECTION 11

1   corporation, for eligible residents who are at least 2 years of age but not more than

2   16 years of age.

3   **(5)** BENEFIT AND HEALTH SAVINGS ACCOUNT DEPOSIT REDUCTIONS. (a) If the

4   corporation determines, based on information and recommendations received from

5   its actuaries, that the cash balance in the health insurance purchasing trust fund is

6   likely to be insufficient for providing the health care benefits under subs. (1) to (4),

7   the corporation shall inform the governor and the legislature of all of the following:

8   1. That expenses will exceed revenues for one or more specified years.

9   2. What increase in revenues would be required to maintain the current health

10   savings account and benefit levels and bring revenues and expenses into balance for

11   the year or years specified in subd. 1.

12   3. Alternative reductions in the amount deposited into health savings accounts

13   under s. 260.10 (1) (b) 2. or in the benefits under this section that would be

14   appropriate to bring revenues and expenses into balance for the year or years

15   specified in subd. 1.

16   4. The revenue increase, health savings account deposit reduction, or benefit

17   reductions, or the combination of increase and reductions, that the corporation

18   recommends to bring revenues and expenses into balance for the year or years

19   specified in subd. 1.

20   5. The health savings account deposit reduction or benefit reductions that the

21   corporation prefers to bring revenues and expenses into balance for the year or years

22   specified in subd. 1. if legislation that increases revenues, reduces the health savings

23   account deposit under s. 260.10 (1) (b) 2., or reduces benefits provided under this

24   section is not enacted before the beginning of the first year specified in subd. 1.

1   (b) If legislation to bring revenues and expenses into balance for the year or

2   years specified in par. (a) 1. is not enacted before the beginning of the first year

3   specified, the corporation shall implement the health savings account deposit

4   reduction or benefit reductions specified in par. (a) 5.

5   **260.25 Cost sharing. (1)** PREMIUMS. (a) An eligible resident who selects or

6   is assigned to coverage under a Tier 1 health care plan shall pay no premium in

7   addition to the amount paid by the corporation under s. 260.10 (1) (a) to the eligible

8   resident's health care plan.

9   (b) An eligible resident who selects coverage under a Tier 2 or Tier 3 health care

10   plan shall be required to pay to the selected Tier 2 or Tier 3 health care plan, as a

11   condition of enrollment, the out–of–pocket monthly premium determined by the

12   corporation under s. 260.15 (2) (b).

13   **(2)** DEDUCTIBLES. Except as provided in s. 260.20 (2) and subject to sub. (4), in

14   a year, an eligible resident shall pay the following annual deductible amount:

15   (a) For an eligible resident who is 18 years of age or older on January 1 of that

16   year, $1,200.

17   (b) For an eligible resident who is under 18 years of age on January 1 of that

18   year, $100.

19   **(3)** COINSURANCE AND COPAYMENTS. Except as provided in s. 260.20 (2) and

20   subject to sub. (4), in a year, after the deductible under sub. (2) has been satisfied,

21   an eligible resident shall pay all of the following:

22   (a) Coinsurance that is equal to at least 10 percent but not more than 20 percent

23   of medical, hospital, related health care services, and prescription drug costs, as

24   determined by the corporation.

2005 - 2006 Legislature   - 18 -   LRB-2922/3

PJK/RAC/MES:lmk:rs

ASSEMBLY BILL 1140   **SECTION 11**

1   (b) For each prescription of a brand-name drug that is on the preferred list

2   determined by the corporation under s. 260.20 (3) (a) or by the eligible resident's

3   health care plan under s. 260.20 (3) (b), in addition to the coinsurance required under

4   par. (a), either coinsurance of at least 10 percent but not more than 20 percent or a

5   copayment, as determined by the corporation.

6   (c) For each prescription of a brand-name drug that is not on the preferred list

7   determined by the corporation under s. 260.20 (3) (a) or by the eligible resident's

8   health care plan under s. 260.20 (3) (b), in addition to the coinsurance required under

9   par. (a), either coinsurance of at least 20 percent but not more than 40 percent or a

10   copayment, as determined by the corporation.

11   **(4)** MAXIMUM AMOUNTS. (a) Subject to par. (c), an eligible resident under sub.

12   (2) (a) may not be required to pay more than $2,000 per year in total cost sharing

13   under subs. (2) and (3).

14   (b) Subject to par. (c), an eligible resident under sub. (2) (b) may not be required

15   to pay more than $500 per year in total cost sharing under subs. (2) and (3).

16   (c) A family consisting of 2 or more eligible residents may not be required to pay

17   more than $3,000 per year in total cost sharing under subs. (2) and (3).

18   **(5)** ADJUSTMENTS. (a) Notwithstanding subs. (2) to (4), the corporation shall

19   reduce the deductible, coinsurance, copayment, or maximum cost-sharing amounts,

20   or any combination of those amounts, for low-income eligible residents, as

21   determined by the corporation, to ensure that the cost sharing required does not

22   deter low-income eligible residents from seeking and using appropriate health care

23   services.

24   (b) Notwithstanding subs. (2) to (4), beginning in 2010, the corporation

25   annually shall adjust the deductible and maximum cost-sharing amounts to reflect

1   the annual percentage change in the U.S. consumer price index for all urban

2   consumers, U.S. city average, as determined by the U.S. department of labor, for the

3   12-month period ending on December 31 of the preceding year.

4   **260.30 Preexisting condition exclusion. (1)** TO WHOM APPLICABLE. Subject

5   to sub. (2), a health care plan may not provide coverage for any preexisting condition,

6   as defined by the corporation, of an eligible resident who, at any time during the

7   18-month period before becoming an eligible resident, resided outside of Wisconsin

8   and did not have health insurance coverage that was substantially similar to the

9   coverage provided under this chapter, as determined by the corporation.

10   **(2)** LENGTH OF EXCLUSION. A preexisting condition exclusion under sub. (1) may

11   not extend beyond the date on which the eligible resident has been continuously

12   covered under this chapter for a total of 18 months.

13   **260.40   Health care advisory committee; health care policies.   (1)**

14   ESTABLISHMENT OF COMMITTEE. (a) The corporation shall establish a health care

15   advisory committee to advise it on all matters related to promoting healthier

16   lifestyles; promoting health care quality; increasing the transparency of health care

17   cost and quality information; preventive care; disease management; the appropriate

18   use of primary care, medical specialists, prescription drugs, and hospital emergency

19   rooms; confidentiality of medical information; the appropriate use of technology;

20   benefit design; the availability of physicians, hospitals, and other providers; and

21   reducing health care costs.

22   (b) The committee shall consist of the following:

23   1. Three members designated by the Wisconsin Medical Society.

24   2. Three members designated by the Wisconsin Hospital Association.

1   3. One member designated by the dean of the University of Wisconsin School

2   of Medicine and Public Health.

3   4. One member designated by the president of the Medical College of

4   Wisconsin.

5   5. One member designated by the Wisconsin Nurses Association.

6   6. One member designated by the Wisconsin Federation of Nurses and Health

7   Professionals.

8   7. One member designated by the Wisconsin Chiropractic Association.

9   8. One member designated by the Wisconsin Dental Association.

10   (c) The committee members shall elect a chairperson from among the members.

11   The chairperson, or his or her designee, shall attend every meeting of the board to

12   communicate to the corporation the advice and recommendations of the committee.

13   The chairperson, or his or her designee, shall communicate to the committee any

14   questions on which the corporation is seeking the committee's advice or

15   recommendations. The corporation shall vote on each recommendation submitted

16   to it by the committee as to whether the recommendation should be implemented.

17   (d) Annually, on or before September 1, the committee shall submit to the

18   corporation a summary of all of its recommendations during the previous 12 months

19   for improving the health insurance purchasing arrangement under this chapter. The

20   corporation shall include those recommendations and the votes taken by the

21   corporation on them in its annual report under s. 260.05 (2) (f).

22   **(2)** ADOPTION OF HEALTH CARE POLICIES. The corporation shall do all of the

23   following:

24   (a) In consultation with the health care advisory committee and experts on

25   creating effective incentives for individuals and employers relating to healthier

2005 – 2006 Legislature – 21 – LRB-2922/3
PJK/RAC/MES:lmk:rs
ASSEMBLY BILL 1140

1   lifestyles, adopt evidence–based policies that create incentives for eligible residents

2   to adopt healthier lifestyles and for employers to institute work–based programs

3   that have been shown to improve the health status of employees and their families.

4   (b) In consultation with the health care advisory committee and experts on

5   increasing the transparency of health care cost and quality information, and in

6   collaboration with the health care advisory committee and health care plans and

7   health care providers, adopt policies that provide eligible residents with current,

8   comprehensive, easily accessible, and easily understandable information about the

9   cost and quality of the care provided by Wisconsin health care providers and by any

10   physicians, clinics, or hospitals outside of Wisconsin that are included in a network

11   of a health care plan offered under the health insurance purchasing arrangement

12   under this chapter.

13   (c) In consultation with the health care advisory committee, the Wisconsin

14   Health Information Organization, the Wisconsin Collaborative for Health Care

15   Quality, and other medical and nonmedical experts on health care quality, promote

16   evidence–based improvements in the quality of health care delivery in Wisconsin.

17   **260.60 Including certain residents who are eligible for Medical**

18   **Assistance. (1)** PLAN. The corporation and the department of health and family

19   services shall jointly develop a plan for providing health care coverage under the

20   health insurance purchasing arrangement established under this chapter to

21   individuals who satisfy the criteria under s. 260.01 (3) (a) 1. to 4. and who are eligible

22   for Medical Assistance under subch. IV of ch. 49 in the low–income families category,

23   as determined under 2005 Wisconsin Act .... (this act), section 14 (1) (b), or for health

24   care coverage under the Badger Care health care program under s. 49.665.

1   **(2)** WAIVER REQUEST. The department of health and family services shall, no

2   later than July 1, 2010, submit to the legislature under s. 13.172 (2) the plan

3   developed under sub. (1), together with its recommendations concerning the

4   desirability of requesting waivers from the secretary of the federal department of

5   health and human services for all of the following purposes:

6   (a) To implement the plan developed under sub. (1).

7   (b) To allow the use of federal financial participation to fund, to the maximum

8   extent possible, health care coverage under the arrangement established under this

9   chapter for individuals specified in sub. (1).

10   **(3)** PROPOSED LEGISLATION. If the legislature authorizes or requires the

11   department of health and family services to request the waivers specified in sub. (2)

12   and if the waivers are granted, the department of health and family services shall

13   submit to the appropriate standing committees under s. 13.172 (3) proposed

14   legislation that will implement the provisions approved under the waivers.

15   SECTION 12. 632.755 (1g) (a) of the statutes is amended to read:

16   632.755 **(1g)** (a) ~~A~~ Except as provided under ch. 260, a disability insurance

17   policy may not exclude a person or a person's dependent from coverage because the

18   person or the dependent is eligible for assistance under ch. 49 or because the

19   dependent is eligible for early intervention services under s. 51.44.

20   SECTION 13. 632.755 (1g) (b) of the statutes is amended to read:

21   632.755 **(1g)** (b) ~~A~~ Except as provided under ch. 260, a disability insurance

22   policy may not terminate its coverage of a person or a person's dependent because the

23   person or the dependent is eligible for assistance under ch. 49 or because the

24   dependent is eligible for early intervention services under s. 51.44.

25   **SECTION 14. Nonstatutory provisions.**

1   (1) PROPOSED LEGISLATION ON ELIGIBILITY OF AND APPROPRIATIONS FOR MEDICAL

2   ASSISTANCE AND BADGER CARE RECIPIENTS.

3   (a) *Definition.* In this subsection, "department" means the department of

4   health and family services.

5   (b) *Eligibility categories for Medical Assistance.*

6   1. The department shall review the statutes and determine which statutory

7   provisions specify eligibility criteria for Medical Assistance by each of the following

8   categories of persons:

9   a. Low–income families.

10   b. Elderly or disabled persons.

11   2. No later than April 1, 2008, the department shall submit the findings of its

12   review under subdivision 1. to the appropriate standing committees of the

13   legislature in the manner provided under section 13.172 (3) of the statutes. If the

14   department determines that one or more statutory provisions provide eligibility

15   criteria that apply to both categories of persons under subdivision 1., along with its

16   findings the department shall submit proposed legislation specifying eligibility

17   criteria for Medical Assistance that clearly separates the 2 categories of persons

18   under subdivision 1. so that any single statutory unit applies to only one of the 2

19   categories.

20   (c) *Appropriations for Medical Assistance and Badger Care.*

21   1. The department and the legislative fiscal bureau shall review the following

22   Medical Assistance and Badger Care health care program appropriations to

23   determine what amount of each of the total amounts appropriated under each of the

24   appropriations is attributable to benefits provided to, or the administrative costs of

1   providing benefits to, Medical Assistance recipients in the category under paragraph

2   (b) 1. a. or Badger Care health care program recipients:

3   a. Section 20.435 (2) (gk) of the statutes.

4   b. Section 20.435 (4) (a), (b), (bc), (bm), (bn), (gp), (iL), (im), (in), (kt), (L), (vt),

5   (w), (wm), (wp), and (x) of the statutes.

6   c. Section 20.435 (6) (ga) and (k) of the statutes.

7   d. Section 20.435 (7) (b) of the statutes.

8   2. No later than April 1, 2008, the department and the legislative fiscal bureau

9   shall submit the findings of the review under subdivision 1. to the appropriate

10   standing committees of the legislature in the manner provided under section 13.172

11   (3) of the statutes, along with proposed legislation that does all of the following:

12   a.   Creates, effective January 1, 2009, separate Medical Assistance

13   appropriations for the state's share of benefits and administrative costs for the

14   category of persons under paragraph (b) 1. a., along with the appropriate amounts

15   in the schedule, and funds those appropriations from the health insurance

16   purchasing trust fund.

17   b. Creates, effective January 1, 2009, separate appropriations for the state's

18   share of benefits and administrative costs for the Badger Care health care program,

19   along with the appropriate amounts in the schedule, and funds those appropriations

20   from the health insurance purchasing trust fund.

21   c. Modifies, effective January 1, 2009, the Medical Assistance and Badger Care

22   health care program appropriations in current law that are affected by the creation

23   of the appropriations under subdivision 2. a. and b., along with the amounts in the

24   schedule, to account for the creation of the appropriations under subdivision 2. a. and

1   b., and funds the modified appropriations in the same manner as those

2   appropriations are funded under current law.

3   SECTION 15. **Initial applicability.**

4   (1) HEALTH SAVINGS ACCOUNTS. The treatment of sections 71.83 (1) (ce) and

5   subchapter XVI of chapter 71 of the statutes first applies to taxable years beginning

6   on January 1, 2008.

7   **(END)**

CHAPTER 21

Reforming America's Health Insurance System
YoungMedicare

DAVID RIEMER

This chapter presents a case for David Riemer's version of Medicare for All that is termed YoungMedicare. A unique differentiator of this proposal, relative to the "Medicare for All" proposal being advocated elsewhere, is that it would have private insurance companies competing with each other, and it would have different levels of coverage, including most likely a high-deductible plan at the basic and fully funded level. Participants could then pay more to get higher levels of coverage if they wanted, from one of the competing plans. Thus, while it is universal and government-funded, it maintains a private market and some level of competition. Riemer would not characterize his plan as a safety net, since he would have everyone participate—although, to the extent that only the basic level of coverage is fully financed by the government, it could still be viewed as a safety net for everyone.

Background

We can argue whether healthcare is a right or not, but surely it is a necessity. Without excellent health insurance, we face a higher probability of death and illness. We also face a high risk of asset depletion and bankruptcy. We can literally be wiped out—personally and financially—if we lack the insurance needed to cover giant healthcare costs, whether because of a chronic illness or a one-off accident.

Lack of any health insurance is of course a cause for fear. But insurance itself can also be a source of anxiety. Policies that zap families with high deductibles, co-pays, and coinsurance are common. Obamacare not only permits such policies; it requires their availability. The Affordable Care Act's bronze, silver, and even gold plans expose families to deductibles and

David Riemer is a policy expert who worked with then Wisconsin representative Curt Gielow to draft the bipartisan legislation presented in chapter 20, which would have created universal healthcare in Wisconsin. This chapter was previously published online at https://www.govinplace.org/content/ReformingHealthInsurance.pdf. © 2019 David R. Riemer. All rights reserved.

other cost-sharing that on average add up to 40%, 30%, and 20%, respectively, of total health costs. The combination of up-front premiums to buy these plans, *plus* the deductibles and co-pays they impose, add to individuals' worries about their financial future even as they alleviate fear of a financial wipeout.

Uninsured health expenses can stress children as well. When parents must agonize about whether to pay the rent, buy food, or take an ailing child to the doctor or a wounded child to the hospital, the dread filters down to the kids. Injecting children with anxiety impairs their physical health, heightens their risk of mental illness, and compromises their chances of success in school. The shadow of growing up in fear can last well beyond childhood, undermining children's subsequent adult decisions about careers, childbearing, homeownership, and life in general.

Because of the severe economic damage that lack of good health insurance can so easily and so quickly inflict, economic security—as well as improved health itself—requires that every American have comprehensive health insurance. It should provide excellent benefits. It should offer a choice of plans and providers. Its structure should controls costs.

Unfortunately, the American health insurance system is none of the above. It is not comprehensive: Over 25 million Americans in 2016 remained uninsured, despite the gains made under the Affordable Care Act (ACA). Nor do the insured have excellent benefits. Tens of millions among the insured have sparse benefits, exposing them to thousands of dollars of costs for deductibles, co-pays, and coinsurance. Indeed, the ACA's "benchmark" silver plan requires that insurance pay on average for only 70% of costs. Nor does everyone have affordable choices among competing healthcare plans or providers. Nor does the system keep costs under control. Rather, costs continue to exceed inflation each year. Americans have not gotten any healthier in recent years, but the system continues to suck up a growing share of gross domestic product (GDP).

Voltaire famously quipped that the Holy Roman Empire was neither holy, nor Roman, nor an empire. In the same spirit, we might say that the American healthcare system is far less than all-American, delivers neither optimal health nor acceptable care, and is so chaotic and costly that it hardly deserved to be called a system.

The private sector by itself is incapable of fixing the system. Government action is essential. Unfortunately, much of what government has done in the past has made matters worse.

Despite past false starts and dead ends, the nation's dysfunctional health insurance system can be fixed by the federal government's adoption of a fairly small number of major policy changes. The problem America faces in cleaning up the current mess is not the lack of a proven alternative or the cost of the alternative. Rather, the problem is a toxic brew of confusion about the causes of the mess, fear of change, and self-interested clinging to a status quo. Once the federal government gets its policies right, however, it can fairly quickly make the system work right.

This chapter spells out a policy redesign that will result in the system that most Americans want: everyone covered, excellent benefits, choice of plans and providers, and costs controlled. I call it YoungMedicare. It resembles Medicare in many respects, but improves on it. In time, this new program and Medicare itself could be merged into a single program.

To put the proposal for YoungMedicare in context, there follows (1) a caution against expecting health insurance reform to dramatically improve health outcomes, (2) a brief account of the evolution of U.S. health insurance policy, and (3) an examination of the strengths and weaknesses of Medicare. The YoungMedicare proposal is then spelled out in detail.

Better Health vs. Better Insurance

Before proceeding, we should pause to remember that the single most important step the United States can take to improve the overall health of the American people is not to reform the health insurance system. There are many sound reasons for health insurance reform. But even the best redesign will do little to make Americans healthier. Rather, tackling what public health experts call the "economic and social determinants" of health—such as unemployment, poverty, and inequality—will have a far greater impact on health outcomes than any health insurance reform can possibly produce (Swain et al., 2014).

According to the University of Wisconsin-Madison Population Health Institute and the Robert Wood Johnson Foundation (2017), economic and social factors are responsible for 40% of health outcomes, with individual behaviors next in importance (30%) and the healthcare system itself of less importance (20%).

Poverty's negative effect on children's health is especially strong. As the Academic Pediatric Association's Task Force on Childhood Poverty concluded in 2013:

> The effects of poverty on children's health and well-being are well documented. Poor children have increased infant mortality, higher rates of low birth weight and subsequent health and developmental problems, increased frequency and severity of chronic diseases such as asthma, greater food insecurity with poorer nutrition and growth, poorer access

to quality health care, increased unintentional injury and mortality, poorer oral health, lower immunization rates, and increased rates of obesity and its complications. There is also increasing evidence that poverty in childhood creates a significant health burden in adulthood that is independent of adult-level risk factors and is associated with low birth weight and increased exposure to toxic stress (causing structural alterations in the brain, long-term epigenetic changes, and increased inflammatory markers). (American Academy of Pediatrics, 2013, p. 1)

Even if it is true that economic and social factors are the major causes of negative health outcomes, can improving those factors—for example, by reducing poverty—actually make Americans healthier? The answer is a clear yes. There is a growing body of evidence that improving the economic and social determinants of health yields gains in health outcomes. Expanding the value of the earned income tax credit (EITC), for instance, reduced the incidence of low birth weights for children (Simon, 2015). Increasing the EITC also improved the health (including the mental health) of mothers (Evans & Garthwaite, 2014). More research is needed to show the full extent to which providing the unemployed jobs, raising wages, increasing earning supplements, and otherwise shrinking poverty will produce which measurable gains in what dimensions of health. But the cause-and-effect relationship is clear. Economic security makes us healthier.

Thus, reforming the New Deal settlement to greatly improve America's economic security structure—that is, creating transitional jobs, raising wages, increasing incomes, and adopting the other measures proposed in my book, *Putting Government in Its Place: The Case for a New Deal 3.0* (Riemer, 2019)—will do much more to improve Americans' health than any cure of the nation's dysfunctional health insurance system. We should nonetheless not slacken in pushing for a vastly better U.S. health insurance system that adds YoungMedicare and improves regular Medicare. Doing so will further enhance economic security. It will also make millions of people healthier. It would be the icing on the cake.

A Brief Account of Health Insurance Reform: Progress and Frustration

Since the launch of the New Deal in 1933, we have already made enormous progress on a tortuous path. Major milestones marking the way include the enactment of Medicaid and Medicare in 1965; the creation of the State Children's Health Insurance Program (SCHIP) in 1997; and most recently, the passage of the Affordable Care Act (aka Obamacare) in 2010. Much credit also goes to the private sector. Unions and corporations increasingly recognized during and after World War II that worker productivity and business profits would improve if employees worried less about their families' health and could pay for the medical care, occasional hospitalization, and prescription drugs they themselves needed to stay on the job.

But 28.5 million Americans, 8.8% of the population, were still uninsured as of 2017 (Berchick et al., 2018, p. 1). The number will increase sharply if the Congress and president obstruct Obamacare or fail to fix its problems (some of which arise from the original 2010 law, but most of which result from subsequent legislative or judicial decisions).

Healthcare costs, meanwhile, continue to rise faster than inflation. From 2005 through 2015, the rate of healthcare inflation outpaced the Consumer Price Index in 10 out of 11 years (Patton, 2015). Compared to the long, 55-year stretch from 1960 to 2015 (i.e., from before the enactment of Medicare to after passage of the ACA), the period from 2005 to 2015 shows an improved trend, however. The gap between healthcare inflation and the general rate of inflation was worse in the past. It was extremely large during the period from 1980 to 1995. The gap has shrunk—and stayed shrunk—for most of the past two decades. One can make the case that while the passage of Obamacare has not solved the problem of hyperinflation in healthcare, it has helped to diminish the problem (Lambrew & Montz, 2017).

Yet the problem of excessive healthcare inflation remains. However measured, and whether accelerating or moderating, what we might call "hyperinflation without benefits" continues (with only occasional relapses) year after year. American businesses and taxpayers keep on spending more and more on health insurance, doctors, hospitals, and drugs. Yet we do not get any healthier.

In short: Despite the important gains in health insurance coverage that the United States has experienced since World War II, and despite the recent slowing down in the overall trend of hyperinflation in health costs, the U.S. still has a long, long way to go. To hit the health insurance trifecta—cover everyone, provide excellent benefits while expanding choices, and permanently bring down cost to (or even close to) the rate of inflation—we need to do something different.

Why Not Medicare for All?

The current system would be greatly improved if everyone were simply enrolled in Medicare. But that would be a second-best solution. The under-65 population should be enrolled in a health insurance program even better than Medicare. Seniors would benefit if Medicare itself were improved.

Medicare has indeed solved some of the big problems that must be tackled to create a rational health insurance system. It provides the age 65+ population with nearly universal coverage. Once seniors select not only Part A but also Parts B and D—or if they choose a Medicare Advantage Plan under Part C that folds in Parts A, B, and possibly D— Medicare pays for the "big three" healthcare costs: hospitals, doctors, and drugs.

Medicare now also offers lots of choice. Enrollees may choose among *types* of plans (an HMO or PPO under Medicare Advantage or a fee-for-service plan under regular Medicare). Enrollees may choose among different HMOs and PPOs. Thus, Medicare offers a wide range of choices among providers.

But Medicare is far from an optimal health insurance program. It has three major problems: a benefit problem, a cost-control problem, and a set of problems arising from the departure of its financing mechanism from basic social insurance principles.

Medicare's benefit problem. Medicare falls short in the benefits it provides. Following is list of the cost-sharing that Medicare imposed in 2017 that significantly limits its benefits to seniors:

- Part A coverage for hospital care required payment in 2017 of (1) a $1,316 deductible for each benefit period, (2) $329 coinsurance per day of each benefit period for days 61–90, (3) $658 coinsurance per each "lifetime reserve day" after day 90 for each benefit period (up to 60 days over your lifetime), and (4) all costs beyond "lifetime reserve days" (Centers for Medicare and Medicaid Services [CMS], n.d.e).
- Part B coverage for medical care, in addition to requiring a monthly premium of $134 (which, depending on income, may be lower or higher), also imposed a deductible of $183 per year and coinsurance 20% of the Medicare-approved amounts for most doctor services (CMS, n.d.e).
- Part D coverage for prescription drugs requires payment of a monthly premium (CMS, n.d.f), imposes an initial deductible that can be as much as $405 (CMS, n.d.h), then imposes a deductible or coinsurance (CMS, n.d.b), and then requires enrollees to pay up to 40% of the plan's cost for covered brand-name prescription drugs during the so-called donut hole (coverage gap) that starts after spending, out of pocket, $3,700 and lasts until spending $4,950 on covered drugs (CMS, n.d.c; n.d.a).

Medicare recipients who enroll under Part C in a Medicare Advantage Plan may face significantly less cost-sharing in exchange for accepting the limitations that an Advantage Plan imposes. The number of seniors who choose to sign up for an Advantage Plan is rapidly growing. In 2017, enrollment reached 19 million, 33% of Medicare's 57 million total recipients (Kaiser Family Foundation [KFF], 2017). In some states, the share of Medicare enrollees in an Advantage Plan has reached 40% or higher. In one state, Minnesota, it is 56% (KFF, 2017). Nearly two-thirds of those who select an Advantage Plan decide to enroll in a health maintenance organization (HMO), with the remainder largely selecting a preferred provider organization (PPO) (KFF, 2017).

But choosing an Advantage Plan is not cost free. Both a monthly premium and cost-sharing apply. In 2017, the average monthly premium for an Advantage Plan that covers prescription drugs was $36 (KFF, 2017). The average cost-sharing out-of-pocket limit imposed by such plans for services covered under Parts A and B was $5,219 (KFF, 2017). Since 2011, all Advantage Plans have been required to limit enrollees' out-of-pocket expenses for services covered under Parts A and B to no more than $6,700, with higher limits allowed for services received from out-of-network providers, prescription drugs, and services not covered by the plan" (Jacobson et al., 2015).

In brief: Whether seniors in Medicare choose regular Medicare or an Advantage Plan, they face significant costs in addition to any premiums they must pay. If they get sick or have an accident, they must pay deductibles, co-pays, or coinsurance that could total thousands of dollars. Compared to the nonexistent coverage or paltry benefits that tens of millions of seniors endured before Medicare's enactment in 1965, Medicare's benefits are wonderful. An optimal health insurance program, however, would provide better benefits than Medicare by virtually eliminating its deductibles, co-pays, and coinsurance. And Medicare itself would provide better healthcare, and achieve better health outcomes, by shedding cost-sharing at the time of obtaining care.

Cost-sharing at the time of obtaining care in the form of deductibles, co-pays (with rare exceptions), and coinsurance is a bad idea. It is bad for health. It is also a counterproductive, and thus ineffective, tool for controlling costs.

Cost-sharing is bad for health because it is healthcare financing's equivalent of an atomic bomb. The A-bomb destroys everything. Cost-sharing deters everything that it touches. It deters both necessary *and* unnecessary care. It prevents the urgently needed visit to the doctor as well as the pointless trip to the clinic. It discourages ill and injured people from seeking the care they need, just as it equally inhibits them from seeking care they really do not need. Imposing deductibles, co-pays, and coinsurance at the point of service thus worsens health outcomes for many at the same time that, for others, it may improve health outcomes.

Dollar incentives—that is, simple, understandable price signals to make or avoid major health decisions—*can be* a good way to improve health outcomes. But the price signal must be finely designed both to encourage needed care and discourage unnecessary care. Co-pays and coinsurance at the point of service are the wrong type of price signal to use because they crudely inhibit all care. They inherently cannot distinguish between whether they are deterring better health or worse health.

Human life is too precious to entangle it with such indifference to health. What we need—and what YoungMedicare incorporates—is the use of price signals that promote only positive health decisions. The appendix to this chapter, "How Price Signals Lower Health Costs and Improve Quality," is an example of the best way to use price signals to achieve desirable cost and quality outcomes.

The second strike against using cost-sharing at the point of service is that it does nothing to constrain overall cost. Deductibles, co-pays, and coinsurance shift costs to patients, thus reducing the health costs that the insurer (whether private or public) bears. But cost-sharing does not lower total health costs. Indeed, it may actually increase total health costs, as explained next.

Medicare's cost-control problem. Controlling costs has been a huge problem for Medicare. The program, which covers 57 million people, cost $588 billion in 2016, which is 24% of the federal budget (Cubanski & Neuman, 2017). From 2000 to 2010, per capita Medicare spending rose annually by an average of 7.4%, nearly three times faster than the general rate of inflation (Cubanski & Neuman, 2017).

To its credit, the program has steadily put mechanisms in place that, with growing effectiveness, have helped to control costs. Per capita spending from 2010 to 2016 grew at an annual average rate of 1.3%, somewhat below the general inflation rate. Medicare's cost-control problem, however, has hardly been solved. Per capita growth in Medicare spending is projected to grow by 4.0% from 2016 through 2021, then rise to 5.0% from 2021 through 2026 (Cubanski & Neuman, 2017). In short, the recent improvement in Medicare's approach to controlling costs has thrown a saddle on the cost monster, but the monster is far from tamed.

Medicare's historically heavy reliance on cost-sharing to control costs is a big part of the problem. There are three major reasons that imposing deductibles, co-pays, and coinsurance at the point of service does little to lower—and may indeed raise—overall Medicare spending on a per capita basis.

First, there is the pay-me-less-now or pay-me-more-later problem. If an ill or injured person avoids necessary care because of the deductible, co-pay, or coinsurance, the savings may be offset by the higher health costs ultimately incurred when the person finally turns up in the emergency room or operating table. It is both healthier and cheaper to fix a wound instead of amputating a foot or to treat high blood pressure rather than deal with a full-blown heart attack.

Second, once cost-sharing reaches an out-of-pocket (OOP) maximum—which is the case for the increasingly popular Medicare Advantage Plan—by definition it becomes impotent in influencing costs. The patient has at that point paid 100% of what the patient will pay, at least for the rest of the year. And a fair number of patients have such serious illnesses or accidents that they quickly breeze past their OOP maximums, at which point the program has no price-based mechanism left to deter costly care. As mentioned earlier, in 2017 the average OOP maximum for a Medicare Advantage Plan was $5,219. Most enrollees in Advantage Plans select HMOs, which have an even lower average OOP maximum of $4,928 (KFF, 2017). It does not take much of an illness or accident to rack up $5,000 or $6,000 in costs. From then on, Medicare's reliance on cost-sharing at the point of service to hold down costs becomes utterly irrelevant.

Third, there may be a "behavioral economics" impulse that causes cost-sharing to push up costs even further. Most of us have friends who, knowing they have passed their OOP maximum for the year, hurry to schedule an appointment with a doctor or dentist before year's end in order to get "free" treatment? Have you, dear reader, not done this yourself? In many cases, of course, the care will be justified. But in some cases, the certainty that "free" care before December 31 will turn into a deductible on January 1 may induce us to pressure our doctors and dentists (or agree when they pressure us) to "fit us in," even though the health justification for care at that time is weak.

Medicare has never relied exclusively on cost-sharing at the point of service to control its costs. With each wave of reform, the program has increasingly turned to other tools, such as the diagnosis-related group (DRG) hospital payment methodology, to try to constrain costs. The creation of the Medicare+Choice program in 1997, which became Medicare Advantage in 2003, was driven in large part by the ambition of holding down spending. Nonetheless, cost-sharing at the point of service remains an integral part of Medicare.

It would be a mistake, therefore, to put all Americans into a Medicare for All health insurance program as long as Medicare continues to rely heavily on cost-sharing at the point of service, both as a way to shift costs to patients and as a device (albeit an ineffective one) to constrain overall spending. The under age 65 population cannot tolerate the high out-of-pocket cost burden that Medicare recipients must endure any more than Medicare recipients themselves can bear the deductibles, co-pays, and coinsurance they are compelled to pay. The American people and economy cannot afford to expand Medicare *per se* until Medicare has created a far better and long-lasting mechanism to keep costs under control.

None of this should be understood, however, as an argument against price signals. The enemy here is the specific use of deductibles, co-pays (with rare exceptions), and coinsurance at the point when healthcare is received. Other price signals—ones that encourage lower healthcare costs, higher quality, and better health outcomes without inhibiting patients from seeking or receiving necessary care—are fine. What America needs— both outside of Medicare and within Medicare—is a new paradigm that uses price signals to control costs in a way that rewards the results we want (universal access, low cost, high quality, good outcomes) and does no collateral damage in the form of avoided necessary care and hyperinflation in costs.

Medicare's payment problem. Medicare's third major structural problem involves its financing mechanism.

Medicare is a social insurance program. The financing of the program's Part A coverage of hospital care takes full advantage of the logic, simplicity, and fairness of social insurance principles. Contributions by workers and employers are obligatory.[1] Payment by workers is automatic, and by employers is routine.[2] The amounts owed are proportionate to earnings.[3]

---

1. Workers' earnings are subject to a 1.45% Medicare tax, and their employers pay another 1.45% of earnings. Self-employed individuals pay both the worker's and the employer's 1.45% of earnings.

2. The vast majority of individuals who pay Medicare taxes do not have to think or worry about whether their payments will be accurate or made on time. They do not have to write a check or instruct their banks to transfer funds. Rather, Medicare taxes are deducted periodically from workers' paychecks by their employers. Employers are responsible for submitting the amounts accrued each calendar quarter, together with their own quarterly payments, to the Internal Revenue Service. Only self-employed individuals have to take the trouble to calculate what they owe (i.e., the combined employee and employer share) and write a check or electronically transfer the funds.

3. Medicare does not apply a lower tax rate to low-income workers and a higher tax rate to those who earn a lot more. However, the formula—1.45% applied to every dollar earned, with no cap on taxable earnings—causes low-income workers' to make smaller dollar contributions while high-income workers make larger ones.

The financing of the rest of Medicare, however, is another story. Several key features of the social insurance financing model do not apply to Part B for medical care, Part D for prescription drugs, or Part C Medicare Advantage plans.

To begin with, payment is *not* obligatory for Parts B, D, or C. No payroll tax or mandatory premium applies. Seniors must decide not only to enroll (which is technically true for Part A), but they must also choose to pay monthly premium for Parts B or D. They likewise must choose to pay monthly premiums for a Part C Medicare Advantage Plan (which folds in Part B medical coverage and, at the enrollee's discretion, may also fold in Part D drug coverage). Not surprisingly, there is a drop-off between the 46.0 million seniors in 2015 who enrolled in "prepaid" Medicare Part A versus the 42.5 million and 41.8 million who signed up, respectively, for optional, premium-demanding, Parts B and D programs (National Committee to Preserve Social Security, 2017).

The other major way in which Medicare Parts B, D, and C depart from the classic social insurance model is that the premiums they charge do *not* vary with income, unless it is quite high. In 2017, the overwhelming majority of Medicare Part B enrollees, regardless of their annual income between $1 and $85,000 (for single filers) or $170,000 (for married joint filers), paid the same $134 per month. Only those with incomes higher than $85,000/$170,000 paid in relationship to ability to pay (CMS, n.d.g). Similarly, the overwhelming majority of Medicare Part D enrollees, regardless of income as long as it is under $85,000 (for single filers) or $170,000 (for married joint filers), pay the same monthly premium for the same benefit package. Only those with higher incomes pay extra (CMS, n.d.d).

Medicare's departure from Part A's classic social insurance financing principles, when it came to Parts B, D, and C, is not just a matter of inelegance. It helps seniors that their hospital insurance program, Part A, is simple, automatic, and paid for in a way that is proportionate to their income. It may harm seniors that Parts B and D are not obligatory. It particularly harms seniors that, whether their income is $40,000 or $80,000 (if single) or $80,000 or $160,00 (if married), they must pay exactly the same premiums for Parts B and D, as well as for the same Part C benefit package.

To sum up: As long as Medicare remains a program that, despite its many strengths, provides seniors with inadequate benefits, falls short on controlling costs, and does not consistently apply social insurance principles in its financing mechanism, we should refrain from enrolling all Americans in a Medicare for All program.

The Shape of Rational Health Insurance:
A New Approach

It would instead be better to enroll Americans under age 65 in a better version of Medicare, which I call YoungMedicare.[4] In time, if Medicare itself changes to absorb all of the principles of YoungMedicare into its approach, the two programs could be fully integrated into a single program: an improved Medicare for All.

YoungMedicare would:

1. Provide all Americans under age 65 with the resources they need to buy health insurance.
2. Require all participating healthcare plans to provide excellent uniform benefits (even better than Medicare's).
3. Use the most basic of market forces—competition, choice, prices, and incentives—to deliver low premiums, improve quality of care, and strengthen health outcomes, by driving out the massive error, waste, and inefficiency that permeate our healthcare system.
4. Organize and finance the program as a new social insurance program that (akin to workers' compensation) relies on an employer mandate and payroll-based premiums.

Here are the details:

Universal coverage: Health insurance purchasing accounts. Every American would have a Health Insurance Purchasing Account (the Account) that, every fall, would be replenished with a dollar amount equal to 100% of the lowest premium bid in the individual's county of residence (or, if the individual wishes, another county) by a High-Quality Health Insurance Plan (the Plan).

The dollar amount in the Account would be actuarially adjusted for the individual's age and sex. It would also reflect the Plan's obligation to provide a defined, comprehensive, excellent, and uniform package of health insurance benefits that includes the ACA's Essential Health Benefits (that benefit package is discussed shortly.)

During an open enrollment period in November and December, adults (age 18 or older) would direct the actuarially adjusted amount in their Accounts to their choice of a Plan. Parents or guardians, on behalf of their children under age 18, would direct the amounts in their children's Accounts to the parents' or guardians' choice of a Plan.

---

4. I wish to acknowledge the influence of Stanford University Emeritus Professor Alain Enthoven, and his explanation of what he calls "cost-conscious consumer choice," in shaping this proposal.

The next year, individuals with Accounts could stay in the same Plan (if available) or switch to a different Plan on offer. Those who make no choice would be reassigned to their prior Plans (if available). If they have no prior Plan, they would be assigned to the lowest-bidding Plan.

At age 65, seniors who qualify for Medicare would decide, as they now do, whether to enroll in a Medicare Advantage Plan or regular Medicare.

Excellent benefits: No cost-sharing. Every Plan would be an insurance plan that complies with applicable state law. The Plan could be a HMO or another type of integrated delivery system, a PPO, or a fee-for-service plan.

Each Plan would provide comprehensive benefits. As with the ACA's set of Essential Health Benefits, each plan would cover medical care, hospital care, prescription drugs, and more (CMS, n.d.h).[5]

All Plan benefits would also be uniform. No deductibles, no co-pays (with one exception), and no coinsurance would apply. Thus, the "actuarial value" of all Plans would be nearly 100%. The only exception is that a Plan could charge a co-pay if a physician decides not to prescribe a lower-cost generic drug but instead prescribes a pharmacologically equivalent brand-name drug.

Use of market forces to control costs, improve quality, enhance outcomes. Basic market forces—choice, competition, prices, and incentives—would cause YoungMedicare to hold down health costs, improve the quality of care, and enhance health outcomes. Government would not fix prices. Government would not regulate supply. Rather, government's role would be to create a structure of price-based signals and across-the-board incentives (for enrollees, Plans, and providers) that put strong and enduring pressure on Plans and providers to submit low risk-adjusted bids, strengthen quality, and generate better outcomes as the only way to attract customers, increase revenue, and maximize profit. (The appendix to this chapter illustrates how these basic market forces would interact to constrain costs and improve quality.)

As mentioned above, all Americans would have a Health Insurance Purchasing Account that pays for excellent benefits and would use their Account to make an annual choice among competing Plans.

Unlike the current system, however, the Plans' competition would not be based on (a) denying or limiting coverage for high-risk individuals or groups, (b) shortchanging benefits, or (c) baffling consumers with irrelevant differences among different insurers' cost-sharing arrangements. No American with an Account could be denied coverage or offered a limited benefit

---

5. Plans would be required to provide all Essential Health Benefits defined in the Affordable Care Act.

package. All Plans would offer the same excellent benefit package. Since cost-sharing at the point of service would almost entirely vanish, Plans could no longer compete based on confusing customers about which Plan's incomprehensible matrix of deductibles, co-pays, and coinsurance is worse or better than some other Plan's equally incomprehensible matrix of cost-sharing.

Rather, as Americans with an Account decide which Plan to join, their decisions would be based on four differences among the competing Plans: (1) monthly extra price, (2) network, (3) quality, and (4) outcomes.

The most important of these Plan differences is monthly extra price.

Recall that YoungMedicare would guarantee all Americans with an Account that it pays for 100% of the actuarially adjusted dollar amount bid per month by the *lowest-bidding* Plan, but no more. That means that an individual with an Account would be obliged to pay, out of pocket, the full *extra amount* per month that has been bid by any *higher-bidding* Plan if the person wanted to obtain health insurance coverage from such a higher-bidding Plan.

For example, if the Account for a 30-year-old male in Milwaukee is credited with $500 per month because lowest-bidding Plan A submitted a $500 monthly bid on an actuarial basis to provide 30-year-old males with the required excellent benefit package, then the individual would pay the following extra monthly amounts to join different Plans:

Plan	Amount Bid/Month	Extra Cost to Join/Month
A	$500	$500 – $500 = $0
B	$525	$525 – $500 = $25
C	$550	$550 – $500 = $50
D	$575	$575 – $500 = $75

The appendix to this chapter provides a visual illustration of how these price signals work.

The formula for actuarial adjustment would of course be designed so that, regardless of an America's age or sex, the difference in each county between the lowest-bidding Plan and each higher-bidding Plan would be the same. In other words, if the 30-year-old male in Milwaukee had to spend an extra $25 per month to join Plan B, any other male or female or any age in Milwaukee (prior to Medicare) would also pay $25 to enroll in Plan B.

The lower price of a product or service is of course a compelling reason to select it in lieu of a higher-priced product or service. But the price signal is only the starting point in making a choice. All of us decide to spend more for any number of products or services because we conclude that the extra cost is "worth it" because of the extra value we obtain. Extra value can be almost anything: greater speed, freshness, color, taste, durability, warranty, popularity, politeness, etc.

In the case of health insurance, three kinds of extra value might well induce a YoungMedicare user of an Account to spend more than the dollar value in the Account, which is attributable to Plan A's low bid, in order to sign up for a more expensive Plan B, C, or D.

- **Network.** An enrollee may prefer a higher-cost Plan's network of providers. Plans will have different (if sometimes overlapping) networks of doctors, hospitals, and other providers, operating at different (if sometimes overlapping) facilities. At least one fee-for-service plan would provide a network comprised of all providers in the United States. In choosing a plan, an individual may decide to spend extra to join a more costly Plan because of the appeal of its provider network or the location of its facilities. Some may be willing to spend a lot more to join a Plan with no limitation on available providers.
- **Quality.** In YoungMedicare, all Plans would have to meet high standards of quality. Nonetheless, the Plans will have different reputations and rankings for quality of care. This could be a relevant factor in deciding to spend extra to join a more expensive Plan.
- **Outcomes.** Finally, the Plans will also have different reputations and rankings for health outcomes. This too may be a relevant factor in spending more to join a particular Plan.

Prior to bid unsealing, of course, the competing Plans will not know whose bid is the low bid. Each Plan *could* be the low bidder, but only one Plan *will* be the low bidder. Thus, each Plan faces the high probability—and all but one Plan face the reality—of having to persuade individuals to spend money out of pocket in order sign up for that Plan. As a consequence, every year each Plan will be under powerful and enduring pressure to do four things to position itself for success:

1. Keep its bid as low as possible: If you cannot be the low bidder, you do not want to cost too much more.
2. Have a desirable network: If you must sell consumers on your higher price, you will want to point to the convenient location of your facilities, your easily accessible hours of service, the reputation of your doctors and hospitals, and so forth.

3. Score well on quality: You will have an edge in persuading consumers to spend more if you can highlight objective (and nonobjective) evidence of how excellent your doctors, nurses, hospitals, and other providers have proved to be.
4. Score well on outcomes: Finally, you may be able to induce consumers to spend more if you can highlight objective (and nonobjective) evidence that your Plan delivers healthy babies, avoids illness, saves lives, and achieves other health outcomes.

This exertion of relentless pressure on health insurance Plans and health-care providers to lower their costs, strengthen their networks, and improve their quality and outcomes is exactly what YoungMedicare is meant to do. It is a core aim of the YoungMedicare model to inject such strong—and appropriate—market forces into the U.S. health system so that, to make money, the nation's health insurers and providers have no choice but obey the new incentives that surround them and produce the cost-containing, quality-improving, outcome-enhancing healthcare system Americans have long desired and the nation desperately needs.

But do America's health insurers and providers have "room" to respond to market pressure by holding down costs, pushing up quality, and strengthening outcomes? The evidence points to a resounding Yes! According to several reports published in 2012, the level of waste in the U.S. health system at the time was roughly $700 billion.

By looking at regional variations in Medicare spending, researchers at the Dartmouth Institute for Health Policy and Clinical Practice have estimated that 30 percent of all Medicare clinical care spending could be avoided without worsening health outcomes. This amount represents about $700 billion in savings when extrapolated to total U.S. healthcare spending, according to the Congressional Budget Office.

More recently, an April 2012 study by former Centers for Medicare and Medicaid Services (CMS) administrator Donald M. Berwick and RAND Corporation analyst Andrew D. Hackbarth estimated that five categories of waste consumed $476 billion to $992 billion, or 18 percent to 37 percent of the approximately $2.6 trillion annual total of all health spending in 2011. Spending in the Medicare and Medicaid programs, including state and federal costs, contributed about one-third of this wasteful spending, or $166 billion to $304 billion. . . . Similarly, a panel of the Institute of Medicine (IOM) estimated in a September 2012 report that $690 billion was wasted in U.S. healthcare annually, not including fraud. (Health Affairs, 2012, pp. 1–2)

This estimate that the U.S. health system wastes $700 billion appeared in 2012. Even if the mind-boggling amount lost to waste has been reduced in the last few years, the opportunity remains to lower cost *and* improve quality by squeezing hundreds of billions of dollars of waste out of the healthcare system. While it is superficially convenient to equate lower health costs with worse health quality, the opposite is true. Higher costs are driven by poor quality. Lower costs and better quality go together, and both result from squeezing out waste.

The following table, summing up findings of Donald Berwick and Andrew Hackbarth, explains that the current U.S. health system is wasting hundreds of billions of dollars because of three types of poor quality care: (1) failures of care delivery, (2) failures of care coordination, and (3) overtreatment. Three other categories of waste that add up to additional hundreds of billions of dollars—that is, administrative complexity, pricing failures, and fraud and abuse—are not the result of care decisions but stem from the byzantine design and misdirecting incentives that permeate our healthcare system. Those design flaws and perverse incentives also expand the niches where "bad actors" (patients, insurers, and providers) can try to fleece the system.

Estimates of waste in U.S. healthcare spending in 2011, by category.

	Cost to Medicare and Medicaid[a]			Total cost to US healthcare[b]		
	Low	Midpoint	High	Low	Midpoint	High
Failures of care delivery	$26	$36	$45	$102	$128	$154
Failures of care coordination	21	30	39	25	35	45
Overtreatment	67	77	87	158	192	226
Administrative complexity	16	36	56	107	248	389
Pricing failures	36	56	77	84	131	178
Subtotal (excluding fraud and abuse)	166	235	304	476	734	992
Percentage of total health care spending	6%	9%	11%	18%	27%	37%
Fraud and abuse	30	64	98	82	177	272
Total (including fraud and abuse)	197	300	402	558	910	1,263
Percentage of total health care spending				21%	34%	47%

Source: Berwick and Hackbarth (2012). Copyright © 2012 American Medical Association. All rights reserved.

Notes: Dollars in billions. Totals may not match the sum of components due to rounding. [a]Includes state portion of Medicaid. [b]Total U.S. healthcare spending estimated at $2,687 trillion.

The YoungMedicare model opens up two new fronts in the effort to lower cost and improve quality by squeezing out waste:

The incentive front. Most important, the model creates three interlocking incentives that work together to put pressure on wasteful practices:

1. Enrollees' have a strong incentive to select a low-cost Health Care Plan that is better in quality, since they must spend cash out of pocket to join a higher-bidding Plan and will tend to shy away from selecting a costlier Plan that ranks worse in quality. Thus . . .
2. Each Plan has a powerful incentive to be a low-cost, high-quality Plan—which the Plan can best accomplish by squeezing out waste— because submitting low bids (that low cost justifies) and achieving a sterling reputation for quality positions the Plan to attract more enrollees, earn greater revenue, and make a handsome profit. As a result . . .
3. Healthcare providers—doctors, hospitals, and others—have a strong incentive to be affiliated with low-cost/high-quality Plans that they assist in squeezing out waste, since that is how they too most likely will gain the patients, revenue, and profit they also seek.

The tail end of this chain of incentives is a steady reduction in the massive waste that permeates the U.S. healthcare system. Within the Young-Medicare framework, the *only* way to respond to enrollees' incentive to enroll in low-cost/high-quality Plans is for the Plans themselves, and their affiliated providers, to work together to aggressively attack the waste that saturates the system. Gaming the system, to avoid risk or dump it on others, is no longer a possibility. Indifference to cost, quality, and outcomes is no longer a viable business option but a ticket to failure. A new, stern, market discipline would henceforth issue the following instruction to the health insurance industry and healthcare providers: "Either lower your costs and improve your quality by driving out the waste you now tolerate or shrink and vanish."

The appendix ("How Price Signals Lower Health Costs and Improve Quality") illustrates in greater detail how the YoungMedicare model would effectively use price signals to reward low-cost/better-quality Plans and discourage enrollees and income from flowing to high-cost/worse-quality Plans.

The administrative front. In addition, YoungMedicare's organizational structure and financial arrangements, because of their simplicity, will help to shrink the portion of waste in the U.S. health insurance system that Berwick and Hackbarth (2012) attribute to administrative complexity, pricing failures, and fraud and abuse.

Under the YoungMedicare model, Americans make only two decisions each year with a financial consequence: which Plan to join and, if they do not select the low-bidding plan, how to pay the extra required to enroll in their alternative choice. This automatically eliminates millions of dollars in costs that in the current health insurance system are needlessly piled onto—that is, wasted.

To begin with, since the YoungMedicare benefit package includes virtually no cost-sharing, the administrative costs associated with the following practices will disappear.

- **Benefit manuals.** Since every enrollee in YoungMedicare has the same benefits, few services are excluded, and cost-sharing at the point of service (deductible, co-pay, coinsurance) is essentially gone, the program's benefit manuals will be simpler, shorter, and less expensive to produce. No longer will insurance plans, at considerable expense, need to send out giant volumes with incomprehensible explanations of what cost-sharing you must pay for different services or what your plan does not cover at all.
- **Explanation of benefits (EOB).** In addition, EOBs will become dramatically simpler and less expensive. They can focus on the details of the actual care you got. Today's lengthy, indecipherable, and costly lists of billed charges versus actual charges, versus what your insurer has paid for, versus what some other insurer is being billed for, versus what you might be charged—all will disappear.
- **Billing.** YoungMedicare will never bill any enrollee for any healthcare service. (If a patient wants to forego a generic drug and purchase a pharmacologically equivalent brand-name drug, the patient will simply pay the extra price at a pharmacy.) The elimination of billing for services will lower administrative costs.
- **Arrears.** Since YoungMedicare patients will never be billed for healthcare services, they will never fall behind in their payments to Plans or providers for those services. Nor will they ever be hassled by collection agencies, or taken to court, or drawn into bankruptcy proceedings, because of unpaid hospital or medical bills. The only risk of arrears arises if an individual chooses a Plan other than the low-bidding plan but fails to pay the extra monthly cost. Even here, the patient's liability will be limited to the number of delinquent months times the extra out-of-pocket monthly cost the patient voluntarily chose to incur. This shrinkage in

the necessity to chase after patients in arrears will help to lower administrative cost.

■ **Coordination of benefits (COB).** Finally, YoungMedicare will result in a decline in the need for health insurance plans to coordinate benefits. There will be no need to coordinate with a workers' comp healthcare component or Medicaid coverage, since both of those programs would end (Riemer, 2019).[6] Nor will there be a need to coordinate benefits when an individual is covered by two different employer-sponsored healthcare plans, since one of the effects of YoungMedicare is to make employer-sponsored health insurance unnecessary.[7] Under Young-Medicare, each covered person will have a single plan with the same benefits. COB will not end entirely, but its costs will greatly shrink.

Another cost-related outcome of the YoungMedicare model is that patients will no longer feel pressure to "use up the benefits" before another calendar year starts and a new deductible kicks in. The elimination of deductibles and other cost-sharing means that patients will seek care at the time of need, not at a time arbitrarily dictated by the calendar.

Organization and finance: A new social insurance program. The final facet of YoungMedicare to consider is its organization and financing. The program would be organized outside the structure of the federal government. Akin to what typically happens with workers' compensation, employers of all sizes would be required to carry YoungMedicare coverage by remitting payroll-based premiums. (The premiums paid by self-employed persons and small firms may need to be treated as taxes, rather than mandatory payments, in order to satisfy the U.S. Supreme Court's narrowing vision of what regulations of commercial activity are allowed under the Commerce Clause of the Constitution.)

YoungMedicare would be run by a new government-sponsored enterprise (GSE): the National YoungMedicare Corporation (NYMC). Employers' premium revenue would be used immediately to enable the under-65 population—overwhelmingly workers, workers' spouses, and workers' children—to purchase an excellent health insurance plan. All funds would flow into and out of the NYMC's independent trust fund.

---

6. In *Putting Government in Its Place: The Case for a New Deal 3.0* (Riemer, 2019, chapter 7, "Outside the Labor Market"), I discuss why the workers' compensation health insurance component should be ended, and in chapter 11 ("Ending Welfare") the logic of ending means-tested welfare programs, including Medicaid.

7. Employers would of course be free to continue to offer other kinds of health-related insurance (e.g., dental and vision, as well as a variety of other insurance and noninsurance benefits such as life insurance, supplemental disability insurance, and defined benefit annuities).

The Medicaid program would be eliminated. Its long-term care function would be taken over by Medicare. In the future, it may make sense for YoungMedicare and Medicare to be combined into a single program.

How many people would YoungMedicare cover? What would Young-Medicare cost? How would it be funded? Estimates for coverage, cost, and funding are as follows. (These estimates assume that employers would require their workers—as permitted—to absorb half of the cost, via payroll deductions, of the payroll-based premium that the employers would be required to remit to the NYMC.)

Covered Individuals (2015)	$254.0 million
Estimated Cost (2015)	$1,326.5 billion
Medicare Part A Taxable Earnings (2015)	$7,580.0 billion
Total Employer Premium: 17.5% of Part A Earnings	$1,326.5 billion
Maximum Worker Deduction: 8.75% of Earnings	$663.2 billion
Minimum Employer Share: 8.75% of Wages/Salaries	$663.2 billion

There would be no individual mandate to obtain health insurance. Rather, individuals under age 65 would just automatically *have* health insurance. Their Health Insurance Purchasing Accounts would include the funds necessary to pay 100% of the premium of the lowest-bidding, high-quality, healthcare plan available in their county. The same dollar amount would pay close to the full premium of other available plans. If individuals do not select a plan, they would be automatically enrolled in the lowest-bidding, high-quality healthcare plan available, which would impose no additional cost.

Although individuals would face no individual mandate to obtain insurance, workers would be subject to the possibility that their employers would exercise the right to deduct from the worker's paycheck up to 50% of the payroll-based premium that employers themselves are obliged to remit to the NYMC. Employers could, of course, implement a smaller payroll deduction, or none at all, for individual workers or the entire workforce.

No worker, however, would bear the full cost of any deduction. Rather, all workers would be able to claim a refundable tax credit for a large portion of it—up to 70%—when they submit their annual federal income tax returns. This would reduce workers' out-of-pocket share to less than they now pay for premiums.

The employers' premium (assuming they deduct half from their workers' paychecks) would also be *less* than what employers as a whole actually spend on private health insurance premiums.

Riemer (2019) explains these fiscal details in full.

Collateral Benefits

I began by arguing that greatly improving the U.S. economic security structure (by guaranteeing transitional jobs, raising the minimum wage, and substantially increasing incomes for workers, the disabled, and retired seniors) is the most important way to improve the American population's health. The converse is also true. A top-notch health insurance system for all Americans under-65—one that provides excellent benefits, a choice of health insurance plans and care providers, and an effective incentive-based mechanism for controlling costs—will strengthen economic security. Bankruptcies will decline. Savings will rise.

Beyond improving economic security, YoungMedicare has several other important collateral benefits. One obvious consequence is that workers' health, including their mental health, will be somewhat improved. As a result, more individuals will be able to find jobs and stay on the job. Workers will be able to keep more regular hours, and they will experience less on-the-job stress. All this means a gain in employee productivity, which translates into business profits and national wealth.

Yes, some firms will have to spend more for their workers' health insurance than they now get away with. But the firms that spend little today do not do so because they are smart at buying good insurance. They typically save on health insurance by using three different types of cost-shifting: skimming, sticking, and skimping.

Skimming. To begin with, some employers intentionally favor hiring younger or otherwise healthier workers in order to reduce their health insurance costs. The responsibility for insuring older or less healthy workers thus gets shifted to the taxpayers or other employers.

Sticking. Some employers "stick it" to the taxpayers by requiring their workers (or their workers' spouses and dependent children) to make use of Medicaid, the Affordable Care Act, or government employee health plans if at all possible. Alternatively, the employers may offer cash bonuses to workers who enroll (or arrange for spouses or children to enroll) in government insurance arrangements.

The taxpayers are not the only victims of such schemes. Some employers—including public employers as well as private ones—insist that their workers enroll (or have their spouses or children enroll) in available private employers' health insurance plans. An alternative is often to offer cash bonuses to workers who agree to "stick it" to a different private firm.

Skimping. Finally, some employers try to save money—for themselves, not for the overall healthcare system—by providing skimpy benefits. They typically saddle their workers with high deductibles in order to slice the price of their premiums. The cost of the deductibles, however, does not vanish. Workers absorb them. And where workers are unable or unwilling to pay up, the unpaid healthcare providers will attempt to embed their lost revenue in the charges they collect (or try to) from other individuals, employers, or government.

A government-overseen system that offers excellent coverage to all Americans, and finances it fairly, avoids all of these forms of cost-shifting. Everybody's covered. Every worker and every employer pays a fair share, based on a simple formula, for the national necessity of having excellent health insurance for all Americans under 65. Just as doctors no longer bleed their patients, employers that engage in the practice of skimming, sticking, and skimping in order to save a buck would become a relic of a bygone era.

The biggest boon to business is likely to be the liberation of employers from the burden of thinking about, worrying over, and being frustrated by the complexity and cost of health insurance. For most employers, public and private, health insurance is not a "core business." Rather, preoccupation with health insurance diverts them from their core business. Its baffling rules and ever-escalating costs soak up energy and creativity that should be focused on the stuff that matters: employee recruitment and management, product development, marketing and sales, and customer relations. YoungMedicare would liberate America's private sector to concentrate fully on its primary mission.

Both large and small businesses will gain when, for a simple and predictable price, they can get the health insurance monkey off their backs. Small firms will benefit in particular. One reason is that a program like Young-Medicare will promote the formation of more small businesses. All over America, would-be entrepreneurs are locked into their jobs in government agencies or large firms because they cannot go without insurance. If their incomes exceed 400% of the poverty line (not that much for a single person in the middle-or-upper ranks of a high-tech corporations), Obamacare offers no subsidy if they quit their insured job and go off on their own to invent the next Apple computer or launch the next Facebook.

Only in the United States are such entrepreneurs thus trapped inside government agencies or big corporations by their fear of losing health insurance for themselves, their spouses, and their children. Their Chinese, British, French, German and Japanese competitors—insured in very different ways no matter what ventures they may pursue—face no similar handicap. YoungMedicare would instantly eliminate "job lock." Entrepreneurs could immediately begin to form the start-ups they dream about and hire other adventurous employees, knowing that all of them (and all of their spouses and children) will retain excellent health insurance through a choice of healthcare plans.

A final collateral benefit will be the slowing down in the share of U.S. GDP that is poured into the healthcare sector (without making us any healthier). This is not merely a matter of getting in line with how much our international competitors spend on healthcare as a percent of their GDP. The reason for slowing the flow of dollars into healthcare is to accelerate the flow of dollars into the other sectors of the economy that (directly or indirectly) make the overall U.S. economy more productive, competitive, and wealthier.

Summary

Whether health insurance is a "right" or not, it is a necessity. Every American should have it. Coverage should include medical care, hospitalization, prescription drugs, and all the other types of care listed in the Affordable Care Act. Benefits should also be excellent. This means getting rid of deductibles, co-pays (except in rare cases), and coinsurance. The harm they do in preventing sick and injured Americans from obtaining necessary care far exceeds any good they do in preventing frivolous or inappropriate care, particularly when a better price-signal mechanism exists to avoid unneeded treatment. To achieve the five essential goals of a good health insurance system—(1) universal coverage, (2) excellent benefits, (3) choice of healthcare plans and providers, (4) effective control of insurance premiums and healthcare costs, and (5) improved healthcare quality leading to gains in health outcomes—we should create a new model, here called YoungMedicare, for the entire under-65 population.

Under YoungMedicare, all covered individuals would have a Health Insurance Purchasing Account credited with a dollar amount equal to the lowest premium bid by competing healthcare plans, on a risk-adjusted basis, to provide a uniform set of excellent health insurance benefits in the county where they live or work. Individuals could buy the uniform benefit package from any of the competing plans. If they passed over the low-bid plan in order to enroll in a higher-bid plan, however, they would pay out of pocket the full difference between the low bid and the higher-premium bid by the plan they selected. This use of clear and simple price signals will cause market forces to exert powerful and enduring pressure on insurers and providers to lower their prices and costs by squeezing out the enormous waste that pervades the U.S. healthcare system, which amounts to as much as one-third of all health spending.

To pay for the amounts credited to every owner of a Health Insurance Purchasing Account for the purpose of choosing a YoungMedicare healthcare plan, the program would be organized as a new social insurance program. Akin to workers' compensation, YoungMedicare would require employers to remit payroll-based premiums. Workers' could be required to absorb payroll deductions for up to half of the employer's premium cost, but workers would be able to reduce the burden by claiming a refundable federal income tax credit for up to 70% of their cost. Both workers and employers would (in aggregate) pay less than the health insurance premiums they now pay.

Medicare would continue to operate as is for the age 65+ population. In time, it may make sense to integrate the two programs—YoungMedicare and the existing Medicare program—into a single program.

APPENDIX
How Price Signals Lower Health Costs and Improve Quality

Price signals, *if* properly designed, can lower health costs and improve health quality. Two assumptions underpin the following explanation—and visual guide—of how properly designed price signals can lead to both lower costs and better quality.

First Assumption: Most Americans already gain access to healthcare through a health insurance plan (the Plan), whether a health maintenance organization (HMO), preferred provider organization (PPO), or fee-for-service (FFS) plan. The Plan ensures that, when covered individuals need a defined set of healthcare services from the Plan's network of doctors, hospitals, and other healthcare providers, the individuals covered will pay far less than full cost of their care. The Plan instead will bear most of the cost. If an individual needs a lot of care, the Plan is likely to pay most of the total cost and nearly all of the "latest" cost (until at least the end of the year).

Second Assumption: Despite these common features, Plans vary a lot. They vary in the location of their facilities. They vary in their networks of providers (i.e., which doctors and hospitals are in their respective networks). HMOs have narrower networks, PPOs broader networks, and FFS plans the widest (often unlimited) networks. Most important for this discussion, Plans vary in how much they cost. Even if providing exactly the same benefits for exactly the same persons of the same age, sex, and other risk factors, premiums (or equivalent) will differ. They also vary in their quality of care.

Figure 21.1 shows the two axes along which Plans vary. Along one axis, Plans vary by cost. Along another axis, Plans vary by quality.

Cost axis. Let us begin by looking at Plan variation based on cost. Let us further assume that all Plans have identical benefits and enrollment "risk profiles" (or have been actuarially risk-adjusted to be identical) and that our cost focus is each Plan's benefit-adjusted, risk-adjusted, per-person premium.

Along the cost axis, some Plans have figured out how to operate more efficiently. Thus, they can keep costs down and charge lower premiums. Other Plans have not succeeded in delivering healthcare as efficiently. Thus, they suffer from higher costs and must charge higher premiums.

In figure 21.2, the more efficient, low-cost, lower-premium Plans occupy the green square and the lower yellow square. The less efficient, high-cost, higher-premium Plans occupy the upper yellow square and the red square.

Quality axis. Now let's look at Plan variation along the quality axis. Again, even if Plans' benefits and risk profiles are identical, their quality varies.

Many Plans provide superb service and excellent care. They give their customers clear and timely information, always treat patients with respect, keep appointments, and provide good follow-up. Their doctors, nurses, and other providers are highly qualified. They make few errors. Care itself is delivered quickly, correctly, and efficiently. These Plans get the highest scores from HEDIS on three measures: customer satisfaction, prevention,

FIGURE 21.1 Plan quality variation based on cost.

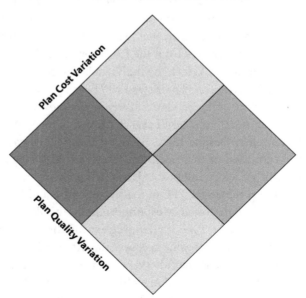

FIGURE 21.2 Plan premium variation.

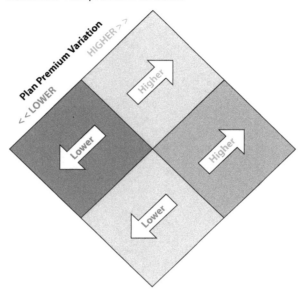

and treatment (National Committee for Quality Assurance, n.d.a; n.d.b).[8] Their hospitals get high grades from Leapfrog.[9]

By contrast, other Plans deliver mediocre-to-terrible quality. Some patients may be quite happy with the service and care they get. But applying objective HEDIS and Leapfrog measures as well as subjective assessments, such Plans fare poorly in quality.

It is typically the efficiency of the Plan—more efficient management, more efficient recruitment and use of personnel, more efficient IT systems, more efficient coordination of the Plan's many complex pieces—that drives its rankings for quality. The more efficient Plans are likely to have higher quality, which helps them keep costs down and keep premiums in check. The less efficient Plans are likely to have lower quality, which inhibits their ability to control costs and pressures them to charge higher premiums.

In figure 21.3, the more efficient, better-quality Plans occupy the green square and the upper yellow square. The less efficient, worse-quality Plans occupy the lower yellow square and the red square.

---

8. HEDIS is the Healthcare Effectiveness Data and Information Set. It is a tool used by more than 90% of America's health plans to measure performance on important dimensions of care and service. Altogether, HEDIS consists of 81 measures across five domains of care.

9. Part of the Leapfrog Group for improving U.S. hospital care, the Leapfrog Hospital Safety Grade assigns letter grades to hospitals based on their record of patient safety, helping consumers protect themselves and their families from errors, injuries, accidents, and infections.

FIGURE 21.3 Plan variation along the quality axis.

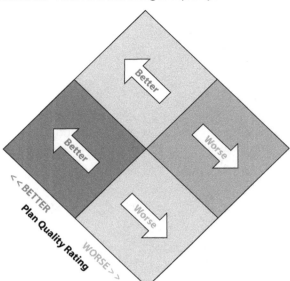

Combining the cost axis and the quality axis. Because Plans vary along *both* a cost/premium axis *and* a quality axis, it is possible to group them into four categories (see figure 21.4):

- Green Square Plans do the best on both measures. They have a lower-cost structure; thus they have the potential to bid lower premiums. They also deliver excellent quality.
- Yellow Square Plans score well on one measure, but they fall short on the other measure. Either (as with the lower-left yellow square) their costs and premiums are low but their quality is mediocre-to-poor, or (as with the upper-right yellow square) their costs and premiums are high, even though their quality is good-to-excellent.
- Red Square Plans do the worst on both measures: They not only suffer from higher costs, compelling them to bid higher premiums. They also have the worst quality.

People are funny. But it is likely that Americans, if they have the choice of enrolling in any one of several healthcare Plans and get accurate information, will at least *say* that they are more likely to enroll in the Green Square Plans whose lower cost justifies lower premiums *and* that earn high ratings for better quality.

FIGURE 21.4 Combining the cost axis and quality axis.

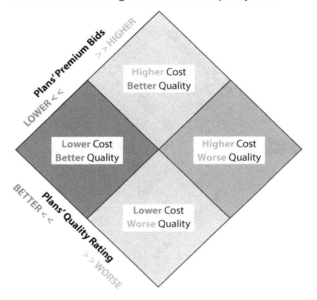

It is also likely that, given a choice, Americans will *say* that they will shy away from Yellow Square Plans that only do well on one measure (cost/premium *or* quality) but fare badly on the other measure (cost/premium *or* quality).

And of course it is likely that Americans will *say* that they will never enroll in a Red Square Plan. Who in their right mind, they might indignantly ask, would go out of the way to enroll in a costly plan that charges higher premiums yet delivers terrible healthcare quality?

Figure 21.5 illustrates what Americans are likely to *say* about their behavior in choosing among competing healthcare Plans (or any other product or service, for that matter). Who does not want the lowest-cost product or service that also happens to be the best product or service? Who would spurn such a choice in order select the highest-cost option that also has the worst record of quality?

But in the absence of a clear and simple price signal that creates a powerful incentive—a strong economic reason—to pick a low-premium/high-quality plan, many Americans will not bother to do so.

They may be suspicious of the lowest-cost option. ("If it's so cheap, how can it possibly be so good?") They may not wish to spend time looking at HEDIS, Leapfrog, or other information about comparative quality. Even if they have no objection to low-cost options *per se* and pay careful attention to quality rankings, they may nonetheless decide—if no cost signal makes

FIGURE 21.5 Optimal enrollee choices.

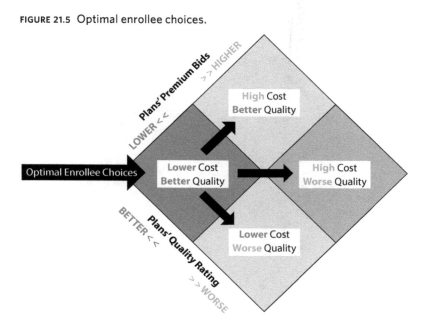

them think twice about choosing a more expensive, worse-quality Plan—to enroll in it solely based on familiarity.

The lack of price signals to induce Americans to select low-cost, high-quality plans is not just a theoretical concern. It drives up the overall cost of the U.S. healthcare system, causing healthcare to absorb an ever-growing share of GDP without improving health outcomes and thus choking off resources for other public and private investments that could better improve U.S. health and wealth. The lack of price signals also takes the pressure off the improvement of the quality of care. As a result, more people die and get sick than would otherwise be the case.

It is fairly simple, however, to create clear and simple price signals that encourage Americans to prefer low-cost/high-quality Plans. Such price signals would not deprive anyone of choice. Americans would be free to select any Plan they want, regardless of premium and quality.

What the price signals would do is induce the Plans to become more efficient, hold down their costs, lower their premiums, and improve their quality. They would not be required to do anything. They could manage their costs, set their premiums, and try to improve their quality any way they want. But they would face the stern and constant discipline of the market. They would gain price-sensitive customers, increase revenue, and make higher profits by greatly improving their efficiency, lowering their costs, holding down their premiums, and enhancing the quality of the care they provide. Conversely, they would lose customers, revenue, and profits if they failed to become more efficient and if they cost more, charged higher premiums, and offered poor quality care.

Figures 21.6 and 21.7, which are again four-square diagrams, show how a clear and simple system of price signals would operate. They illustrate one basic concept: a coin whose two sides are stated below:

- When enrollees pick a Plan, they *must personally save money* when they select a Plan that is lower in cost, bids a lower premium, and delivers high-quality care.
- Conversely, enrollees *must personally lose money*—out of pocket—if they join a plan that is higher in cost, bids a higher premium, and delivers lower-quality care.

For this price-signal mechanism to work, five things are necessary:

1. The Plans must be required to bid on a single, uniform benefit package.
2. The actual monthly dollar amount that enrollees *personally will either save or lose out of pocket* in joining each Plan must be clearly presented, along with objective information (e.g., HEDIS scores, Leapfrog rankings, etc.) on the competing Plans' quality.
3. Enrollees must *save the most money* (i.e., pay the least) if they join the Plan that bids the lowest premium. Ideally, they should be able to join for free the lowest-bidding Plan with high-quality ratings.
4. Enrollees must *lose money* (i.e., pay more) if they enroll in any Plan that bids a premium greater than that of the lowest-bidding Plan.
5. Enrollees must *lose more and more money* in proportion to the difference between the lowest-bidding Plan's premium bid and the premium bid by the Plan they actually join. Ideally, they should pay out of pocket the *full entire extra cost* of enrolling in a higher-bidding Plan—that is, 100% of the difference between the lowest-bidding Plan's premium and the premium bid by the Plan they select.

Figure 21.6 shows a hypothetical variety of monthly premiums bid by competing healthcare Plans. The actual dollar amounts are arbitrary. It is the relationship between them—lowest premiums in the green square, higher premiums in the yellow squares, and the highest Premium in the red square—that matters. Remember: All the Plans are assumed to have the same benefits (or are actuarially adjusted to achieve that outcome, and all the premiums are risk-adjusted.)

FIGURE 21.6 Hypothetical monthly premiums bid by competing health care plans.

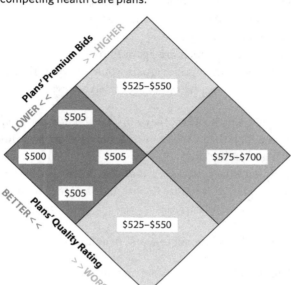

Figure 21.7—keying off the above—shows how much *extra* an enrollee would be obliged to pay, out of pocket, to join the various Plans available:

- Ideally, if the enrollee joins the Plan with the very lowest bid (i.e., in figure 21.6, the Plan with the $500 monthly premium) and high quality, the enrollee's extra out-of-pocket cost would be zero.[10]
- If the enrollee joins any other Plan, the enrollee's extra out-of-pocket cost would be the difference between the lowest-premium bid and the higher-premium bid by the more expensive Plan selected. (In figure 21.7, the extra cost ranges from an extra $5 per month to an extra $200 per month.)

Any insured individual would be free to join any plan. But with strong price signals like this, enrollees will have a powerful incentive to choose the lowest-bidding Plan, or at least a relatively low-bidding Plan, in order to avoid the substantial additional extra out-of-pocket cost of enrolling in a higher-bidding Plan.

---

10. Part of the Leapfrog Group for improving U.S. hospital care, the Leapfrog Hospital Safety Grade assigns letter grades to hospitals based on their record of patient safety, helping consumers protect themselves and their families from errors, injuries, accidents, and infections.

FIGURE 21.7 Additional out-of-pocket cost to join health plans.

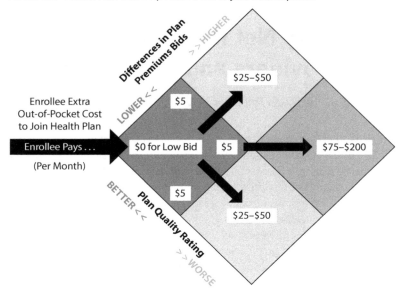

This inducement to enrollees creates exactly the kind of market pressure needed to impel the more expensive Plans and their networks of providers to improve their efficiency, lower their costs, constrain their premiums, and improve the quality of their care.

Isn't this picture that we want? An American health insurance system where:

- Everyone has coverage.
- Benefits are excellent.
- All individuals can select the specific Plans and healthcare providers they want.
- Individuals can freely change their Plans every year.
- Many of the choices require enrollees either to pay none of the premium or only a modest monthly amount.
- The price signals that flow through the system create powerful and enduring incentives to health insurers (whether HMOs, PPOs, or FFS plans) and healthcare providers (hospitals, doctors, and drug companies) to improve their efficiency, lower costs, hold down premiums, improve quality, and perhaps even improve health outcomes.

CHAPTER 22

Safety Net Alternatives for Providers and Employers

JAMES J. TARASOVITCH AND CHARLES P. STEVENS

Previous chapters in section 4 presented an economist's perspective on healthcare safety nets (chapter 19), as well as attempts to create a universal healthcare plan in Wisconsin that provided healthcare that was not tethered to employment (chapters 20 and 21). Those plans were not pure public options because they included private insurance and providers and had some level of market competition. This chapter explores what type of safety net ideas make sense from the perspectives of those in the trenches of healthcare delivery—first from a provider-hospital system perspective and then from a payer-employer perspective. In both cases, while a universal single-payer healthcare plan is not proposed, some variation of catastrophic coverage or stop loss insurance is explored, paid for either by the federal government or as a payroll tax. This is intended to protect patient-consumers and employers from rare but expensive medical events that could be financially devastating for individuals or the companies that pay for their healthcare. Other important considerations, like meeting the needs of vulnerable populations, are also discussed.

The Provider Perspective: From a Hospital CFO

J. TARASOVITCH

Current Environment

The conversation regarding healthcare policy continues to be a topic of great interest in the United States today, as it directly impacts everyone in our country. Both employers and individuals are facing rising costs in addition to access, quality, cultural, and geographic disparities. Healthcare has drawn a great deal of attention from lawmakers in the past decade, culminating in the passage of the Affordable Care Act (ACA) on March 23, 2010, and efforts by President Donald Trump's administration to repeal this

James J. Tarasovitch, CPA, is regional chief financial officer for the south market of Ascension Wisconsin. Charles P. Stevens, JD, is an employee benefits attorney and a partner in the Milwaukee, Wisconsin, office of the law firm of Michael Best & Friedrich, LLP.

policy. Both providers and patients continue to be impacted by the consequences of our country's current healthcare policy.

While most individuals receive *good* care from providers, there are many
who do not receive *effective* care—meaning cost-effective care with quality
outcomes. Why does this continue to be an ongoing issue? The easy response
is that it is an extremely complex issue and there is no "silver bullet" that
can solve it. Some of the reasons that contribute to the complexity of healthcare in the United States have been well documented: limited access, affordability, and cultural and geographical disparities, to name a few. However,
there are other issues that need to be addressed that are not fully the responsibility of the healthcare industry. It is widely accepted that only 10–20%
of health relates to an individual's physical well-being. The other 80–90%
relates to environment and societal factors, called *social determinants*, such
as access to housing, transportation, employment, and affordable and nutritious food (Magnan, 2017).

To fully address the complicated issues that impact the health of our
nation and face our healthcare providers, these social determinants must be
included in the discussion to find solutions.

Each of these issues is interdependent and impacts an individual's ability
to access the care they need. To adequately address the social determinants of
health, it will take a holistic approach that includes the combined efforts
of healthcare providers, community partners, and the government.

Case Study of Work Being Done by Ascension Wisconsin to Address Social Determinants of Health

Food insecurity is an example of this interdependence. According to
Hunger Task Force, "People who are food insecure are [disproportionately]
affected by diet-sensitive chronic diseases such as diabetes and high blood
pressure, and according to research, food insecurity is also linked to many
adverse effects to overall health." To get upstream and address the issues
caused by food insecurity, providers at Milwaukee's Ascension SE Wisconsin
Hospital–St. Joseph Campus targeted two patient groups who were viewed
to be most at-risk: expectant mothers and senior citizens.

Nearly half of the at-risk moms cared for at Ascension St. Joseph qualify for food assistance through the Women, Infants, and Children (WIC)
program, but are unenrolled. To tackle the issue, the Ascension St. Joseph
team reached out to the City of Milwaukee Health Department to offer the
hospital as a location for a satellite WIC office. WIC is a nutrition program
for pregnant women, women who are breastfeeding, and families with children younger than five. WIC provides nutrition education, breastfeeding

education and support, supplemental nutritious foods, and connections to other community services (Wisconsin Department of Health Services, 2019).

Similarly, the rate of hunger among seniors age 60 and older has increased by 45% since 2001, and 63% of senior households served by the Feeding America network are forced to choose between food and medical care (Feeding America, n.d.). Recognizing this trend, Ascension St. Joseph collaborates with Hunger Task Force, Milwaukee's food bank, as a pickup location for the senior stockbox program. A stockbox is a box of healthy foods that Hunger Task Force delivers to low-income seniors free of charge. Each box contains 16 nutritious items including rice, cereal, juice, beef stew, pasta, and vegetables. Each month, more than 70 boxes are distributed at Ascension St. Joseph to vulnerable seniors living in the Sherman Park neighborhood (Hunger Task Force, n.d.).

The Challenges of the Current Healthcare Policy

Public and Private Insurance. The United States currently has a blended healthcare model that comprises both public and private insurers. Each segment of the model has provided access and benefits to most Americans. The ACA expanded the opportunity for affordable insurance for many, yet it did not cover everyone and it has proved to be less affordable than originally intended. While the ACA has provided some advantages, such as removing the preexisting conditions clause, eliminating the lifetime benefit limit, and expanding coverage to dependents up to age 26, it has had some unintended consequences that affect both patients and providers.

The ACA and the Impact of Not Rejecting Preexisting Conditions. In the era before the Affordable Care Act, it was acceptable for insurance companies (payers) to deny coverage to individuals with preexisting conditions, leaving these patients unable to obtain a health insurance plan to cover their higher cost of care. Since the adoption of the ACA, insurers may no longer refuse coverage to these patients, which increases the pool of individuals participating in the insurance market. With more participants in the marketplace, premiums should decrease and provide patients with a better opportunity to obtain insurance at an affordable cost. While this has been positive for patients, it has created an additional burden for payers, who previously were not responsible for new patients with preexisting conditions. This has required payers to either raise their premiums to offset these losses or exit the health insurance exchange, thereby reducing the insurance plans available for consumers.

This increased cost of ACA insurance exchange plans had a negative impact on patients and providers, leaving patients with two options. The first is to purchase a plan with much higher deductibles and co-pays. This lowers their monthly premiums, making these types of plans the only real affordable options under the Affordable Care Act. The other option is to choose to not purchase the mandated coverage and pay the penalty. This latter option has proved to be a viable solution for many individuals, who have discovered that the elimination of the preexisting clause penalty means they can purchase insurance later when they have the need for insurance. This has resulted in a smaller pool of healthy patients obtaining health insurance through the ACA insurance exchanges. Those premiums were expected to offset the costs associated with patients who require more expensive care. This dynamic results in the exchange plans' costs increasing when it was expected that costs would be lowered overall. In both scenarios, the providers are incurring higher bad debt expenses because the patients are not able to pay the out-of-pocket costs from these plans, or they require higher charity care because they opted out of the mandatory coverage. So, what can be done to provide a baseline of healthcare to everyone, or at least most people, and especially people who are vulnerable?

Potential Safety Net Solutions

Many Americans believe that there needs to be a change in our healthcare. The disparity issues among different population segments, coupled with continued rising costs—especially pharmaceutical costs and the costs of our public programs and private insurance options—all contribute to the need for change. Despite this, many individuals are concerned about the costs associated with a new national healthcare policy and how it will impact them. Whatever the final policy change(s) may be, it will need to provide a sustainable safety net for people who are the most vulnerable in society and include the funding mechanisms to ensure that it will be available for future generations. Below are some potential safety net solutions for both the public and private sectors:

"Medicare for All" is a 2020 presidential election topic. Some politicians are espousing the benefits of a universal plan for the United States, like those in Canada or the United Kingdom (see chapter 1). While the universal plans in these countries have had some positive impacts, they are experiencing similar economic realities as in the United States. These nations are seeing healthcare costs rapidly increase because of aging populations and greater usage of services, coupled with an eroding tax base that negatively impacts their ability to properly fund the healthcare system. What are some of the impacts to patients in these countries?

In January 2018 the combination of underfunding and a bad flu season stretched Britain's National Health Service to the breaking point. Then Prime Minister Theresa May ended up offering apologies to British patients for the conditions they faced:

- Up to 55,000 operations postponed
- An emergency room doctor who felt the need to publicly apologize to patients for "Third World conditions of the department due to overcrowding"
- Advisories that patients should not go to the emergency room "unless they are very seriously ill"
- Up to two dozen ambulances parked outside a hospital, "with an average of 10–14 vehicles waiting to drop off patients throughout the day" because the hospitals had no place to put the incoming patients

(Jacobs, 2019)

If the United States chose to implement a universal health plan, issues experienced by countries with government-mandated plans should be studied closely to determine if we would experience similar issues. As noted earlier in this chapter, the United States currently experiences access to care issues. To be successful, this proposed change in healthcare policy assumes that the government can implement and operate a national healthcare plan at an affordable cost that will cover the needs for all individuals living or visiting the United States, while ensuring the providers have adequate reimbursement to continue to properly invest in their employees, facilities, and technology. This option has been met with significant opposition for many reasons including cost, fear of healthcare rationing, investment in healthcare infrastructure, and the potential for fewer individuals seeking careers in healthcare. More important, by trying to provide benefits to everyone, the system could become so expensive that it becomes unaffordable for everyone.

One healthcare program that serves vulnerable populations is Medicaid (see chapter 1). Some lawmakers have suggested a policy change that would convert the current open-ended federal Medicaid funds into a block grant system. A block grant refers to grant funding from the federal government to individual state and local governments to help support a specific broad-purpose program, such as housing, health, or social services. "Caps on spending could be designed in a number of ways, such as a block grant under which states would receive a limited, pre-budgeted amount of money from the federal government, or on a per capita basis, which would predetermine the amount of money spent per person enrolled in Medicaid" (Sachs & Huberfeld, 2019).

This proposal presents several challenges to overcome, including many legal barriers along with concerns about the proposal's potential to harm patients and providers. Opponents of this concept also have suggested that "block grants are simply bad policy. Proposals of this kind are predictably harmful to both beneficiaries and to the state's economic interests" (Sachs & Huberfeld, 2019). This could add financial stress to both the patient and the provider—with potentially fewer eligible patients, providers seeing an increase in unreimbursed services, and cost-conscious patients needing expensive emergency room visits after choosing not to seek lower-cost preventative healthcare services.

Public-private Hybrid Solutions—Catastrophic Insurance. The above discussion focused only on potential safety net solutions from the government sector. Given the complexities, it is hard to imagine that only one sector, the government, could solve this issue by itself. Any solution must have participation from many segments of society. A possible safety net solution that both the public and private sectors could work on together could be the establishment of a catastrophic insurance plan. Such a plan could be funded through tax contributions, new or redistributed, coupled with financial incentives for healthcare providers to reduce the cost of care. It could be established to protect individuals and employers from catastrophic claims exceeding $1 million, which is the same lifetime benefit limit that was eliminated by the ACA law.

A catastrophic plan funded through the public sector and operated by private insurance would require both sectors to work together to establish the plan requirements and benefit coverages. It is well known that most personal bankruptcy claims stem from healthcare issues, with the highest instances being associated with long-term cancer treatment (Konish, 2019). Even though the ACA has eliminated the lifetime benefit for treatment, which is positive for patients, it has resulted in significant financial hardships for employers, particularly for small business employers. Small business owners who experience this may be forced to reduce benefits or simply stop offering healthcare insurance coverage altogether, neither of which is favorable for the employer or the employee. A catastrophic healthcare plan solution could assist employers and their employees who need unusually high cost care by reducing their financial burden while maintaining adequate healthcare benefits for both. It would serve as a kind of publicly funded stop loss insurance to protect against these rare but expensive events.

It could be argued that the creation and implementation of a new insurance plan that is funded through taxpayer contributions would be ineffective and costly. However, a catastrophic safety net may lower premiums and enhance overall benefits for individuals, because the employers would have lower risk than is associated with high-cost claims. There needs to be a deeper analysis into the concept of a new safety net for both the individual and employer, including catastrophic limits and where the plan would actually assume the liability.

Summary

Whatever path we take as a nation to address the complex healthcare issues that are present today, a new healthcare policy should meet these simple principles:

- Assure access to affordable healthcare for all.
- Preserve and extend the safety net for those who are poor and vulnerable.
- Provide a safety net to protect against rare but extremely expensive medical events that can bankrupt a person (e.g., expensive cancer therapies).
- Stabilize and strengthen the individual (private insurance) market, because a vibrant and sustainable individual and small group market is essential to a successful, equitable healthcare system.

Likewise, the following should be included or retained in the new policy:

- **Health insurance portability:** individuals need to have the security of no lapse in coverage because of a career change, loss of job, or any other reason that would result in a loss of coverage. This is a problem associated with linking healthcare insurance coverage to employment. Covid-19 has made even more clear how important this is.
- **Coverage for preexisting conditions:** The current provision of covering individuals with preexisting conditions should be retained. Without this clause many individuals would lose coverage because of a lack of affordability.

■ **Incentives for value-based care:** For providers, financial incentives need to be established to help them transition to a value-based, preventative care model and away from the current volume-based model that can incentivize unnecessary procedures and treatments (e.g., the relative value units, or RVUs, discussed in chapter 1). This is the key to lowering healthcare costs in the long run.

Given the complexity of the issue, it is clear that both the private and public sectors will need to work together to develop a solution. Given the political realities, any solution will most likely address a piece of the puzzle while working toward a more comprehensive solution.

The Employer Perspective: From a Healthcare Benefits Attorney

C. STEVENS

The Health Benefits Crisis for Employers and a Proposed Solution

For attorneys representing employers in employee benefits matters, often concerning health insurance, the issues have evolved over the last 10 years from mundane to "bet the company." Indeed, there is a significant difference between the era of "before the ACA" and "10 years after the ACA." Let's illustrate with a scenario, then and now.

November 2009

ABC Company is a medium-sized family-owned business with 300 employees. Over the years, the cost of health insurance for the company's employees has grown more expensive. Recently, the company received a quote for a 20% increase in premiums when renewing for 2010, and ABC has been told by its health insurance broker/consultant that it might want to consider self-funding the company health plan (i.e., act as an insurer itself rather than use an outside insurance provider). This would involve canceling the company's group health insurance policy and hiring a claims administrator to process and pay the claims, which would be directly funded by ABC. However, to avoid excess medical claims that could severely damage the company, ABC would also take out "stop loss" insurance coverage on both an *aggregate* and *specific* basis.

ABC expects about $1.8 million in claims, so under this arrangement, if total health claims paid by ABC exceed $2 million during the year, the

stop loss carrier will step in and reimburse ABC for any claims it is required
to pay in excess of the aggregate limit. Furthermore, if any one person's paid
claims exceed a specific dollar limit during the year (ABC selects $80,000
per person), the stop loss carrier will reimburse those claims as well.

ABC's health plan has a lifetime benefit limit of $1 million (which for
2008 is common and no one at ABC ever had claims that high). That limit,
the exclusion of coverage for preexisting conditions, and the stop loss coverage, which is not very expensive, permits ABC to go the self-funded route.
To be safe, ABC decides that it should set aside funds to cover its maximum
potential liability, so it deposits $167,000 per month into a separate account
to pay claims. In addition, ABC pays the premiums for the stop loss coverage and the fees charged by the claims administrator to administer the plan.
Even with these expenses, ABC is projected to save money as compared to
staying with fully insured medical coverage. However, because ABC does
not expect to hit the annual or specific stop loss limit, ABC is likely to have
unused claims money at the end of year if it is a "normal" year.

It turns out ABC does save money. Some additional details are associated
with self-funding that create more administrative burden, including more
work in complying with the privacy issues associated with federal regulations that include the Health Insurance Portability and Accountability Act
(HIPAA) and the Employee Retirement Income Security Act (ERISA), but
ABC figures these out and, on the whole, the new arrangement turns out to
have been a good decision.

March 2010

The Affordable Care Act is enacted and health insurance carriers and
employers with self-funded health plans must comply with certain new
rules. Notably, ABC must eliminate its $1 million lifetime maximum limit
on benefits paid under its health plan and the exclusion of coverage for preexisting conditions. ABC must also extend coverage for employees' children
up to their 26th birthday. Certain additional items now must be covered
at no cost to the patient because they have been determined to be "preventative." Because ABC has a self-funded plan that soon becomes "non-
grandfathered," it must adhere to additional requirements. Employees with
employer-provided coverage appreciate the changes as do individuals with
individual market insurance coverage where the same changes are mandated. Healthcare providers, hospital systems, and pharmaceutical companies appreciate that there are fewer limits on covered claims. Medical
insurance carriers realize premiums will have to increase; so do the stop
loss carriers.

November 2019

Since 2010, ABC has had some good years and some bad years with its self-funded health plan, but the cost of coverage has continued to rise. The annual aggregate stop loss limit is now at $4 million and the annual specific stop loss limit is now at $100,000 per person. ABC's broker/consultant schedules a meeting with ABC's president and human resources director and tells them that they have had a very high health claim and it is causing a problem with the renewal of their stop loss coverage for 2020. The HR director points out that the company has already had large increases in the cost of stop loss coverage over the last several years, and paid claims are now anticipated to be about $3.3 million in 2020 (averaging now about $11,000 per employee). The broker, however, relates an even greater issue.

A dependent of an employee is receiving a drug called Tusdotin. The broker looked it up and Tusdotin is an "orphan drug" (see chapter 15 on Orphan drugs) developed to treat a rare and horrible genetic disease called Hypophosphatasia, where the child lacks a particular enzyme necessary for bone creation and health. Without this enzyme, calcium and phosphate do not bond in adequate amounts and children with the disease have bones that are soft or weak. The disease has historically been painful, crippling, and often fatal. Tusdotin, however, has now been approved by the Food and Drug Administration (FDA) and it is typically effective in treating the illness, but it is not a cure and must be taken "for life." The dosage of the drug depends on the weight of the patient, and as the child gets older and reaches adult size it becomes even more expensive.

ABC's president asks, "How expensive?"

The broker responds that because Tusdotin is the only drug of its kind, it is extraordinarily expensive.

"How expensive?" repeats the president.

"So expensive, it is not covered under the Canadian health system."

"How much is our plan paying?" asks ABC's president.

"The claim paid by the ABC health plan in 2019 has so far exceeded $800,000. The company paid the first $80,000 and the stop loss carrier has picked up the rest," the broker says.

ABC's president says, "So this is good, that we have stop loss coverage, right?"

The broker responds, "We did for 2019, but we can't renew this coverage unless we agree to a 25% premium increase and a $1 million laser."

The president asks, "What's a laser?"

The broker explains that when a stop loss carrier imposes a laser on a person covered by the plan, the carrier will not reimburse any claims before they exceed the amount of the laser. Also, the child's medical claims paid by the employer between the specific stop loss point of $80,000 and the amount of the $1 million laser are ignored for aggregate stop loss purposes. The broker also explains that stop loss coverage is not medical insurance; it only provides some protection for the employer against excess claims. The stop loss carrier is permitted by state and federal law to do this—that is, to take the person's health status and healthcare costs into account. The president realizes that the company's cost of providing health coverage has now gone through the roof.

ABC's president says, "We only have a projected annual profit of $800,000! Does this mean all of our profit is going away because of one health claim?"

As the president and the HR director attempt to brainstorm with the broker about possible solutions, the broker has no answers. The Affordable Care Act now provides that employer group health plans cannot impose benefit limits. Furthermore, attempting to take the company back to a fully insured plan is not a solution because ABC is of a size that no group insurance carrier will provide a quote under these circumstances. Finally, the broker suggests that the company call its lawyer.

I am the lawyer. The above fact pattern is not specific to a child or a client of mine, ABC is fictional, and Tusdotin is not the real name of the drug. However, scenarios like this one have caused my phone to ring numerous times since the enactment of the Affordable Care Act. Make no mistake: Times were difficult before the ACA for individuals with serious health conditions where they had to deal with preexisting conditions, annual and lifetime maximums, and concerns over who would pay for expensive new medical treatments and drugs. Nevertheless, the Affordable Care Act not only left these problems unsolved, it made them worse in some cases, and so my phone rings more and more.

New Problems for Employers, Because of the ACA and Unusually Expensive Treatments

From the point of view of a certain small number of seriously afflicted individuals, the ACA brought good news and bad news. First the good news. The Orphan Drug Act of 1983 created a strong incentive for pharmaceutical companies to develop drugs for small populations with significant health problems (see chapters 10 and 15), and with the ACA, which eliminated benefit limits and required that most people now have insurance coverage, pharmaceutical companies also began to develop many new lifesaving but expensive drugs. Moreover, new extraordinarily expensive medical treatments have been developed, such as proton radiation therapy. Now the bad news: The United States continues to have a health-care system where employers are largely viewed as responsible for paying for healthcare (see chapter 1). However, whether the health coverage is insured or self-funded, employers find it is much more expensive than it used to be.

If an employer is lucky, it has not had a significant health problem among its employees or their covered family members. But how an employer looks at medical coverage is much different now than it was 10 years ago. In 2009, it was difficult to imagine how one person could generate $1 million in health claims. The thought was that the patient would not survive to a point where the hospital had a chance to provide $1 million in treatment. Even when the ACA was enacted in 2010, the elimination of annual and lifetime limits was not viewed to be a problem for insurance carriers and employers. It is a problem for employer-sponsored coverage now, however.

Another Post-ACA Healthcare Crisis Scenario

Imagine another scenario in which the problem is nothing but amazing bad luck and a very good hospital. Joe and Beth are returning to their home from a restaurant one evening when they are involved in a serious car accident. It does not matter who is at fault, but the Jaws of Life are required to get them out of their mangled vehicle and both require very long hospitalizations, physical therapy, vocational therapy, wheelchairs, prosthetics, and ongoing treatment. Both are covered under Joe's employer's health plan. Over a six-month period, Joe's claims are $950,000 and Beth's claims are $1.3 million. Hopefully, Joe's employer is not ABC Company.

If Joe's employer's health plan is self-funded, the stop loss carrier could impose a million-dollar laser in the next year on Joe and on Beth (each) as well as throw in a very significant premium increase. However, even if the health plan is fully insured, a very large increase in premiums would be likely.

Note that the size of the employer is very important here. If the employer has 50 or fewer full-time employees, it is a "small employer plan" and the insurance carriers in this sector of the industry offer "community rated" coverage. That is, premiums are set for each employer's plan based on the ages of the participants but not on their health status. The claims experience of the participating employers are pooled. For small employers, this is mostly good because they would find it much more difficult to deal with a high health claim for one of their employees. However, for small employers with healthy employees, they have to pay more than they would if their good claims experience were taken into account.

On the other side of the spectrum are large employers of, say, 1,000 employees. These employers have enough employees covered by the plan that their health claims are much more statistically reliable and the stop loss carrier is more comfortable in underwriting the case that it can sometimes offer a "no lasers" commitment. Granted, a "no lasers" commitment is never permanent and a history of very large claims may result in very large premium increases. Whether or not a no-lasers commitment would be made by the carrier will vary. However, at least from year to year, large employers who are not subject to possible lasers can engage in self-funding with greater assurance that the employer's financial position will not be turned upside down by high health claims.

Where does this leave those employers with more than 50 and fewer than 1,000 employees, who employ a significant percentage of working Americans? Many have been required to turn to not only their insurance brokers and consultants, but to their lawyers.

The problem: *protecting and insuring against rare but unusually large claims.*

High health claims create a complicated mix in terms of balancing different laws, managing the employer's risk of being sued, and determining what other options exist for the employer and employee that provide for optimal care while reducing employer cost and risk. These are all very sensitive situations in which families are already frustrated with carriers and claims administrators becoming involved with medical decision-making; now we add the employer to the dialogue.

We need to recognize that some claims are so large that they are beyond the capacity of individuals, hospitals (where the patient is uninsured), employers, and even some insurance carriers to handle without causing the current system to break down. We need to acknowledge that only a very large payer has the best ability to handle very large claims. We need a government-funded safety net.

Proposal: A Safety Net

Rare and Expensive Conditions. What if we were to have a safety net not simply for people but for certain rare and costly health conditions? Many previous state and federal solutions (most of which were eliminated by the ACA) involved taking responsibility for the individual and all of their health claims. Such arrangements included Wisconsin's former Health Insurance Risk Sharing Plan (HIRSP), which was funded by state health insurance carriers and offered coverage for individuals who were not eligible for employer or governmental coverage and who had been turned down by an insurance carrier. It covered all conditions for all people on the program and in these respects was similar to Medicare and Medicaid. Furthermore, precedent exists for focusing on individual conditions. In just one example, Congress recognized in 1972 that it would add a Medicare-based program for individuals with end-stage renal disease. The proposed safety net would have the federal government recognize that other rare and expensive medical conditions require special attention and funding.

The safety net would *not* be an arrangement where all of those with the most serious health conditions would be put on Medicare. Instead, only as to certain extraordinary conditions, the high cost of treating that condition would be handled by a large payer and not by other coverage the individual might have. This arrangement would make employer-provided coverage much more cost-efficient in terms of premium setting and permitting fewer employers to be struck by the lightning of a high health claim.

The Uninsured. The envisioned safety net would also be available to individuals who do not have employer-provided coverage and also do not have Medicare or Medicaid, where the individual is expected to pay out of pocket and the hospital has to determine whether or not to seek collection or instead provide the care without payment.

Federal Funding, Local Control. I am not prepared to assume that we will have perfect decision-making in terms of what conditions would be on the schedule (of what is covered) and how they would be handled for purposes of determining appropriate payments for treatment. My fear is that a decision-maker like the Centers for Medicare and Medicaid Services (CMS) could be too centralized and inflexible. The conditions that make it onto the schedule will not permit a one-treatment-fits-all approach. Accordingly, it would make more sense to have the funding come through the federal government, but the decision-making as to what is covered and how could be state-based so there is greater local responsibility and accountability. As different states implement different ideas for running the safety net, successful approaches will stand out. Such an arrangement would permit the safety net to evolve through an initial limited group of conditions for which treatment is funded through the program, which can be expanded as states determine whether the arrangement is working.

Employers Should Not be Responsible for Catastrophic Claims. Anyone considering the history of health insurance coverage in the United States will realize that, as employer-provided coverage evolved, it was understood to be a "fringe" benefit; that is, in addition to wages, the employer would help with some doctor bills (see chapters 1 and 4). Only in recent decades has the cost of health coverage become a significant component of an employee's wage and benefit "package." Indeed, in a case I argued before the Seventh Circuit of the U.S. Court of Appeals, the issue was whether or not an employer could modify a benefit commitment for retirees made in the 1970s, where the employee paid $2.00 at the pharmacy counter and the employer paid the rest. We advised the court that in the 1970s, the average prescription drug cost was $3.50 and the employer was paying less than half the cost.

We need to remind ourselves that the vast majority of employers never said they would be responsible for all of the costs of medical care and, notwithstanding the attempts by Congress through the ACA to place more responsibility on employers, it does not work in all conditions. That is, employers can cover some things. Hospitals, when a patient does not have health insurance or governmental coverage, can provide care for some things without being paid. Even individuals can handle some things. But, there are some conditions that only a very large payer can adequately handle, such as for certain expensive orphan drugs (chapters 12 and 15).

We should let employer-provided insured and self-funded health plans provide coverage for reasonable ordinary care, and even for some expensive but not rare conditions that insurance companies have adequately built into their underwriting. But perhaps there should be a schedule of certain extraordinary and rare conditions with their related treatments and drugs where the federal government takes over the funding, not for the entire person, but only to support the cost to treat the condition.

Just as Congress recognized the need for the Orphan Drug Act of 1983 (chapter 15) so that certain rare conditions would benefit from research and development of drugs, so too Congress could recognize that the next step in addressing these conditions is to find a rational way to pay for their treatment rather than expecting employers to somehow do so.

CHAPTER 23

Purple Solutions for the Needed Safety Net

DANIEL SEM

The previous chapters in section 4 gave an overview of potential safety net solutions that would provide a baseline of healthcare services to everyone, including vulnerable populations. The perspectives came from an: economist (chapter 19), politician (chapter 20), policymaker (chapter 21), and provider and employer-payer (chapter 22). Based on those chapters, a series of potential safety net solutions, which strive to be economically sound and sustainable, are presented in this final chapter. Section 4 on safety nets is meant to be the Blue counterpart to the somewhat Red section 2, which emphasizes the need for free and competitive markets, setting prices at reasonable values, and using competition to drive increases in quality and decreases in price. It is felt that a truly reasonable healthcare solution—a Purple solution—needs to consider both the need for free and competitive markets and a humane safety net that is economically sustainable. It is a compromise that spans both parties, and the hope is that our politicians would be willing to make reasonable compromises so that we can have better healthcare in America—perhaps even the best healthcare in the world.

Background

This book began with an analysis of the various causes of the high cost of healthcare in America (chapter 1), noting our frustration with the lack of up-front price transparency and the shocking surprise bills (figure 23.1) that get thrust on us. At the end of section 2, we concluded that one favorable and viable *Purple solution* to control cost and provide us with quality healthcare would be to implement a version of the system proposed by David Goldhill, similar to that used in Singapore, whereby (a) we use insurance only for more costly, rare, and catastrophic events, and (b) routine medical expenses are paid out of pocket using a health savings account (HSA). In fact, our current high-deductible plans—even the bronze Affordable Care Act (ACA) plan—are like this already in some respects, but without a flexible and mobile (i.e., usable for out-of-network direct-pay options) HSA in place. The HSA could be funded either by the government, if you

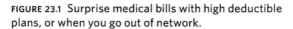

FIGURE 23.1 Surprise medical bills with high deductible plans, or when you go out of network.

Source: Art by John Alberti, reproduced with permission.

are on the Blue end of the political spectrum, or by individuals and/or their employers, if you are on the Red end of the political spectrum. Thus, with the system we currently have, we are not far from this model of healthcare delivery—we just need to expand and improve the form of HSA that we have. We just need barriers removed for us, as patient-consumers, so we can shop for healthcare out of network. In addition to a portable HSA, we need (a) easy-to-understand, transparent, and bundled prices and (b) a centralized electronic medical record system that we own and can grant others access to. We also need to take charge of and ownership of our healthcare. This was discussed at length in section 2, and in chapter 11.

What remains is to better define a safety net that provides a baseline of healthcare services to (a) vulnerable populations, (b) those employers and individuals that are hit with rare and expensive/catastrophic medical events, and (c) possibly everyone, according to some on the Blue side of the political spectrum. And as Covid-19 has taught us, we are all vulnerable to job loss and in need of a healthcare safety net that is not connected to employment.

Protecting the Poor and Vulnerable in Society

In our current healthcare system, those without insurance can and do use emergency rooms to receive care, even if they cannot pay. That is a result of the Emergency Medical Treatment and Labor Act (EMTALA) of 2012 (chapter 18). This is not a good or sustainable way to obtain healthcare because it is expensive and sometimes forces people to wait too long to get care—and arguably is not a humane way to treat the most vulnerable in our society. As was argued by James Tarasovitch (chief financial officer at a large provider) in chapter 22, this is a problem that needs to be addressed. Tarasovitch also argued for the need to have some sort of insurance to address catastrophic claims for employers and suggested the best solution might not be purely government funded, but rather a public-private hybrid.

Catastrophic Event Insurance—A Role for Government-sponsored Insurance?

Like Tarasovitch, Charles Stevens also argued for some sort of government-funded catastrophic insurance, to protect both individuals and employers from extremely large claims (over $1 million, which is the ACA threshold). If that level of claim hits an individual, it can drive them into bankruptcy, and if it hits a company and exceeds what the company's insurance can cover, it leads to higher premiums for everyone and potential costly "laser" policies. From these two perspectives (provider and payer-employer), a clear proposal emerged for limited government intervention to protect individuals and payers-employers from rare and extremely high cost medical events. These events include, especially, expensive treatments for rare diseases that are now emerging from the Orphan Drug Act (discussed in chapters 15 and 16). These are lifesaving treatments that were expensive to create (see chapter 12). But to date, we as a society have not developed any strategy to pay for them (chapter 17). Thus, when individuals or companies that pay for insurance are hit with these huge claims, it is financially devastating. We have a choice. Either we find a way to pay for these orphan drugs, or scientists stop trying to develop drugs to treat and cure people of rare diseases. Price controls are not an option in this case—because, quite simply, it costs a lot of money to make these drugs, and those expenses need to be recouped (chapter 12). Government funding to reimburse unusually large (and sometimes justified) claims above a certain limit, as a kind of publicly funded "stop loss" insurance, is one safety net solution—a bit like the Federal Deposit Insurance Corporation (FDIC) protecting banks from rare but financially devastating financial crises. This would effectively be government-funded "stop loss" insurance, which is called "level-2" insurance in this chapter. As noted by Charles Stevens, in chapter 22:

> Just as Congress recognized the need for the Orphan Drug Act of 1983 in terms of recognizing certain rare conditions that would benefit from research and development of drugs, so too Congress could recognize that the next step in addressing these conditions is to find a rational way to pay for their treatment rather than expecting employers to somehow do so.

In this proposed government-funded plan, according to Stevens, some schedule for what would or would not be covered under the plan would need to be created, by medical experts, to decide which extraordinary and rare conditions should be covered and at what level.

What About a Safety Net for the Poor and Vulnerable?

This is a tricky area for which to find a Purple solution, but I think both parties do care about our most vulnerable and do not want them to suffer without some healthcare or to be using emergency rooms for reasons not intended. Arguably, even a true free market advocate might agree to some sort of safety net considering that the father of free market thinking, Friedrich Hayek, seemed to think it made sense (chapter 1). But, as noted in chapter 19, there are more economically sustainable ways to do a safety net that provide needed support and help in a compassionate manner but also recognize that free and competitive markets are the best way to control prices and increase quality of services. The proposal put forth by Dr. Tyler Watts, an economist himself, is to provide the poor with vouchers to fund their HSA accounts, analogous to food stamps used to pay for food. In this way, as for food, markets get to actually function as they should, and because of the efficiency of markets, the poor would get better healthcare in a more sustainable manner than if the government ran and financed one healthcare provider network for everyone. It puts the healthcare consumer in control and also makes them responsible for smart spending of their healthcare dollars (in this case, dollars provided by a government voucher program). This, combined with HSAs, might encourage use of more routine preventative medical services and minimize unnecessary usage of emergency rooms (ERs), since a portion of the large fees for ER visits would be deducted from the HSAs—something any smart healthcare consumer would want to avoid, unless necessary, given the choice. Residual unused HSA funds, later in life, could go into either a retirement account or to a person's estate, so healthcare consumers feel like they are spending their own money, which puts it in Milton Friedman's most desirable Category I of spending (chapter 19).

What About Healthcare for the Rest of Society?

Expanding on the above plan, everyone in society could have an HSA account, but only those that are within some threshold of the poverty line (as for Medicaid) would be given this government-financed HSA voucher. Some fraction of the current Medicaid budget could be used to fund these HSA vouchers, as it is money still going to fund healthcare for the poor, just through a different mechanism. For everyone else, they would use the same HSA, but either they would fund it directly themselves or their employers would fund it. In all likelihood, some combination of both would likely occur. Companies could fund the HSA from some of the savings they get from (a) the government-sponsored stop loss insurance mentioned previously (which, because of risk shifting, would significantly lower the company's insurance premiums and decrease their financial risk) and (b) the lower insurance premiums they have because now higher-deductible plans can be used, since routine medical expenses would be paid from the HSA using lower-cost direct pay options (like those in chapters 6, 8–10). Employees would be happy, because now they can cover the cost of their exorbitant deductibles and co-pays using this new HSA account.

If you are on the Blue end of the political spectrum, you may be saying the government should fully fund the HSA account for everyone. While those on the Red side might oppose this, it is still a much better option than a universal healthcare plan like Medicare for All, from an economics perspective (chapter 19), since it has us as end-consumers (i.e., patient-consumers) making the buying decisions instead of our disinterested surrogates in government or insurance companies. We would be spending what feels like our own money, whatever the source, on our own personally selected healthcare service.

Can Some Version of Medicare for All Work?

As long as we are venturing deeper into the Blue political realm, what about Medicare for All? As discussed in chapters 1 and 19, having exclusive control of healthcare by the government, as Canada does, will eventually lead to rationing and to limited options and longer wait times. If America wants a single-payer universal plan, it should at least look to other countries like Germany and Switzerland that have a national plan but also allow private options in free and competitive markets. Only that public-private hybrid approach is sustainable and has some way to constrain costs while giving consumers options. As noted earlier, there are plans being proposed by moderate Democrats that permit both public and private options and that maintain free and competitive markets.

A plan called the Wisconsin Health Plan was also put forth in 2005 as Assembly Bill (AB) 1140 by Curt Gielow working with policy expert David Riemer (chapter 20). David Riemer also has a similar proposal that he calls YoungMedicare (chapter 21). The Gielow legislation was intended to be a bipartisan and Purple solution, but it never passed. Both plans were intended to provide universal healthcare coverage (AB 1140 was to be for all Wisconsin residents) and have several tiers of private insurance to choose from, with the most basic tier being "free" to individuals. People could purchase higher tiers of coverage in a competing private insurance marketplace, a bit like the ACA exchanges. The Wisconsin plan was to be funded by a payroll tax, although other funding options were on the table. The state was also to provide an HSA account, to help people pay for medical expenses. At some level, this is similar to the ACA, but with an HSA and universal coverage. This, and the idea of expanding ACA and providing an HSA, is certainly far on the Blue end of the Purple spectrum, but it is still far from being Medicare for All in a pure single-payer system with no private options. It is still a hybrid plan that has a competitive private market, which is essential according to the economic arguments presented in chapter 19, and espoused by economist Milton Friedman.

Summary

The best solutions to healthcare will retain some sort of free and competitive market, where we—patient-consumers—are making Friedman's Category I buying decision. This can be achieved if we all have some sort of HSA that lets us shop for healthcare, including in direct pay markets. The poor and vulnerable could be provided with HSA funds via a voucher system, like food stamps. These HSA accounts would be our money that we are spending and would be used ultimately for our retirement or our estate, if any is left toward the end of our lives.

In addition, we would need some level-1 insurance for more expensive and less frequent healthcare expenses. This could be a high-deductible plan like we currently get through our employers or like the ACA bronze plan (which, if the deductible were higher, would have a lower monthly premium). Furthermore, there could be a government-sponsored insurance program for extremely expensive and rare catastrophic medical events (e.g., rare diseases treated by expensive orphan drugs) and level-2 high-risk insurance (e.g., $1 million stop loss insurance) to serve as a safety net for everyone, for even more rare and expensive events. Having this level-2 stop loss insurance would have the added benefits, because of the risk it removes, of lowering the cost of (a) ACA premiums (from insurers on the private exchanges) and (b) insurance premiums that employers pay, along with the insurance "lasers" they get hit with.

Thus, there are three levels to this healthcare proposal:

1. HSAs: for routine healthcare needs, to purchase our healthcare using direct pay options; this includes vouchers for the poor
2. Level-1 insurance: high-deductible plans (ACA or private insurance) for less common and higher-cost medical needs (events that happen every three to 10 years)
3. Level-2 insurance: government-funded stop loss insurance, for extraordinary and rare but unusually expensive claims (e.g., greater than $1 million)

That third item may not be of interest to the average consumer at first blush—but here is why it should be: If you remove that rare but costly risk from a pool of people covered by the ACA or your company insurance, then that will significantly lower your insurance premium. Because that is how insurance works.

Still, the advocates of Medicare for All may want more than what was outlined above—they perhaps want some sort of universal healthcare insurance (not just HSAs). I would say to them, if that is what you want, just make sure you *also* allow there to be complementary private markets where there is competition. In fact, we could use some variation of the Wisconsin Health Plan put forth by a Democrat and a Republican in Wisconsin, that provided universal healthcare, but also let there be private insurance and HSAs that at least satisfied Milton Friedman's requirement for Category I purchasing decisions, where we as consumers feel like we are spending our own money. Only when that happens will we as healthcare consumers be put at the center of healthcare, allowed to make our own decisions and thereby forcing the Medical-Industrial Complex (or government-run program) to yield to our needs. It would also put market pressure on the healthcare system to keep it affordable and drive technological innovations, as markets tend to do (chapter 2). How about it—are you ready for a grassroots healthcare revolution, with you—the patient-consumer—at the center and empowered?

References

Chapter 1

Abelson, R. (2019, December 5). Hospitals sue Trump to keep negotiated prices secret. *The New York Times*. https://www.nytimes.com/2019/12/04/health/hospitals-trump -prices-transparency.html

Access HealthNet. (n.d.). https://accesshealthnet.com/

Ali, A. (2019). *Affordable healthcare: Challenges and solutions* [Google Books version]. https://books.google.com/books?id=c0q1DwAAQBAJ&ppis=_c&dq=healthcare +fee+doctor%27s+eat+what+you+kill&source=gbs_navlinks_s

Aliferis, L. (2014, November 17). In California, that MRI will cost you $255—or maybe $6,221. *NPR*. https://www.npr.org/sections/health-shots/2014/11/17/364719763/in -california-that-mri-will-cost-you-255-or-6-221

Alltucker, K. (2019, June 4). "Really astonishing": Average cost of hospital ER visit surges 176% in a decade, report says. *USA Today*. https://www.usatoday.com/story /news/health/2019/06/04/hospital-billing-code-changes-help-explain-176-surge-er -costs/1336321001/

Amadeo, K. (2019, September 25). What is the federal budget? *The Balance*. https://www .thebalance.com/what-is-the-federal-budget-3306305

Amadeo, K. (2020, January 14). The rising cost of health care by year and its causes. *The Balance*. https://www.thebalance.com/causes-of-rising-healthcare-costs-4064878

American College of Private Physicians. (n.d.). *CN Health Solutions*. https://www .acpp.md/

American Society for Aesthetic Plastic Surgery. (n.d.). *2016 Cosmetic surgery national data bank statistics*. https://www.surgery.org/sites/default/files/ASAPS-Stats2016.pdf

Appleby, J., & Ostrov, B. F. (2019, January 4). As hospitals post sticker prices online, most patients will remain befuddled. *Kaiser Health News*. https://khn.org/news /as-hospitals-post-sticker-prices-online-most-patients-will-remain-befuddled/

Association of American Medical Colleges. (n.d.). *Brief history of the hospital charge description master ("charge master")*. https://www.aamc.org/system/files/c/2/449996 -pricetran_chargemaster.pdf

Association of American Physicians and Surgeons. (2020). https://aapsonline.org

Biernat, N. (2019, May 22). Now 2 decades old, does HIPAA have the muscle to protect patient rights? *HealthChampion*. https://myhealthchampion.com/now-two-decades -old-does-hipaa-have-the-muscle-to-protect-patient-rights/

Caldwell, B. (Ed.). (2007). *The road to serfdom. Text and documents—the definitive edition*. Chicago: University of Chicago Press.

Cannon, C. M. (2019, May 15). "Medicare for All" support is high . . . but complicated. *RealClearPolitics*. https://www.realclearpolitics.com/real_clear_opinion_research /new_poll_shows_health_care_is_voters_top_concern.html

Carroll, A. (2019, April 22). What can the U.S. health system learn from Singapore? *The New York Times*. https://www.nytimes.com/2019/04/22/upshot/singapore -health-system-lessons.html

Centers for Medicare and Medicaid Services. (n.d.). *Eligibility*. https://www.medicaid .gov/medicaid/eligibility/index.html

Centers for Medicare and Medicaid Services. (2012). *Emergency medical treatment and labor act (EMTALA)*. https://www.cms.gov/Regulations-and-Guidance/Legislation /EMTALA

Centers for Medicare and Medicaid Services. (2020). *History: CMS' program history*. https://www.cms.gov/About-CMS/Agency-Information/History

Centers for Medicare and Medicaid Services, Medicare Learning Network. (n.d.). *National health expenditures 2017 highlights*. https://www.cms.gov/Research -Statistics-Data-and-Systems/Statistics-Trends-and-Reports/NationalHealth ExpendData/Downloads/highlights.pdf

Centers for Medicare and Medicaid Services, Medicare Learning Network. (2017). *Medicare physician fee schedule*. https://www.cms.gov/Outreach-and-Education /Medicare-Learning-Network-MLN/MLNProducts/downloads/MedcrePhysFee Schedfctsht.pdf

Cohen, R. A., & Zammitti, E. P. (2018, August). High-deductible health plan enrollment among adults aged 18–64 with employment-based insurance coverage. *Centers for Disease Control and Prevention/National Center for Health Statistics*. https://www.cdc.gov/nchs/products/databriefs/db317.htm

Committee for a Responsible Federal Budget. (2019, February 27). *How much will Medicare for All cost?* [Blog post]. http://www.crfb.org/blogs/how-much-will -medicare-all-cost

Concierge Choice Physicians. (2019). https://www.choice.md/

Davis, M. A., Nallamothu, B. K., Banerjee, M., & Bynum, J. P. W. (2016, July 1). Patterns of healthcare spending in the last year of life. *Health Affairs*. 35(7), 1316–1323. https://www.ncbi.nlm.nih.gov/pmc/articles/PMC5046841/

Ellis, R. P., Chen, T., & Luscombe, C. E. (2014). *Comparisons of health insurance systems in developed countries*. In A. Culyer (Ed.), *Encyclopedia of health economics* (pp. 12–17). Elsevier Press.

Enthoven, A. (2005, April 10). The rise and fall of HMOs shows how a worthy idea went wrong. *CommonWealth Magazine*. https://commonwealthmagazine.org/arts -and-culture/emthe-rise-and-fall-of-hmosem-shows-how-a-worthy-idea-went-wrong/

Ericsson. (n.d.). *From healthcare to homecare: The critical role of 5G in healthcare transformation*. https://www.ericsson.com/en/reports-and-papers/consumerlab /reports/transforming-healthcare-homecare

Forbes, S. (2019, May 7). Capitalism will save us—if only we let it. *Forbes*. https://www. forbes.com/sites/steveforbes/2019/05/07/capitalism-will-save-us-if-only-we-let -it/#668534c362d6

Gee, E. (2019, June 26). The high price of hospital care. *Center for American Progress*. https://www.americanprogress.org/issues/healthcare/reports/2019/06/26/471464 /high-price-hospital-care/

Gee, E., & Gurwitz, E. (2018, December 5). Provider consolidation drives up health care costs. *Center for American Progress*. https://www.americanprogress.org/issues /healthcare/reports/2018/12/05/461780/provider-consolidation-drives-health-care -costs/

Goldhill, D. (2013). *Catastrophic care: Why everything we think we know about health care is wrong.* New York: Vintage Books.

Gruber, L. R., Shadle, M., & Polich, C. L. (1988, Summer). From movement to industry: The growth of HMOs. *Health Affairs, 7*(3). https://www.healthaffairs.org/doi/full/10.1377/hlthaff.7.3.197

Healthcare Bluebook. (2019). *CAREOperative.* https://www.healthcarebluebook.com/

HealthPocket. (2020). *Bronze plan.* https://www.healthpocket.com/individual-health-insurance/bronze-health-plans#.Xis8nKJMGM8

HealthViewX. (2020). Referral leakage and ways to prevent it. *Payoda Technology.* https://www.healthviewx.com/referral-leakage-and-ways-to-prevent-it/

Hellmann, J. (2020, January 14). Warren, Buttigieg spar over health care costs. *The Hill.* https://thehill.com/homenews/campaign/478317-warren-buttigieg-spar-over-health-care-costs

Hunt, J. (2019, April 13). Direct primary care alternatives to health insurance. *The Balance.* https://www.thebalance.com/direct-primary-care-alternatives-for-health-insurance-4164823

Kelley, E. (2013). Medical tourism [Presentation]. *World Health Organization.* https://www.who.int/global_health_histories/seminars/kelley_presentation_medical_tourism.pdf

Klein, S. (n.d.). "Hospital at home" programs improve outcomes, lower costs but face resistance from providers and payers. *The Commonwealth Fund.* https://www.commonwealthfund.org/publications/newsletter-article/hospital-home-programs-improve-outcomes-lower-costs-face-resistance

MarketWatch. (2018, September 4). *New report shows the harmful effect rising health care costs have on wage stagnation* [Press release]. https://www.marketwatch.com/press-release/new-report-shows-the-harmful-effect-rising-health-care-costs-have-on-wage-stagnation-2018-09-04

Masterson, L. (2019, November 7). Health deductible health plan—what's an HDHP? *Insurance.com.* https://www.insure.com/health-insurance/high-deductible-health-plan-hdhp

Mather, M., Scommegna, P., & Kilduff, L. (2019, July 15). Fact sheet: Aging in the United States. *Population Reference Bureau.* https://www.prb.org/aging-unitedstates-fact-sheet/

Mayer, C. E. (2009, November/December). The health care claim game. *AARP.* https://www.aarp.org/health/medicare-insurance/info-09-2009/health_claim_game.html

MDsave. (2020). https://www.mdsave.com/

MDVIP. (2020). http://www.mdvip.com

Mihm, S. (2017, February 24). *Employer-based health care was a wartime accident* [Op-ed]. https://www.chicagotribune.com/opinion/commentary/ct-obamacare-health-care-employers-20170224-story.html

Ministry of Finance Singapore. (2019). *Injecting more into Singapore's healthcare as we age.* https://www.mof.gov.sg/singapore-budget/curated-budget-reads/injecting-more-into-singapore-s-healthcare-as-we-age

Morris, S. (2019, June 28). How telemedicine is changing healthcare. *HealthTechZone.* http://www.healthtechzone.com/topics/healthcare/articles/2019/06/28/442557-how-telemedicine-changing-healthcare.htm

National Bureau of Economic Research. (2020). *Managed care has slowed growth in medical spending.* https://www.nber.org/digest/may98/w6140.html

National Conference of State Legislatures. (2018, December 4). *Health insurance: Premiums and increases.* https://www.ncsl.org/research/health/health-insurance-premiums.aspx

Paavola, A. (2019, September 23). How CVS, Walgreens and Walmart health-focused stores compare. *Becker's Hospital Review.* https://www.beckershospitalreview.com /pharmacy/how-cvs-walgreens-and-walmart-health-focused-stores-compare.html

Parnell, S. (2014). *The self-pay patient: Affordable healthcare choices in the age of Obamacare.* Alexandria, VA: Self-Pay Patient, LLC.

Patient Protection and Affordable Care Act of 2010. Pub. L. No. 111–148, 124 Stat. 119–1024 (2010).

Pear, R. (2019, January 13). Hospitals must now post prices. But it may take a brain surgeon to decipher them. *The New York Times.* https://www.nytimes.com/2019/01/13/us /politics/hospital-prices-online.html

Peltzer, K., Williams, J. S., Kowal, P., Negin, J., Snodgrass, J. J., Yawson, A., . . . Chatterji, A. (2014, October). Universal health coverage in emerging economies: Findings on health care utilization by older adults in China, Ghana, India, Mexico, the Russian Federation, and South Africa. *Global Health Action, 7.* https://www.ncbi.nlm.nih .gov/pmc/articles/PMC4216816/

Perry, M. J. (2017, March 22). If cosmetic surgery has a working market, why can't medical care? *FEE: Foundation for Economic Education.* https://fee.org/articles/if -cosmetic-surgery-has-a-working-market-why-can-t-medical-care/

Pete Buttigieg for America. (n.d.). *Medicare for all who want it: Putting every American in charge of their health care with affordable choice for all.* https://peteforamerica .com/policies/health-care/

Premier Private Physicians. (n.d.). http://premiermd.com/

Price, G., & Norbeck, T. (2018, April 9). U.S. health outcomes compared to other countries are misleading. *Forbes.* https://www.forbes.com/sites/physicians foundation/2018/04/09/u-s-health-outcomes-compared-to-other-countries-are -misleading/#211c019f1232

Pricepain.com. (2020). http://www.pricepain.com/

Proval, C. (2014, June 12). Cost comparison map underscores price variation for MRI, CT. *Radiology Business.* https://www.radiologybusiness.com/topics/healthcare -economics/cost-comparison-map-underscores-price-variation-mri-ct

Relman, A. S. (1980, October 23). The new medical-industrial complex. *The New England Journal of Medicine.* https://www.nejm.org/doi/full/10.1056/NEJM198010233031703.

Ren, F., & Labrie, Y. (2017, June 29). Leaving Canada for medical care, 2017. *Fraser Institute.* https://www.fraserinstitute.org/studies/leaving-canada-for-medical-care-2017

Richman, B. D., Kitzman, N., Milstein, A., & Schulman, K. A. (2017, April). Battling the chargemaster: A simple remedy to balance billing for unavoidable out-of-network care. *American Journal of Managed Care, 23*(4), e100–e105. https://www .ajmc.com/journals/issue/2017/2017-vol23-n4/battling-the-chargemaster-a-simple -remedy-to-balance-billing-for-unavoidable-out-of-network-care

Robinson, J. C., Pozen, A., Tseng, S., & Bozic, K. J. (2012, September 19). Variability in costs associated with total hip and knee replacement implants. *Journal of Bone and Joint Surgery, 94*(18), 1693–1698. https://www.ncbi.nlm.nih.gov/pubmed/22878562

Rosato, D. (2018, May 4). How paying your doctor in cash could save you money. *Consumer Reports*. https://www.consumerreports.org/healthcare-costs/how-paying -your-doctor-in-cash-could-save-you-money/

Roth, M. (2018, November 27). Virtual care is no longer optional: What's now, what's next, and how to get there. *HealthLeaders*. https://www.healthleadersmedia.com /innovation/virtual-care-no-longer-optional-whats-now-whats-next-and-how-get-there

Roy, A., & The Apothecary. (2019, May 11). RAND study: Hospitals charging the privately insured 2.4 times what they charge Medicare patients. *Forbes*. https://www .forbes.com/sites/theapothecary/2019/05/11/rand-study-hospitals-charging-the -privately-insured-2-4-times-what-they-charge-medicare-patients/#6339010058d9

Sawyer, B., & Cox, C. (2018, December 7). How does health spending in the U.S. compare to other countries? *Peterson–KFF Health System Tracker*. https://www .healthsystemtracker.org/chart-collection/health-spending-u-s-compare-countries /#item-average-wealthy-countries-spend-half-much-per-person-health-u-s-spends

SimpleCare. (n.d.). *American Association of Patients and Providers*. https://simplecare .com/providers.asp

Solomon, N. A. (2017, March 20). How telemedicine is making its way into the home. *HomeCare*. https://www.homecaremag.com/operations-software/march-2017/how -telemedicine-making-its-way-home

Stabilization Act of 1942. Pub. L. No. 77–729, 56 Stat. 765–768 (1942).

Tikkanen, R. (2019, March 22). Variations on a theme: A look at universal health coverage in eight countries. *The Commonwealth Fund*. https://www .commonwealthfund.org/blog/2019/universal-health-coverage-eight-countries

Torinus, J. (n.d.a). At last, a silver bullet for health care costs: *Transparency on prices, quality* [Blog post]. http://johntorinus.com/blog/transparency-on-prices-quality /last-silver-bullet-health-care-costs/

Torinus, J. (n.d.b). *The grassroots healthcare revolution*. http://johntorinus.com/opt-out -on-obamacare-opt-into-the-private-health-care-revolution/

Torinus, J. (2010). *The company that solved health care: How Serigraph dramatically reduced skyrocketing costs while providing better care, and how every company can do the same*. Dallas: BenBella Books.

TRICARE. (n.d.). *Defense Health Agency*. https://www.tricare.mil/

U.S. Department of Health and Human Services. (n.d.). *HHS FY 2018 budget in brief*. https://www.hhs.gov/about/budget/fy2018/budget-in-brief/index.html

U.S. Department of Health and Human Services. (2019a). *HHS leadership*. https://www.hhs.gov/about/leadership/index.html

U.S. Department of Health and Human Services. (2019b, November 15). *Trump administration announces historic price transparency requirements to increase competition and lower healthcare costs for all Americans* [Press release]. https://www.hhs.gov/about/news/2019/11/15/trump-administration-announces -historic-price-transparency-and-lower-healthcare-costs-for-all-americans.html

Woolf, S. H., & Aron, L. (Eds.). (2013). *U.S. health in international perspective: Shorter lives, poorer health*. Washington, DC: National Academies Press. https://www.ncbi .nlm.nih.gov/books/NBK154469/

Yglesias, M. (2010, February 26). Hayek on health care. *ThinkProgress*. https://think progress.org/hayek-on-health-care-e29ae2d600e6/

Chapter 2

American Academy of Physician Assistants. (2017, December 12). WY PA unable to care for patients after physician death. https://www.aapa.org/news-central/2017/12/wy-pa-unable-care-patients-physician-death/

Bryan, D. N. (2019, October). Promoting maternal health in rural and underserved areas. *Mercatus Policy Brief*. https://www.mercatus.org/publications/healthcare/promoting-maternal-health-rural-and-underserved-areas

Bryan, D. N., Rhoads, J, & Graboyes, R. (2018). Healthcare openness and access project: Mapping the frontier for the next generation of American healthcare. *Mercatus Center*. https://www.mercatus.org/system/files/bryan-healthcare-hoap-mercatus-project-overview-v1.pdf

Cellscope. (n.d.). https://rockhealth.com/companies/cellscope/

Centers for Medicare and Medicaid Services. (2018). *NHE Fact Sheet*. https://www.cms.gov/Research-Statistics-Data-and-Systems/Statistics-Trends-and-Reports/NationalHealthExpendData/NHE-Fact-Sheet

Choi, E., & Sonin, J. (2017). Determinants of health. *GoInvo*. https://www.goinvo.com/vision/determinants-of-health/

Cochrane, J. H. (2014). "After the ACA: Freeing the market for health care. In Anup Malani and Michael H. Schill (Eds.), *The Future of Healthcare Reform in the United States*. Chicago: University of Chicago Press.

Das, S. (2014, February 24). Devi Shetty opens low-cost healthcare venture in Cayman Islands outside U.S. regulatory reach. *Economic Times*. https://economictimes.indiatimes.com/small-biz/entrepreneurship/devi-shetty-opens-low-cost-healthcare-venture-in-cayman-islands-outside-us-regulatory-reach/articleshow/30917552.cms

Ganjoo, A. (2019, August 22). A deep dive into UTM and the flight information management system for drones. *DroneLife*. https://dronelife.com/2019/08/22/a-deep-dive-into-utm-and-the-flight-information-management-system-for-drones-long-form/

Graboyes, R. (2016a, September 28). Patient as diagnostician: David Albert and AliveCor. *Inside Sources*. https://www.insidesources.com/patient-as-diagnostician-david-albert-and-alivecor/

Graboyes, R. (2016b, October 15). Telemedicine as lifesaver: Ian Tong and Doctor on Demand. *Inside Sources*. https://www.insidesources.com/telemedicine-as-lifesaver-ian-tong-and-doctor-on-demand/

Graboyes, R. (2016c, November 30). Direct primary care: Rushika Fernandopulle and Iora. *Inside Sources*. https://www.insidesources.com/direct-primary-care-rushika-fernandopulle-and-iora/

Graboyes, R. (2017a, February 22). The invention of the chicken and innovation in healthcare. *Inside Sources*. https://www.mercatus.org/commentary/invention-chicken-and-innovation-health-care

Graboyes, R. (2017b, March 15). Defending volunteers: Ron Hines and Carroll Landrum. *Inside Sources*. https://www.insidesources.com/defending-volunteers-ron-hines-carroll-landrum/

Graboyes, R. (2017c, September 13). High quality and low price converge at Narayana and Health City Cayman Islands. *Inside Sources*. https://www.insidesources.com/high-quality-low-price-converge-narayana-health-city-cayman-islands/

Graboyes, R. (2018, October 1). The din of healthcare: Myths and maybes. *Mercatus Center: The Bridge.* https://www.mercatus.org/bridge/commentary/din-healthcare -myths-and-maybes

Graboyes, R., & Bryan, D. N. (2019, January 18). Drones delivering medical supplies and more can help save American lives. *Stat.* https://www.statnews.com/2019/01/18 /drones-deliver-medical-supplies-united-states/

Graboyes R., & Rogers, S. (2018, September 12). As free innovation encounters health care regulation, think "soft laws." *Stat.* https://www.statnews.com/2018/09/12/free -innovation-health-care-regulation/

Gupta, A., & Sao, D. (2012) The constitutionality of current legal barriers to telemedicine in the United States: Analysis and future directions of its relationship to national and international health care reform, *Health Matrix: The Journal of Law-Medicine, 21*(2), 385–442. https://scholarlycommons.law.case.edu/healthmatrix /vol21/iss2/4/

Institute of Medicine. (2012). *Best care at lower cost: The path to continuously learning health care in America.* Washington, DC: National Academies Press. http:// nationalacademies.org/hmd/Reports/2012/Best-Care-at-Lower-Cost-The-Path-to -Continuously-Learning-Health-Care-in-America.aspx

Kim, E., Teague-Ross, T. J., Greenfield, W. W., Williams, K., Kuo, D., & Hall, R. W. (2013). Telemedicine collaboration improves perinatal regionalization and lowers statewide infant mortality. *Journal of Perinatology, 33*(9). https://www.ncbi.nlm.nih .gov/pmc/articles/PMC4138978/

Magann, E. F., Bronstein J., McKelvey S. S., Wendel P., Smith D. M., & Lowery C. L. (2012). Evolving trends in maternal fetal medicine referrals in a rural state using telemedicine. *Archives of Gynecology and Obstetrics, 286*(6). https://www.ncbi.nlm .nih.gov/pubmed/22821508

Mitchell, M. (2017, August). Certificate-of-need laws: Are they achieving their goals? *Mercatus on Policy.* https://www.mercatus.org/system/files/mitchell-con-qa-mop -mercatus-v2.pdf

NightScout. (n.d.). http://www.nightscout.info/

Office of the National Coordinator for Health Information Technology. (2017, September 28). *Telemedicine and telehealth.* https://www.healthit.gov/topic/health -it-initiatives/telemedicine-and-telehealth

Office of the National Coordinator for Health Information Technology. (2019). *Are there state licensing issues related to telehealth?* https://www.healthit.gov/faq/are -there-state-licensing-issues-related-telehealth

Organization for Economic Cooperation and Development. (n.d.a). *Life expectancy at birth.* https://data.oecd.org/healthstat/life-expectancy-at-birth.htm

Organization for Economic Cooperation and Development. (n.d.b). *Infant mortality rates.* https://data.oecd.org/healthstat/infant-mortality-rates.htm

Poss, J. (2019, January 7). The "why's" of the 2018 FAA Reauthorization Act. *Inside Unmanned Systems.* https://insideunmannedsystems.com/the-whys-of-the-2018 -faa-reauthorization-act/

Robeznieks, Andis. (2019, October 11). Interstate medical licensure by the numbers. *American Medical Association.* https://www.ama-assn.org/practice-management /digital/interstate-medical-licensure-numbers

Saslow, E. (2019, November 16). The most remote emergency room: Life and death in rural America. *The Washington Post*. https://www.washingtonpost.com/national /the-most-remote-emergency-room/2019/11/16/717d08e2-063e-11ea-b17d -8b867891d39d_story.html

Stratmann, T., Koopman, C., Mitchell, M. D., Philpot, A., Baker, M. C., & Wille, D. (2017, August 29). Certificate-of-need laws: How CON laws affect spending, access, and quality across the states. *Mercatus Center*. https://www.mercatus.org/publications /corporate-welfare/certificate-need-laws-how-con-laws-affect-spending-access -and-quality

Thierer, A. (2016, March 15). Permissionless innovation: The continuing case for comprehensive technological freedom. *Mercatus Center*. https://www.mercatus .org/publication/permissionless-innovation-continuing-case-comprehensive -technological-freedom

Timmons, E. J. (2016). Healthcare license turf wars: The effects of expanded nurse practitioner and physician assistant scope of practice on Medicaid patient access. *Mercatus Working Paper*. https://www.mercatus.org/publications /healthcare/healthcare-license-turf-wars-effects-expanded-nurse-practitioner -and

Ullah, H., Nair, N. G., Moore, A., Nugent, C., Muschamp, P., & Cuevas, M. (2019, March 18). 5G communication: an overview of vehicle-to-everything, drones, and healthcare use-cases, *IEEE Access, 7*, 37251–37268. https://ieeexplore.ieee.org /document/8668495

Wamala, D. S., & Augustin K. (2013). A meta-analysis of telemedicine success in Africa. *Journal of Pathology Informatics 4*(6). https://www.ncbi.nlm.nih.gov /pubmed/23858382

Williams, R., Graboyes, R., & Thierer, A. (2015, October 21). U.S. medical devices: Choices and consequences. *Mercatus Center*. https://www.mercatus.org /publications/regulation/us-medical-devices-choices-and-consequences

Chapter 3

American Hospital Association. (2017, November 3). *Regulatory overload*. https://www.aha.org/guidesreports/2017-11-03-regulatory-overload-report

Arndt, B. G., Beasley, J. W., Watkinson, M. D., Temte, J. L., Tuan, W.-J., Sinsky, C. A., & Gilchrist, V. J. (2017). Tethered to the EHR: Primary care physician workload assessment using EHR event log data and time-motion observations. *Annals of Family Medicine, 15*(5), 419–426. https://www.doi.org/10.1370/afm.2121

Blue Button 2.0. (n.d.). https://bluebutton.cms.gov/

Bouri, S., Shun-Shin, M. J., Cole, G. D., Mayet, J., & Francis, D. P. (2014, March 15). Meta-analysis of secure randomised controlled trials of β-blockade to prevent perioperative death in non-cardiac surgery. *Heart, 100*(6). http://heart.bmj.com /content/early/2013/07/30/heartjnl-2013-304262.full?eaf

Bush, G. (2004, April 27). Exec. Order No. 13335—Incentives for the use of health information technology and establishing the position of the national health information technology coordinator. *Federal Register*, 69 FR 24057. https:// www.federalregister.gov/documents/2004/04/30/04-10024/incentives-for-the-use -of-health-information-technology-and-establishing-the-position-of-the

Casalino, L. P., Gans, D., Weber, R., Cea, M., Tuchovsky, A., Bishop, T. F., . . . Evenson, T. B. (2016). U.S. physician practices spend more than $15.4 billion annually to report quality measures. *Health Affairs (Millwood)*, *35*(3), 401–406. https://doi.org/10.1377/hlthaff.2015.1258

Centers for Disease Control and Prevention. (2011). *History of the statistical classification of diseases and causes of death*. https://www.cdc.gov/nchs/data/misc/classification_diseases2011.pdf

Centers for Medicare and Medicaid Services. (n.d.). *Adopted standards and operating rules*. https://www.cms.gov/Regulations-and-Guidance/Administrative-Simplification/HIPAA-ACA/AdoptedStandardsandOperatingRules

Centers for Medicare and Medicaid Services. (2011, July). *Medicare physician group practice demonstration*. https://web.archive.org/web/20110813031323/http://www.cms.gov/DemoProjectsEvalRpts/downloads/PGP_Fact_Sheet.pdf

Centers for Medicare and Medicaid Services. (2018, August 2). *CMS finalizes changes to empower patients and reduce administrative burden*. https://www.cms.gov/newsroom/press-releases/cms-finalizes-changes-empower-patients-and-reduce-administrative-burden

CRISP Hospital Services. (n.d.). *Care alerts*. https://www.crisphealth.org/wp-content/uploads/2016/03/Care-Alerts_SSO_Readmission-Flyer-1_16.pdf

Federal Register. (2009, January 16). *Health insurance reform; modifications to the Health Insurance Portability and Accountability Act (HIPPA); Final rules*. https://www.govinfo.gov/content/pkg/FR-2009-01-16/pdf/E9-740.pdf

Federal Register. (2017, February 3). *Reducing regulation and controlling regulatory costs*. https://www.federalregister.gov/documents/2017/02/03/2017-02451/reducing-regulation-and-controlling-regulatory-costs

Finkelstein, A., Zhou, A., Taubman, S., & Doyle, J. (2020). Health care hotspotting: A randomized, controlled trial. *The New England Journal of Medicine*, *382*, 152–162. https://www.nejm.org/doi/10.1056/NEJMsa1906848

Fonarow, G. C. (2018, December 25). Unintended harm associated with the hospital readmissions reduction program. *JAMA*, *320*(24), 2539–2541. https://doi.org/10.1001/jama.2018.19325

Foote, S. B., Virnig, B. A., Town, R. J., & Hartman, L. (2008). The impact of Medicare coverage Policies on health care utilization. *Health Services Research*, *43*(4), 1285–1301. https://doi.org/10.1111/j.1475-6773.2008.00836.x

Hanson, K. (2020, January). Next generation accountable care organization model evaluation: Second evaluation report. *NORC at the University of Chicago*. https://innovation.cms.gov/Files/reports/nextgenaco-secondevalrpt.pdf

History of the Development of the ICD. (n.d.). https://www.who.int/classifications/icd/en/HistoryOfICD.pdf

Howell, C. (2009, 18 February). Stimulus package contains $19 billion for health care technology spending and adoption of electronic health records. *Foley & Lardner LLP*. https://www.foley.com/en/insights/publications/2009/02/stimulus-package-contains-19-billion-for-health-ca

Intensive versus Conventional Glucose Control in Critically Ill Patients. (2009). *The New England Journal of Medicine*, *360*(13), 1283–1297. https://doi.org/10.1056/nejmoa0810625

Kocher, B. (2016, July 31). How I was wrong about Obamacare. *The Wall Street Journal*.
https://www.wsj.com/articles/i-was-wrong-about-obamacare-1469997311

Kocher, R., Emanuel, E. J., & DeParle, N.-A. M. (2010). The Affordable Care Act and
the future of clinical medicine: The opportunities and challenges. *Annals of Internal
Medicine*, 153(8), 536. https://doi.org/10.7326/0003-4819-153-8-201010190-00274

Lapar, D., Isbell, J. M., Kern J. A., Ailawadi. G., & Kron, I. L. (2014, March). Surgical
care improvement project measure for postoperative glucose control should not
be used as a measure of quality after cardiac surgery. *Journal of Thoracic and
Cardiovascular Surgery*, 147(3), 1041–1048. http://www.ncbi.nlm.nih.gov
/pubmed/24418668

LaPointe, J. (2018, May 30). VUMC sees operating income decrease after EHR
implementation. *RevCycleIntelligence*. https://revcycleintelligence.com/news/vumc
-sees-operating-income-decrease-after-ehr-implementation

Library of Congress. (n.d.). *A Century of Lawmaking for a New Nation:
U.S. Congressional Documents and Debates, 1774–1875*. http://memory.loc.gov/cgi
-bin/ampage?collId=llsl&fileName=001/llsl001.db&recNum=728

Melnick, E. R., Dyrbye, L. N., Sinsky, C. A., Trockel, M., West, C. P., Nedelec, L., . . .
Shanafelt, T. (2019). The association between perceived electronic health record
usability and professional burnout among us physicians. *Mayo Clinic Proceedings*.
https://doi.org/10.1016/j.mayocp.2019.09.024

Modern Healthcare. (2020, January 8). *Program meant to curb repeat hospital stays fails
big test*. https://www.modernhealthcare.com/clinical/program-meant-curb-repeat
-hospital-stays-fails-big-test?utm_source=modern-healthcare-am-thursday&utm
_medium=email&utm_campaign=20200108&utm_content=article2-readmore

Office of the National Coordinator for Health Information. (2018, August 13).
Technology medical practice efficiencies and cost savings. https://www.healthit
.gov/topic/health-it-and-health-information-exchange-basics/medical-practice
-efficiencies-cost-savings

Promoting Healthcare Choice and Competition Across the United States. (2017,
October 17). *Federal Register*. https://www.federalregister.gov/documents/2017/
10/17/2017-22677/promoting-healthcare-choice-and-competition-across
-the-united-states

Romano, M. J., & Stafford, R. S. (2011). Electronic health records and clinical decision
support systems. *Archives of Internal Medicine*, 171(10). https://doi.org/10.1001
/archinternmed.2010.527

Samarghandi, A., & Qayyum, R. (2019, September 18). Effect of hospital readmission
reduction program on hospital readmissions and mortality rates. *Journal of Hospital
Medicine*. https://doi.org/10.12788/jhm.3302

Selvaraj, S., Fonarow, G. C., Sheng, S., Matsouaka, R. A., DeVore, A. D., Heidenreich,
P. A., . . . Bhatt, D. L. (2018). Association of electronic health record use with quality
of care and outcomes in heart failure: An analysis of Get With the Guidelines—
heart failure. *Journal of the American Heart Association*, 7(7), e008158. https://doi
.org/10.1161/jaha.117.008158

Shrank, W. H., Rogstad, T. L., & Parekh, N. (2019, October 7). Waste in the U.S. health
care system estimated costs and potential for savings. *JAMA*, 322(15), 1501–1509.
https://jamanetwork.com/journals/jama/article-abstract/2752664

Sibert, K. S. (n.d.). The dark side of quality. *Anesthesia Business Consultants.* https://www.anesthesiallc.com/component/content/article/20-communique /past-issues/spring-2014/305-the-dark-side-of-quality

U.S. Department of Health and Human Services. (n.d.). *Appendix A. Medicare and Medicaid EHR incentive programs.* https://aspe.hhs.gov/system/files/pdf/76706 /EHRPI-appendA.pdf

U.S. Department of Health and Human Services. (2017, June 16). *HITECH act enforcement interim final rule.* http://www.hhs.gov/hipaa/for-professionals/special -topics/HITECH-act-enforcement-interim-final-rule/index.html

U.S. Department of Health and Human Services, U.S. Department of the Treasury, & U.S. Department of Labor. (n.d.). *Reforming America's healthcare system through choice and competition.* https://www.hhs.gov/sites/default/files/Reforming-Americas -Healthcare-System-Through-Choice-and-Competition.pdf

Wadhera, R. K., Joynt Maddox, K. E., Wasfy, J. H., Haneuse, S., Shen, C., & Yeh, R. W. (2018). Association of the hospital readmissions reduction program with mortality among Medicare beneficiaries hospitalized for heart failure, acute myocardial infarction, and pneumonia. *JAMA, 320*(24), 2542–2552. https://doi.org/10.1001 /jama.2018.19232

Weston, A., Caldera, K., & Doron, S. (2012). Surgical care improvement project in the value-based purchasing era: More harm than good? *Clinical Infectious Diseases, 56*(3), 424–427. https://doi.org/10.1093/cid/cis940

Young, R., Burge, S., Kumar, K., Wilson, J., & Ortiz, D. (2018). *Family Medicine, 50*(2), 91–99. https://doi.org/10.22454/FamMed.2018.184803

Chapter 4

Affordable Care Act (ACA). (n.d.). Glossary. *HealthCare.gov.* https://www.healthcare .gov/glossary/affordable-care-act/

Aliferis, L. (2014, November 17). In California, that MRI will cost you $225—or maybe $6,221. *National Public Radio.* https://www.npr.org/sections/health-shots /2014/11/17/364719763/in-california-that-mri-will-cost-you-225-or-6221

Amadeo, K. (2019, December 7). The rising cost of health care by year and its causes: See for yourself if Obamacare increased health care costs. *The Balance.* https:// www.thebalance.com/causes-of-rising-healthcare-costs-4064878

Beaton, T. (2017, September 18). More payers, more providers increase price negotiation power. *HealthPayerIntelligence.* https://healthpayerintelligence.com /news/more-payers-more-providers-increase-price-negotiation-power

Brill, J. (2015, January 26). Competition in health care markets. *Health Affairs.* https://www.healthaffairs.org/do/10.1377/hblog20150126.043409/full/

Calandra, R. (2018, November 12). Bundled payments for joint replacements reduce expenditures, don't compromise quality. *Managed Care.* https://www.managedcaremag .com/archives/2018/11/bundled-payments-joint-replacement-reduce-expenditures -don-t-compromise-quality

Capps, C., Kmitch, L., Zabinski, Z., & Zayats, S. (2019, April). The continuing saga of hospital merger enforcement. *Antitrust Law Journal, 82*(2), 441–496. https://www .bateswhite.com/newsroom-insight-230.html

Carroll, A. E. (2017, September 5). The real reason the U.S. has employer-sponsored health insurance. *The New York Times*. https://www.nytimes.com/2017/09/05 /upshot/the-real-reason-the-us-has-employer-sponsored-health-insurance.html

Casalino, L. P., Pesko, M. F., Ryan, A. M., Mendelsohn, J. L., Copeland, K. R., Ramsay, P. P., . . . Shortell, S. M. (2014, September). Small primary care physician practices have low rates of preventable hospital admissions. *Health Affairs*. https://www.healthaffairs.org/doi/full/10.1377/hlthaff.2014.0434

Centers for Medicare and Medicaid Services. (n.d.). *CMS's program history*. https:// www.cms.gov/About-CMS/Agency-Information/History/index/

Ducharme, J. (2018, March 13). The U.S. spends twice as much on health care as other high-income countries. *Time*. https://time.com/5197347/us-health-care-spending/

eHealth Medicare. (n.d.) *What are the Medicare plan star ratings and how are they measured?* https://www.ehealthmedicare.com/faq/what-are-medicare-plan-star-ratings/

Finnegan, J. (2018, July 10). What kind of doctors experience dramatically lower levels of burnout? Study offers new perspective. *FierceHealthcare*. https://www.fiercehealthcare .com/practices/doctors-small-independent-practices-experience-less-burnout

Floyd, P. (2014). Roadmap for physician compensation in a value-based world. *BDC Advisors*. https://www.bdcadvisors.com/roadmap-for-physician-compensation-in -a-value-based-world/

Friedberg, M., Chen, P., White, C., Jung, O., Raaen, L., Hirshman, S., . . . Lipinski, L. (2015). Effects of health care payment models on physician practice in the United States. *Rand Health Q, 5*(1). doi: 10.7249/rr869

Fulton, B. D. (2017, September 1). Health care market concentration trends in the United States: evidence and policy responses. *Health Affairs*. https://www .healthaffairs.org/doi/abs/10.1377/hlthaff.2017.0556?url_ver=Z39.88-2003&rfr _id=ori:rid:crossref.org&rfr_dat=cr_pub=pubmed

Health and Human Services Office of the Secretary & Office of Budget. (2017, May 23). *HHS FY 2018 budget in brief*. https://www.hhs.gov/about/budget/fy2018/budget-in -brief/index.html

HealthPayerIntelligence. (2016, October 17). *How the Affordable Care Act changed the face of health insurance*. https://healthpayerintelligence.com/features/how-the -affordable-care-act-changed-the-face-of-health-insurance

Hollaran, S. (2018, May 25). The history of HMOs. *Capitalism Magazine*. https:// www.capitalismmagazine.com/1999/11/the-history-of-hmos/

Institute of Medicine. (1993). *Origins and evolution of employment-based health benefits*. In M. J. Field & H. T. Shapiro (Eds.), *Employment and health benefits: a connection at risk*. Washington, DC: National Academies Press, ch. 2. https:// www-ncbi-nlm-nih-gov.cuw.ezproxy.switchinc.org/books/NBK235989/

Kate, R. (2016, April 16). Physician incentives—how to structure them the right way? [Blog comment]. *HBS Digital Initiative*. https://digital.hbs.edu/platform-mhcdsolutions /submission/physician-incentives-how-to-structure-them-the-right-way

Kumar, P. D. (2019, May 9). Antitrust laws in health care: Evolving trends. *American Association for Physician Leadership*. https://www.physicianleaders.org/news /antitrust-laws-health-care-evolving-trends

LaPointe, J. (2019, June 25). Healthcare merger and acquisition activity up 14.4% in 2018. *RevCycleIntelligence*. https://revcycleintelligence.com/news/healthcare -merger-and-acquisition-activity-up-14.4-in-2018

LaPointe, J. (2020, January 3). 5 hospital merger and acquisition moves kicking off 2020. *RevCycleIntelligence*. https://revcycleintelligence.com/news/5-hospital-merger -and-acquisition-moves-kicking-off-2020

Livingston, S. (2017, February 11). Paying for population health. *Modern Health*. https://www.modernhealth.com/article/2010211/Magazine/302119984/paying-for -population-health?ptid

Luthra, S. (2019, May 10). Market muscle: study uncovers differences between Medicare and private insurers. *Kaiser Health News*. https://khn.org/news/market -muscle-study-uncovers-differences-between-medicare-and-private-insurers/

Matthews, A. W., & Evans, M. (2018, December 27). The hidden system that explains how your doctor makes referrals. *The Wall Street Journal*. https://www.wsj.com /articles/the-hidden-system-that-explains-how-your-doctor-makes-referrals -11545926166

McGrail, S. (2020, January 7). Beaumont Health signs $6.1 B hospital merger deal with Summa Health. *RevCycleIntelligence*. https://revcycleintelligence.com/news /beaumont-health-signs-6.1b-hospital-merger-deal-with-summa-health

Merck, G. W. (1950, December 1). *Medicine is for the patient, not for the profits*. Speech at Medical College of Virginia at Richmond. https://www.merck.com/about/our -people/gw-merck-doc.pdf

Milwaukee Journal Sentinel. (2018, April 2). *Merger of Aurora Health Care and Advocate Health Care is completed*. https://www.jsonline.com/story/money/business /health-care/2018/04/02/merger-aurora-health-care-and-advocate-health-care -completed/478565002/

Nation, G. (2016). Hospital chargemaster insanity. *Pepperdine Law Review, 43*(3), 745–784. https://digitalcommons.pepperdine.edu/cgi/viewcontent.cgi?article =2411&context=plr

National Health Policy Forum. (2015, January 12). *The basics: Relative value units (RVUs)*. https://www.nhpf.org/library/the-basics/Basics_RVUs_01-12-15.pdf

National Law Review. (2018, January 11). *Will antitrust review of CVS/Aetna shed additional light on vertical theories?* https://www.natlawreview.com/article/will -antitrust-review-cvsaetna-shed-additional-light-vertical-theories

Palmer, K. S. (2020, January). Speech at the Physicians for a National Health Program (PNHP) meeting, San Diego.

Quality Payment Program. (n.d.). *MIPS [merit-based incentive payment system] overview*. https://qpp.cms.gov/mips/overview

Relman, A. S. (1980, October 23). The new medical-industrial complex. *The New England Journal of Medicine*. https://www.nejm.org/doi/full/10.1056/NEJM198010233031703

Roberts-Grey, G. (2019, December 3). Direct primary care: what is it and should I try it? *GoodRx*. https://www.goodrx.com/blog/guide-to-direct-primary-care/

Schenker, L. (2018, April 2). Advocate Health Care finalizes merger with Wisconsin hospital system. *Chicago Tribune*. https://www.chicagotribune.com/business/ct-biz -advocate-aurora-merger-done-20180403-story.html

Short, M. N., & Ho, V. (2019, February 9). Weighing the effects of vertical integration versus market concentration on hospital quality. *Medical Care Research and Review*. https://journals.sagepub.com/doi/10.1177/1077558719828938

U.S. Census Bureau. (2019, November 8). *Health insurance coverage in the United States: 2018*. https://www.census.gov/library/publications/2019/demo/p60-267.html

Chapter 5

Avalere Health. (2015, June 8). *Hospital acquisitions of physician practices and the 340B program* [White paper]. https://avalere.com/insights/avalere-white-paper-hospital -acquisitions-of-physician-practices-and-the-340b-program

Beaulieu, N. D., Dafny, L. S., Landon, B. E., Dalton, J. B., Kuye, I., & McWilliams, J. M. (2020, January 2). Changes in quality care after hospital mergers and acquisitions. *The New England Journal of Medicine, 382*, 51–59. https://www.nejm.org/doi/full /10.1056/NEJMsa1901383

Centers for Medicare and Medicaid Services. (2019b, November 29). *Trustees report & Trust Funds.* https://www.cms.gov/Research-Statistics-Data-and-Systems/Statistics -Trends-and-Reports/ReportsTrustFunds

Centers for Medicare and Medicaid Services. (2019b, December 17). *National health expenditure data.* https://www.cms.gov/Research-Statistics-Data-and-Systems /Statistics-Trends-and-Reports/NationalHealthExpendData

Centers for Medicare and Medicaid Services. (2019c, December 26). *Physician fee schedule.* https://www.cms.gov/medicare/medicare-fee-for-service-payment /physicianfeesched

Centers for Medicare and Medicaid Services. (2020, February 4). *Oncology care model.* https://innovation.cms.gov/initiatives/Oncology-Care/

Consolidated Omnibus Budget Reconciliation Act of 1985. (2019, November 14). *Wikipedia.* https://en.wikipedia.org/wiki/Consolidated_Omnibus_Budget_ Reconciliation_Act_of_1985

Coombs, B. (2017, August 05). As Obamacare twists in political winds, top insurers made $6 billion (not that there is anything wrong with that). *CNBC.* https://www .cnbc.com/2017/08/05/top-health-insurers-profit-surge-29-percent-to-6-billion -dollars.html

Ginsburg, P. (2016, March 16). Health care market consolidations: Impacts on costs, quality, and access. *Informational hearing before California Legislature, Senate Committee on Health.* https://www.brookings.edu/wp-content/uploads/2016/07 /Ginsburg-California-Senate-Health-Mar-16-1.pdf

Hayes, J., Hoverman, R., Brow, M., Dilbeck, D., Verrilli, D., Garey, J., . . . Beverridge, R. (2015, March 31). Cost differential by site of service for cancer patients receiving chemotherapy. *American Journal of Managed Care.* https://www.ajmc.com/journals /issue/2015/2015-vol21-n3/cost-differential-by-site-of-service-for-cancer-patients -receiving-chemotherapy

Health Resources and Services Administration. (2019, March). *340B Office of Pharmacy Affairs information system.* https://www.hrsa.gov/opa/340b-opais/index.html

Himmelstein, D., Lawless, R., Thorne, D., Foohey, P., & Woolhandler, S. (2019, February 6). Medical bankruptcy: Still common despite the Affordable Care Act. *AJPH.* https://ajph.aphapublications.org/doi/10.2105/AJPH.2018.304901

MCOL.com. (2018, February 28). Growth of physicians and administrators [1970–2009]. *Medical-Executive-Post.* https://medicalexecutivepost.com/2018/02/28/growth-of -physicians-and-administrators-1970-2009/

Medicare Learning Network. (2019, February). Hospital prospective payment system— HOPPS. *Centers for Medicare and Medicaid Services.* https://www.cms.gov/Outreach -and-Education/Medicare-Learning-Network-MLN/MLNProducts/downloads /HospitalOutpaysysfctsht.pdf

Medicare Sustainable Growth Rate. (2019, September 30). *Wikipedia.* https://en.wikipedia.org/wiki/Medicare_Sustainable_Growth_Rate

National Academies of Sciences. (2011, June 1). Geographic price cost indexes (GPCIs). *National Center for Biotechnology Information (NCBI).* https://www.ncbi.nlm.nih.gov/books/NBK190061/

New Mexico Cancer Center. (n.d.). Home page. https://nmcancercenter.org/

Rosenberg, J. (2018, March 21). Hospital acquisition of independent physician practices continues to increase. *American Journal of Managed Care.* http://www.ajmc.com/focus-of-the-week/hospital-acquisition-of-independent-physician-practices-continues-to-increase

Ross, H. (2013, September 28). The great healthcare bloat: 10 administrators for every 1 U.S. doctor. *Healthline: Health News.* https://www.healthline.com/health-news/policy-ten-administrators-for-every-one-us-doctor-092813#1

Sarasohn-Kahn, J. (2019, March 18). Medical issues are still the #1 contributor to bankruptcy in the U.S., an AJPH study asserts. *Health Populi.* https://www.healthpopuli.com/2019/03/18/medical-issues-are-still-the-1-contributor-to-bankruptcy-in-the-u-s/

Sawyer, B., & McDermott, D. (2019, March 28). How does the quality of the U.S. healthcare system compare to other countries? *Peterson-KFF Health System Tracker.* https://www.healthsystemtracker.org/chart-collection/quality-u-s-healthcare-system-compare-countries/#item-start

Sood, N., Shih, T., Van Nyus, K., & Goldman, D. (2017, June 13). Follow the money: The flow of funds in the pharmaceutical distribution system. *Health Affairs.* https://www.healthaffairs.org/do/10.1377/hblog20170613.060557/full/

Watanabe, J., McInnis, T., & and Hirsch, J. (2018, March 26). Cost of prescription drug-related morbidity and mortality. *Annals of Pharmacotherapy, 52*(9), 829–837. https://doi.org/10.1177/1060028018765159

Chapter 6

Alexander, G. C., Kurlander, J., & Wynia, M. (2005). Physicians in retainer ("concierge") practice: A national survey of physician, patient, and practice characteristics. *Journal of General Internal Medicine, 20*(12), 1079–1083. https://www.ncbi.nlm.nih.gov/pmc/articles/PMC1490281/

American Academy of Family Physicians. (n.d.). Direct primary care: Delivering exceptional care. On your terms. *AAFP.* https://www.aafp.org/practice-management/payment/dpc.html

American Academy of Family Physicians. (2014). Direct primary care: An alternative practice model to the fee-for-service framework. *AAFP.* https://www.aafp.org/dam/AAFP/documents/practice_management/payment/DirectPrimaryCare.pdf

Anderson, W. (2019, June 6). Rudy's BBQ expects to slash health costs with major change to employee benefits. *Austin Business Journal.* https://www.bizjournals.com/austin/news/2019/06/06/rudys-bbq-expects-to-slash-health-costs-with-major.html

Balat, D., O'Connor, E., Minjarez, J., & Heubaum, E. (2019, October 22). A brief history of government intervention in the U.S. healthcare system. *Texas Public Policy Foundation.* https://www.texaspolicy.com/a-brief-history-of-government-intervention-in-the-u-s-healthcare-system/

Basu, S., Berkowitz, S., Phillips, R., Bitton, A., Landon, B., & Phillips, R. (2019, February 18). Association of primary care physician supply with population mortality in the United States, 2005–2015. *JAMA Internal Medicine, 179*(4), 506–514. https://jamanetwork.com/journals/jamainternalmedicine/article-abstract/2724393

Burger, D. (2018, June 22). In-office membership plans could build patient loyalty, revenue. *American Dental Association.* https://www.ada.org/en/publications/ada-news/2018-archive/june/in-office-membership-plans-could-build-patient-loyalty-revenue

Cohen, R., & Zammitti, E. (2018, August). High-deductible health plan enrollment among adults aged 18–64 with employment-based insurance coverage. *NCHS Data Brief No.317.* https://www.cdc.gov/nchs/data/databriefs/db317.pdf

Cooper, Z., & Morton, F. (2016). Out-of-network emergency-physician bills—an unwelcome surprise. *The New England Journal of Medicine, 375,* 1915–1918. https://www.nejm.org/doi/full/10.1056/NEJMp1608571

DirectRX. (n.d.). *About us.* https://www.directrx.com/about/

DPC Frontier. (n.d.a). *2019 DPC laws + pilots.* https://www.dpcfrontier.com/states/

DPC Frontier. (n.d.b). *DPC frontier mapper.* https://mapper.dpcfrontier.com/

Erickson, S., Rockwern, B., Koltov, M., & McLean, R. (2017, May 2). Putting patients first by reducing administrative tasks in health care: A position paper of the American College of Physicians. *Annals of Internal Medicine, 166*(9), 659–661. https://annals.org/aim/fullarticle/2614079/putting-patients-first-reducing-administrative-tasks-health-care-position-paper

Eskew, P., & Klink, K. (2015, November 6). Direct primary care: Practice distribution and cost across the nation. *Journal of the American Board of Family Medicine, 28*(6), 793–801. https://www.jabfm.org/content/jabfp/28/6/793.full.pdf

Forrest, B. (2007, June). Breaking even on four visits per day. *Family Practice Management, 14*(6), 19–24. https://www.aafp.org/fpm/2007/0600/p19.html

Ghany, R., Tamariz, L., Chen, G., Dawkins, E., Ghany, A., Forbes, E., Tajiri, T., & Palacio, A. (2018, August 28). High-touch care leads to better outcomes and lower costs in a senior population. *American Journal of Managed Care.* https://www.ajmc.com/journals/issue/2018/2018-vol24-n9/hightouch-care-leads-to-better-outcomes-and-lower-costs-in-a-senior-population?p=1

Heartland Institute. (2019, August 30). Direct primary care offers cost savings, privacy, personalized care. *Heartland Institute.* https://www.heartland.org/news-opinion/news/direct-primary-care-offers-cost-savings-privacy-personalized-care

Herrick, D. (2013, May). The market for medical care should work like cosmetic surgery. *National Center for Policy Analysis Policy Report No. 349.* http://www.ncpathinktank.org/pdfs/st349.pdf

Kirzinger, A., Lopes, L., Wu, B., & Brodie, M. (2019, March 01). KFF Health tracking poll—February 2019: Prescription drugs. *Kaiser Family Foundation.* https://www.kff.org/health-reform/poll-finding/kff-health-tracking-poll-february-2019-prescription-drugs/

Lucia, K., Giovannelli, J., Corlette, S., Volk, J., Palanker, D., Kona, M., & Curran, E. (2018, March 29). State regulation of coverage options outside of the Affordable Care Act: Limiting the risk to the individual market. *The Commonwealth Fund.* https://www.commonwealthfund.org/publications/fund-reports/2018/mar/state-regulation-coverage-options-outside-affordable-care-act

Madrian, B. (1994, February 1). Employment-based health insurance and job mobility: Is there evidence of job-lock? *The Quarterly Journal of Economics, 109*(1), 27–54. https://academic.oup.com/qje/article-abstract/109/1/27/1850075

Pickett, S., O'Connor, E., & Balat, D. (2020, January). Choosing your care: How direct care can give patients more choice. *Texas Public Policy Foundation Policy Perspective.* https://files.texaspolicy.com/uploads/2020/01/16092834/Balat-Pickett -OConnor-Direct-Care-Gives-Patients-More-Choice.pdf

Primary Care Collaborative. (2019). Investing in primary care: A state-level analysis. *PCC.* https://www.pcpcc.org/slider-post/investing-primary-care-state-level-analysis

Raymond-Allbritten, J. (2019, April 1). In-office membership plans 101. *Registered Dental Hygienist.* https://www.rdhmag.com/patient-care/article/16408879/inoffice -membership-plans-101

Rohal, P. (2015, November 8). Why in the world would I pay TWICE for healthcare? *CovenantMD.* https://www.covenantmd.net/blog/2015/11/8/why-in-the-world

Rowe, K., Rowe, W., Umbehr, J., Dong, F., & Ablah, E. (2017, February 15). Direct primary care in 2015: A survey with selected comparisons to 2005 survey data. *Kansas Journal of Medicine, 10*(1), 3–6. https://www.ncbi.nlm.nih.gov/pmc/articles/PMC5733409/

Sadusky, A. (2018, July 1). The dental drilldown: Dental membership plans 101. *Dental Economics.* https://www.dentaleconomics.com/practice/patient-communication -and-patient-financing/article/16385005/the-dental-drilldown-dental-membership -plans-101

Schimpff, S. (2014, February 24). How many patients should a primary care physician care for? *MedCity News.* https://medcitynews.com/2014/02/many-patients-primary -care-physician-care/?rf=1

Seeley, E., & Kesselheim, A. (2019, March 26). Pharmacy benefit managers: Practices, controversies, and what lies ahead. *The Commonwealth Fund.* https://www .commonwealthfund.org/publications/issue-briefs/2019/mar/pharmacy-benefit -managers-practices-controversies-what-lies-ahead

Surgery Center of Oklahoma. (n.d.). *Surgery pricing.* https://surgerycenterok.com /pricing/

Texas Free Market Surgery. (n.d.). *Surgery prices in Austin, TX.* https://texasfreemarket surgery.com/pricing/

Texas Occupation Code. (n.d.). Chapter 162 §162.253. https://statutes.capitol.texas .gov/Docs/OC/htm/OC.162.htm

Thornton, K. (2019, February 19). The cost-savings for direct primary care patients. *Elation Health.* https://www.elationhealth.com/direct-care-blog/cost-patients/

Tuohy, C. (2017, December 14). Dental savings plan enrollment rises 20 percent. *InsuranceNewsNet.* https://insurancenewsnet.com/innarticle/dental-savings-plan -enrollment-rises-20-percent#.XiXq_shKg2z

Vujicic, M., Buchmueller, T., & Klein, R. (2016, December). Dental care presents the highest level of financial barriers, compared to other types of health care services. *Health Affairs, 35*(12). https://www.healthaffairs.org/doi/10.1377/hlthaff.2016.0800

Chapter 7

Altman, S., Butler, A. S., & Shern, L. (2015). *The future of nursing: Leading change, advancing health.* Washington, DC: National Academies Press.

Burrow, J. G. (1977). *Organized medicine in the progressive era: The move toward monopoly*. Baltimore: Johns Hopkins University Press.

Feldstein, M. S. (2020). Medical licensure in the age of uberization. *Cato Institute*. In press.

Flexner, A. (1910). *Medical education in the United States and Canada*. New York: Carnegie Foundation. Reproduced 1972.

Global Knowledge Exchange Network. (2009, September). *An overview of education and training requirements for global healthcare professionals: Physician*. http://gken .org/Docs/Workforce/Physician Educ Reqs_FINAL 102609.pdf

Goodman, J. C. (1980). *The regulation of medical care: Is the price too high?* (Vol. 9). San Francisco: Cato Institute.

Hiatt, M. D., & Stockton, C. G. (2003). The impact of the Flexner report on the fate of medical schools in North America After 1909. *Journal of American Physicians and Surgeons, 8*(2), 37–39. https://www.jpands.org/vol8no2/hiatt.pdf

Johnston, G. A. (1984). The Flexner report and Black medical schools. *Journal of the National Medical Association, 76*, 223–225.

Ludmerer, K. M. (1985). *Learning to heal: The development of American medical education*. New York: Basic Books.

Lyu, H., Xu. T., Brotman, D., Mayer-Blackwell. B., Cooper, M., Daniel, M., . . . Makary, M. A. (2017). Overtreatment in the United States. *PLoS ONE, 12*(9), e0181970. https://doi.org/10.1371/journal.pone.0181970

Marescaux, J., Leroy, J., Rubino, F., Smith, M., Vix, M., Simone, M., & Mutter, D. (2002). Transcontinental robot-assisted remote telesurgery: Feasibility and potential applications. *Annals of Surgery, 235*(4), 487–492. doi: 10.1097/00000658 -200204000-00005

Nash, D. A. (2012, April 10). A review of the global literature on dental therapists. *W. K. Kellogg Foundation*. https://www.wkkf.org/resource-directory/resource /2012/04/nash-dental-therapist-literature-review

Roda, R. (2018, May). Asymmetrical conflicts. *Inscriptions, 32*(5), 8–14. https:// inscriptions.azda.org/Sample/files/assets/common/downloads/Inscriptions.pdf ?uni=ffa11ac6e80642ea29b534ef794d656f

Scarberry, K., Berger, N. G., Scarberry, K. B., Agrawal, S., Francis, J. J., Yih, J. M., . . . Abouassaly, R. (2018). Improved surgical outcomes following radical cystectomy at high-volume centers influence overall survival. *Urologic Oncology: Seminars and Original Investigations, 36*(6), 308. doi: 10.1016/j.urolonc.2018.03.007

Schlomach, B., Feldstein, M., & Sandefur, C. (2018). A win-win for consumers and professionals alike. *Goldwater Institute*. https://goldwaterinstitute.org/article/a-win -win-for-consumers-and-professionals-alike-an-alternative-to-occupational-licensing/

Starr, P. (1982). The consolidation of professional authority 1850–1920. In *The social transformation of American medicine*, chap. 3. New York: Basic Books.

Svorny, S. (2008, September 17). Medical licensing: An obstacle to affordable, quality care. *Cato Institute Policy Analysis No. 621*. https://www.cato.org/sites/cato.org/files /pubs/pdf/pa-621.pdf

Svorny, S. (2017, November 15). Liberating telemedicine: Options to eliminate the state-licensing roadblock. *Cato Institute Policy Analysis No. 826*. https://www.cato .org/publications/policy-analysis/liberating-telemedicine-options-eliminate-state -licensing-roadblock

U.S. Department of Health and Human Services. (2018, December 3). *Reforming America's healthcare system through choice and competition*. https://www.hhs.gov /about/news/2018/12/03/reforming-americas-healthcare-system-through-choice -and-competition.html

Chapter 8

Carter, S. M. (2018, November 29). Over half of Americans delay or don't get health care because they can't afford it—these three treatments get put off most. *CNBC*. https://www.cnbc.com/2018/11/29/over-half-of-americans-delay-health-care -becasue-they-cant-afford-it.html

Kaiser Family Foundation. (2019, September 25). *Employer health benefits survey*. https://www.kff.org/health-costs/report/2019-employer-health-benefits-survey/

Kirzinger, A., Munana, C., Wu, B., & Brodie, M. (2019, June 11). Data note: Americans' challenges with healthcare costs. *KFF*. https://www.kff.org/health-costs/issue-brief /data-note-americans-challenges-health-care-costs/

Chapter 9

Amadeo, K. (2020, January 14). The rising cost of health care by year and its causes. *The Balance*. https://www.thebalance.com/causes-of-rising-healthcare-costs-4064878

Berchick, E. R., Barnett, J. C., & Upton, R. D. (2019, November 8). Health insurance coverage in the United States: 2018. *US Census*. https://www.census.gov/library /publications/2019/demo/p60-267.html

Hartman, M., Martin, A. B., Benson, J., & Catlin, A. (2019, December 5). National health care spending in 2018: Growth driven by accelerations in Medicare and private insurance spending. *Health Affairs*. https://www.healthaffairs.org/doi/full /10.1377/hlthaff.2019.01451

Kaiser Family Foundation. (2019, September 25). *2019 employer health benefits survey*. https://www.kff.org/report-section/ehbs-2019-summary-of-findings/

Chapter 10

Christensen, C. M., Raynor, M. E., & McDonald, R. (2015, December). What is disruptive innovation? *Harvard Business Review*, 44–53. https://hbr.org/2015/12 /what-is-disruptive-innovation

Collins, H. (2014, June 10). Will federal privacy laws impede health-care consumerization? *Government Technology*. https://www.govtech.com/health /Will-Federal-Privacy-Laws-Impede-Health-Care-Consumerization.html

Deegan Winters, A. (2019, September 27). Personal communications.

Friedman, Z. (2019, June 12). Walmart expands college for $1 a day. *Forbes*. https://www.forbes.com/sites/zackfriedman/2019/06/12/walmart-college-education /#444e6e53613f

Japsen, B. (2019a, September 3). As CVS rolls out health hubs, Walmart prepares clinic expansion. *Forbes*. https://www.forbes.com/sites/brucejapsen/2019/09/03/as-cvs -rolls-out-health-hubs-walmart-prepares-clinic-expansion/#46df63c961b2

Japsen, B. (2019b, September 13). Walmart's first healthcare services "super center" opens. *Forbes*. https://www.forbes.com/sites/brucejapsen/2019/09/13/walmarts -first-healthcare-services-super-center-opens/#29d4c58579d2

Kokosky, G., & Hall, C. (2018, June 28). Amazon enters the pharmacy world with acquisition of PillPack. *Pharmacy Times*. https://www.pharmacytimes.com/news /amazon-enters-the-pharmacy-world-with-acquisition-of-pillpack—

Pifer, R. (2019, April 24). "Meet PillPack": Amazon rolls out Rx delivery direct marketing. HealthcareDive. https://www.healthcaredive.com/news/meet-pillpack -amazon-rolls-out-rx-delivery-direct-marketing/553364/

Remedium eXchange. (2019, November 8). The 2019 healthcare economics summit in review. Concordia University, Wisconsin. http://rxthinktank.org/the-2019 -healthcare-economics-summit-in-review

Robson, C. (2019, November 8). Delivering healthcare in every neighborhood, via drugstore-based medical homes as portals to primary care. *The 2019 Healthcare Economics Summit in Review*. http://rxthinktank.org/the-2019-healthcare-economics -summit-in-review

Walgreens. (2020, March 13). Walgreens joins collaboration with administration and industry partners to provide access to government-run COVID-19 testing facilities. https://news.walgreens.com/press-releases/general-news/walgreens-joins -collaboration-with-administration-and-industry-partners-to-provide-access-to -government-run-covid-19-testing-facilities.htm

Wicklund, E. (2019, October 30). Walgreens shutters retail health clinics, eyes telehealth partnerships. *mHealth Intelligence*. https://mhealthintelligence.com/news/walgreens -shutters-retail-health-clinics-eyes-telehealth-partnerships

Chapter 11

Lights on Econ. (2015, October 15). Boris goes shopping [Video]. https://www.youtube .com/watch?v=8adfNdGR2i0

Chapter 12

Agrawal, M. (1999). *Global competitiveness in the pharmaceutical industry*. New York: Pharmaceutical Products Press.

American Academy of Actuaries. (2018, March). *Prescription drug spending in the U.S. health care system: An actuarial perspective*. https://www.actuary.org/content /prescription-drug-spending-us-health-care-system

American College of Physicians. (2015, November). *Doctors should prescribe generic medications whenever possible rather than more expensive brand name drugs*. https://www.acponline.org/acp-newsroom/doctors-should-prescribe-generic -medications-whenever-possible-rather-than-more-expensive-brand-name

Boustany, C. (2018, September). America funds much of the world's drug research; here's how Trump can end that. *The Virginia Gazette*. https://www.dailypress.com /virginiagazette/va-vg-tr-edit-drugs-0919-story.html

Caffrey, M., & Inserro, A. (2018, September). Senate votes 98–2 to ban pharmacist gag clauses. *AJMC Managed Markets Network*. https://www.ajmc.com/newsroom /senate-votes-982-to-ban-pharmacist-gag-clauses

Centers for Medicare and Medicaid Services. (2019). *National health expenditures 2017 highlights*. https://www.cms.gov/Research-Statistics-Data-and-Systems /Statistics-Trends-and-Reports/NationalHealthExpendData/Downloads/highlights .pdf

Clark, D., & Breslauer, B. (2018, October). Trump signs bills lifting pharmacist "gag clauses" on drug prices. *NBC News.* https://www.nbcnews.com/politics/white -house/trump-signs-bills-lifting-pharmacist-gag-orders-drug-prices-n918721

Coppock, K. (2018, October). Legislation signed into law prohibiting "gag clauses" for pharmacies. *Pharmacy Times.* https://www.pharmacytimes.com/conferences/ncpa -2018/legislation-signed-into-law-prohibiting-gag-clauses-for-pharmacies

Davio, K. (2018, March). Price and clinical factors impact Canadian orphan drug recommendation rates. *AJMC Managed Markets Network.* https://www.ajmc.com /newsroom/in-canada-price-and-clinical-factors-impact-recommendation-rates

DiMasi, J. A., Grabowski, H. G., & Hansen, R. W. (2016). Innovation in the pharmaceutical industry: New estimates of R&D costs. *Journal of Health Economics, 47,* 20–33. doi: 10.1016/j.jhealeco.2016.01.012

DiMasi, J. A., Hansen, R. W., & Grabowski, H. G. (2003) The price of innovation: New estimates of drug development costs. *Journal of Health Economics, 22,* 151–185.

The Economist. (2019, September). A dire scarcity of drugs is worsening, in part, because they are so cheap. https://www.economist.com/international/2019/09/14 /a-dire-scarcity-of-drugs-is-worsening-in-part-because-they-are-so-cheap

Federal Trade Commission. (2020, January). *Price fixing.* https://www.ftc.gov/tips-advice /competition-guidance/guide-antitrust-laws/dealings-competitors/price-fixing

Frank, R. G. (2001). Prescription drug prices: Why do some pay more than others do? *Health Affairs, 20,* 115–128.

Gassmann, O., & Zedtzitz, G.R.M. (2004). *Leading pharmaceutical innovation.* New York: Springer.

Goldman, D., & Lakdawalla, D. (2018, January). The global burden of medical innovation. *Brookings.* https://www.brookings.edu/research/the-global-burden-of -medical-innovation/

Jaffe, S. (2018, October). No more secrets: Congress bans pharmacist "gag orders" on drug prices. *Kaiser Health News.* https://khn.org/news/no-more-secrets-congress -bans-pharmacist-gag-orders-on-drug-prices/

Kacik, A. (2019, October). Low generic-drug prices exacerbate drug shortages: FDA. *Modern Healthcare.* https://www.modernhealthcare.com/technology/low-generic -drug-prices-exacerbate-drug-shortages-fda

Kim, T. (2017, October). Biotech, pharma shares drop after Trump says "drug prices are out of control." *CNBC.* https://www.cnbc.com/2017/10/16/biotech-pharma-shares -drop-after-trump-says-drug-prices-are-out-of-control.html

Lyman, S. (2014, September). Which countries excel in creating new drugs? It's complicated. *Xconomy.* https://xconomy.com/seattle/2014/09/02/which-countries -excel-in-creating-new-drugs-its-complicated/

Mangan, D. (2019, April). "Pharma bro" Martin Shkreli moved from federal prison after claim he was running drug company with banned cellphone. *CNBC.* https://www.cnbc.com/2019/04/24/pharma-bro-martin-shkreli-moved-from -prison-after-rule-breaking.html

Marsh, T. (2019a, June 12). Most expensive drugs, period. *GoodRx* [Blog post]. https://www.goodrx.com/blog/most-expensive-drugs-period/

Marsh, T. (2019b, October 11). The 20 most expensive prescription drugs in the U.S.A. *GoodRx* [Blog post]. https://www.goodrx.com/blog/20-most-expensive-drugs-in -the-usa/

Martin, B., & Raynor, B. (2008). An empirical test of pricing techniques. *Proceedings of the American Marketing Association Advanced Research Techniques Forum.*

Njardarson, J. T. (2009, April). *Top 200 drugs.* http://www.chem.cornell.edu/jn96/outreach.html

NPR. (2020, January 27). When insurance won't cover drugs, Americans make "tough choices" about their health. *NPR Shots.* https://www.npr.org/sections/health-shots/2020/01/27/799019013/when-insurance-wont-cover-drugs-americans-make-tough-choices-about-their-health

Paraxel Pharmaceutical. (2002). *Parexel Pharmaceutical R&D Statistical Sourcebook, 2002–2003.* San Diego: Barnett Educational Services.

Parks, J. (2009, October 29). Phone discussion with then Director of International Pricing and Access at Schering Plough.

Pitts, P. (2017, February). How other countries freeload on U.S. drug research [Op-ed]. *The Wall Street Journal.* https://www.wsj.com/articles/how-other-countries-freeload-on-u-s-drug-research-1487722580

Pope, C. (2019, November). Issues 2020: Drug spending is reducing health-care costs. *Manhattan Institute.* https://www.manhattan-institute.org/issues-2020-drug-prices-account-for-minimal-healthcare-spending

Rémuzat, C., Urbinati, D., Mzoughi, O., Hammi, E. E., Belgaied, W., & Toumi, M. (2015). Overview of external referenced pricing systems in Europe. *Journal of Market Access and Health Policy, 3.* doi: 10.3402/jmahp.v3.27675

Sanders, B. [SenSanders]. (2015, October 9). The greed of the pharmaceutical industry is a public health hazard to the American people [Tweet]. https://twitter.com/sensanders/status/652562701525323776

Seal, D., Jackson, S., Brooks, J., Harris, K., Haskell, A, & Ransom, R. (2016, June). Direct-to-consumer sale of prescription drugs by pharmaceutical companies. *Journal of Pharmacy Technology, 32*(3), 98–103. doi: 10.1177/8755122515627361

Tsai, A. (2016). The rising cost of insulin: Why the price of this lifesaving drug is reaching new heights. *Diabetes Forecast: The Healthy Living Magazine.* http://www.diabetesforecast.org/2016/mar-apr/rising-costs-insulin.html

Turner, T. (2019). Avandia. *Drugwatch.* https://www.drugwatch.com/avandia/

U.S. Department of Health and Human Services. (2020). *Drug pricing.* https://www.hhs.gov/about/leadership/secretary/priorities/drug-prices/index.html

U.S. Food and Drug Administration. (2020, January). *Drug shortages.* https://www.fda.gov/drugs/drug-safety-and-availability/drug-shortages

U.S. Patent and Trademark Office. (2001, July 31). *First U.S. patent issued today in 1790.* [Press release]. https://www.uspto.gov/about-us/news-updates/first-us-patent-issued-today-1790

Ventola, C. L. (2011). The drug shortage crisis in the United States. *Pharmacy & Therapeutics. 36*(11), 740–742, 749–757. https://www.ncbi.nlm.nih.gov/pmc/articles/PMC3278171/

Willingham, E. (2016). Why did Mylan hike EpiPen prices 400%? Because they could. *Forbes.* https://www.forbes.com/sites/emilywillingham/2016/08/21/why-did-mylan-hike-epipen-prices-400-because-they-could/#3ae126df280c

Zamora, B., Maignen, F., O'Neill, P., Mestre-Ferrandiz, J., & Garau, M. (2019). Comparing access to orphan medicinal products in Europe. *Orphanet Journal of Rare Diseases. 14*(95). doi: 10.1186/s13023-019-1078-5

Chapter 13

Beck, J. (2015, September 22). The drug with a 5,000 percent markup: The story of Daraprim's huge price hike is part of a trend of exorbitant pharmaceutical pricing. *The Atlantic.* https://www.theatlantic.com/health/archive/2015/09/daraprim-turing-pharmaceuticals-martin-shkreli/406546/

Candisky, C. (2019, March 18). Ohio sues pharmacy middleman OptumRx to recover $16 million in overcharges. *The Columbus Dispatch.* https://www.dispatch.com/news/20190318/ohio-sues-pharmacy-middleman-optumrx-to-recover-16-million-in-overcharges

Candisky, C., & Sullivan, L. (2018, June 27; updated June 28). Drug middlemen charging Ohioans triple the going rate—or more. *The Columbus Dispatch.* https://www.dispatch.com/news/20180627/drug-middlemen-charging-ohioans-triple-going-rate—-or-more

Centers for Medicare and Medicaid Services. (n.d.). *State drug utilization data.* https://www.medicaid.gov/medicaid/prescription-drugs/state-drug-utilization-data/index.html

Centers for Medicare and Medicaid Services. (2020, January 14). *NADAC (National Average Drug Acquisition Cost): Drug pricing and payment.* https://data.medicaid.gov/Drug-Pricing-and-Payment/NADAC-National-Average-Drug-Acquisition-Cost-/a4y5-998d

DiMasi, J. A., Grabowski, H. G., & Hansen, R. W. (2016). Innovation in the pharmaceutical industry: New estimates of R&D costs. *Journal of Health Economics, 47*(5), 20–33. https://doi.org/10.1016/j.jhealeco.2016.01.012

Dunn, A. (2018, August 13). Drugmakers say R&D spending hit record in 2017. *BioPharma Dive.* https://www.biopharmadive.com/news/phrma-research-development-spending-industry-report/529943/

Faget, K. Y., & Waltz, J. A. (2019, February 1). HHS proposes new rules to eliminate drug rebates and encourage direct discounts for federal beneficiaries [Blog post]. *Foley & Lardner LLP Health Care Law Today.* https://www.foley.com/en/insights/publications/2019/02/hhs-proposes-new-rules-to-eliminate-drug-rebates-a

Fein, A. J. (n.d.). 2018 MDM market leaders: Top pharmaceutical distributors. *Modern Distribution Management (MDM).* https://www.mdm.com/2017-top-pharmaceuticals-distributors

Fein, A. J. (2016, October 14). Follow the vial: The buy-and-bill system for distribution and reimbursement of provider-administered outpatient drugs. *Drug Channels.* https://www.drugchannels.net/2016/10/follow-vial-buy-and-bill-system-for.html

Feldman, R. (2019, April 11). The perils of value-based pricing for prescription drugs. *The Washington Post.* https://www.washingtonpost.com/outlook/2019/04/11/perils-value-based-pricing-prescription-drugs/

46brooklyn. (2019). *Are we paying too much for prescription drugs?* http://www.46brooklyn.com

Gagnon, M.-A., & Lexchin, J. (2008, January). The cost of pushing pills: A new estimate of pharmaceutical promotion expenditures in the United States. *PLoS Medicine, 5*(1), 29–33. https://pdfs.semanticscholar.org/1e44/fb439bf41fd6e01fd5e8a2a22016c05e6022.pdf

Health Resources and Services Administration. (2020, January). *340B drug pricing program.* https://www.hrsa.gov/opa/index.html

Joint Medicaid Oversight Committee. (2020). *JMOC—Ohio General Assembly.*
    http://jmoc.state.oh.us/home

Kaltenboeck, A., & Bach, P. B. (2018, June 5). Value-based pricing for drugs: Theme
    and variations. *Journal of the American Medical Association, 319*(21), 2165–2166.
    https://jamanetwork.com/journals/jama/article-abstract/2680422

Marketplace. (2018, January 30). *Amazon, Buffett, JPMorgan Chase tackle U.S. health
    care tapeworm* [Audio podcast]. https://www.marketplace.org/2018/01/30/amazon
    -buffett-jpmorgan-chase-tackle-us-health-care-tapeworm/

McCain, J. (2012, Summer). Distribution models for biologics and other specialty
    pharmaceutical products. *Biotechnology Healthcare, 9*(2), 8–13. https://www.ncbi
    .nlm.nih.gov/pmc/articles/PMC3411231/

Office of Population Affairs. (2016, August 17). 340B drug pricing program.
    U.S. Department of Health and Human Services. https://www.hhs.gov/opa/grants
    -and-funding/340b-drug-pricing-program/index.html

Paavola, A. (2019a, April 10). The top insurers all have PBMs: Here's who they are.
    Becker's Hospital Review. https://www.beckershospitalreview.com/pharmacy/the
    -top-insurers-all-have-pbms-here-s-who-they-are.html

Paavola, A. (2019b, May 30). Top PBMs by market share. *Becker's Hospital Review.*
    https://www.beckershospitalreview.com/pharmacy/top-pbms-by-market-share
    .html

Patient Protection and Affordable Care Act (2010). Pub. L. No. 111–148, 124 Stat.
    119–1024.

Popovian, R. (2019, December 6). Debunking the myth of who funds biomedical
    innovation [Op-ed]. *Morning Consult.* https://morningconsult.com/opinions
    /debunking-the-myth-of-who-funds-biomedical-innovation/

Remedium eXchange. (2019, November 8). *The 2019 healthcare economics summit in
    review.* Concordia University Wisconsin. http://rxthinktank.org/the-2019
    -healthcare-economics-summit-in-review/

Schwartz, L. M., & Woloshin, S. (2019, January). Medical marketing in the United
    States, 1997–2016. *Journal of the American Medical Association, 321*(1), 80–96.
    https://www.ncbi.nlm.nih.gov/pubmed/30620375

Socal, M., Bai, G., & Anderson, G. F. (2019). Favorable formulary placement of
    branded drugs in Medicare prescription drug plans when generics are available.
    JAMA Internal Medicine, 179(6), 832–833. https://jamanetwork.com/journals
    /jamainternalmedicine/article-abstract/2728446

U.S. Department of Health & Human Services. (2018, May). *American patients first:
    The Trump administration blueprint to lower drug prices and reduce out-of-pocket
    costs.* https://www.hhs.gov/sites/default/files/AmericanPatientsFirst.pdf

U.S. Department of Health & Human Services. (2019, May 8). *CMS drug pricing
    transparency fact sheet* [HHS news release]. https://www.hhs.gov/about/news
    /2019/05/08/cms-drug-pricing-transparency-fact-sheet.html

U.S. Department of Health and Human Services, Office of Inspector General. (2019,
    February 6). *Fraud and abuse; removal of safe harbor protection for rebates
    involving prescription pharmaceuticals and creation of new safe harbor protection
    for certain point-of-sale reductions in price on prescription pharmaceuticals and
    certain pharmacy benefit manager service fees* [HHS 42 CFR Part 1001].
    https://s3.amazonaws.com/public-inspection.federalregister.gov/2019-01026.pdf

Ventola, C. L. (2011, October). Direct-to-consumer pharmaceutical advertising: Therapeutic or toxic? *Pharmacy and Therapeutics, 36*(10), 669–674, 681–684. https://www.ncbi.nlm.nih.gov/pmc/articles/PMC3278148/

Winegarden, W. (2017, December). Addressing the problems of abuse in the 340B drug pricing program. *Pacific Research Institute.* https://www.pacificresearch.org /wp-content/uploads/2017/12/340B-Study_FINAL.pdf

Chapter 14

Albaek, S., Mollgaard, P., & Overgaard, P. B. (2015). Government-assisted oligopoly coordination? A concrete case. *Journal of Industrial Economics, 45*(4), 429–443. doi: 10.1111/1467-6451.00057

Alexander, L. (2019, June 26). Lower Health Care Costs Act, S.1895, 116th Congress (2019–2020).

Association of American Medical Colleges. (2019, June). *Results of the 2018 medical school enrollment survey.* http://store.aamc.org/downloadable/download/sample /sample_id/287/

Bryant, D. (2017, March 21). *Interim hearing on data collection and price transparency by David Bryant, MD.* Texas Senate Health and Human Services Committee.

Byrne, D. P., & de Roos, N. (2019, February). Learning to coordinate: A study in retail gasoline. *American Economic Association, 109*(2), 591–619. https://pubs.aeaweb.org /doi/pdfplus/10.1257/aer.20170116

Capretta, J. (2019, June). Toward meaningful price transparency in health care. *American Enterprise Institute,* 1–17. https://www.aei.org/wp-content/uploads/2019/06/Toward -meaningful-price-transparency-in-health-care.pdf

CMS Price Transparency Push Trails State Initiatives. (2019, February 8). *The National Law Review.* https://www.natlawreview.com/article/cms-price-transparency-push -trails-state-initiatives

Cutler, D., & Dafny, L. (2011). Designing transparency systems for medical care prices. *The New England Journal of Medicine, 364*(10), 894–895. doi:10.1056/nejmp1100540

Danzon, P. M. (2000). Making sense of drug prices. *Regulation, 23*(1), 56–63. https:// pdfs.semanticscholar.org/0a8a/b55896a0532339666f682772c9ff97d5a866.pdf

Desai, S., Hatfield, L. A., Hicks, A. L., Chernew, M. E., & Mehrotra, A. (2016, May 3). Association between availability of a price transparency tool and outpatient spending. *JAMA, 315*(17), 1874–1881. doi: 10.1001/jama.2016.4288

DiMasi, J., Grabowski, H. G., & Hansen, R. (2016, February). Innovation in the pharmaceutical industry: New estimates of R&D costs. *Journal of Health Economics, 47:* 20–33. doi: 10.1016/j.jhealeco.2016.01.012

Emanuel, E., Tanden, N., Altman, S., Armstrong, S., Berwick, D., de Brantes, F., ... Spiro, T. (2012, September 6). A systemic approach to containing health care spending. *The New England Journal of Medicine, 367,* 949–954. https://www.nejm .org/doi/full/10.1056/NEJMsb1205901

Flier, J. S., and Rhoads, J. M. (2018). The U.S. health provider workforce: Determinants and potential paths to enhancement. *Mercatus Working Paper.* https://www.mercatus .org/system/files/flier-health-provider-mercatus-working-paper-v1.pdf

Fulton, B. (2017, September). Health care market concentration trends in the United States: evidence and policy responses. *Health Affairs, 36*(9). https://www.healthaffairs .org/doi/pdf/10.1377/hlthaff.2017.0556

Gabel, J. R., Whitmore, H., Stromberg, S., & Green, M. (2018, November 15). Why are the health insurance marketplaces thriving in some states but struggling in others? *The Commonwealth Fund.* https://www.commonwealthfund.org/publications/issue-briefs/2018/nov/marketplaces-thriving-some-states-struggling-others

Garthwaite, C. (2019, May 23). What Martha's Vineyard's gas stations can teach us about drug pricing. *Forbes.* https://www.forbes.com/sites/craiggarthwaite/2019/05/23/what-marthas-vineyards-gas-stations-can-teach-us-about-drug-pricing/#53eed9a162dc

Goldhill, D. (2013, September). How American health care killed my father. *The Atlantic.* https://www.theatlantic.com/magazine/archive/2009/09/how-american-health-care-killed-my-father/307617/

Gorke, J. (2019, August 7). Price transparency—again: Eating the elephant in little bites. *Forbes.* https://www.forbes.com/sites/jeffgorke/2019/08/07/price-transparency-again-eating-the-elephant-in-little-bites/#2a40b1de134a

Harris, J. (2016, May 5). I tried to find out how much my son's birth would cost. No one would tell me. *Vox.* https://www.vox.com/2016/5/5/11591592/birth-cost-hospital-bills

Jenkins, J. (2019, April 30). We must stop Rx greed now: Expensive prescription drugs are a problem for us all. AARP. https://www.aarp.org/politics-society/advocacy/info-2019/jenkins-fight-prescription-drug-prices.html

Koslov, T. I., & Jex, E. (2015, July 21). Price transparency or TMI? *Federal Trade Commission* [Blog post]. https://www.ftc.gov/news-events/blogs/competition-matters/2015/07/price-transparency-or-tmi

Lao, M., Feinstein, D. L., & Lafontaine, F. (2015, June 29). Amendments to the Minnesota government data practices act regarding health care contract data. *Federal Trade Commission.* https://www.ftc.gov/system/files/documents/advocacy_documents/ftc-staff-comment-regarding-amendments-minnesota-government-data-practices-act-regarding-health-care/150702minnhealthcare.pdf

Lipinski, D. (2019, July 26). Hospital Price Transparency and Disclosure Act, H.R. 3965, 116th Congress (2019–2020). https://www.congress.gov/bill/116th-congress/house-bill/3965

Mankiw, G. (2018). *Principles of microeconomics.* Mason, OH: South-Western, Cengage Learning.

Mencken, H. L., & Thompson, G. H. (2005). *Prejudices* (2nd ed.). Whitefish, MT: Kessinger.

Mitchell, M. D., & Koopman, C. (2016, September 27). 40 years of certificate-of-need laws across America. *Mercatus Center.* https://www.mercatus.org/publications/corporate-welfare/40-years-certificate-need-laws-across-america

Musgrave, F. W. (2006). *The economics of U.S. health care policy: The role of market forces.* London: Routledge.

National Center for Education Statistics. (2018, May). *Trends in student loan debt for graduate school completers.* https://nces.ed.gov/programs/coe/indicator_tub.asp

National Conference of State Legislature. (2017, March). *Transparency and disclosure of health costs and provider payments: State actions.* https://www.ncsl.org/research/health/transparency-and-disclosure-health-costs.aspx

Pauly, M. V. (2019). Giving competition in medical care and health insurance a chance. *Mercatus Research.* https://www.mercatus.org/system/files/pauly-competition-medical-care-mercatus-research-v1.pdf

Perlmutter, E. (2019, February 27). Transparency in All Health Care Pricing Act of 2019, H.R. 1409, 116th Congress (2019–2020). https://www.congress.gov/bill /116th-congress/house-bill/1409

Rentoul, J. (2016, March 29). Review of Utopia for Realists: The case for a universal basic income, open borders and a 15-hour workweek, by Rutger Bregman. *Independent*. https://www.independent.co.uk/voices/comment/for-every-problem -there-is-a-solution-that-is-comprehensive-simple-and-wrong-a6956191.html

Schultz, C. (2002, May). *Transparency and tacit collusion in a differentiated market*. https://www.ifo.de/DocDL/730.pdf

Stigler, G. J. (1964, February). A theory of oligopoly. *The Journal of Political Economy*, *72*(1), 44–61. http://home.uchicago.edu/~vlima/courses/econ201/Stigler.pdf

Stühmeier, T. (2014). Price disclosure rules and consumer price comparison. *The B.E. Journal of Economic Analysis and Policy*, *15*(2). https://www.degruyter.com /view/j/bejeap.2015.15.issue-2/bejeap-2014-0053/bejeap-2014-0053.xml

U.S. Department of Health and Human Services. (2019, January 31). *Trump administration proposes to lower drug costs by targeting backdoor rebates and encouraging direct discounts to patients* [Press release]. https://www.hhs.gov/about /news/2019/01/31/trump-administration-proposes-to-lower-drug-costs-by -targeting-backdoor-rebates-and-encouraging-direct-discounts-to-patients. html

Van Norman, G. (2016, April). Drugs, devices, and the FDA: Part 1: An overview of approval processes for drugs. *JACC: Basic to Translational Science*, *1*(3), 170–179. https://www.sciencedirect.com/science/article/pii/S2452302X1600036X

Werble, C. (2017, September 14). Pharmacy benefit managers. *Health Affairs*. https://www.healthaffairs.org/do/10.1377/hpb20171409.000178/full/

William White v. R.M. Packer Co., Inc., No. 10-1130. (2011).

Wyden, R. (2019, February 13). Stopping the Pharmaceutical Industry from Keeping Drugs Expensive (SPIKE) Act of 2019, S.474, 116th Congress (2019–2020).

Chapter 15

FAQs About Rare Diseases. (2017, November 30). *National Institutes of Health, National Center for Advancing Translational Sciences*. https://rarediseases.info.nih. gov/diseases/pages/31/faqs-about-rare-diseases

Food and Drug Administration. (2020, January 29). *FDA-Led Patient-Focused Drug Development (PFDD) public meetings*. https://www.fda.gov/industry/prescription -drug-user-fee-amendments/fda-led-patient-focused-drug-development-pfdd -public-meetings

Global Genes. (n.d.). *Rare facts*. https://globalgenes.org/rare-facts/

Global Genes. (2019, September). *Next: Imagining the future of rare disease*. https://global genes.org/wp-content/uploads/2019/09/Global_Genes_NEXT_Report_2019.pdf

Lanthier, M. (2017, October 17). Insights into rare disease drug approval: Trends and recent developments [PowerPoint slides]. *U.S. Food and Drug Administration (FDA)*. https://www.fda.gov/files/about%20fda/published/Insights-into-Rare -Disease-Drug-Approval—Trends-and-Recent-Developments-%28October-17 —2017%29.pdf

Mikami, K. (2019, August). Orphans in the market: The history of orphan drug policy. *Oxford Journals: Social History of Medicine*, *32*(3): 609–630. https://www.ncbi.nlm .nih.gov/pmc/articles/PMC6664588/

National Institutes of Health. (1990, May 4). Report of the workshop on methods for determining the prevalence of rare diseases. *National Institutes of Arthritis and Musculoskeletal and Skin Diseases and the Office of National Policy and Legislation.*

National Organization for Rare Disorders. (2018). Trends in orphan drug costs and expenditures do not support revisions in the Orphan Drug Act: Background and history. *NORD.* https://rarediseases.org/wp-content/uploads/2018/05/NORD-IMS -Report_FNL.pdf

PhRMA. (n.d.). Progress in fighting rare diseases. *Pharmaceutical Research and Manufacturers of America.* https://www.phrma.org/en/Media/Progress-in-Fighting -Rare-Diseases

PhRMA. (2016, May 3). Medicines in development for rare diseases 2016 report. *Pharmaceutical Research and Manufacturers of America.* https://www.phrma.org/ en/Report/Medicines-in-Development-for-Rare-Diseases-2016-Report

Redfearn, S. (2018, May 14). Tufts: Facing many challenges, orphan drugs take 18% longer to develop. *WCG Clinical Services: CenterWatch.* https://www.centerwatch .com/articles/12603-tufts-facing-many-challenges-orphan-drugs-take-18-longer -to-develop

Statista. (2019, April). Top 20 pharmaceutical companies worldwide by orphan drug revenue market share in 2024 compared to 2018. *Statista.* https://www.statista.com /statistics/373373/top-companies-based-on-global-orphan-drug-market-share/

Woodcock, J. (2020, January 7). Innovation in new drug approvals as 2019 advances patient care across a broad range of diseases. *U.S. Food and Drug Administration (FDA).* https://www.fda.gov/news-events/fda-voices-perspectives-fda-leadership -and-experts/innovation-new-drug-approvals-2019-advances-patient-care-across -broad-range-diseases

Chapter 16

American Cancer Society. (2015). *Cancer facts and figures 2015.* http://www.cancer.org /research/cancerfactsstatistics/cancerfactsfigures2015/index

Bren, L. (2001). Frances Oldham Kelsey: FDA medical reviewer leaves her mark on history. *FDA Consumer Magazine.* https://web.archive.org/web/20090512235601/ http://www.fda.gov/fdac/features/2001/201_kelsey.html

Congressional Budget Office. (2006). *Research and development in the pharmaceutical industry.* https://www.cbo.gov/sites/default/files/cbofiles/ftpdocs/76xx/doc7615 /10-02-drugr-d.pdf

Cruzan v. Dir., Mo. Dep't of Health. (1990). 497 U.S. 261, 278–79.

Doe v. Bolton. (1997). 410 U.S. 179, 218 (Douglas, J., concurring).

Drug Amendments Act. (1962). Pub. L. No. 87–781, 76 Stat. 780.

Fiore, K. (2019). Desperate families pursue "n-of-1" trials for ultra-rare diseases: Technology dangles hope of cure—for those able to pay. *MedPage Today.* https://www.medpagetoday.com/publichealthpolicy/generalprofessionalissues/81725

Flatten, M. (2016). Dead on arrival: Federal "compassionate use" leaves little hope for dying patients. *Goldwater Institute.* http://righttotry.org/dead-on-arrival

Food and Drug Administration Modernization Act. (1997). Pub. L. No. 105–115, 105 Stat. 1677.

Griffin v. Tatum. (1970). 425 F.2d 201, 203 (5th Cir.).

Kelo v. City of New London. (2005). 545 U.S. 469, 489.

Kravitz, R. L., & Duan, N. (2014). Design and implementation of n-of-1 trials: A user's guide. *Agency for Healthcare Research and Quality.* https://effectivehealthcare.ahrq .gov/sites/default/files/pdf/n-1-trials_research-2014-5.pdf

Madara, M. (2009). Constitutional law—sacrificing the good of the few for the good of the many: Denying the terminally ill access to experimental medication. *Western New England Law Review, 31*(2), 535–580. https://digitalcommons.law.wne.edu /lawreview/vol31/iss2/8/

Metropolitan Life Insurance Co. v. Massachusetts. (1985). 471 U.S. 724, 756.

President's Council of Advisors on Science and Technology. (2012). *Report to the president on propelling innovation in drug discovery, development, and evaluation.* https://permanent.access.gpo.gov/gpo32081/pcast-fda-final.pdf

Pure Food and Drug Act. (1906). Pub. L. No. 59–384, 34 Stat. 768.

Rochin v. California. (1952). 342 U.S. 165, 172–74.

Rush Prudential HMO, Inc. v. Moran. (2002). 536 U.S. 355, 387.

Trickett Wendler, Frank Mongiello, Jordan McLinn, and Matthew Bellina Right to Try Act. (2018). Pub. L. No. 115–176, 132 Stat. 1372.

Tufts Center for the Study of Drug Development. (2014). *Cost to develop and win marketing approval for a new drug is $2.6 billion.* https://www.sciencedirect.com /science/article/abs/pii/S0167629616000291?via%3Dihub

United States v. Rutherford. (1979). 442 U.S. 544.

U.S. Food and Drug Administration. (2015, April 13). Balancing premarket and postmarket data collection for devices subject to premarket approval: Guidance for industry and Food and Drug Administration staff. https://www.fda.gov/media /88381/download

U.S. Food and Drug Administration. (2018, January 4). *The drug development process: Clinical research.* http://www.fda.gov/ForPatients/Approvals/Drugs/ucm405622 .htm#Clinical_Research_Phase_Studies

White, J. B. (2015). "Right to Try" bills would let dying Californians use experimental drugs. *Sacramento Bee.* http://www.sacbee.com/news/politics-government /article21718809.html

Chapter 17

Amadeo, K. (2019, September 25). What is the federal budget? *The Balance.* https://www.thebalance.com/what-is-the-federal-budget-3306305

American Pharmacists Association. (2018, October 10). APhA applauds law prohibiting PBM "gag clauses." https://www.pharmacist.com/press-release/apha -applauds-laws-prohibiting-pbm-gag-clauses

Assistant Secretary for Public Affairs. (2018, June 14). Drug pricing. *U.S. Department of Health and Human Services.* https://www.hhs.gov/about/leadership/secretary /priorities/drug-prices/index.html

Centers for Medicare & Medicaid Services. (2018, October 21). *International pricing index (IPI) model.* https://innovation.cms.gov/initiatives/ipi-model/

Centers for Medicare and Medicaid Services. (2019, May 15). *CMS issues new guidance addressing spread pricing in Medicaid, ensures pharmacy benefit managers are not up-charging taxpayers* [CMS news release]. https://www.cms.gov/newsroom/press -releases/cms-issues-new-guidance-addressing-spread-pricing-medicaid-ensures -pharmacy-benefit-managers-are-not

Commonwealth Fund. (n.d.). *International health care system profiles.* https://international.commonwealthfund.org/

Davis, S. (2019, August 9). Top senate republican pushes forward with drug bill that divides GOP. *NPR.* https://www.npr.org/2019/08/09/749669233/top-senate-republican-pushes-forward-with-drug-bill-that-divides-gop

Dearment, A. (2019, July 12). Trump administration ends key drug pricing proposal. *MedCity News.* https://medcitynews.com/2019/07/trump-administration-ends-key-drug-pricing-proposal/

Enthoven, A. (2005, April 10). The rise and fall of HMOs shows how a worthy idea went wrong. *CommonWealth Magazine.* https://commonwealthmagazine.org/arts-and-culture/emthe-rise-and-fall-of-hmosem-shows-how-a-worthy-idea-went-wrong/

Erman, M., & O'Donnell, C. (2019, December 18). Trump proposes rule for importing drugs from Canada; industry says it won't cut costs. *Reuters.* https://www.reuters.com/article/us-usa-healthcare-drugpricing/trump-proposes-rule-for-importing-drugs-from-canada-industry-says-it-wont-cut-costs-idUSKBN1YM1LX

Frakt, A., & Mehrotra, A. (2019, April 16). What type of price transparency do we need in health care? *Annals of Internal Medicine, 170*(8), 561–562. https://annals.org/aim/article-abstract/2729812/what-type-price-transparency-do-we-need-health-care

Guynn, R. D. (2010, November 20). The financial panic of 2008 and financial regulatory reform. *Harvard Law School Forum on Corporate Governance.* https://corpgov.law.harvard.edu/2010/11/20/the-financial-panic-of-2008-and-financial-regulatory-reform/

HealthCare.gov. (n.d.). "Navigator." https://www.healthcare.gov/glossary/navigator/

Heath, S. (2017, August 22). What are healthcare navigators, patient-centered care benefits? *Patient Engagement HIT.* https://patientengagementhit.com/news/what-are-healthcare-navigators-patient-centered-care-benefits

Huetteman, E. (2019, November 11). Voters say Congress needs to curb drug prices, but are lawmakers listening? *USA Today.* https://www.usatoday.com/story/news/health/2019/11/11/mcconnell-pelosi-clash-over-drug-price-bill-congress-act/2558426001/

IGES Institute GmbH. (2019). *Reimbursement and pricing of pharmaceuticals in Europe.* Berlin: IGES Group.

Junod, S. W. (n.d.). FDA and clinical drug trials: A short history. *Food and Drug Administration.* https://www.fda.gov/media/110437/download

Kaiser Health News. (2019, November 14). Trump wants to demand U.S. pays lowest price for drugs out of developed countries, Azar says. *Kaiser Family Foundation.* https://khn.org/morning-breakout/trump-wants-to-demand-u-s-pays-lowest-price-for-drugs-out-of-developed-countries-azar-says/

Kliff, S. (2019, February 12). Private health insurance exists in Europe and Canada. Here's how it works. *Vox.* https://www.vox.com/health-care/2019/2/12/18215430/single-payer-private-health-insurance-harris-sanders

Miller, E. (2018, January 25). U.S. drug prices vs. the world. *Drugwatch.* https://www.drugwatch.com/featured/us-drug-prices-higher-vs-world/

Ministry of Health, Labour, and Welfare, Economic Affairs Division, Health Policy Bureau. (n.d.). *Update of drug pricing system in Japan.* https://www.pmda.go.jp/files/000221888.pdf

Ministry of Health, Labour, and Welfare Insurance Bureau. (2016, November 30). *Drug pricing system in Japan.* http://www.jpma.or.jp/english/parj/pdf/17_supplement.pdf

Nathan-Kazis, J. (2019, August 8). An international drug-price index is coming, a Trump advisor says. *BARRON'S.* https://www.barrons.com/articles/international-drug-price-index-trump-advisor-medicare-drugmakers-health-care-51565269669

Organization for Economic Development. (2014). *Pharmaceutical spending.* https://data.oecd.org/chart/4NYS

Pipes, S. (2019, August 16). Trump's drug price controls could cost lives. *Washington Examiner.* https://www.washingtonexaminer.com/opinion/trumps-drug-price-controls-could-cost-lives

Sagan, A., & Thomson, S. (2016). *Voluntary health insurance in Europe: Role and regulation.* Geneva: World Health Organization. http://www.euro.who.int/__data/assets/pdf_file/0005/310838/Voluntary-health-insurance-Europe-role-regulation.pdf

Schulthess, D. (2019, June 5). International pricing index: What will be the impact on patients, outcomes, and innovation? *Vital Transformation.* http://vitaltransformation.com/wp-content/uploads/2019/06/IPI_June_5.pdf

Sullivan, P. (2019, December 12). House passes sweeping Pelosi bill to lower drug prices. *The Hill.* https://thehill.com/homenews/house/474294-house-passes-sweeping-pelosi-bill-to-lower-drug-prices

Thoma, M. (2007, March 27). The marginal cost and marginal benefit of cancer drugs. [Blog post]. *Economist's View.* https://economistsview.typepad.com/economistsview/2007/03/the_marginal_co.html

Torinus, J. (n.d.). *The grassroots healthcare revolution.* http://johntorinus.com/opt-out-on-obamacare-opt-into-the-private-health-care-revolution/

U.S. Department of Health and Human Services. (2019a, January 31). *Trump administration proposes to lower drug costs by targeting backdoor rebates and encouraging direct discounts to patients* [HHS news release]. https://www.hhs.gov/about/news/2019/01/31/trump-administration-proposes-to-lower-drug-costs-by-targeting-backdoor-rebates-and-encouraging-direct-discounts-to-patients.html

U.S. Department of Health and Human Services. (2019b, November 15). *Trump administration announces historic price transparency requirements to increase competition and lower healthcare costs for all Americans* [HHS news release]. https://www.hhs.gov/about/news/2019/11/15/trump-administration-announces-historic-price-transparency-and-lower-healthcare-costs-for-all-americans.html

U.S. Department of Health and Human Services. (2019c, December 18). Trump administration takes historic steps to lower U.S. prescription drug prices [HHS news release]. https://www.hhs.gov/about/news/2019/12/18/trump-administration-takes-historic-steps-to-lower-us-prescription-drug-prices.html

U.S. Food and Drug Administration. (2018, December 20). *Developing products for rare diseases and conditions.* https://www.fda.gov/industry/developing-products-rare-diseases-conditions

U.S. Securities and Exchange Commission. (2013). *What we do.* https://www.sec.gov/Article/whatwedo.html

Vital Transformation (2019, July 12). *Pfizer's John Doyle champions value-based healthcare* [Vital Health podcast]. https://podtail.com/en/podcast/vital-health-podcast/pfizer-s-john-doyle-champions-value-based-healthca/

Vitry, A., Nguyen, T., Entwistle, V., & Roughead, E. (2015). Regulatory withdrawal of medicines marketed with uncertain benefits: The bevacizumab case study. *Journal of Pharmaceutical Policy and Practice, 8*(25). https://www.ncbi.nlm.nih.gov/pmc/articles/PMC4610052/

World Health Organization. (2003). Equitable pricing of newer essential medicines for developing countries: Evidence for the potential of different mechanisms. *WHO Essential Medicines and Health Products Information Portal.* http://apps.who.int /medicinedocs/en/m/abstract/Js18815en/

Wynne, B., & Llamas, A. (2019, October 24). New legislation to control drug prices: How do house and senate bills compare? [Blog post]. *The Commonwealth Fund.* https://www.commonwealthfund.org/blog/2019/new-legislation-control-drug -prices-how-do-house-and-senate-bills-compare

Young, K. (2015, January 9). Pharma heavily markets "me-too" drugs to physicians. A. Sofair & W. E. Chavey (Eds.). *NEJM Journal Watch.* https://www.jwatch.org /fw109727/2015/01/09/pharma-heavily-markets-me-too-drugs-physicians

Chapter 18

Caldwell, N., Srebotnjak, T., Wang, T., & Hsia R. (2013). "How much will I get charged for this?" Patient charges for top ten diagnoses in the emergency department. *PLoS ONE, 8*, 2. https://doi.org/10.1371/journal.pone.0055491

Centers for Medicare and Medicaid Services. (2012, March 26). *Emergency Medical Treatment and Labor Act.* https://www.cms.gov/Regulations-and-Guidance /Legislation/EMTALA/

Luthra, S. (2017, January 24). Everything you need to know about block grants: The heart of GOP's Medicaid plans. *Kaiser Health News.* https://khn.org/news/block -grants-medicaid-faq/

New England Healthcare Institute. (2010, March). A matter of urgency: Reducing emergency department overuse. *NEHI Research Brief.* https://www.nehi.net/writable /publication_files/file/nehi_ed_overuse_issue_brief_032610finaledits.pdf

Pipes, S. (2017, July 28). Yes, we should block-grant Medicaid. *National Review.* http:// www.nationalreview.com/article/449926/medicaid-block-grants-would-put-states -budget

Pope, C. (2015, July 6). Assuring hospital emergency care without crippling competition. *Health Affairs Blog.* ttps://www.healthaffairs.org/do/10.1377/hblog20150706.049122 /full/

Sem, D. S., Gou, S., & Aljabban, T. (2018). Celebrating Wisconsin entrepreneurs: Lessons learned from Wisconsin entrepreneurs and businesses, and future prospects for a healthcare sector that is driving healthcare reform. *Marquette Intellectual Property Law Review 22*, 51. https://scholarship.law.marquette.edu/iplr/vol22/iss1/6/

Texture Health. (2020). *We believe every population deserves access to high quality, coordinated care.* https://www.texturehealth.com/

Chapter 19

Adolphsen, S., & Ingram, J. (2018, February 28). Three myths about the welfare cliff. *The Foundation for Government Accountability.* https://thefga.org/wp-content /uploads/2018/02/Three-myths-about-the-welfare-cliff-2-28-18.pdf

Cannon, M., & Tanner, M. (2007). *Healthy competition: What's holding back health care and how to free it.* Washington, DC: Cato Institute.

Education Next. (2019, August 19). EdNext poll: Democrats divided over school choice. *Harvard Graduate School of Education.* https://www.gse.harvard.edu/news/19/08 /ednext-poll-democrats-divided-over-school-choice

Eisenhower, D. D. (1953, April 16). Chance for peace. *Miller Center, University of Virginia.* https://millercenter.org/the-presidency/presidential-speeches/april-16 -1953-chance-peace

Farenthold, K. (2014, May 30). How the VA developed its culture of coverups. *The Washington Post.* https://www.washingtonpost.com/sf/national/2014/05/30/how -the-va-developed-its-culture-of-coverups/?utm_term=.f5eb46d82a7c

FMI—The Food Industry Association. (2020). *Supermarket facts.* https://www.fmi.org /our-research/supermarket-facts

Friedman, M., & Friedman, R. (1980). *Free to choose: A personal statement.* New York: Harcourt

Goodman, J. (2020, January 17). What the left doesn't understand about health care prices. *Forbes.* https://www.forbes.com/sites/johngoodman/2020/01/17/what-the -left-doesnt-understand-about-health-care-prices/#66e6ed19664e

Jones, L. (2012). Small donors allow St. Jude Children's Research Hospital to take the hardest cases—without charging families a dime. *Philanthropy Magazine.* https://www .philanthropyroundtable.org/philanthropy-magazine/article/millions-from-millions

Kaiser Family Foundation. (2018a). *Health insurance coverage of the total population.* https://www.kff.org/other/state-indicator/total-population/?dataView=0&current Timeframe=0&selectedDistributions=employer&sortModel=%7B%22colId%22: %22Location%22,%22sort%22:%22asc%22%7D

Kaiser Family Foundation. (2018b). *Distribution of the nonelderly with Medicaid by federal poverty level (FPL).* https://www.kff.org/medicaid/state-indicator /distribution-by-fpl-4/?currentTimeframe=0&sortModel=%7B%22colId%22: %22Location%22,%22sort%22:%22asc%22%7D

Kaiser Family Foundation. (2018c). *Distribution of Medicare beneficiaries by federal poverty level.* https://www.kff.org/medicare/state-indicator/medicare-beneficiaries -by-fpl/?currentTimeframe=0&sortModel=%7B%22colId%22:%22Location%22 ,%22sort%22:%22asc%22%7D

Kreuger, A. (1974, June). The political economy of the rent-seeking society. *The American Economic Review, 64(3).*

Maltais, K. (2019, June 4). What chocolate shortage? Cocoa prices steady as record output projected. *The Wall Street Journal.* https://www.wsj.com/articles/what -chocolate-shortage-cocoa-steadies-as-record-output-projected-11559649601

Randolph, E. (2014, December). Modeling potential income and welfare assistance benefits in Illinois: Single parent with two children household and two parents with two children household scenarios in Cook County, City of Chicago, Lake County and St. Clair County. *Illinois Policy Institute.* https://files.illinoispolicy.org/wp -content/uploads/2015/06/Welfare_Report_finalfinal.pdf

Resendes, S. (2020, January 22). 50+ restaurant industry statistics restaurateurs should know in 2020. *Upserve.* https://upserve.com/restaurant-insider/industry -statistics/

U.S. Department of Agriculture. (2019, September 20). Ag and food sectors and the economy. *USDA Economic Research Service.* https://www.ers.usda.gov/data -products/ag-and-food-statistics-charting-the-essentials/ag-and-food-sectors-and -the-economy/

Wilson, K. (2019, May 21). Health care costs 101: 2019 edition. *California Health Care Foundation.* https://www.chcf.org/publication/2019-edition-health-care-costs-101 -national-spending/

Chapter 20

Lewin Group. (2007, June 4). *The Wisconsin Health Plan (WHP): Estimated cost and coverage impacts.*

Small Business Times. (2005, August 5). *Special reports: State of health care.*

Chapter 21

American Academy of Pediatrics. (2013, April 30). *APA task force on childhood poverty: A strategic road-map.* http://www.ncdsv.org/images/APA_Task-Force-on-Childhood-Poverty-a-Strategic-Road-Map_4-30-2013.pdf

Berchick, E. R., Hood, E., & Barnett, J. C. (2018, September). Health insurance coverage in the United States: 2017, Current population report P60–264. *U.S. Census Bureau.* https://www.census.gov/content/dam/Census/library/publications/2018/demo/p60-264.pdf

Berwick, D. M., & Hackbarth, A. D. (2012, April 11). Eliminating waste in U.S. health care. *JAMA, 307*(14) 1513–1516.

Centers for Medicare and Medicaid Services. (n.d.a). *Catastrophic coverage.* https://www.medicare.gov/drug-coverage-part-d/costs-for-medicare-drug-coverage/catastrophic-coverage

Centers for Medicare and Medicaid Services. (n.d.b). *Copayment/coinsurance in drug plans.* https://www.medicare.gov/drug-coverage-part-d/costs-for-medicare-drug-coverage/copaymentcoinsurance-in-drug-plans

Centers for Medicare and Medicaid Services. (n.d.c). *Costs in the coverage gap.* https://www.medicare.gov/part-d/costs/coverage-gap/part-d-coverage-gap.html

Centers for Medicare and Medicaid Services. (n.d.d). *How much does Part D cost?* https://www.medicare.gov/drug-coverage-part-d/costs-for-medicare-drug-coverage

Centers for Medicare and Medicaid Services. (n.d.e). *Medicare 2017 and 2018 costs at a glance.* https://www.medicare.gov/your-medicare-costs/costs-at-a-glance/costs-at-glance.html

Centers for Medicare and Medicaid Services. (n.d.f). *Monthly premium for drug plans.* https://www.medicare.gov/part-d/costs/premiums/drug-plan-premiums.html

Centers for Medicare and Medicaid Services. (n.d.g). *Part D premiums by income.*

Centers for Medicare and Medicaid Services. (n.d.h). *What marketplace health insurance plans cover.* https://www.healthcare.gov/coverage/what-marketplace-plans-cover/

Cubanski, J., & Neuman, T. (2017, July 18). The facts on Medicare spending and financing. *Kaiser Family Foundation.* https://www.kff.org/medicare/issue-brief/the-facts-on-medicare-spending-and-financing/

Evans, W. N., & Garthwaite, C. L. (2014). Giving mom a break: The impact of higher EITC payments on maternal health. *American Economic Journal: Economic Policy, 6*(2), 258–290.

Health Affairs. (2012, December 13). *Health policy brief: Reducing waste in health care.* https://www.healthaffairs.org/do/10.1377/hpb20121213.959735/full/

Jacobson, G., Gold, M., Damico, A., Neuman, T., & Casillas, G. (2015, December 3). Medicare advantage 2016 data spotlight: Overview of plan changes—limits on out-of-pocket spending. *Kaiser Family Foundation.* https://www.kff.org/report-section/medicare-advantage-2016-data-spotlight-overview-of-plan-changes-limits-on-out-of-pocket-spending/

Kaiser Family Foundation. (2017, October 10). *Medicare advantage*. https://www.kff .org/medicare/fact-sheet/medicare-advantage/

Lambrew, J., & Montz, E. (2017, March 22). ObamaCare vs. TrumpCare in 10 charts. *The Century Foundation*. https://tcf.org/content/commentary/obamacare-vs-trumpcare -10-charts/

Leapfrog Group. (n.d.). *Raising the bar for safer health care*. http://www.leapfroggroup .org/about

National Committee for Quality Assurance. (n.d.a). *HEDIS and performance measurement*. http://www.ncqa.org/hedis-quality-measurement

National Committee for Quality Assurance. (n.d.b). *NCQA health insurance plan ratings 2017–2018—summary report (private)*. http://healthinsuranceratings.ncqa.org /2017/Default.aspx

National Committee to Preserve Social Security. (2017, February). *Number of people receiving Medicare (2015)*. http://www.ncpssm.org/Medicare/MedicareFastFacts

Patton, M. (2015, June 29). U.S. health care costs rise faster than inflation. *Forbes*. https://www.forbes.com/sites/mikepatton/2015/06/29/u-s-health-care-costs-rise -faster-than-inflation/#11eac1426fa1

Riemer, D. R. (2019). *Putting government in its place: The case for a New Deal 3.0*. Milwaukee, WI: HenschelHAUS Publishing.

Riemer, D. R. (2019, February 27). *Reforming America's health insurance system: YoungMedicare*. https://www.govinplace.org/content/ReformingHealthInsurance.pdf

Simon, D. (2015, June 9). Expansions to the earned income tax credit improved the health of children born to low income mothers [Blog post]. *London School of Economics and Political Science*. http://blogs.lse.ac.uk/usappblog/2015/06/09 /expansions-to-the-earned-income-tax-credit-improved-the-health-of-children -born-to-low-income-mothers/

Swain, G. R., Grande, K. M., Hood, C. M., & Inzeo, P. T. (2014, December). Health care professionals: Opportunities to address social determinants of health. *Journal of the Wisconsin Medical Society, 113*(6).

University of Wisconsin-Madison Population Health Institute and Robert Wood Johnson Foundation. (2017). County health rankings and roadmaps. *County Health Rankings*. https://www.countyhealthrankings.org/about-us

Chapter 22

Feeding America. (n.d.). *Hunger in America: Senior hunger facts*. https://www .feedingamerica.org/hunger-in-america/senior-hunger-facts

Hunger Task Force. (n.d.). Stockbox. *Hunger Task Force: Free & Local*. https://www .hungertaskforce.org/volunteer/stockbox/

Jacobs, C. (2019). *The Case against single payer: How "Medicare for All" will wreck America's health care system—and its economy*. Alexandria, VA: Republic Book Publishers.

Konish, L. (2019, February 11). This is the real reason most Americans file for bankruptcy. *CNBC*. https://www.cnbc.com/2019/02/11/this-is-the-real-reason -most-americans-file-for-bankruptcy.html

Magnan, S. (2017, October 09). Social determinants of health 101 for health care: Five plus five. *National Academy of Medicine*. https://nam.edu/social-determinants-of -health-101-for-health-care-five-plus-five/

Sachs, R., & Huberfeld, N. (2019, July 24). The problematic law and policy of Medicaid block grants. *Health Affairs Blog.* https://www.healthaffairs.org/do/10.1377 /hblog20190722.62519/full/

Wisconsin Department of Health Services. (2019, December 18). *WIC (Women, Infants, and Children) Program.* https://www.dhs.wisconsin.gov/wic/index.htm

About the Authors

David Balat is the director of the Right on Healthcare initiative with the Texas Public Policy Foundation. He is a former congressional candidate in the 2nd congressional district in Texas and a seasoned hospital executive with more than 20 years of healthcare industry leadership and executive management experience, with special expertise in healthcare finance.

Catherine Bodnar was a research associate and is currently an MBA student at Concordia University and a medical student at Medical College of Wisconsin. She has interests at the interface of science, medicine, and business.

Murray S. Feldstein, MD, is currently a Visiting Fellow for Health Care Policy at the Goldwater Institute in Phoenix. Dr. Feldstein started his urology practice in Flagstaff, Arizona, in 1974 and practiced there until 2000. He then joined Mayo Clinic Arizona as a urologic consultant and engaged in clinical, educational, and research activities. Retiring in 2015 as an assistant professor of urology, he remains on the emeritus staff. Dr. Feldstein was also twice elected to the Flagstaff City Council and served as vice-mayor for two years.

Anne Marie Finley, MS, RAC, is a former policymaker with 25 years of experience at the Food and Drug Administration (FDA), the Department of Health and Human Services (HHS), and Congress. She served in the administration of President George H. W. Bush as special assistant for Legislative and Public Affairs in the Office of the Commissioner, U.S. FDA. More recently, she served as vice president of Government Relations and Public Policy at Celgene, and VP of Regulatory Policy at GE Healthcare. In 2014, she was named a top 50 Thought Leader in Orphan Drugs and Rare Diseases. Currently, she is president of Biotech Policy Group LLC, a healthcare government relations and regulatory policy consulting firm.

Curt Gielow holds an undergraduate degree in pharmacy, a graduate degree in healthcare administration from the Washington University School of Medicine, and an honorary doctorate from Concordia University in Ann Arbor, Michigan. He was the founding dean of the Concordia University School of Pharmacy and served 13 years in elected office as a local alderman, mayor, and Wisconsin State representative. A Republican, Gielow is the 2005 coauthor, with Representative Jon Richards (D), of the Wisconsin Health Plan, a bipartisan attempt to create a universal healthcare plan that failed consideration in the Wisconsin state legislature during his tenure.

Robert Graboyes is a senior research fellow and healthcare scholar at the Mercatus Center at George Mason University. Author of *Fortress and Frontier in American Health Care*, his work asks, "How can we make healthcare as innovative in the next 30 years as information technology was in the past 30?" Previously, he was the healthcare adviser for the National Federation of Independent Business, economics professor at the University of Richmond, and regional economist/director of education at the Federal Reserve Bank of Richmond.

Eric Haberichter is a serial healthtech entrepreneur with 25 years of medical imaging and health business experience, specializing in market-based healthcare solutions for providers, self-insured employers, and those looking for quality-assured, high-value alternatives. Haberichter is CEO and cofounder of Access HealthNet, which develops episodic case rates (i.e., procedural bundles) for employers, health plans, and providers. Previously, he cofounded Smart Choice MRI, which brought affordable and transparently priced MRIs, at less than $700, to Wisconsin.

Naomi Lopez-Bauman is the director of healthcare policy at the Goldwater Institute. Previously, she served as the director of research and the director of health policy at the Illinois Policy Institute. Before that she worked as an entitlements policy analyst at the Cato Institute. She also served as special policy adviser to the state of Michigan's Secchia Commission, which provided recommendations for state government reform. A frequent media guest and public speaker, Lopez-Bauman has authored hundreds of studies, opinion articles, and commentaries.

Barbara L. McAneny, MD, FASCO, MACP, is a board-certified medical oncologist/hematologist from Albuquerque, New Mexico. She draws on her personal experience from the oncology medical practice group she founded in 1987, and as managing partner, since 1999, of the New Mexico Cancer Center, which she built as the first physician-owned multidisciplinary cancer center in the state. She became the 173rd president of the American Medical Association in June 2018. *Modern Healthcare* ranked Dr. McAneny no. 5 on its list of most influential clinical executives for 2019.

Katie Nemitz is a doctoral student at Concordia University Wisconsin, and is passionate about healthcare, healthcare quality, and healthcare transformation. She started her career as a registered nurse and discovered that while patients were getting care, there were many opportunities to deliver both better care and a better patient experience, while keeping in mind that those providing the care need to be considered as well. After finishing her doctorate, she hopes to continue writing, researching, teaching, and working as a consultant to healthcare organizations trying to change the way they deliver healthcare.

Elizabeth O'Connor is originally from Long Island, New York. As an undergraduate, she attended Manhattan College, where she studied government, international studies, and economics. Following her undergraduate career, Elizabeth chose to attend the Bush School of Government and Public Service at Texas A&M University for a master of public service and administration. There, she focused her studies on public policy analysis and public management in a state government context. While at the Bush School, she had the opportunity to spend a summer in Wales at the Wales Centre for Public Policy as a visiting fellow.

Stephen Pickett is a healthcare economist for the Right on Healthcare Initiative at the Texas Public Policy Foundation. Prior to joining the foundation in October 2019, Stephen worked in the health insurance industry. There, he primarily researched the relationship between different insurance products and healthcare utilization and outcomes, as well as alternative provider reimbursement strategies. His research during graduate school focused on the impacts of the Affordable Care Act's marketplaces on Texans and how providers change their behavior when alternative payment models are introduced. Stephen is a native Texan. He received his BBA in business fellows and mathematics in 2013 from Baylor University and his PhD and MA in economics in 2018 from Rice University.

David Riemer, JD, has worked closely with both Democrats and Republicans to create path-breaking public policy at the state level and influence national policy. A graduate of Harvard College and Harvard Law School, Riemer held administrative, legal, and policymaking positions with the mayor of Milwaukee, two governors of Wisconsin, and the late Senator Edward Kennedy's health subcommittee. He was the policy expert who worked with Curt Gielow to draft the bipartisan legislation presented in chapter 20, which would have created universal healthcare in Wisconsin. Active in politics as both an adviser and candidate, Riemer has focused for the last decade on advocacy and writing that aim to reshape the role of government in ensuring economic security, equal opportunity, and an effective market economy.

Christina Sandefur, JD, is the executive vice president of the Goldwater Institute. Sandefur develops policies and litigates cases advancing healthcare freedom, free enterprise, private property rights, free speech, and taxpayer rights. She is a co-drafter of the 41-state Right to Try initiative, now federal law, which protects terminally ill patients' right to try safe investigational treatments that have been prescribed by their physician but are not yet FDA approved for market. Sandefur is a frequent guest on national television and radio programs, has provided expert legal testimony to various legislative committees, and is a frequent speaker at conferences.

Daniel Sem, PhD, MBA, JD, received his PhD in biochemistry from the University of Wisconsin–Madison and his MBA and JD degrees from Marquette University. Currently, he is dean and professor of business, professor of pharmaceutical sciences, and director of technology transfer at Concordia University in Wisconsin. He also serves as director of the Rx Think Tank, focused on healthcare policy reform. Dr. Sem has 25 years of experience in healthcare innovation and 10 issued patents and has published over 60 papers. Previously, he cofounded four drug discovery and development companies (Triad, AviMed, Estrigenix, and Retham) and one social venture (Bridge to Cures). Triad was voted one of the top 10 biotech startups in the United States in 2001 by Drug Discovery Today, and licensed drug leads to Novartis. Dr. Sem's passion is leading healthcare innovation and policy initiatives with the goal of achieving better healthcare outcomes for patients, whether through development of new medicines or new ways to deliver healthcare.

Charles P. Stevens, JD, is an employee benefits attorney and a partner in the Milwaukee, Wisconsin, office of the law firm of Michael Best & Friedrich, LLP. He represents employers and benefits plans in court and is an expert at fixing problems in healthcare benefits plans. He counsels on Affordable Care Act compliance and has litigated before the U.S. Court of Appeals. He was named a "Leader in the Field" by Chambers USA.

James J. Tarasovitch, CPA, is regional chief financial officer for the south market of Ascension Wisconsin. As one of the leading nonprofit and Catholic health systems in the United States, Ascension is committed to delivering compassionate, personalized care to all, with special attention to persons living in poverty and those most vulnerable. Before joining Ascension, Tarasovitch was the regional CFO for Mayo Clinic Health System Minnesota and the CFO for Bradford Regional Health System. He is also an adjunct faculty member at Concordia University Wisconsin.

John Torinus is former CEO and now chairman of Serigraph Inc., a manufacturing company with about 550 employees. The company and its coworkers spend about $6 million per year on healthcare. He has written two books with a company perspective on healthcare reform and cost containment and how to provide better care: *The Grassroots Health Care Revolution* and *The Company That Saved Health Care.*

Greg Watchmaker, MD, is a graduate of Washington University School of Medicine and a practicing hand surgeon at the Milwaukee Hand Center. His outcomes research in carpal tunnel syndrome received the top editorial honors by the *Journal of Hand Surgery* in 2020 for the most impactful published work in the field of hand surgery. Though a practicing surgeon, Dr. Watchmaker started his education in the field of computer science, developing financial software for UW-Madison in the 1980s and later heading a team that developed medical software to map abnormal heart rhythms during open-heart surgery. He has developed applications used to facilitate quality reporting between hospitals and the federal government and, more recently, patient-facing web-based outcomes assessment tools.

Tyler Watts, PhD, is an assistant professor of economics at Ferris State University and an adjunct faculty member at Concordia University. Previously, he was an assistant professor of economics at Ball State University and a visiting assistant professor of economics at Grand Valley State University. Watts earned his PhD in economics at George Mason University in 2010 and a master of finance from Colorado State University–Global Campus in 2019. While at George Mason, he was a Mercatus Center PhD Fellow. His research has appeared in the *Eastern Economic Journal, Independent Review, Review of Austrian Economics,* and *Journal of Private Enterprise.*

Index

CPSIA information can be obtained
at www.ICGtesting.com
Printed in the USA
LVHW050146210820
663573LV00009B/353